T0287944

# General Eisenhower

RHETORIC AND PUBLIC AFFAIRS SERIES

# GENERAL EISENHOWER
## *Ideology and Discourse*

Ira Chernus

Michigan State University Press
East Lansing

Copyright © 2002 by Ira Chernus
∞ The paper used in this publication meets the minimum requirements of ANSI/NISO
Z39.48–1992 (R 1997) (Permanence of Paper).

Michigan State University Press
East Lansing, Michigan 48823–5202

Printed and bound in the United States of America.

08  07  06  05  04  03  02     1  2  3  4  5  6  7

LIBRARY OF CONGRESS CATALOGING-IN-PUBLICATION DATA

Chernus, Ira, 1946-
General Eisenhower, ideology and discourse / Ira Chernus.
    p.  cm. — (Rhetoric and public affairs series)
Includes bibliographical references (p. ) and index.
ISBN 0-87013-616-X (hardcover : alk. paper)
    1.  Eisenhower, Dwight D. (Dwight David), 1890-1969—Political and social
views. 2.  Eisenhower, Dwight D. (Dwight David), 1890-1969—Language.
3. Rhetoric—Political aspects—United States—History—20th century.
4. Eisenhower, Dwight D. (Dwight David), 1890-1969—Military leadership.
5. Presidents—United States—Biography. 6. Generals—United States—Biography.
7. United States. Army—Biography. 8. United States—Politics and government—
1945-1953. 9. United States—Politics and government—1953-1961. I. Title.
II. Series.
E836 .C47 2002
973.921'092—dc21

                                                                        2002007210

Cover design by Heidi Dailey
Book design by Michael J. Brooks

Visit Michigan State University Press on the World Wide Web at:
www.msupress.msu.edu

# Contents

# Acknowledgments

Parts of this book were written with financial support from the University of Colorado at Boulder, through its Council for Research and Creative Work, its Graduate Committee on Arts and Humanities, and its Twentieth Century Humanities Fund, and from the Eisenhower World Affairs Institute. My sincere thanks to those institutions.

I have received valuable critical responses to my work from a number of generous historians, including Stephen Ambrose, Robert McMahon, and H.W. Brands, Jr. I especially appreciate the support of two outstanding scholars of Eisenhower's rhetoric, Robert Ivie and Martin Medhurst. I also appreciate the assistance of archivists at the Eisenhower Library (particularly Dwight Strandberg). Jim Glasscock read the entire manuscript with his sharp editorial eye. My colleagues in the Department of Religious Studies have graciously indulged and supported my research, which stretched the boundaries of our discipline. I wish to express my appreciation to all of these people, who helped to make this book possible. They share in whatever credit is due, while the mistakes are wholly my own.

I close with the customary thanks to my family, because in this case custom is also such a genuine pleasure. Ann and Miguel have shared my life, day by day, through the years of preparing this book. Ann's deep caring has shown me the true meaning of the word *spouse*. Miguel has put the zest in my life and kept my work in perspective by asking (more than once): "When will you be done with Eisenhower? And what's so important about Eisenhower anyway?" When I will be done is anyone's guess. As for what is so important, I hope that the following pages are the beginning of a good answer.

# Introduction

If our attitudes are muddled, our language is often to blame.
—Dwight D. Eisenhower, 5 September 1949

What was the cold war all about? Why did it start? Why did it last so long? To the earliest cold war historians in the United States, the answers were quite obvious. It was all a matter of fundamental beliefs: the liberal values of the West, grounded in Judeo-Christian spirituality, were under attack from totalitarian atheistic communism. For several decades now, such an appeal to beliefs has been virtually taboo among professional historians. Political power struggles, national security imperatives, economic rivalries, domestic political needs, and others such factors have all been admitted to the arena of possible explanations. Indeed, almost any factor could be considered, as long as it fell into the category of hard-headed "objective" interests. Now the pendulum is slowly swinging back. Cold war historians are beginning to recognize once again that ideas do matter.

## IDEOLOGY

Of course the ideas under discussion now are rather more subtle and complex than the naive "ideological battle" theory of early cold war days, and the methods used to study these ideas are correspondingly more sophisticated. In an important study of ideology and U.S. foreign policy, Michael Hunt viewed foreign policy ideas as historical products, "rich in symbols and mythology . . . rooted in the process of nation building, in domestic social arrangements broadly understood, and in ethnic and class divisions." Hunt emphasized the hegemonic influence of a small foreign policy elite, composed largely of privileged white men, who interacted in complex ways with other social groups. More recently, Michael J. Hogan has traced the origins of U.S. cold war policy to ideas that generated a profound shift in political culture and national identity. Like any other identity, Hogan explains, a national identity is not naturally given. Rather it is a cultural construction forged out of "principles, ideas, attitudes, and values." He shows that the new U.S. identity constructed during the early cold war years emerged from an ideological battle between competing factions within the U.S. leadership—a battle about national identity. The result was the distinctive new ideology of the national security state.

Frank Ninkovich has also called attention to the "postmodern turn" and its rejection of the simplistic claims to objectivity that marked the cold war enterprise. Neither we nor the people we study can escape the inevitable subjectivity that comes with being human. Nor is the idea of "objective interests" tenable: "Interests are slippery because they have no objective existence apart from the way people constitute and interpret them." Ninkovich goes on to quote the influential sociologist Herbert Blumer: "To indicate anything, human beings must see it from their perspective; they must depict it as it appears to them." Therefore, no one can escape ideological frameworks, Ninkovich concludes, "for the simple reason that these preexisting frameworks are a condition of our knowing." Applying a similar approach, Hogan demonstrates how the new ideology of national security "shaped the way its believers saw the postwar world and America's place within it," leading to the dramatically new policies of the cold war era.[1]

To study ideas is not to deny the importance of political and economic factors. It is rather to recognize that all leaders are motivated by their constructed identities and their perceptions of reality, which are inevitably a complex blend of interests and ideas. The exact blend is different in every case. Some leaders are more influenced by ideas than others. Each individual must be studied carefully on his or her own terms before generalizations can be made about a group or era. Ideas seem to have been particularly important in the career of Dwight D. Eisenhower.

To most Americans who recall the man as president, it would be surprising that ideas were important to him at all, and even more surprising that those ideas are worth studying. When he spoke, particularly at his many presidential press conferences, his words frequently seemed to betray a confused mind. To call him "unsystematic" or "unschematic" would have seemed to many contemporaries a generous characterization. Most historians now, however, agree with Fred Greenstein that Eisenhower's apparent befuddlement was more calculated than real. "Startlingly," Greenstein writes, "for a man who seemed, to as acute an observer as Richard Rovere, to have an 'unschematic' mind, many of his confidential writings display geometric precision in stating the basic conditions shaping a problem, deducing their implication, and weighing the costs and benefits of alternative possible responses."[2] Eisenhower's public speeches and statements also had a clear underlying logic, which in most cases mirrored the logic of the confidential writings. Though not always characterized by geometric precision, both the public and private utterances demonstrated the same overall consistency.

Richard Immerman has called Eisenhower "the first postwar president to produce a systematically articulated body of thought on war, peace, and security in the nuclear age." Immerman admits, though, that "he could be both naïve and simplistic." In a broader vein, Robert Griffith has found a similar pattern: "Eisenhower was not, of course, a profound or original thinker. He did, however, take ideas seriously, especially in the area of political economy; and, although he typically expressed these ideas in platitudes, he did create, beyond the banality of his language, a fairly coherent vision of how society ought to operate—not just a series of vague generalities, but a broad, internally consistent social philosophy."[3]

*Philosophy* is probably too lofty a term for Eisenhower's thinking. He had to work out his vision piecemeal, individually, and self-consciously. The result was not a philosophy, but an ideology. Historian Michael Hunt has shown that ideology has shaped the decisions of all U.S. leaders as they have had to deal with issues of war and peace. Hunt's definition of ideology is useful precisely for its simplicity: "an interrelated set of convictions or assumptions that reduces the complexities of a particular slice of reality to easily comprehensible terms and suggests appropriate ways of dealing with that reality."[4] Hunt, Hogan, and other historians interested in ideology acknowledge the influence of the anthropologist Clifford Geertz. Geertz describes ideology as the conscious elaboration of worldview and ethos, most often applied in political contexts, when myths have lost their persuasive power. For Geertz, a myth is a story that embodies a received, culturally shared, taken-for-granted vision of reality and set of values. It embodies a group's worldview, its ethos, and its sense of perfect fit between the two. The myth is not intended to falsify reality, nor is it intended to tell the truth. It simply ignores the question of empirical reality and creates a more vivid, more compelling reality of its own. An effective myth is compelling enough to persuade the group that, as Geertz puts it, "the world as lived and the world as imagined, fused under the agency of a single set of symbolic forms, turn out to be the same world."[5]

When myths can no longer be taken for granted, they are replaced by ideology:

It is a loss of orientation that most directly gives rise to ideological activity, an inability, for lack of usable models, to comprehend the universe of civic rights and responsibilities in which one finds oneself located. . . . It is in country unfamiliar emotionally or topographically that one needs poems and road maps. So too with ideology. . . . It is in fact precisely at the point at which a political system begins to free itself from the immediate governance of received tradition, from the direct and detailed guidance of religious or philosophical canons on the one hand and from the unreflective precepts of conventional morality on the other, that formal ideologies tend first to emerge and take hold. . . . One constructs arguments for tradition only when its credentials have been questioned. To the degree that such appeals are successful they bring, not a return to naive traditionalism, but ideo-logical retraditionalization—an altogether different matter.[6]

Geertz's view of ideology is especially apt for the study of Eisenhower. It would be hard to find a better description of the function and aim of the general's discourse. He assumed a comprehensive worldview and ethos, which reinforced each other, much as in a myth. His understanding of reality was not derived from empirical observation; it was the lens through which he made all his empirical observations. He assumed that the world as he imagined it was the same as the world in which he and everyone else lived.

Yet Eisenhower understood that his worldview and ethos could no longer be taken for granted, particularly in the political realm. He was quite candid about the anxiety he felt in the face of uncertain or ambiguous values, and he often rued the difficulty of finding clarity and order in the postwar world. This was arguably the main motive that drove him to his ideological rigidity. He felt obliged to artic-ulate and defend his views as clearly and logically as possible. Eisenhower also set optimism and confidence in the future among his highest values, and he related these, as both cause and effect, to ideological clarity. In some of the writ-ten record, particularly in his diary and occasional letters to intimates, the reader can almost watch him consciously figuring out how the pieces of the system fit together and how new phenomena can be incorporated into it. This was proba-bly the primary function of the diary and intimate letters: not to record inner-most feelings, nor to create an artificial record for history, but to figure out what he should say and think, consistent with his already constructed ideology.

Eisenhower's efforts produced the surprising degree of coherence in his dis-course. His expressed ideas were like so many spokes on a wheel. This wheel was all-encompassing, taking in virtually all the political, economic, social, military, and educational issues that came into his purview. This is not to say that his way of tracing the spokes branching out from the hub, and connecting them with each other, was the only possible way, or even the most logically compelling way. In fact he showed little concern for grasping his system as a whole and tracing out all the internal connections. He cared only that each spoke be plausibly connected to some other spoke. Yet virtually all of the spokes were logically linked, making Eisenhower's discourse a wheel with substantial internal consistency.

## DISCOURSE

Now that cold war historians are beginning to turn to ideology, a few are taking the next step: recognizing, as have so many in the social sciences and the humanities, that ideologies and the ideas of which they consist are not invisible entities inside people's heads. Rather, they are constructions built out of words.

Political historians have given too little attention to language. Until quite recently, most have been content to study what leaders purportedly wanted and how they tried to get it. In other words, they have studied leaders' beliefs and policy actions. Language, the link between beliefs and policies, has been treated as an epiphenomenon—often as a smokescreen hiding reality, or at best as "mere ideology" that can somehow be analytically separated from other causal factors. But to investigate the "true beliefs" of any historical figure is inevitably to chase a chimera of inner mental events. There is no way to ascertain with any certainty a causal link between palpable external language and hypothesized mental events. The effort to infer beliefs from policy actions is an even more slippery slope.[7]

Language is the essential matrix of policy, for policy depends largely on how policymakers talk about the world and the meanings they find there. Thus policy is embedded in the realm of discourse —the way people have learned to talk about the world. John Fiske has offered a convenient definition: "Discourse is a language or system of representation that has developed socially in order to make and circulate a coherent set of meanings about an important topic area. These meanings serve the interests of that section of society within which the discourse originates and work ideologically to naturalize those meanings into common sense." Not all discourse is as ideologically laden as Fiske suggests. But his definition is particularly appropriate for a study of Eisenhower, whose discourse was consistently and pervasively rooted in ideological patterns.[8]

Every political policy, and every policymaker, begins already enmeshed in the web of signifiers that constitutes discourse. That web includes not only verbal representations, but also nonverbal images, actions, and behaviors. These cannot be separated from the many perceptions, judgments, emotions, and motivations already interwoven with the representations. No one can decide to pursue power, wealth, pleasure, or any other goal, and then manipulate language for their ends, as if they were standing outside the nexus of language. Every desire and decision is shaped from the very beginning within that nexus. Language is neither more nor less real and influential than any other causal factor. In a recent survey of the "linguistic turn" in political science, Francis Beer and Robert Hariman have summarized the point: "What we say influences how we see the world, which in turn influences how we act in the world, and how, by acting, we remake the world in the image of our discourse." Daniel Rodgers, who has traced this interaction between language and behavior through U.S. political history, concludes that "the making of words is indeed an act, not a business distinct from the hard, behavioral part of politics. . . . The old dichotomy between behavior and ideas, intellectual history and the history of politics, never in truth made much sense. Political talk is political action of a particular, often powerful, sort." Furthermore, as Rodgers and others have shown, the history of political change has not only been reflected in, but has largely consisted of, struggles to control the meanings of words.[9]

The term *discourse* implies this inevitable intertwining of language with other factors. A historian may (and perhaps must) privilege some factors over others in any particular study, for heuristic purposes. Any one factor can serve as a lens to illuminate others. In this study I focus on Eisenhower's discourse. I ask how public and private words, as well as other forms of behavior, were woven together (perhaps in highly contradictory or paradoxical ways) on particular occasions to yield particular results. As a historian of religions, I am particularly interested in the constantly shifting meanings of symbols within a system of discourse. I view the behaviors and discourse of political leaders as symbols that function in some ways like religious symbols. These symbols reflect and reshape society's sense of ultimate meanings and values. They are interwoven in a seamless web in which each modifies all the others. Of course Eisenhower would have claimed that his words merely reflected, as accurately as possible, objective truths about world affairs and human life. Looking back a half-century later, with the new perspective on discourse that a half-century has produced, we must demur from that claim. Like everyone else, he was constructing discourse, and thereby constructing the world that he claimed merely to reflect. He was using verbal signifiers to construct rhetorical notions, ideological concepts, cultural symbols and, at the broadest level, a comprehensive vision of human life.

He was also using words to make things happen. Martin Medhurst has mounted an impressive effort to interpret Eisenhower as a "strategic communicator," stressing his "consistent concern for the strategic dimensions of rhetoric": "The key was Eisenhower's purpose in speaking. Everything else, including his use of language, bent to this end. To Eisenhower, language was a means only; it was the end that ultimately mattered"; rhetoric was "a valuable Cold War weapon and one that Eisenhower employed repeatedly." Similarly, Robert Ivie says that his rhetoric was "calculated and crafted" to pursue cold war aims, and Michael Hogan argues that Eisenhower "pursued an astute—and perfectly consistent— rhetorical approach premised upon the notion that the cold war would be won, not with bombs and bullets, but through persuasion." This is certainly a very valuable corrective to the traditional view of Eisenhower as an ineffective communicator. His career offers abundant evidence that words must be understood as a form of action.[10]

Medhurst's approach may be misleading, however, if it suggests a picture of Eisenhower as a strict "realist," whose goals were always in the realm of practical policy and political power. He never employed words merely as means to pragmatic ends; the words, and the ideology constructed from them, were integral parts of the ends themselves. Thus he himself dictated that he could and should be best understood by using discourse as the historian's focal lens. His insistence on articulating principles within a rigid, unified, and totalizing structure of discourse makes it hard to avoid the conclusion that he was an ideologue—a man always shaping practical goals in light of his ideology, a man for whom the clear and distinct contours of ideology were more real and more vital than the fuzzy landscape of reality. As Geertz explains, ideology is always related to power and interests, but it must never be reduced to power and interests. Ideologues can be well aware of the effects of their words, as Eisenhower clearly was, yet still be motivated primarily by their ideas. "An unduly Machiavellian view of ideology as a form of higher cunning" neglects its other crucial functions, such as "defining (or obscuring) social categories, stabilizing (or upsetting) social expectations, maintaining (or undermining) social norms, strengthening (or weakening) social consensus."[11]

Eisenhower clearly announced his intention to define categories, stabilize expectations, maintain norms, and strengthen consensus. He also announced his intention to promote the interests of the United States, its economic and political system, and its military establishment (particularly his beloved army). But he said repeatedly that he wanted to protect U.S. economic or political interests, not as ends in themselves, but as means to protecting "a way of life"; i.e., a set of ideological values. He wanted, in John Fiske's terms, to "naturalize" his ideology through public rhetoric, so that it would gain the taken-for-granted status characteristic of myth. He wanted to pronounce a particular vision so often and so effectively that the whole "free world" would adopt that vision as its official guiding story. He saw that as the key to both cold war victory and a lasting peace. He asked to be taken as an ideologue, one for whom conformity to, perpetuation of, and dissemination of an ideology were ends in themselves. There is good reason to take him at his word and see him as a true believer.

Practical success and ideological commitment were so closely intertwined in Eisenhower's discourse that the former cannot be separated from the latter, even for analytical purposes. Language could never be a mere means, strictly separated from practical ends. Just as he used ideology to advance practical goals, so he also saw practical goals as means to the end of legitimating and reinforcing ideology. The language that forged his ideological commitments could shape policy as much as policy shaped language. The language chosen in pursuit of any end could reshape the end, or even commit the speaker unwittingly to quite a different end. Once uttered or written, words had an independent power to act back upon their author. Eisenhower took words seriously, particularly his own. As he produced them, he was creating new constructions of reality and thereby reshaping his lived world. Since his most important words were expressions of his ideological commitments, the very act of producing those words defined the ideology more precisely and committed him to it more powerfully. As with ideology so with language: what appear at first glance as mere means might turn out to be ends in themselves.

Indeed, the whole corpus of Eisenhower's discourse from 1941–52 shows a striking tendency to focus on words more than actions, particularly during the postwar years. Once the war was won, he seemed to lose interest in day-to-day policymaking. He was more concerned with the long-term plight of the United States and its allies, and he said repeatedly that it could best be remedied with inspiring words. When he wrote and spoke about the things that mattered most to him, he focused not on policy debates but on ideological themes. If the study I offer here seems to some readers excessively preoccupied with words, and insufficiently attentive to events and concrete policy decisions, that reflects the methodological choices I have made. But it also reflects the person I am studying. Historians often assume that the real "stuff" of history must be made up of events and policies. We may come closer to an accurate historical record, though, if we assume the perspective of the people who made history. In this case, that dictates an emphasis on ideological discourse.

Some historians will hesitate to accept a picture of Eisenhower as a true believer. Some have already suggested that he was pursuing some unstated goal while hiding behind disingenuous, fine-sounding words. If so, what might that goal have been? Had he disappeared from public life in February 1948, it could well be argued that he was a lifelong soldier using skillful words to promote army and military interests. By 1950, however, this argument was much harder to sustain. He was not seeking unlimited appropriations for the military. His arguments for specific configurations of military power were couched within his larger ideological framework, which he used at times to justify limits on military planning and action as well as spending. He was seeking unlimited donations for Columbia, and particularly his pet projects there, but he certainly could have used other lines of persuasion for that purpose. He was not a corporate tycoon. He had some investments, and he stood to profit from a general expansion of U.S. business, but he was not a wealthy businessman seeking primarily to increase his wealth or the wealth of any particular business.

Was he maneuvering in a subtly calculated way for the Republican nomination for the presidency in 1952? If so, he planned to get there using words that were perfectly compatible with virtually everything he had said since 1941. There is no persuasive evidence that he was shifting his rhetorical stances to comply with shifting political winds. The evidence tends to support his own claim that he finally felt free to say what he had really wanted to say all along. Finally, it might be argued that he aimed primarily to secure U.S. world domination, or at least a preponderance of power. This was certainly among his goals. But again he set power as a means to promote or (far more often) to save the U.S. ideological system. Power was said to serve ideology, not vice versa. Absent that ideological motive, it is not clear what he stood to gain from increased U.S. political power. If he was being disingenuous, the historian must reckon with the problem of evidence. If there ever was an alternative body of words to show that Eisenhower was using his ideological discourse in Machiavellian ways, that evidence has disappeared. The surviving record shows a remarkable logical consistency built on the primacy of ideology. This consistency, combined with the seeming lack of any ulterior motives, leaves the impression that Eisenhower was a true ideologue.

Fred Greenstein has rightly stressed the need to differentiate between Eisenhower's public and private life. He had "a striking propensity," Greenstein writes, to establish "'space' between his private and public self . . . [which] required considerable effort, self-discipline, and a conception of his duties in which eschewing expression of impolitic impulses was taken for granted."[12] It would be tempting to assume that Eisenhower's private language, his diary entries, personal conversations, and private letters represent his true beliefs, while his public speeches and pronouncements were merely conscious manipulations. But it would be misleading. When it comes to language, Greenstein's point should be taken with some caution. Public and private language interacted in close and complex ways.

Eisenhower biographer Peter Lyon has written: "Precisely what the private Eisenhower privately thought may never be known. His true thoughts had in all likelihood never been committed to paper, or if so, quickly destroyed. . . . The terms of the debate he carried on with himself on a more public level are defined in letters he wrote to Beetle Smith, his brother Milton, and others. . . . All such evidence must, however be discounted as having been quite consciously spread on the record for history."[13] Here Lyon asserts both too little and too much. It should be said more accurately that what Eisenhower thought privately will surely never be known. Yet there is no evidence to conclude with any certainty that his true thoughts were not contained in his diary or letters to his most intimate correspondents; that, too, will surely never be known. Lyon offers no evidence to support his bald skepticism about the letters. Indeed none could be offered, unless there were other, more private, writings to contradict these letters. If any such writings once existed, they have surely disappeared, as Lyon himself acknowledges. The only certainty is that Eisenhower left behind a massive amount of private language, which embodies a fairly complex and relatively consistent ideological pattern.

The same can be said of Eisenhower's public rhetoric. Surely he was conscious of its manipulative power. There is copious evidence that he shaped his public language to suit the occasion of its utterance. But it is equally evident that his public and private words often show a striking congruence. The public words do not show an ideological pattern distinct from the private words. The public words are best understood in light of the private, and vice versa. With due attention to the distinction between the two, they must be studied in their mutual interaction. The private language often revealed the source of and motive for strategic public communication. But the public language, particularly the words and themes that were frequently repeated, created public commitments and ideological patterns that were later reflected in the private language. The two together formed a single, dense web of discourse. This was the web within which Eisenhower lived, the web that he took with him into the White House. That web must be studied as a unified whole.

It must also be studied in close detail. By re-creating the full pattern of Eisenhower's discourse, it becomes possible to study the history of his own policymaking from the inside, to see the logic of his decision-making patterns in a new and clearer light. This requires a carefully detailed study of his language. Eisenhower's words deserve such careful study, for he was very careful with words. Extant drafts of letters show how painstakingly he edited his words, even to his closest family and friends. Much of his language may not seem to merit such close attention, since it is filled with banal clichés and platitudes. No one of these expressions might be worth studying separately, but the ensemble reveals an inner logic that provides valuable clues to the structure of discourse and policy in the Eisenhower administration and its effect on U.S. culture. Only by looking at each of the pieces individually, and seeing how they all fit together, can the full structure be revealed.

This approach does run the risk of creating more logical order than Eisenhower himself could ever muster. As Halford Ross Ryan observes, one will search his public rhetoric in vain for sustained logical argument: "There is generally no unifying theme or proposition, merely just [sic] a stringing together of miscellaneous observations and thoughts." Although there are occasional flashes of argumentation, he was far more likely merely to assert the truth of his own views and rely on the force of his personality to persuade his audience.[14] The same was generally true of his private correspondence. Therefore, the logical patterns and connections I shall trace out are sometimes only implicit in the discourse, but these implicit patterns often exercised a strong effect on later discourse and policy. To understand the totality of Eisenhower's influence, it is necessary to reconstruct the inner logic of his discourse, even though he himself might not always have been able to—and rarely cared to—fully articulate it. The following pages will show that, at least in the case of one influential figure of the early cold war, ideological discourse was far more than mere window dressing. It was absolutely central to the life, commitments, and political decisions of a cold warrior. So I offer this study as a contribution to the emerging understanding of ideology and discourse as central factors in interpreting the origins of the cold war. That emerging understanding is bound to change our view of the cold war and U.S. policy.

## THE COLD WAR

The cold war was more than just a forty-five-year geopolitical struggle between two powerful nations and their allies. It was an entire worldview, a set of symbolic expressions of interlocking perceptions and values, built out of a unique structure of discourse. To understand the cold war, then, we must pay close attention to its language. This is true of any war, but particularly of a war that remains cold, because a war stays cold only as long as words are its chosen weapons. As Medhurst points out, "The currency of Cold War combat—the tokens used in the contest—is rhetorical discourse."[15]

In cold war discourse, the highest good is security, both national and personal. Security demands eternal vigilance, for there are always threats to security. Although the particular content of these threats may change from time to time, the threats are always represented with the same formal characteristics, for they all play the same role in the discursive system. That system assumes a polar opposition between security, denoting predictable stable order, and threats to the stability of life. Because that opposition is presented as absolute, the threat must also be absolute; i.e., it must portend a total dissolution of existing structures.

Virtually every study of cold war discourse notes its Manichean and apocalyptic elements. Some scholars have concluded that U.S. leaders used public apocalyptic language to rally support for, and mask the true motives of, their "realist" policies. But Lynn Hinds and Theodore Windt, Jr., in their study of early cold war rhetoric, reject this view because "it presumes that the public explanation of events was one thing and the private bases for action quite a different matter. There is precious little evidence to support such a conclusion. The two arose together." Privately as well as publicly, they conclude, U.S. leaders "chose a universal crusade. . . . The rhetoric of anticommunism created a new political reality for Americans and thus established a new world order."[16]

Windt and Hinds are correct as far as their conclusion goes. But cold war discourse, public as well as private, also includes a copious amount of "realist" language, which is in many respects quite the opposite of apocalyptic language. Most important, while apocalypticism prizes rapid and radical change, "realism" opposes significant change. As Paul Chilton notes, political "realism" is the foundation for the language of "national security." Studying the semantics of the word *security* in cold war discourse, Chilton finds the word now "connected to the absence of motion, to stasis, and more precisely to the physical restraint of undesired motion. Since spatial concepts map metaphorically onto time, we are also talking about absence of and prevention of undesired 'movement' in time, that is undesired change: 'security' is a guarantee of a particular state of affairs over time." Hans Morgenthau, in his classic exposition of "realism," points out that nations often proclaim peace and security as their highest goal because such language, when deployed by "realists," "supports the maintenance of the status quo."[17]

The synthesis of the "realist" and apocalyptic traditions gives the new reality of cold war discourse its unique character. On the one hand, human life is depicted as an endless battle between order and chaos; threats of disorder are assumed to be a permanent fact of life. On the other hand, those threats are portrayed in apocalyptic terms. Every change in the status quo comes to represent an apocalyptic change—a total chaos—and change itself appears to be inherently threatening. But the "realist" component dictates that the battle against change must go on forever. So the best to hope for is to keep the forces of chaos sufficiently under control to preserve the status quo from total dissolution.

Although the roots of this discursive pattern go back far earlier than the cold war, only in that era did it become the foundation of all public discourse. Eisenhower certainly did not originate the elements of cold war discourse. They were all in common use during the Truman presidency. William Graebner, surveying U.S. culture in the 1940s, has found that it was pervaded by doubt, and above all doubt about the possibility of meaningful change: "The core notion of a 'march of time'—consistent, dependable, linear progress—seemed increasingly unrealistic, even deeply flawed." The result, he argues, was a "new and oddly static view of U.S. history . . . an ideological deep freeze. . . . Barriers seemed to be everywhere and change seemed impossible." He links this to growing fears of disintegration and disaster: "Confusion and uncertainty extended to the most basic beliefs, values, and priorities. . . . Americans of the 1940s were more interested in personal survival than in social progress." Finally, he notes a growing sense that "security is a foolish dream of old men, that crisis will always be with us."[18] This was a situation ripe for the reassurance of ideology, in Geertz's sense of the term. The great achievement of cold war discourse was to provide that ideology, to give voice to all these trends within a unified structure that gave them positive meaning.

All the main currents of cold war discourse were evident in Harry Truman's presidential rhetoric. During his first two years or so in office, Truman expressed public hope for peaceful relations with the Soviet Union. As Hinds and Windt note, however, Truman was implying that U.S. principles and policies would have to be the basis for peace. They cite the words of Norman Graebner: "President Truman's principles . . . assumed that there were no conflicts of interest in the world which could not be settled by peaceful adjustment and thus largely on American terms." Soon, they add, the implication would become an explicit demand for Soviet submission to U.S. terms.[19]

As the cold war hardened, Truman turned to more ideological and religious language: "We will win—because God is with us in that enterprise." "Administration rhetoric increasingly emphasized these crusading themes," comments Athan Theoharis; "ultimately this served to limit its options. Because Americans were encouraged to expect victory as inevitable, owing to American purity, to Providence, and to Soviet perfidy and atheism, they were led to reject a policy of compromise and concession. . . . Because the Soviet Union was also portrayed as the anti-Christ, Truman's moralistic tone obviated a policy course that sought to reach some form of accommodation." Diplomacy and the notion of limits on U.S. power "ceased to be a part of administration policy rhetoric."[20]

To legitimate this increasingly dualistic view and the policies that followed from it, Truman had to paint the Soviets not only as anti-Christ but as an imminent threat to the average U.S. citizen. Robert Underhill, in his probing study of Truman's rhetoric, finds that "the drive that is variously called fear, security, or safety . . . was a drive underlying many of Truman's public speeches. Perhaps the clearest example of a Truman speech that appealed to fear is found in his address of March 12, 1947, calling for military and economic aid to Greece and Turkey."

Underhill goes on to recount the advice Truman received from Sen. Arthur Vandenberg, while preparing the Truman Doctrine speech, to "scare hell out of the American people," and he concludes: "Truman did just that. . . . He aroused the fears of millions of Americans that the two superpowers were teetering on the brink of another world conflict." Throughout his presidency, Thomas Paterson puts it, "Truman simplified issues and exaggerated consequences, stirring the heart rather than the mind. . . . He created awesome and frightening images of the foreign adversary. . . . He exploited Cold War tensions through a frequently alarmist, hyperbolic, anti-Communist rhetoric which he thought necessary to insure favorable legislation, to disarm his critics, and to nudge budget-conscious Congressmen to appropriate funds" for cold war programs. Theoharis, agreeing that the president's rhetoric became "distinctly alarmist," adds that this inevitably "heightened insecurity and tension, rather than encouraged dispassion, reason, and confidence." He notes insightfully that "administration policy, both domestic and foreign, reacted against disruptive change. . . . [It] attempted to preclude, not adapt to, change."[21]

The surest way to preclude change was to label every opponent of U.S. policy a threat to the nation's very existence. By late 1950, Truman was warning his National Security Council that the communist threat was a matter of "our survival or destruction." He brought the same dire message to the public. The United States was fighting in Korea not only for "our own national security," but for survival, he proclaimed: "Our homes, our Nation, all the things we believe in, are in great danger." Why did the public respond so readily to such frightening images? Robert Ivie suggests that there was a "rhetorical transaction" between the speaker and his audience. The public brought to the transaction its "underlying fear of chaos, a fear that was itself premised on a convergent image of Christian civilization's inherent fragility." The president played on and exacerbated this fear with his deliberate "plain style," which encouraged the audience to take his words literally. Because his words were so obviously devoid of rhetorical artifice, they seemed even more compellingly alarming. "Together, the public and the president constructed a sense of crisis."[22]

Truman was certainly not the only elite leader responsible for generating a sense of crisis. One very important figure in this regard was George F. Kennan, whose discourse has recently been given a probing analysis by Ivie. Throughout Kennan's writings, according to Ivie, one finds a "horror of chaos" that "makes him yearn for the order and stability of a balance of power among nations, and causes him to fear for the survival of civilization itself." Kennan's own words reveal his view of the ultimate source of the threat—human nature itself: "We run around . . . encumbered by our demonic side . . . wholly unamenable to reason . . . restrained only by some form of force. Violence is the tribute we pay to original sin." Since such "realist" discourse constitutes "a threat that cannot be allayed," Ivie argues, it only "compounds the threat of national insecurity, exaggerating the external threat by turning it inward." "Kennan's conceptual image of containing ourselves—of controlling our destructive emotional impulses—entails a Platonic constraint on human freedom in order to insure the welfare and happiness of the republic." Kennan's famous metaphor of containment of communism and his yearning for stability rested upon his Platonism; human constraint in the name of unchangeable realities constituted the essence of the good.[23]

These pervasive ideological themes were not simply produced for public consumption, to legitimate private nonideological goals of the elite. Michael J. Hogan has devoted a detailed study to the ideology underlying the development of the national security state during the Truman administration. He finds these themes just as basic to the secret documents shaping policy as to the rhetoric justifying that policy: the rigidly bipolar worldview, the obsession with security, the despair of negotiated agreements, the fear of impending catastrophe, the assumption that crisis was a permanent condition, the sense of a sacred mission to preserve civilization, and the need to mobilize the entire nation in a crusade to fulfill that mission. Hogan adds that all this was woven together in a totalizing context. Policymakers assumed that "a new era of total war had dawned." A perceived threat to peace or freedom anywhere was taken to be an immediate threat to the peace and freedom of the United States. Therefore, the country had to mobilize itself and the entire "free world" on a permanent war footing, ready to fight anywhere on a moment's notice; and this national security state had no foreseeable end.[24]

As Hogan's study makes clear, the language of eternal threat used by Truman, Kennan, and so many others was a discursive construction, not an objective description of external reality. Other descriptions of reality were equally available, even among the nation's political elite. Hogan depicts an intense ideological struggle between proponents of the new doctrine of national security and defenders of a more traditional view. The latter, led by Sen. Robert Taft, saw the rising power of the executive branch and the military as a threat to individual political and economic freedoms. They warned that the United States was on its way to becoming a "garrison state." They also feared that entangling alliances such as NATO would undermine, not enhance, U.S. security. These conservative critics saw communism as a great threat, but they wanted to fight it in more unilateral and less massively militarized ways. The primary interests at stake for them, Hogan argues, were not political or economic but ideological.

Ideological resistance also came, though less successfully, from the left.[25] Truman's own secretary of commerce, Henry A. Wallace, told his boss: "We should make an effort to counteract the irrational fear of Russia which is being systematically built up in the American people. . . . We should not act as if we too felt that we were threatened in today's world. We are by far the most powerful nation in the world." Seeing no imminent threat, Wallace urged acceptance of Soviet policies in eastern Europe and a peaceful coexistence between the two world powers. The "slogan" that capitalism could not coexist with communism was, he asserted, "pure propaganda."[26] When he persisted in voicing such ideas publicly, Wallace was fired. After his disastrous bid for the 1948 presidency, he was largely eclipsed from the public scene. The example of Wallace may have ensured that no other elite figure would express similar views. By the end of the 1940s, in any event, his interpretation simply was not available as a legitimate option in mainstream discourse. That discourse was then free to depict Truman's warnings about the "red menace" as a necessary response to an objective reality.

## THE PATTERNS OF EISENHOWER'S IDEOLOGICAL DISCOURSE

Eisenhower's discourse had much in common with the proponents of the national security state. During World War II he had already rejected, privately, any possibility of the kind of accommodation Henry Wallace advocated. As time went on, the general was increasingly influenced by the conservative critique of Truman's policies. Overall, he may be best seen as a bridge between the two camps (though he ran for president largely to prevent the Taft forces from taking control of the government).[27] In this book, I do not compare Eisenhower's discourse with that of Truman or any other public figures. I have no stake in proving any uniqueness or originality for Eisenhower; I make no effort to determine what was unique, innovative, or unusual in his words. That would surely be an interesting project, well worth doing. As comparative studies of the ideology and discourse of cold war leaders progress, we will gain a clearer picture of the overall shape and effects of the language of cold war. That scholarship will probably reveal significant similarities between Eisenhower and others, since Eisenhower's discourse included all of the basic themes and patterns of 1940s cold war discourse. I will be pleased to know that my work has helped to provide data for such a synthesis.

This book will also show that, whatever may prove to be the case for other elite leaders, Eisenhower's motivations lay primarily in the realm of ideology and discourse. The key to his discourse, the center of his ideological wheel, was his view of human nature, which was basically a religious view. Like his Christian forebears, he saw every individual permanently seized by an inner struggle between selfish desire (which his forebears called sin) and the virtue of voluntary self-restraint.[28] This fixed center gave his discourse its unexpected degree of consistency and logical coherence. His political, economic, and social fears, including a deep-rooted fear of communism, all grew out of his fear that unchecked selfishness would destroy civilized order. That danger could be averted, he repeatedly said, only if a unified American public led the world in fighting against it. Unity required a clearly defined, universally shared vision and purpose. That vision and purpose would come from the clarifying and inspiring words of leaders like himself. Public discourse was the vital weapon of national security, and it had to be ideological discourse. The purpose of discourse was to defend traditional values in the face of disorienting change. Clear, orderly thinking was the only way to fend off the growing chaos, Eisenhower assumed. In form as well as content, he intended his words to reassure the nation that the old order still endured.

Unfortunately the general's efforts at ideological discourse, so widely heard and read throughout the land, were constructed on a superficial clarity that masked deep underlying contradictions. As his language was disseminated by the media, it helped to increase not clarity, but confusion. The confusion was compounded because it passed as common sense, so its deeper confusions went unanalyzed, and even unnoticed. The contradiction responsible for much of the confusion was in the central notion of human nature. On the one hand, Eisenhower saw humanity's only salvation in self-restraint undertaken purely voluntarily. The call to self-restraint implied that victory over the inner enemy was possible. On the other hand, perhaps influenced by his ancestors' belief in original sin, he ascribed a powerful and eternal strength to the selfish impulses. They could never be vanquished; the best to hope for was to keep them under some degree of control, through constant vigilance and powerful exertions. In theological terms, Eisenhower constructed the human dilemma as an apocalyptic one: an implacable battle between good and evil, with no compromise possible. But he ruled out a priori the possibility of the apocalyptic solution, the final abolition of evil.

From this basic contradiction in his discourse many others flowed. The orderly ideology he saw as a prerequisite for a stable, orderly society became impossible. And without stable order, his ideology asserted, there could be no security, nor hope for a better life. What he wanted, above all, was to create a discourse that would give the nation (and, very probably, him) that security and hope. But he constructed his discourse on the foundation of a fear that could never go away, because it was, at base, fear of the eternal structure of human nature. Fear and hope were inextricably linked; more of one meant more of the other. The more Eisenhower pronounced his words of hope, therefore, the more he exacerbated the insecurity and fear that were discursively tied to hope. The more he offered what he took to be his clear, logical understanding of the world, the more he exacerbated the confusions of the time. This inevitably heightened the very fear of chaos he wanted to diminish.

This pattern was perhaps most evident, and most important, in Eisenhower's discourse on the subject for which he was best known: war and peace. Halford Ross Ryan, the only previous scholar to study the pre-presidential rhetoric in detail, finds that "Eisenhower's basic rhetorical proposition which he argued from 1945 to 1951 was: 'Lasting peace must be maintained.' This was Eisenhower's *a priori* assumption." This claim goes too far. As the following pages will show, the general's rhetorical commitment to peace was neither his most basic proposition nor an a priori assumption. It was, however, a theme that he sounded consistently and it was the one theme, above all others, that would win him his immense public popularity. For this reason I give it special attention throughout this study.

In this theme he was not wholly original. All U.S. leaders had traditionally proclaimed the nation's desire for peace. The public mood of the late 1940s demanded that the theme be especially salient. As William Graebner says, "After long years of war, Americans turned to peace with an almost desperate self-consciousness."[29] The outbreak of war in Korea intensified the desperation. During his last two and a half years in office, Harry Truman never missed a chance to explain how and why the Korean War would bring world peace. In Truman's discourse peace meant, above all, a situation in which the Soviet Union's innate aggressive instinct was held in check. This, Truman insisted, was the primary purpose of the Korean War; if U.S. resolve were not clearly communicated, Stalin would feel free to aggress elsewhere, and the inevitable result would be a total war. The United States was depicted as merely a static wall holding back the dynamic force of the aggressor. As Theoharis says, Truman "stressed the need to 'win the peace' (not negotiate a compromise peace). . . . Truman thought that superior military strength, not yet achieved, was essential to a lasting peace."[30]

Since images of compromise were inadmissible, all policy change had to come from the enemy. And those changes would be produced only by overwhelming U.S. strength. So virtually every reference to peace in Truman's speeches was bracketed by calls for more weaponry, more military spending, and more support for the war effort in Korea. Perhaps that is why Truman's many words in praise of peace had so little effect on his public image. Listening to a leader whose image was etched in the phrase "give 'em hell," the press and the public naturally heard his fighting words more clearly than his hopes for peace.

Eisenhower's public image was strikingly different. He was the "warrior for peace," who hoped to be remembered not for waging cold war but for "waging peace."[31] Some historians believe he sincerely wanted peace. Others argue that he really wanted cold war victory and used peace moves as cold war tactics, dooming his chances for achieving real peace. But all seem to assume that empirical research can determine whether or not he truly desired peace, how he could have moved the nation closer to it, and why it remained so distant. In making this assumption, all treat *peace* as an objective reified reality, a simple word with a univocal meaning. The debate thus fails to recognize that every historian builds his or her own interpretation on a particular a priori construction of peace, which remains unthematized. I hope to advance the debate by asking a question that has not yet been systematically investigated: What did Eisenhower mean when he spoke of "peace"?

In the 1950s, C. Wright Mills recognized that peace, far from being a univocal term, had become a semantic marker for a host of different and often conflicting values. "Peace is such an altogether 'good' word that it is well to be suspicious of it," he wrote. "It has meant and it does mean a great variety of things to a great variety of men. Otherwise they could not all 'agree' upon it so readily and so universally. . . . Everybody agrees upon peace as the universal aim—and into it each packs his own specific political fears, values, hopes, demands."[32] As Mills suggested, *peace* meant more than simply avoiding war. The hope for "world peace" became a sort of mythic vision, and the term itself took on mythic proportions. It became the focal point for the eschatological hope that had always been so central in U.S. public discourse.

There was no single myth of world peace. *Peace* was simply a word, a verbal token set within a constantly changing body of discourse. The word took on a wide range of meanings. Each meaning carried the weight of a particular worldview, a particular set of values and political concerns. The debate about "world peace" and the paths to it was essentially a battle among competing mythic visions, each using the word peace as a central weapon. Treating peace as a symbolic concept with variable meanings, I ask not whether Eisenhower "really" wanted peace, but how his discourse transformed the meaning of peace as it responded to new historical circumstances with a new blend of religious and political language.

The answer rests, again, on the religious foundation of Eisenhower's ideology. Publicly, he spoke of peace as the total triumph of "the American way," which meant an unconditional victory over unrestrained selfishness. Privately, though, he never dared hope for that victory; it simply was not possible, given his ideological premises. When the general concurred with Truman's view of peace as rigid containment, he was only projecting his view of human nature onto a global geopolitical canvas. And, of course, he was projecting the evil inherent in human nature (as he understood it) onto the political and economic structures of communism. Fear of communism was just part, though a central part, of the range of interlocking fears central to his ideology, which became the primary motive force driving his policy views. When those views were enacted as policy, political behavior was bound to reinforce the fears, particularly the fear of war.

Discourse and policy were both produced in the name of fighting and winning the war, not only against communism but against all forces of selfishness and disorder. The apocalyptic tones of cold war discourse made those forces seem infinitely threatening. Every call for victory over communism and chaos only reinforced the images of the threat and the fears they conjured up. The more the general exhorted the nation to a spiritual crusade against the external foe, the more he institutionalized and thus exacerbated this vicious cycle. Yet in Eisenhower's discourse there was no way to imagine an end to that war and the fear it generated. A genuine harmony among nations was not possible; nor, in the nuclear age, was a war to eliminate the enemy possible. The best to hope for was endless containment, a permanent stability that would prevent disaster by preventing any fundamental change. So the cold war situation—neither war nor peace—would continue indefinitely, with all its uncertainty and anxiety. In all these ways and more, the language of national security was bound to make the nation feel less secure. Words of peace, stability, and hope paradoxically ended up exacerbating conflict, instability, and fear.

Again, although Eisenhower did not create this basic dynamic of cold war discourse, he did contribute to it and typify it in many ways. To understand it fully, we shall need careful discursive biographies of all cold war leaders. This is not a full-scale discursive biography. Ideally, the story should begin with Eisenhower's childhood (or even earlier, with his forebears). The sources for that study, however, and indeed for the first fifty years of his life, are too sparse to allow any meaningful conclusions.[33] I begin my study with World War II, which seemed to force Eisenhower, for the first time, to set his thoughts about himself and his nation in a consistently global and world-historical context. Only during the war did he set forth fully the foundations of the ideology he would develop on his way to the White House. World War II and the early cold war years had a similar effect on all U.S. leaders. Although this study is intended primarily to understand one very interesting and important person, I trust that it will also help other scholars illuminate the whole era in which he developed his ideas.

The debates about cold war origins are still so heated because so much is at stake. The question of origins is pivotal for the larger issues of what the cold war was all about, and how to evaluate U.S. policy throughout that era. Our interpretation of those larger issues remains crucial for charting our future. The cold war is apparently gone for good. The geopolitical situation of the early twenty-first century is vastly different than the world of Truman and Eisenhower. The cultural world, however, shaped by discourse and ideology, is not so different. Cultural realities change rather more slowly than geopolitical situations. Our publicly shared way of speaking about the world, and the U.S. role in it, is still largely under the impress of discourse forged at the outset of the cold war. To comprehend that discourse is to know a bit more, not only about the past, but also about the present. By untangling the web of one person's discourse, we can better understand the world of U.S. public discourse and culture today, and therefore better understand ourselves. Public action stems from public language. Confused public action, and the insecurity it breeds, is most often a result of confused public language. To clarify the prevailing mode of public action—or inaction—in the face of massive global problems in the twenty-first century, we would do well to understand more clearly the rich, complex, all-enveloping ideology and discourse of the cold war. We can come one step closer to that understanding by studying the ideology and discourse of Dwight D. Eisenhower.

# Part I

## THE WAR AND ITS AFTERMATH

## CHAPTER 1

# Supreme Commander: World War II

When the United States entered World War II, there was no reason to think that the war would catapult Dwight D. Eisenhower to world fame and, eventually, to the White House. At the time, he was a fifty-one-year-old colonel, apparently stuck permanently in that rank. His chances of becoming a general were "nil," he told his son John, requiring nothing short of a miracle. As Stephen Ambrose has written, he must have wondered why he stayed on in the army at all.[1] In hindsight his biographers saw that his thirty-five years of prewar service had prepared him very well for his rise to eminence. Eisenhower had served in a wide range of military jobs, he had met and worked with political leaders of all sorts, and he had earned the respect of most of the army's top-ranking officers. Nevertheless, his unexpected ascent, from 1942–44, seemed at the time nearly miraculous. If World War II was the defining experience for all U.S. military officers of that era, it was even more defining for General Eisenhower. Not only did it bring him to the pinnacle of fame and power, it also allowed, and in some sense forced, him to crystallize in writing his most basic ideas about himself, his nation, the global community of nations, and human life in its broadest terms.

### EISENHOWER AND FASCISM

It is widely assumed that the war confirmed Eisenhower as a moral crusader, fighting for liberal democracy against the evils of totalitarianism. H. W. Brands, Jr., sums up this view when he says that "Eisenhower emerged from [World War II] convinced of America's moral preeminence," with "an ideology of unquestioning righteousness . . . the product of a conflict in which the world neatly divided into camps of good and evil."[2] There are many expressions of strong antifascist sentiment in his World War II writings that support this claim. Explaining the title of his war memoir, for example, Eisenhower wrote:

Daily as [the war] progressed there grew within me the conviction that as never
before in a war between many nations the forces that stood for human good and
men's rights were this time confronted by a completely evil conspiracy with
which no compromise could be tolerated. Because only by the utter destruction
of the Axis was a decent world possible, the war became for me a crusade in the
traditional sense of that often misused word.[3]

Eisenhower's biographers have raised serious doubts about his claim to have
crusaded against fascism. A crusade denotes a battle to expand the realm in which
one's own values hold sway. Yet Stephen Ambrose says that he was primarily concerned with defending and sustaining, not expanding, American values: "His passion for democracy was essentially conservative. It was not offensive, a vigorous
attempt to spread democracy or its meanings." Merle Miller similarly contends
that he was never a reformer and never had any desire to be one.[4] Others go even
further. Piers Brendon finds Eisenhower "strangely oblivious to the fascist character of the Vichy regime and consistently insensitive to issues of civil liberties,"
which are so essential to American democracy, a view echoed by Robert Burk.
Peter Lyon goes so far as to argue that "his crusade in Europe was never antifascist. He spoke rarely of the Nazis and often of the Boche or the Hun."[5]

These sentiments echo the doubts that were first raised in November 1942,
when the Allies invaded North Africa. Eisenhower, as commander of the invading forces, allowed Jean Darlan and other French political leaders to retain their
civil authority, despite their well-known fascist credentials; this raised a large
public outcry. During the invasion of North Africa, and indeed throughout sixteen months of U.S. involvement in the war, he said virtually nothing about combating fascism. He did once tell his brother Edgar:

> I was one of those that for the past two years has preached preparedness and tried
> to point out the deadly peril into which the United States was drifting. We have
> got a fearful job to perform and everybody has got to unify to do it. . . . If they
> should win, we would really learn something about slavery, forced labor, and the
> loss of individual freedom. We have got to win and any individual in this coun-
> try, so far as I am concerned, that doesn't do his very best to fulfill his part of the
> job is an enemy.[6]

This statement, however, was his only substantial comment about the ideological values at stake in the war during those first sixteen months. His public
messages, in which one would have expected appeals to defend American ideals

in the face of the Nazi evil, carried no such ideological pleas.[7] As late as 4 April 1943, he told Gen. Charles Herron: "I am completely weary of banalities, generalities, and slogans, in the effort to win this war. Honesty, sincerity, and complete devotion to duty are the only things that count."[8]

Yet just three days later he wrote to his boyhood friend and confidant Swede Hazlett, who had lamented that his physical condition kept him out of military action. Eisenhower insisted that everyone, whatever their job, could contribute effectively to the war effort. Then he added:

> It seems to me that in no other war in history has the issue been so distinctly drawn between the forces of arbitrary oppression on the one side and, on the other, those conceptions of individual liberty, freedom and dignity, under which we have been raised in our great Democracy. I do have the feeling of a crusader in this war, and every time I write a letter or open my mouth, I preach the doctrine that I have so inadequately expressed above.[9]

This was Eisenhower's first reference to the war as a crusade.

The very next day he again proclaimed his antifascist passion to Gen. Harold Alexander: "The whole democratic world is applauding your successes against forces that have outraged our concepts of freedom and human rights."[10] To be sure, this was written for public consumption. But on the same day he wrote a private letter to his son, which revealed something of the motivation for this new turn:

> Within the past few days another tempest in a teapot broke out about French politics. It is nothing but tripe . . . [and] an aid to the enemy. I have been called a Fascist and almost a Hitlerite—actually, I have one earnest conviction in this war. It is that no other war in history has so definitely lined up the forces of arbitrary oppression and dictatorship against those of human rights and individual liberties. My single passion is to do my full duty in helping to smash the disciples of Hitler.[11]

What was the "tempest in a teapot"? On 6 April, the day before the Hazlett letter, Charles de Gaulle had publicly blamed Eisenhower for preventing him from coming to North Africa to form a new antifascist government. Eisenhower warned Marshall: "It is possible that this statement may cause considerable repercussion in the American press."[12] He was obviously expecting renewed criticism for his seeming complicity with and support of the fascist French government.

(Eisenhower explained privately that he was following the advice of British political leaders, who wanted to avoid a political crisis while the battle for Tunisia was still on.) He had been surprised by the intensity and duration of the criticism directed at him for the Darlan deal, and had been exasperated by the time and energy he felt compelled to give to defending that deal. By March 1943 the issue had pretty well died down. Now the whole political mess threatened to flare up again, and in light of the unexpected intensity of the earlier criticism, there was no way to predict where this incident might lead.

It seems apparent that the general sounded his new ideological note because he was expecting another round of criticism, and perhaps a renewal of the previous autumn's imbroglio. Ironically, the criticism never came. Yet the expectation of it stung so badly that the supreme commander felt compelled to attest—or protest—his commitment to the ideological aims of the war, employing the generalities and slogans of which he had just proclaimed himself so weary. Eisenhower formulated his antifascist language in response to a specific historical circumstance, not as a fundamental principle shaping his attitude toward the war from the outset. He had not set out to wage a crusade against fascism, nor one for civil liberties and human rights.

## WHAT WAS EISENHOWER CRUSADING FOR?

Eisenhower had indeed been crusading from the very first days of the war, although not against fascism. The essence of his crusade was summed up in his 4 April affirmation to Herron that the imperative need was for devotion to duty, not political generalities, if disaster were to be avoided. This was the message he preached at every opportunity. It was also the theme he stressed in the letters just cited—to his brother, his son, and his closest confidant. His views on fascism were secondary to this overriding concern.

For Eisenhower the soldier, fidelity to duty meant always being prepared for the worst. Serving in the War Department office in 1930, he had written a report on planning for wartime industrial mobilization. That experience had led him to take seriously the threat of a future war at a time when he believed that few others did. His report had stressed the advantages of laying detailed plans well in advance to mobilize all the nation's resources in the next war.[13] Just a week after Pearl Harbor, when Army Chief of Staff George Marshall brought him to Washington again as a chief planner for the Pacific theater, his first concern was for mobilization. "Ships! Ships! All we need is ships. Also ammunition—AA—guns—tanks—airplanes—what a headache!" he noted to himself.[14] The war reinforced Eisenhower's longstanding conviction that peacetime preparedness was the key to victory in war and thus to national security. It reinforced, too, his conviction that he himself would have to bear the stress—the headache—of preparedness more than others.

The mobilization headaches were particularly galling to Eisenhower because, as he told Edgar, he felt that the present dangers could have been avoided had his earlier warnings about preparedness been heeded. Early in 1942 he told Alfred Gruenther that he took "a certain amount of smug and mean satisfaction in recalling the name of 'Alarmist Ike' that some of the boys tried to fasten on me almost two years ago." The "boys" were presumably fellow officers, all of whom were professionally inclined to prepare for worst-case scenarios. Yet even among these military men Eisenhower apparently stood out, and wanted to stand out, as unusually apprehensive and alarmist. In early 1940 Eisenhower told his junior officers: "This country is going to war, and I want people who are prepared to fight that war." One of those officers later commented: "Nobody, *nobody* was talking like that at the time. People were going around saying, 'War? What war? I don't see any war.'" But Eisenhower told his friends that the nation would soon choose to go to war: "The public will get infuriated at the necessity of building, spending, and defending against a threat, and will get in the frame of mind that it will be better, cheaper and quicker to *remove* the threat."[15] "Alarmist Ike" was alarmed primarily by the prospect that his army and his nation, insufficiently prepared, might lose the war. The motives underlying the war were a secondary issue. In fact in May 1940, Eisenhower told his son that he did not know the real causes of the war, either in Europe or in Asia.[16]

Throughout the war Eisenhower remained an alarmist, foreseeing all the different ways in which the war effort might fail, and crusading for his chosen way to avoid each of these pitfalls. In addition to insufficient preparedness and inefficient mobilization, he was also alarmed about inadequate strategic planning. He developed an early version of the domino theory, stressing the threat that the Japanese would take all of Southeast Asia and then go on to conquer India. His greatest early fear was that the Japanese would then hook up with German troops advancing through the Middle East. "If we're to keep Russia in, save the middle East, India and Burma; we've got to begin slugging with air at West Europe; to be followed by a land attack as soon *as possible,*" he wrote in his diary, and then, "Strange that no one sees the danger." When others failed to share his enthusiasm for an early invasion of northwest Europe, he lamented: "The actual fact is that not 1 man in 20 in the Government . . . realizes what a grisly, dirty, tough business we are in! They think we can buy victory!" He called the canceling of plans for Operation Sledgehammer, an initial small incursion into France, "the blackest day in history." Such comments typified Eisenhower's penchant for overly dramatic and even melodramatic language.[17]

A certain amount of this alarmism can be ascribed to Eisenhower's impatience to get out of Washington and into the theater of combat. But when he got his wish, as commander of Operation Torch (the allied invasion of North Africa), he still worried that others were not worried enough. Throughout the first months of the North African campaign, according to Ambrose, he "consistently harped on what a tough business war is and on the overwhelming need to impress that fact on the troops." No doubt Eisenhower, like every commander, used images of alarm in wartime as a ploy to demand more strenuous exertion from his troops. But he seems to have been genuinely convinced that others were complacent in the face of great danger; his official statements to this effect were mirrored in his most private writings.[18]

To stress Eisenhower's alarmism is not to deny that the dangers he and the nation faced were real and urgent. His quality of alarmism was less exaggerated in wartime than in peacetime. But it is important to see how his alarmism and his need to see himself as an alarmist played a central role in the larger ideological framework within which he organized his experience. The stress on danger and preparedness was a crucial part of his self-image. It was the quality that he believed (probably correctly) set him apart from his fellow officers. This became a hallmark of his ideology during the war and remained so ever after.

Not only was Eisenhower convinced that others were consistently ignoring dangers that he clearly recognized, but he was also quite sure he knew why. The following quotes come from several different sources: "Most advice [from staff officers] is, of course, colored by individuals who subconsciously think of their own power or opportunities for advancement"; "I get exceedingly weary of the little people that spend their time worrying about promotion, personal prestige, prerogatives, and so on, rather than forgetting everything in the desire to get on with the work"; "The struggle to secure the adoption by all concerned of a common concept of strategical objectives is wearing me down. Everybody is too much engaged with small things of his own—or with some vague idea of larger political activity to realize what we are doing—rather *not* doing." Teamwork was essential to planning a proper strategy, in Eisenhower's view. As long as competing planning officers advanced their own strategic concepts, the military as a whole would "just be thrashing around in the dark."[19]

"War creates such a strain," he told Mamie, "that all the pettiness, jealousy, ambition, greed and selfishness begin to leak out the seams of the average character

. . . Everyone pursues their own selfish or political concerns and fails to understand what is not being done to win the war." "All these trials and tribulations," he told her in another letter, "must come upon the world because of some great wickedness." Man's intelligence and "spiritual perceptions" should find a way to put an end to it.[20] The wickedness that spawned war was thus a spiritual failure. It was, in fact, Eisenhower's version of what his sectarian Christian ancestors called original sin: humanity's persistent unwillingness to voluntarily restrain its innate selfishness.

Ultimately, his idea of teamwork and a common concept of strategical objectives meant unanimous agreement on his own concept, the only one that he believed could win the war. Fred Greenstein points out that Eisenhower's fine mind and great self-confidence were liabilities as well as assets: "His confidence in the correctness of his own views could lead him to forget that what was self-evident to him might be obscure to others. His rationality was accompanied by a distrust of the emotionalism of others." The emotion he distrusted, above all, was selfishness. When others disagreed with him, he was quick to ascribe it to their petty desires for self-advancement and their desire to avoid making the sacrifices entailed in facing the danger. So he consistently equated his own advice on strategy not only with correct strategy, but also with preparedness, sufficient alarm, and above all with selfless devotion to a common cause, the virtue on which he especially prided himself. Competing views were equated not only with complacency, but also with the selfish and political aims of others. Seeing himself as one of the few wise, selfless planners battling against widespread ignorance, complacency, and selfishness, he naturally felt worn down.[21]

Eisenhower was generally confident that the Allies were fully capable of winning the war. His alarm was consistently expressed in terms of doubts about whether the Allies had the will to win, which meant the willingness to restrain their own selfishness. This was a question of character, of morality, and ultimately of spirituality. "Never forget," he told his son John, "that in the soldier's life the first tenet of his religion must always be the immediate and proper performance of duty. Everything else is secondary." In other correspondence he wrote: "The only unforgivable sin in war is not doing your duty. . . . The soul of an army . . . is nothing but discipline"; and "It is impossible to exaggerate the importance of this subject."[22] Placing duty above selfish desire was the key to discipline, and discipline was the key to victory. Therefore, the question of discipline was central to Eisenhower for both ideological and practical reasons.

Eisenhower stressed that discipline could not be based on externally imposed punishments. It meant an internalized attitude of voluntary self-restraint and selfless concern for the group. The officer's primary task was to produce voluntary self-restraint in his men by setting a convincing example of selfless devotion to duty. "You have got to look on that word 'discipline' as something different from mere punishment for commission of crime," he told his son. At other times, he said, "Discipline is that quality in an organization that gives the Commander the assurance that every man in it will do exactly as he is told"; and "Leadership can produce the all important discipline in an army with minimum resort to punishment."[23]

"I have developed almost an obsession as to the certainty with which you can judge a division, or any other large unit, merely by knowing its commander intimately," he told Gen. Vernon Prichard; a good commander "has to be able to forget himself and personal fortunes." He praised Gen. Alfred Gruenther as "a grand, self-effacing officer" because "he apparently never thinks of himself or his personal fortunes—a quality that I assure you has come to be one that means much to me in any officer." Discipline was the only antidote to selfishness, divisiveness, and complacency. Without it, there could be no military victory, nor any decent social order, but only chaos: "Discipline is the thing that distinguishes an army from a mob."[24]

## THE MILITARY AND CIVILIAN SOCIETY

Eisenhower extended his ideology beyond the military to encompass civilian society. He often complained that the public and government leaders were unwilling to make sufficient sacrifices because they failed to appreciate the magnitude of the dangers facing the nation. After the first Allied victories, he became even more concerned about civilian overconfidence, and commented on it in separate letters: "I deplore the acceptance of the winning of the war as a foregone conclusion"; and "Nothing disturbs me more than a complacent attitude." In a letter to his wife, he lamented, "God—how I wish I could help make all Americans feel the *deadly* seriousness of this task."[25]

Recognizing the danger meant responding with the same kind of self-sacrifice demanded of soldiers, Eisenhower told some of his most intimate correspondents. To his brother Edgar: "Any individual in this country, so far as I am concerned, that doesn't do his very best to fulfill his part of the job is an enemy." To his brother Arthur: "Every man, soldier and civilian alike, must recognize the enormity of the difficulty still facing us and buckle right down to the job of doing his own best." To his father-in-law: "Everyone must put his shoulder to the wheel and push with all he has." To an old friend: "If all Democratic nations, and every citizen in them, put their shoulders to the wheel, and shove to the limit of endurance, then we will do the job." To Gen. Vernon Prichard: "Battlefield discipline is what we need . . . absolute obedience, instant obedience—I wish that it were within the power of my tongue and pen to convince every individual in the United States of this necessity." Again to Arthur: "It is the duty of every one of us, civilian and soldier alike, to carry out the orders of our government when a war emergency arises." Discipline and duty were the antidotes to complacency for soldiers and civilians alike. In wartime, the first tenet of the soldier's religion had to become the foundation of everyone's faith.[26]

For Eisenhower the home front extended beyond the United States to include all the Allied nations. Discipline was the sine qua non of every successful alliance, from the alliance of a few soldiers in a squad to the alliance of great nations in a United Nations. For many of his contemporaries (as for many historians), his ability to hold an international wartime alliance together was his most impressive achievement. The intensive effort that this required also shaped his thoughts and his fears. His alarmism, his perception of pervasive selfishness, and his insistence on duty and self-control were all tied together in his commitment to the United Nations alliance. Having led the invasion of North Africa, Eisenhower still feared that the Allied nations, each pursuing its own interests, would fracture the unity needed for the final thrust into northwest Europe. He was convinced that only a sufficiently alarmed, sufficiently mobilized, and dutifully selfless alliance could win the war. This was the key to "teamwork," a value that he prized as highly, and as often, as any other. As supreme commander of Allied forces, Eisenhower criticized not only Americans but also members of all the Allied nations for insufficient dedication to the common effort. Dire predictions of the consequences of disunity were certainly calculated to produce a more effective war effort, but they came naturally to "Alarmist Ike"; his emerging discursive framework made them not merely appropriate but necessary.

Eisenhower's ideological commitments to duty and self-restraint, like his alarmism, were surely shaped in part by his lifelong military career, as well as by the immediate exigencies of war. Every military commander stresses discipline and uses dire warnings to enforce it, especially in wartime. Moreover, Eisenhower shared almost all of the ideological beliefs typical of professional officers, as delineated in a classic study by Morris Janowitz. This included his conviction that the moral fiber of the nation was degenerating because "the materialism and hedonism of American culture [was] blocking the essential military virtues of patriotism, duty, and self-sacrifice."[27] Janowitz, however, gave this particular point relatively little attention, finding other factors of greater importance in the typical officer's ideology. If he was correct, then in this respect the supreme commander stood out from his colleagues. He stood out, too, in the intensity of his expressions of foreboding. He was also unusual because he relied upon an explicitly formulated, logically consistent ideology linking the call to danger with the belief in duty and self-restraint as religious virtues. Moreover, the same ideological commitments generally informed both his public and his private discourse as it touched on both military and civilian life. Most important, of course, Eisenhower stood out from his colleagues because he alone would bring his ideology into the White House. The worldview he was crystallizing during the war would strongly influence his policymaking as president through some of the most formative years of the cold war.

## MORAL DUALISM AND APOCALYPTIC STRUGGLE

Anyone who forms policies on the basis of an explicit, consistent, relatively unified ideology with a strong religious foundation stands a good chance of becoming a crusader. Although Eisenhower's letter to Swede Hazlett in April 1943 marks the first time he used the word *crusade,* he had been crusading for quite some time—for preparedness, for the high state of alarm that it demanded, for strict discipline and adherence to duty, and for an attitude of selfless harmonious teamwork. His crusading, his alarmism, and his approach to military strategy all reflected his tendency to view military issues in terms of the religious tradition most typical of crusades: the apocalyptic tradition. His support for an all-out air and land attack in northwest Europe made him an early champion of what Russell Weigley has called the "strategy of annihilation." This approach, typically favored by army strategists since the days of Ulysses Grant, is essentially an apocalyptic stance.[28] It assumes that the outcome of a war will be determined in a single cataclysmic collision between massed armies, which will yield total victory for one side and absolute defeat for the other; no compromise is possible. Eisenhower's alarmism went hand-in-glove with this strategic view. Apocalypticism sees every encounter with the enemy forces as part of, or a step toward, the decisive battle. Every battle, therefore, represents a global and deadly danger. Since any defeat in war appears to be an absolute, unmitigated disaster, every battle and every military decision takes on infinite significance and urgency. One is either wholly right or wholly wrong, wholly victorious or wholly defeated; there is no room for error.

Behind the cognitive dualism of apocalypticism, however, lies a moral dualism. When war is legitimated by an apocalyptic paradigm, it is framed as a contest between the upholders of a just cosmic order and those who would overthrow this order and supplant it with an unjust order or (what may be even worse, in this view) no order at all. Each instance of disorder becomes a harbinger of total chaos. This moral dualism generates and legitimates the kind of urgency (and consequently the kind of melodramatic imagery) typified by "Alarmist Ike." It not only legitimates, but demands, a belief that the end—victory—justifies every means, since the structure of the world itself seems to be at stake. It calls logically for war to be waged as a crusade: enemy forces must be fought directly, without quarter, by all available means, until they are exterminated.

Apocalypticism must identify and account for the source of the threat that it confronts. For Eisenhower, a crusade was justified and necessary because humanity was divided into those who were selfless and those who were not. There was no in-between; no one, soldier or civilian, was exempt from making the choice. The world now stood on the brink of this fateful decision. Alarm, mobilization, and preparation for battle, like the "strategy of annihilation," thus became issues of moral as well as strategic urgency—signs that one was moral enough to support good over evil. It might be argued that Eisenhower was an alarmist, a crusader, and an advocate of "annihilation" because he was, from the beginning, committed to an apocalyptic vision of war. His discourse, however, during the first sixteen months of the war lacked crucial components of apocalypticism. He did not insist that the enemy must be totally destroyed because of its absolute moral evil. Nor did he directly address the question of unconditional surrender before the Casablanca Conference, when President Roosevelt declared it the war aim of the Allies. He could readily adopt these elements of the apocalyptic vision, though, because the whole vision was quite congenial to him.

In order to understand Eisenhower's ideology it is crucial to recognize that, for at least the first sixteen months of U.S. participation in the war, he never directly identified the Allies with selflessness or the enemy with selfishness; he never suggested that the war was a crusade to defend or spread a selflessness already inherent in the Allied nations. Indeed the selfishness he decried was almost wholly what he saw displayed on his own side. So the apocalyptic dualism that defined the two sides in the war was not the Allies versus the Axis, but the forces of orderly selflessness versus the forces of disorderly selfishness. It was a sort of global moral civil war being fought within as well as among all nations; and the most important battlefield was within the Allied nations, for restraining the enemy ultimately depended on restraining the true source of all threat—the unbridled self.[29] The root of Eisenhower's alarmism was his deep fear that his soldiers might not have enough moral virtue to push on to victory. Yet the reason for winning the war was, ultimately, so that one would be free to go on voluntarily restraining oneself. This was the core of his crusade in Europe.

## IDEOLOGY AND PERSONALITY

Many of Eisenhower's wartime ideological reflections come from his first year as commander of the Allied forces in Europe, the year in which he rose so rapidly to become a commanding general with responsibilities on a world-historical scale. As he developed a discourse to reflect upon his situation, he articulated a corresponding self-image. The crux of this self-image was that he held himself to the same disciplinary standard he expected of others. He tied his hope for victory directly to his own adherence to the first tenet of his religion. "All these people will keep working for me at top speed as long as they are convinced I'm completely selfless," he told Mamie. But if subordinates began to think that their chief was out for personal glory "the whole thing will go flop. *And I want to get this d——war won!! So the publicity seekers can have the headlines; all I want is another victory.*"[30]

Yet that victory was far from certain. Given the massive problems the Allies faced, there was good reason for doubt. As he prepared for Operation Torch he faced "profound gloom and a protracted shambles," as Peter Lyon says, and the picture did not improve greatly until the spring of 1943.[31] Throughout the first sixteen months, a peril greater than fascism was the danger of losing the war, which would mean failure in his life's most important task. As Lyon notes, once he took control of Torch, he was no longer advising his superiors on the overall coordination of war plans. He became something of an outside observer of those global plans, as his focus turned to the immediate problems of a specific theater. This more distant vantage point might have given him more space to reflect on the larger issues involved in fighting a war, but at the same time it might have increased his sense of uncertainty too.

During the North African campaign, he was quite candid about his insecurities, at least in private correspondence. But he turned the problem of fear into a problem of self-discipline. "It is a real exercise in self-control to keep yourself doing your own job and pounding away at it day after day," he told Gen. Joseph McNarney. A telling note to Marshall read: "If a man permitted himself to do so, he could get absolutely frantic." The general, however, would not permit himself to feel such an emotion; he worked consciously at maintaining the greatest possible calm and confidence. When he lamented the problems associated with Torch to his chief of staff, Walter Bedell (Beetle) Smith, he insisted: "I am not crying wolf nor am I growing fearful of shadows. . . . I am disturbed by the apparently bland assumption that this job is finished." But even such an implicit expression of doubt was quite rare for Eisenhower. To confirm his image of himself as an exemplar of self-control, he had to turn his alarmism into a virtue, a farsighted awareness of genuine peril.[32]

Denying his alarmism and fear of failure also forced him to deny the Allied feeling of pessimism. He wrote to John: "I am probably the most optimistic person in this whole world. Everybody else sees all the risks and dangers and I guess I am just a wishful thinker, because I just shut my eyes to such things and say 'We will go ahead and try to win.'" Perhaps he was merely trying to allay John's fears. Perhaps he genuinely believed these words. If so, John was not taken in. Although his father succeeded in appearing "simple, self-confident and stable," he later said, pictures taken of him "give no indication of the tremendous battle he was fighting with himself to combat exhaustion, frustration, and the normal doubts."[33]

Occasionally Eisenhower did admit a discrepancy between the image he was creating and the reality behind it. In a considerable understatement, he told Marshall: "There have been times during the past few weeks when it has been a trifle difficult to keep up, in front of everybody, a proper attitude of confidence and optimism." When he had to cancel a planned attack in Tunisia, he reflected: "In such circumstances it is always necessary for the commander to avoid an attitude of defeatism; discouragement on the part of the high commander inevitably spreads rapidly throughout the command and always with unfortunate results. On that occasion, it was exceedingly difficult to display any particular optimism." Eisenhower's confidence and optimism were only a logical extension of his wartime ideology of military duty and leadership. He had to demand optimism of himself in order to conform to his emerging self-image.[34]

During the North African campaign he wrote to his friend Charles Gailey: "On the whole, I think I keep up my optimism very well, although we have suffered some sad disappointments. . . . Only the sissy indulges in crying and whimpering because everything does not go as he would like. We have constantly got to get tougher and tougher—all of us—take our losses in stride." The same sense of duty that required an outward show of optimism also demanded that one not indulge normal human emotions. In war "a man must develop a veneer of callousness," he told Mamie. Explaining to his brother Edgar why he attended neither his father's nor his brother's funeral in 1942, he invoked his own commitment to duty: "War is a hard task-master, and all personal and family considerations simply must be ignored when they interfere with the military job."

Noting in his diary his decision not to attend his father's funeral, he wrote that he wished he could be with his mother, "But we're at war! And war is not soft—it has no time to indulge even the deepest and most sacred emotions."[35]

The next day, thinking about his father, he added a revealing glimpse into the roots of his commitment to duty: "My only regret is that it was always so difficult to let him know the great depth of my affection for him." Indeed, he would later remark on several occasions that it was characteristic of him, and he believed of all Anglo-Saxon men, to restrain their emotions. After receiving an award from British officers, he reported that his emotions "came so nearly overwhelming me that my only recourse was to keep a very tight hold on myself." This kind of control was precisely what was needed to win wars, he insisted. Only by restraining personal desires and feelings for the sake of the common good could people cooperate together. In Eisenhower's ideology any indulgence in, or concession to, any personal emotion—and especially to a personal desire—constituted an act of selfishness.[36]

## SELF-RESTRAINT AND ANTIFASCISM

When Eisenhower did finally articulate an antifascist attitude he set it firmly in the context of his larger ideological framework. All four of the statements of 7 and 8 April 1943 (see notes 8–11 above) displayed his typical grandiosity and sense of global importance. Three of the four were typically alarmist in their apocalypticism, and all linked fidelity to democratic values with the central importance of mobilization and doing one's duty.[37] For the next two years, whenever Eisenhower repeated his antifascist message, he was likely to refer in the same breath to self-restraint, selfless cooperation, and obedience to duty.[38] On the first anniversary of the Torch invasion, for example, his official statement called the war a crusade to protect American democracy, adding, "The God of Justice fights on our side." He then concluded that the troops, after victory, could go home "with the proud knowledge of having done, in our time, our duty to our beloved country." In another formal statement he described the Allied soldier as a defender of liberty and humanitarianism "against the forces of greed and selfishness and love of power, today typified in Nazism, Fascism, and Shintoism. . . . Just as he in battle has learned the need for disciplined team work, he hopes that [his family and friends at home] understand how necessary it is for each to do his assigned duty."[39]

Eisenhower rarely voiced any antifascist sentiment in his personal letters. On the few occasions he did so, he linked it directly to his characteristic insistence on the first tenet of his religion. While worrying as usual about money in a letter to Mamie, Ike pronounced himself willing to accept a rumored pay cut:

> I'm in favor of lower salaries throughout our whole economic structure and absolute price control, with every man's job looked upon as that of a soldier's. This war is serious—we'll never preserve our accustomed ways of living in the U.S.—free speech—press—and right to worship—unless we all turn in now and fight and work!!

He told an old friend from Abilene:

> This war—more than any other in history—definitely places on one side the forces of liberty and human dignity and, on the other, the forces of evil and enslavement. Moreover, I am of the complete conviction that the only sure way to win this war is for every one of us to do his part, his full part. If each one of us believes that he is contributing something to this great and single purpose, then there is automatically generated that great morale and determination that no dictator can ever stand against.[40]

Why should antifascism be linked so consistently with self-restraint? Eisenhower never explicated the connection clearly until after the war's end, but he foreshadowed his postwar views in two especially revealing letters to his brother Milton and his wife. In May 1944, responding to the idea of a film version of his life story, he told Milton: "If properly handled in a water-tight contract, the theme of the picture could take the slant of glorifying opportunities presented under the American system and tend to support initiative, effort and persistence in an average American family, as opposed to the idea of collectivity that discards self-dependence and is ready to trust to regimentation for a secure future." The film would thus promote "the virtues of the traditional American system." The same day, he told Mamie that he hoped the movie "might encourage kids to work, and to depend upon themselves, rather than to become too complacent with respect to the State's obligation to the individual."[41]

Here was one crux of Eisenhower's postwar discourse: when individuals let governments provide for their needs, rather than working persistently to meet their own needs, the society inevitably becomes increasingly regimented, as in the Axis (later it would be communist) nations. Why would individuals allow this to happen? According to Eisenhower, because persistent hard work meant disciplining oneself, putting duty ahead of immediate indulgence in selfish desires. Those who were complacent and refused self-discipline were bound to end up under the harsher discipline of the State. The Axis powers represented the fate that could overtake all of civilization, including the Allies, in the absence of sufficient self-restraint.

Haunted by this fear, Eisenhower could never feel confident that victory would provide any insurance against totalitarianism. At the very outset of the war, on the day Britain declared war on Germany, he had written in his diary that if this war proved as destructive as World War I, after it was over, "communism and anarchy are apt to spread rapidly, while crime and disorder, loss of personal liberties, and abject poverty will curse the areas that witness any amount of fighting." In September 1942 he addressed similar thoughts to Mamie, with a revealing twist:

> Even after we've won the military victory, the problems facing the world will be such as to require a courage equal to that of the battlefield. Just as the World War brought in an era of almost hysterical change and restlessness, so will this one bring about revolutions in our customs, laws and economic processes. If we could hope for a greater mass discipline—self-imposed—there would be cause for rejoicing; the danger is that special economic, industrial or social groups will apply pressures that will either be disruptive or might force, for a time at least, the adoption of some form of dictatorship in our democracies. Either outcome would be tragic. . . . It looks as if we must face a long struggle.[42]

The ideal outcome of the war, in Eisenhower's view, was a society built on "mass discipline—self-imposed." Without sufficient restraint a society, like an army, would degenerate into a mere mob. But if restraint were not adopted voluntarily, it would have to be imposed by others, which meant dictatorship. This was the evil of fascism (and communism) for Eisenhower: not that individuals were restrained, but that the restraints were externally and forcibly imposed.

Although Eisenhower disliked the idea of giving governments more centralized power, if it ever came to a choice between social chaos and dictatorship, he would surely choose the latter. He had thought through this issue during the early years of the Great Depression. In February 1932, noting in his diary the widespread feeling that "virtual panic is upon us," he predicted: "Things are not going to take an upturn until more power is centered in one man's hands. . . . For two years I have been called 'Dictator Ike' because I believe that virtual dictatorship must be exercised by our president. So now I keep still—but I still believe it! . . . We *must* conform to the President's program regardless of consequences." As

Kenneth Davis noted, his plans for mobilization in case of war gave the federal government emergency powers that it was in fact loathe to take on. And, writing on behalf of the army, he likened the New Deal programs to war, calling them a "powerful offensive against the forces of depression."[43]

He articulated these views after he had taken actual military action as a result of the Depression, watching troops under his command rout the Bonus Marchers in 1932. In his official reports on the Bonus March incident, Eisenhower called the marchers a mob "incited by radicals and hot heads . . . the subversive element"; he described the event as "a riot rapidly assuming alarming proportions."[44] Knowing firsthand what it meant to use force against a "mob" spawned by poverty, he still found centralized governmental power the best answer to social unrest.

As Eisenhower's fuller postwar reflections clearly demonstrate, this intense fear of social disorder and its consequences formed the crux of his concern for discipline and self-restraint. Foreign nations might be the enemy in wartime, but disorder stemming from the unrestrained self was the ultimate enemy in both war and peace. Believing that dictatorships were elicited by unchecked human impulses creating chaos, he was quick to see and fear the threat of government control precisely because he was quick to see and fear the threat of mob rule. So the key question in all of his social and political thinking was how to avoid both social unrest and totalitarianism by getting the masses to restrain themselves voluntarily. Of course this was a mirror image of Eisenhower's most pressing practical question: How to motivate the troops voluntarily to restrain their selfish emotions?

His answer always led him back to the "American system." People had to understand and embrace the essential principle of this system: self-reliance and voluntary self-restraint go hand in hand; those who rely on the state to meet their needs will inevitably cede to the state the right to supply the most important need, social restraint. This was the lesson that would bring victory in war: disciplined soldiers join the team, take the initiative, and get the job done; the self-indulgent wait for someone else to do it for them.

For Eisenhower, "America" was a single community—a fantasy image of his boyhood Abilene writ large. Old-fashioned patriotism, he wrote to his sister-in-law, meant a "sense of loyalty and obligation to the community that is necessary to the preservation of all the privileges and rights that the community guarantees."[45] He told his brother Arthur that, during wartime, loyalty meant obedience to government orders: "Far above my hatred of war is the determination to smash every enemy of my country, especially Hitler and the Japs—or to put it more simply, my hatred of war will never equal my conviction that it is the duty of every one of us, civilian and soldier alike, to carry out the orders of our government when a war emergency arises. . . . Right or wrong, my country."[46] The extreme chauvinism of this statement was quite rare in Eisenhower's wartime discourse. He never suggested that U.S. soldiers and civilians owed loyalty to their nation because it was inherently more virtuous and self-denying than other nations. But one's nation did not have to prove itself worthy of personal sacrifice by embodying self-restraint or any other moral value. Simply because it was one's own nation, facing the supreme emergency of war, it had the right to demand the selfless sacrifice needed for victory.

More important, by demanding that sacrifice, the nation offered the individual an unparalleled opportunity for developing and demonstrating selflessness, the virtue that would be just as vital in peace as in war. But as long as the sacrifice was voluntary, it modeled the enduring (albeit less stringent) peacetime self-restraint that was the ultimate goal of the war. In peace as well as in war, all individuals would have to protect their own freedom as well as that of their neighbors. The only way to forestall a radical loss of freedom was to curtail one's freedom willingly, subordinating individual interests to the good of the whole community.

## THE DARLAN DEAL

The ideological discourse that crystallized for Eisenhower in the early months of World War II provides a valuable framework to interpret his most controversial decision of the war: the Darlan deal. His ideological commitments fostered the fears that made the Darlan deal seem necessary, and the deal's controversial aftermath validated and reinforced those commitments in his discourse. Long before the Torch invasion, he had predicted, in his typically dramatic, alarmist language, that it would be an operation "of a desperate nature . . . sailing a dangerous political sea . . . in which military skill and ability can do little in charting a safe course."[47] As always, he felt it his duty to expect the worst possible outcome, while concealing that expectation from others.

Many historians have concluded that the general's dealings with Darlan yielded something close to the worst possible outcome. It did not save the French fleet, as Eisenhower had hoped. Nor did it yield much tangible military assistance, as he admitted. While it brought some of the more reactionary French over to the Allied side, it alienated many other French and, in the long run, stirred up as many problems in the rear as it solved. From a purely military point of view, it was of doubtful wisdom.[48]

Few historians have noted, though, that Eisenhower knew when he made the deal that it promised little direct military advantage. He knew that Darlan's authority over the French army in Tunisia was highly uncertain. He also knew that there was little chance of obtaining meaningful military performance from French troops or of bringing the French fleet over to the Allied side. On the day after concluding the deal he told Beetle Smith that the military position was already favorable anyway. "However," he added, "there is always the Arab question to think of and the tremendous problem of policing this whole country if we had any unrest."[49]

It was fear of internal disorder that led Eisenhower to put Darlan in charge. He made this clear to Gen. Mark Clark the day before concluding the deal: "It is important that we do not create any dissension among the [Arab] tribes or encourage them to break away from existing methods of control. To organize this country in support of the war effort, we must use French officials and we do not want any internal unrest or trouble." He continued to voice a fear of passive resistance from the French army. This was hardly his main rationale for the deal, however, since he told Beetle Smith he was "convinced that the lower ranks of the [French] Army are pro-Giraud and anti-Vichy. But to uncover and organize that sentiment would take time and, in some instances, an application of force and general policing of region at least for a considerable period." This was his real answer (though offered only in private to his closest aide) to the question so many asked: Why not form a provisional government out of those anti-Vichy forces? Why rely upon known fascists instead? The problem was organizing and policing the region. It had to be done quickly, and Eisenhower had neither the time nor the troops to accomplish such a task.

Darlan, on the other hand, seemed to have an organization already in place that could effectively retain French colonial control. So the general readily appointed him head of the civil government despite his notorious fascist record. As Stephen Ambrose summarizes the situation: "Eisenhower was most concerned with getting on to Tunisia; to that end, he wanted a secure rear area; to get it, he was ready to work with the existing French administration, no matter how bad its fascist reputation." Ambrose concludes that "the Allies had, in short, paid a high political price for a minor material gain. . . . Darlan did deliver those 'proven administrators' whom [U.S. envoy Robert] Murphy felt to be essential to domestic tranquillity in North Africa, but that was about all." This is correct, but it obscures the central point. In Eisenhower's ideology domestic tranquillity was hardly a minor gain. In fact it was the deal's principal aim. From the standpoint of his apocalyptic dualism, the only alternative to guaranteed security was a rapid breakdown of all duly constituted authority, which meant social chaos.[50]

Robert Burk (following other biographers) has criticized Eisenhower's dealings with the Vichy government as "an early example of a consistent willingness
to view military or other international crises in the detached, amoral calculus of
the military strategist." If this was true, it was a source of pride, not shame, for
the general: "With us this whole problem is cold blooded military necessity," he
explained to Marshall. Later he would justify the restoration of the Italian monar-
chy in similar terms as "essential if chaos in Italy is to be avoided. The present
Italian regime is managing to keep comparative order and tranquillity in the
country which according to the General should work to the benefit of the Allies."
Eventually he would extend this to a general principle: "the same thing that
always happens in an invasion of enemy territory, namely the need to drop off
fighting units to protect the rear and to preserve order among the population."[51]

Shortly before his agreement with Darlan he had told a press conference that
he would lie, cheat, and steal to win the war. In his apocalyptic ideology, every
means was justified if it contributed to winning the war. And victory in the war
meant an ultimate victory for selflessness. In February 1943, when he reiterated
to John that "personal fortunes mean nothing—the job is to win the war," he
added that in modern war, "governments are forced to treat individuals as
pawns." Although the comment referred explicitly to his own treatment by the
army, it shows how easily Eisenhower could legitimate his disregard for civil liberties as perfectly rational, and thus selfless.[52]

When Eisenhower claimed to be implementing a rational strategic calculus,
however, he was actually rationalizing a rather irrational decision. He ended up
creating many new problems for himself, placing military success in jeopardy
unnecessarily, while the "Arab problem" he aimed to resolve was surely overesti-
mated. When John J. McCloy visited North Africa in March 1943, he found no
need for continuing the repressive measures enforced by the Vichy government.
"Their repeal would have no effect on 'le Probleme Mussulman,'" he told
Eisenhower, while it would serve U.S. interests. The general was led to an irrational decision in part by his typical penchant for overestimating the threat of
social disorder.[53]

In North Africa his military good sense was also overcome by ideological and
racial prejudice. "Millions of Arabs are a very uncertain quantity, explosive and full
of prejudices," he wrote to Mamie. "Many things done here that look queer are just
to keep the Arabs from blazing up into revolt. We sit on a boiling kettle!!" "Arabs
are everywhere," he wrote to John, "and seem to have very little regard for personal
cleanliness." "The Arab," he told Beetle Smith, "typifies filth, squalor, rags, and laziness. As he stalks along in his stately filthiness, he seems to be perfectly content

with his lot." Eisenhower depicted the Arab populace as a squalid mob, incapable (at least as yet) of self-discipline. Among people without self-discipline, he had told Mamie, rampant selfishness would force—and apparently justify—some form of dictatorship, because it was the only alternative to chaotic disruption. As Ambrose points out, he was following here the principles he had learned serving with MacArthur in the Philippines: "Work through the elite, don't ask questions about local conditions, don't interfere. Given Eisenhower's beliefs and [pre-war] experiences, it never occurred to him not to deal with Darlan."[54]

Unfortunately, he soon came to the conclusion that the French leaders with whom he had to deal were not much better. On three separate occasions he wrote to Beetle Smith on this subject: "All these Frogs have a single thought—'ME.' It isn't this operation that's wearing me down—it's the petty intrigue and the necessity of dealing with little, selfish, conceited worms that call themselves men"; "They are not thinking in terms of a cause but of individual fortunes and opportunities"; and "Once the population looks to us as their benefactors, I can tell all the turncoats and skunks to go to hell."[55] The French leaders were worms and skunks, in his view, not because they were fascists or colonial oppressors, but because they were politicians and thus naturally concerned only about self. Nevertheless, he ceded civil authority to these selfish fascists because they had experience administering an orderly Western-style government.

Many in the United States and England decried Eisenhower's decision. To defend himself publicly would mean confessing his hurt and thus revealing some insecurity about his personal situation—an emotion that the general would never display. Privately, though, he expressed his sensitivity to the criticism. When an old friend wrote that his wife kept Ike's picture prominently displayed in their home, he replied, with typical exaggeration: "I have at least one staunch friend! Sometimes in the midst of these Darlan-Peyrouton and related problems I rather doubt it."[56] He showed his sensitivity most clearly in the numerous private defenses of his actions written to his closest relatives and friends. These self-justifications drew upon and reinforced all of his ideological commitments. They were not just after-the-fact rationalizations, however; they reflected his genuine understanding of the situation.

Eisenhower's first line of defense, predictably, was that he was placing duty above his own best interests. He urged John not to be upset by the unprecedented public criticism of his father, because military leaders "should not be too much disturbed about popularity or newspaper acclaim." He described his critics to Harold Macmillan as "these long-haired, starry-eyed guys [who] keep gunning for me." He added, "I'm no reactionary, Christ on the Mountain! I'm idealistic as Hell!" If the quotation is accurate, it is unique evidence of how Eisenhower felt about the issue privately: one had to be either a reactionary or an idealist. This view allowed him to see the preservation of human rights in wartime as an idealistic hope that only the "starry-eyed" would cling to. As a military leader, he could tell himself, he was duty-bound to restrain his own idealism in favor of a rational calculation of "cold-blooded military necessity."[57]

Just after the Darlan deal was concluded he told Beetle Smith: "I do not repeat not understand why it should be thought I fail to realize crookedness or intense unpopularity of Darlan." A few months later he had integrated this aspect of the affair into his ideology. To Edgar he wrote that he was "a little peeved . . . that anyone should think I was so incredibly stupid as to fail to realize I was doing an unpopular thing, particularly with those who were concerned with things other than winning the war—which is my whole doctrine and reason for existence." A long letter to Mamie a few days earlier, reflecting on his promotion to four-star general, expounded this theme at great length. "I didn't have much feeling" about the promotion, he claimed; a commander is too busy thinking about winning the war to be concerned with "what the world calls success." Promotion and criticism must both be "as completely disregarded as the ant crawling across the floor." Victory comes only through clear logical thinking and fidelity to duty. He had certainly known, he continued, that his "acceptance of Darlan would be bitterly assailed by many, particularly by those who think that all humans think in terms of self only." For himself, he wanted only Mamie's prayer that he would always do his duty to the extreme limit of his ability. Here, as always, there was a clear line between those committed only to duty and victory and those pursuing their own personal gain.[58]

From this perspective, Eisenhower could convince himself that he was the aggrieved party, for he had to deal with such highly selfish politicians only because of his overriding sense of duty. Eisenhower wrote off his critics by finding the same political selfishness in them. "A lot of the columnists at home were very noisy in their objections," he told John, "and quite frequently these people have a very grave influence on political leaders." Eisenhower interpreted all these problems as "political"; i.e., motivated by selfishness and thus outside the scope of a disciplined, selfless, military life. "My concern has nothing whatsoever to do with international or French politics. . . . This matter is purely military," he insisted to Marshall. Naturally he complained to his superior: "The sooner I can get rid of all these questions that are outside the military in scope, the happier I will be."[59]

The experience in North Africa confirmed Eisenhower's view that politicians, being naturally selfish, were a breed quite apart from military officers. Throughout his life, no matter how embroiled he became in politics, he would insist that he was not a politician, because he pursued no personal ambitions or interests. So he could readily convince himself that the question of fascism was not really germane here. That was a political question, to be debated among the selfish. He was above such petty concerns, and could (and in fact must) avoid getting involved. He must do only what was necessary to maintain social order. That was the appropriate job for the selfless. Having survived the Darlan affair with his prestige still intact, he was more certain than ever of his ideological convictions.

Those ideological convictions were clearly articulated in the first months of the war, and they did not include any dedicated opposition to fascism. That did not come until many months later, when Eisenhower's refusal to allow DeGaulle's visit to Algeria threatened to stir up the smoldering ashes of the Darlan deal. Within the structure of Eisenhower's ideology, there was no contradiction between antifascism and the Darlan deal. Rather, the two were perfectly compatible. The ideology had led to the Darlan deal, and thus it led indirectly to the articulation of antifascism. The legacy of both ideological elements would live on in Eisenhower's later discourse. He would often proclaim his fierce opposition to totalitarianism. He would be equally strenuous in calling for rigid control of all threats of disorder. Truly, as Ambrose says, his passion for democracy was essentially conservative. He would praise democracy, above all, as a means of conserving social order through voluntary self-control. He would value democracy, and the freedom it affords, less as ends in themselves than as symbols of the essential ideological value for which he waged his crusade in Europe.

CHAPTER 2

# Head of the Occupation
# of Germany

Eisenhower's forces won their unconditional victory over Germany by destroying every semblance of independent German military and political structure. After the triumph was complete, the Allied military was the de facto government of Germany. It seemed natural for the military commander to stay on as commander of both his own troops and the enemy's territory. So V-E day transformed Eisenhower from supreme commander of the greatest fighting force in history into merely the chief administrator of an occupied territory. "His heart was never in the German occupation," wrote his diplomatic advisor Robert Murphy. Secretary of War Henry Stimson found him "very disappointed" at being forced to take the post. Historian Edward Peterson sustains this judgment: "He showed little interest in his political job. . . . Usually he delegated decisions, so much so that observers were amazed by his lack of command." He was, says biographer Peter Lyon, merely "marking time."[1]

Historians generally focus on policy decisions. Since Eisenhower made few significant decisions in this period of his life, it has received little scholarly study. In the Eisenhower biographies, the brief chapters on this period view it only as a bridge to the future. They focus on his dawning thoughts about the presidency and on his relationships with the Russians, particularly his Soviet counterpart and newfound friend, Marshal Grigori Zhukov, who hosted his reception in Moscow.[2] His greatest impact during that time, and the most valuable clue to his later influence, has been overlooked by historians because it lay in the realm not of policy but of words.[3]

## THE IMPORTANCE OF SYMBOLISM

When Eisenhower did occasionally step in to make a decision on occupation policy, he was usually responding to public relations concerns. During the war, all of his biographers agree, he had shown a great talent for public relations. He saw this realm as absolutely crucial. In 1944 he told journalist William Robinson that "public opinion wins most of the wars and always wins the peace." Now that peace had come, he was sensitive to every nuance of public opinion. He agreed wholeheartedly with George Marshall that the army's biggest postwar problem was its public relations—with its own soldiers, with Congress, and with the American public.[4]

These concerns with public imagery seemed to bother him only sporadically. In early June 1945, he complained to Marshall (with typical exaggeration) about critics who accused the army of moving too slowly toward restoring civilian control in Germany: "They believe that the millennium can be achieved in 24 hours." The next day, discussing his ill-fated policy forbidding U.S. troops to fraternize with Germans, he told Marshall that "the most important thing at the moment seems to be public opinion in the United States." On that same day he urged the Joint Chiefs of Staff to speed the withdrawal of U.S. troops from the Soviet zone of occupation because anything that delayed the establishment of the Allies' Control Council for Germany "would be attributed to us and might well develop strong public reaction."[5] In October, he once again went through a bout of intense concern about public relations. He complained to his former aide Harry Butcher that he needed a good public relations officer more in peacetime than during the war, and a few days later he advised his chief deputy, Gen. Lucius Clay, to stress the PR value in all his reports on army policies.[6]

These occasional administrative issues were only a minor part of Eisenhower's cultivation of symbolism and imagery. The major part came in his public rhetoric. In his six months as head of the occupation, Eisenhower spent much of his time participating in ceremonies honoring him and marking the end of the war, ceremonies at which he often made formal speeches or statements. He was his nation's greatest public relations agent. In the most famous of his speeches, at the London Guildhall on 12 June, he defined his role quite accurately. When a commander receives such postwar tributes, he said, "his position is a symbol" of all the forces he has commanded, and he ought to feel this symbolism.[7] As head of the occupying forces in Germany, Eisenhower was much more a symbol than an active administrator. That was apparently how he wanted it. His many speeches, official statements, and public appearances constituted, in effect, a ritual process that symbolically marked the passage from war to peace.

Some of his symbolic words were celebrations and recapitulations of the victory just achieved. Others were analyses of the postwar era, responding to the perceived needs of the moment and exhorting his audiences to meet those needs. He relied on the clichés that one would expect from any commander celebrating victory: the glorious victory, the heroism of the troops, their amazing triumphs against all odds, their persistence in overcoming every obstacle, the need to mourn those who sacrificed their lives, and the ultimate value of the cause for which they died. His speeches also featured the clichés used by every modern democracy that wins a war: the ordinary soldiers as the true heroes, the triumph of freedom over totalitarianism as the cause for which they fought and died, and the need for continuing vigilance to protect liberal values. These kinds of clichés are an essential, though often overlooked, part of any war. The victors want not only to brag, but to define what the war was about and to stake their claim to controlling the future, as Eisenhower's clichés plainly did.[8]

Postwar rhetoric has an even more crucial function. Success in war always comes at a psychological price. It requires that society value and promote the kind of lethal violence that is, at all other times, most dangerous and therefore most strenuously forbidden. In war all is fair; the rules that normally govern human behavior are suspended. This makes wartime a "liminal" state, to use the terminology of Victor Turner.[9] Turner has written of liminal states as times when the rules and routines of society are suspended, times themselves suspended between the old order that has been destroyed and the new order yet to be created. Precisely because no generally accepted rules prevail, liminal states are potentially creative but also disorienting and disturbing. A chaos reigns that can dissolve every kind of order.

Since war is inherently liminal, the soldier inevitably embodies liminality. He is therefore viewed by others, and by himself, in ambivalent terms, as a creative hero who is also an agent of disruption and danger. "The warrior is both fascinating and terrifying," says James Aho in his study, *Religious Mythology and the Art of War*. "The universal existence of exclusive men's barracks segregated from the community is not simply for disciplinary purposes. It also has authentic religious motives."[10] The warrior must be segregated because he embodies such a powerful threat to norms and order. Often this threat is expressed in some kind of taboo.

When war ends, the taboo must be removed. There must be a symbolic closure to the war experience, creating a clear demarcation between war and peace. The liminal state must be ended, the reversal of values must be undone, and the warriors who have embodied the reversal must be reintegrated into the normal routine of society. The ritual celebrations that typically follow victory in war are crucial to performing this function. In many cultures, as Aho notes, "reentry into the world of ordinary men must be preceded by the performance of intricate lustral rites and in some cases even purification by fire."[11]

World War II had been particularly disorienting for the United States. Until Pearl Harbor, the nation had been reluctant to commit itself to violence. But once that commitment was made, its forces had wreaked violence of unprecedented magnitude. The war had been in many respects a liminal state, and in the summer of 1945 it was time (in the European theater) to mark a return to the norm. Rites of reintegration were in order. Eisenhower, as the best known symbol of the successful wartime violence, was now called upon to preside over the symbolic closure of the war and passage back to the peacetime norm. He would use, not lustration or fire, but his favorite ritual means: the spoken and written word.

Words always play a crucial role in the passage from wartime to the postwar era. The war-torn society seeks to restore order by erasing its sense of disorder. One effective, perhaps necessary, way to accomplish this is to create an interpretive framework—a story about the war, telling how it began, who started it and why, how it was fought and why, etc. By repeating this story, the postwar society gives meaning to its harrowing experience of killing and being killed. It makes sense out of the war by placing the liminal period within a larger picture of a continuing overarching order that preceded the war and will follow it as well. Thus the story serves to deny that there was, in the final analysis, any real disorder at all.

The story, though begun in wartime, is finally created in peacetime. It must explain how peace came, and why. The return to peace inevitably becomes the final chapter in the story of the war. That final chapter defines the meaning of the new peacetime situation and thereby helps to give meaning to the war. The story of the return to peace must somehow demonstrate that a positive change has occurred, if the suffering of the war is to be justified. War and peace must be two correlated chapters of a single story.

Eisenhower, acutely aware of his fame and his unique role as supreme commander of the Allied forces in Europe, took it as his obligation (and his well-enjoyed privilege) to articulate the shared story of war and peace in his time. So, while frequently complaining of the heavy burden of speaking engagements, he kept up a constant round of traveling, appearances, and public statements, which gave him a platform to tell the story as he wanted it to be told. For the first time, he was articulating the meaning of peace as he understood it. He was also doing so in public, making a public commitment to that articulation. The more often he set forth his understanding of peace, the more strongly he committed himself to it. This understanding was framed within a three-layered ideological context: first, concern for the U.S. Army and its public image; second, political and economic concerns of U.S. foreign policy; and third, ideological and spiritual commitments.

## A Booster for the Army

The army, and Eisenhower as the symbol of its success, had received lavish praise during the war. Almost as soon as the war ended, though, criticism of the army's handling of the German occupation began. Eisenhower was unaccustomed to criticism; it was something "he did not like at all," says Stephen Ambrose, and he hoped to mute it. Yet he and the other top army officials knew that this was a typical American pattern. They had all witnessed the rapid evaporation of public support for the military after World War I, and they had reason to fear that the same would happen again. In the first months after V-E day, they were especially concerned that the clamor for rapid demobilization would undermine public support for the army and lead to wholesale cuts in its budget.[12]

Eisenhower was doing more than simply trying to protect his service's budget, however. He was a true believer in military preparedness; this had always been his passion. Throughout the war he thought about how it could be done better the next time. He wanted to be sure that the nation was never caught unprepared again. At the war's end, he agreed with many other army leaders that the two keys to future success were peacetime Universal Military Training (UMT) and unification of the armed services. He told William Robinson that he ranked these among his highest concerns. Toward the end of his tour of duty in Germany, he wrote to Marshall that all his speeches "just keep hammering on two or three points," UMT and unification among them.[13]

His other major concern, he told Robinson, was U.S.–British cooperation. In his speeches, he told Marshall, he spoke more generally of the need for international cooperation. Eisenhower often linked the teamwork of service integration with the teamwork of Allied unity. "Service integration is fully as important as is Allied integration in waging a war," he told a press conference, choosing his tense carefully to include future wars as well as the one just past. His stress on international cooperation also reflected an army orientation. That branch alone among the military services tended to embrace what Daniel Yergin has called the Yalta axioms. These reflected Franklin Roosevelt's trust that a consortium of great powers, including the Soviet Union, could cooperate effectively to police the world and maintain a mutually agreeable form of global stability. Policing was certainly on Eisenhower's mind, for he was in effect the police chief of conquered Germany. Although he delegated day-to-day supervision to others, he played what he thought was a more important role: alerting the world to the dangers of insufficient policing, and thereby cultivating support for the program of the U.S. Army and U.S. Government in Europe.[14]

Eisenhower made the peace seem very fragile and the possibility of another war seem very real to his audiences. This certainly served the purposes of the army, for he could then insist that the combination of international cooperation and overwhelming military strength was just as necessary for keeping the peace as for winning the war: "Weakness cannot co-operate with anything. Only strength can cooperate. If we are going to live the years of peace . . . we must be strong and we must be ready to co-operate." On at least one occasion he stressed the value of massive military production for fighting the only kind of war likely to win public support in the future, a war fought with enough power to give the United States a quick victory with minimal losses: "If you apply overwhelming force losses for your side are negligible. . . . When a bomb can do the work let us not spend an American life for it."[15]

Still, the supreme commander's overriding and constant theme was the need to avoid another war. He invoked his own experience as the ultimate touchstone of truth: "The hard task of a commander is to send men into battle knowing some of them—often many—must be killed or wounded . . . It is a soul-killing task! . . . The blackness of their grief can be relieved only by the faith that all this shall not happen again!" The crucial challenge was to prevent the persistent disorder that might trigger another round of mass slaughter.[16]

This theme also served the interests of the army by defending against critics who accused the army of delaying the institution of civilian government. In October, as the criticisms mounted, Eisenhower suggested to Marshall a public relations campaign stressing the army's desire to turn over government to civilians as soon as basic order was restored. Its theme would be: "Because Government in Germany had to begin from a situation of utter chaos, there was no one capable of initiating it except the Army." The army would turn over government to civilians as soon as possible and thereafter be "strictly a reserve of force to be used when demanded. . . . The peace of Europe demands a long-term occupation by fairly strong forces." This message "should be publicly stated over and over," he added, "because, as I understand it, this is exactly the War Department conviction on the subject."[17]

This last comment should probably be accepted at face value. Eisenhower never really wanted the duties of day-to-day governing. The army's role, as he saw it, was to pursue peace by bringing order out of chaos and to be available for emergencies, when chaos threatened to erupt again.[18] In a larger sense, though indirectly, his speeches were meant to allay public fears of militarism. These fears were natural, in light of the massive militarization of World War II and the unprecedented levels of peacetime money and manpower the military was now seeking. By insisting that military leaders, more than anyone, wanted peace, he was offering an assurance that all of the military's resources would be under civilian control and serve civilian purposes. The military wanted to be used as rarely as possible, he implied, and ultimately it hoped to find itself put out of business.

The longing for peace, the fragility of the peace, the importance of cooperation with allies, the need for a strong army to preserve the peace, and the need to prepare for future military emergencies—all these themes would aid the army in dealing with its postwar problems.

## A LIBERAL INTERNATIONALIST

Eisenhower's readiness to relinquish army control reflected his larger view of the postwar situation. His rhetoric was intended primarily to advocate not just the army's parochial aims, but the broader program of the liberal internationalist establishment. During the war, Eisenhower had met all the establishment's elites, from Roosevelt and Winston Churchill on down. He had come to share their sense of urgency about creating a postwar world order that would preserve and expand the democratic capitalist system. For this reason his discourse reflected the fundamental assumptions of Western liberalism.

Individual freedom and social order were, he said, the goals for which the war had been fought. They were the essence of "those things that we call the American heritage. To preserve that heritage, more than three million of our citizens . . . resolutely faced every terror the ruthless Nazi could devise." According to Eisenhower, "It was for freedom we fought and won this war." It was a heritage rooted in and shared by English society. So the American had joined the Englishman "to preserve his freedom of worship, his equality before the law, his liberty to speak and act as he sees fit." If these were the aims for which so many had died, they should naturally become the hallmarks of the postwar peace.[19]

It was not enough, however, simply to safeguard these values in one's own nation. Eisenhower agreed with all liberal internationalists that peace was now indivisible, for disorder anywhere threatened stable order everywhere. "The substance of peace is a universal appreciation of human values," he proclaimed. But human values, in his discourse, were those values that had made America (and England) great. Only when the truth of Anglo-Saxon values "has permeated to the remotest hamlet and heart of all people may we beat our swords into plowshares." Therefore, the army's immediate task was to institute "systems of justice and order" modeled on the American and English systems. The larger task was to universalize this liberal international order. So he called upon the United States to be "a vast influence of international law and order," to create "agreements and machinery to maintain order and eliminate piracy in international relationships," and thereby to lift "the age old curse, the fear of war." Just as peace follows war, he was saying, so order should follow disorder and freedom should follow the era of triumphant dictatorships. The world would find stability in the universalizing of Anglo-Saxon values.[20]

Eisenhower could have stopped there and created a story rather typical of victors in war: the chaos of war was created by the chaos of foreign values; our own values have now triumphed; we usher in a new order based on the reign of those values. The prevailing discourse of the liberal internationalist elites, however, would not allow for such a simple transition from chaos to stability. After fifteen years of girding themselves to stave off economic depression, socialism, and fascism, these elites could no longer speak in confident tones about endless enlightenment and orderly progress. They could only express a desperate hope that the worst might be avoided. Naturally, then, their language focused attention on what that worst could be. The war just passed, Eisenhower said, had "eliminated one menace to our country's freedom—even her very existence." But he, like others, depicted future dangers in equally dire terms. The orders under which he conducted the occupation, embodied in Joint Chiefs of Staff Paper 1067, asserted that the war had "destroyed the German economy and made chaos and suffering inevitable." Since U.S. elite leaders, such as Undersecretary of State Dean Acheson, had long expected frightening postwar disorder, they readily saw a world plunged into "social *disintegration*, political *disintegration*, . . . and a great deal of economic *disintegration*."[21]

Ike's penchant for alarmism inclined him to share, and perhaps even exaggerate, the widespread apprehensions that postwar Europe would plunge into depression and therefore into social chaos. As early as the day Britain declared war on Germany he had predicted to his brother Milton a postwar rise of communism, anarchy, disorder, and loss of personal liberties. In his 15 September 1942 letter to his wife he had foreseen "an era of almost hysterical change and restlessness . . . revolutions in our customs, laws and economic processes." This was the kind of postwar world Eisenhower had expected to see; naturally, when the war ended, it was the world that he saw. Summing up his experience in the occupation of Germany, he told a congressional committee that "we found a country in complete chaos."

His postwar discourse stressed the same dangers that nearly everyone else in the elite feared: economic and societal collapse in western and central Europe would lead to some form of dictatorship, and the Allies would be forced to go to war yet again. "The triumph in the shooting war will become an empty mockery if democracy fails in the fight against starvation and disease."[22] In the discourse of liberal internationalism the danger was portrayed as so great that Western civilization itself might be destroyed. To cite Acheson again, it was a "confusion that threatens the whole fabric of world organization," the greatest threat to European civilization since the Muslim invasions of the eighth century. "Alarmist Ike" found it appropriate (and perhaps comfortable) to use similarly catastrophic language on several different occasions: "Civilization itself, in the face of another catastrophe such as we have faced in the last three years—and for other nations more—would tremble, possibly decay and be destroyed"; "The mechanical power of destruction has now become so fearfully devastating . . . almost it seems that civilization itself and the freedom of men are in the balance"; and "The preservation of our way of life" depended on proper preparations for national security.[23]

The tension between danger past and danger to come created a corresponding tension between two images of peace in Eisenhower's discourse. On the one hand, since he was celebrating the victorious end of the war, he had to speak of peace as a present, albeit precarious, reality. So, for example, he called on the Allies to "strive as earnestly to preserve peace as to win a war."[24] In order to promote the full liberal internationalist vision, though, he could not tell a simple tale of wartime terror giving way to order, freedom, and peace. He had to tell a story about one set of problems effectively controlled yet unleashing a whole new set of equally daunting difficulties. He could not depict the war as an event now safely in the past, nor as an atypical hiatus in a normally peaceful flow of history. He had to speak of peace as a future goal, something yet to be attained.

Most often, he presented the war as one more episode in an ongoing struggle between civilization and its enemies, between the forces of order and the forces of chaos. That struggle, he insisted, would now have to continue. "At last, *this* part of the job is done," he said in his V-E day message. On one level, he was referring to the continuing Pacific war. But on another level he was referring to the struggle to secure world order after Japan as well as Germany was defeated. His several references, before the victory over Japan, to continuing the war effort made that theme an intrinsic part of his discourse. Therefore it was easy and natural for him to retain this theme in his speeches after both enemies had been defeated. The call to continue the war was sounded throughout his postwar speeches: "With the same determination, the same optimistic resolution and the same mutual consideration among allies" that defeated Germany, "the problems of peace can and must be met"; and "We are going to have peace, even if we have to fight for it."[25]

Eisenhower's stress on continuing threats of disorder played a pivotal and paradoxical role in his postwar story. It deprived his audiences of what they wanted most: an assurance that peace and order had been restored. Yet in doing so it also gave them an assurance, perhaps even more satisfying, that the fundamental order of their lives had never really been disrupted. The image of a struggle between civilization and chaos had been basic to the discourse of Western society for many centuries. By interpreting both the war and the postwar period in such terms, Eisenhower was fitting both into a perfectly familiar structure. In this sense he was denying that there had been any liminal period to be explained. He was denying that there had been any fundamental disorder at all, beyond the continuing manifestations of disorder that evoke war from time to time.

Consequently, he could not speak of peace as an already achieved state, except in tentative and decidedly partial terms. He had to describe the present peace as merely one step toward the larger goal of a permanent peace that could only be attained in some distant future, by implementing perfectly the liberal internationalist values for which the war had been fought. Instead of using his ritual statements to proclaim order and create closure, Eisenhower used them to explain why there could be no order, no real peace, and thus no closure, at present.

He promised that the United States would now lead the world toward the peaceful order that would eventually bring a real close to the war. But he insisted that the United States could not succeed without enlisting all the energies of the Allied nations, civilian as well as military. The reconstruction and preservation of a stable world would require the same close cooperation among the Allies that had been the key to the victory just won: "From common danger we learned lessons of cooperation. . . . We must now enlist the same energy and singleness of purpose in developing the institutions of peace which in the time of our necessity we devoted to the prosecution of war. . . . We cannot doubt that the basic principles of united action which guided us through the war may be turned to the realization and preservation of the peace." Every soldier, he claimed, "knows that in war the threat of separate annihilation tends to hold allies together; he hopes we can find peace a nobler incentive to produce the same unity."[26]

## THE SPIRITUAL FOUNDATION

Eisenhower had interpreted the war as, at bottom, a battle between contending spiritual forces. When he called for a continuation of the war and a continuing commitment to wartime values, he was calling on the public to keep on fighting that spiritual battle. His postwar rhetoric often cited freedom as the ultimate war aim. Although freedom remained a vague term, often mentioned only in passing, this understanding of freedom was assumed in, and fundamental to, everything else he said. The war was fought to restore social order and give people the freedom to control themselves voluntarily—which was, for Eisenhower, the only true freedom, the essence of the American way of life, and the essence of spirituality. When he depicted the war as one more round in an ongoing struggle between civilization and chaos, he made it clear that civilization depended on voluntary self-restraint. So the war was actually another round in the continuing spiritual battle between self-discipline and its enemies: "This was a holy war. More than any other war in history, this war has been an array of the forces of evil against those of righteousness." Its successful conclusion had been not just a military victory but "deliverance."[27]

Eisenhower was more likely to pin the hope for peace on individual moral and religious reform than on systemic political or economic reform. "The peace lies, when you get down to it, with all the peoples of the world, not just for the moment with some political leader," he told a Paris press conference; "If all the peoples are friendly, we are going to have peace." At another time he said, "If we can forget self, if we can forget politics, if we can forget personal ambitions we can solve this problem [of peace], and we must solve the problem or we will all be lost." He called on educators to teach the truth, since democracy was based on truth and dictatorship on falsehood. But he could not separate universal truth, which he defined as the substance of peace, from the specific religious traditions of his native land. So he urged the educators to concern themselves with "the Christian principles on which all true democracy is based." "No man can tell me," he assured another audience, "that America with its glorious mixture of creeds, its Jews, its Catholics, its Protestants, can lose."[28]

This appeal to religious values added to Eisenhower's discourse an ambiguity that was inherent in Christianity, the only religion he really knew. On the one hand, his references to deliverance in a holy war reflected the apocalyptic tradition, with its absolute dualism between good and evil. The general had been raised in a religious community that used such language. Thirty years as a soldier, and three and a half years pursuing unconditional surrender on the battlefield, made him even more comfortable employing its powerful rhetorical effects. In assessing the postwar situation, he often divided humanity into two mutually exclusive groups: the selfless or self-disciplined (his ancestors would have called them the saved) and the selfish (whom his ancestors would have called the damned). In traditional Christian terms these were the forces of God and the Devil. Since God was the absolute, one had to be either absolutely for or

absolutely against him. Most versions of Christian theology allowed for no middle ground.

At the same time, though, he was equally faithful to his Christian heritage
when he reminded his audiences that no one could claim to be free of the taint of
selfishness (his ancestors would have called it sin). Although Eisenhower knew little, if anything, of the foundational Christian theologian, Augustine, he was an
Augustinian to a considerable degree. He implied quite clearly that as long as we
are living in what Augustine called the earthly city, even the best of us will be compounded of virtue and sin. Within Eisenhower's discourse, then, there was a clear
temptation to project all evil onto the other and an equally clear hesitation to yield
to that temptation.

This ambiguity was clearly expressed in Eisenhower's comments on the
denazification controversy. Viewing the German people as the embodiment of
spiritual evil, he ordered his troops to observe strict nonfraternization with
German children, whom he feared had absorbed the evil of their elders; some
individuals were incurably evil, and personal contact with them could be dangerous. This order stirred considerable opposition, and the general soon found
himself telling reporters that U.S. troops could have dealings with German children, if they judged it safe. He justified this new approach to the journalists by
reverting to Augustinian terms: "The fine line sometimes between wickedness
and good is not too clearly drawn."[29]

The ambiguity of Christianity was not the same as the ambiguity of liberal
internationalism. The two set of polarities could be interwoven in various ways,
producing a complex body of discourse that contained several distinct concepts
of peace. At times Eisenhower spoke as if the peace based on the values of liberalism had been attained, as if the apocalyptic battle had been fought and won.
But since this kind of language might encourage apathy in the fight against the
new forms of impending chaos, he used it sparingly. When he did speak of the
peace that had been won, it was almost always a prelude to a call to defend that
peace against continuing threats. This naturally led to a view of peace as something still to be attained in the future.

To rally the Allies for concerted action to achieve peace, he was most likely
to use the language made familiar by Woodrow Wilson during and after World
War I. In this language, peace meant a unified world system of democratic
nations, all cooperating together through a League of Nations to resolve conflicts
peacefully. This world system would be liberal, democratic, and capitalist.
Although Wilson never said so too explicitly, he was assuming the triumph of liberalism over the socialist alternative. Thus he wove into his liberal idealism the

dualistic imagery typical of apocalyptic discourse, which projected all evil onto the "other." He had prepared the ground for this dualism with his apocalyptic language during World War I. Depicting the war as a climactic battle that would banish war and evil forever, he gave peace an eschatological as well as a political value. This implied an eternal state of self-restraint and stability, in which no fundamental changes could ever again occur.

The way in which World War II ended, with the first use of the atomic bomb, made it too frightening to prophesy any final battle. So Eisenhower was more likely to speak of a long, gradual road toward peace. He portrayed the war and the postwar struggle as two connected stages in a long path toward the distant goal of perfect world order. In this sense, peace was less a static state than a continuing process, though that process would eventually lead to a static end.

Eisenhower's Augustinian language led to yet another view of peace. It located the force of otherness not within any particular nation or political group, but within every nation and every individual of every group. Here, too, he left open a possibility of permanent triumph of the good over the evil—a Kingdom of God on earth—to be reached through gradual stages, without any apocalyptic catastrophe. His Augustinian approach, however, made such perfection far less likely. It assumed that the selfishness of human beings was not likely ever to be wholly eradicated. Logically, this meant that the Wilsonian goals for which the general claimed the war had been fought could never be permanently secured. Unlike Wilson, Eisenhower could not fully embrace any image of a world enjoying perfect peace. He could not tell his audiences that the war had once and for all put an end to war or made the world safe for democracy. His Augustinian language could only depict peace as a temporary and precarious state of order, constantly staving off the onslaughts of disorder. Those onslaughts could never end, because the source of disorder was permanently embedded in human nature.

The general's discourse blended these different views of peace, just as it blended the language of spirituality and the language of liberal internationalism. But all yielded the same crucial implication: peace could not be the opposite of war, because there was no essential difference between the two. From the Wilsonian perspective, voluntary self-restraint was the means to victory in war. It was also the goal of war, for it was the essence of the peace and freedom to be won. So fighting the war and enjoying the peace consisted of exercising the same virtue. Since perfect self-restraint had not yet been achieved, the war had not resulted in any fundamental transformation in human, or American, life. But Wilsonian language cast the war as the potential beginning of a religious renewal—if the people of the United States and its allied nations chose to embrace that renewal by continuing the struggle against chaos. This made war and peace two equally essential parts of the same religious renewal.

From the Augustinian perspective, it was impossible to imagine peace as a virtuous kingdom of God on earth; the apocalyptic goal could never be attained. Yet Eisenhower still painted the problems themselves in apocalyptic colors. Enemies would permanently block the way to a more perfect world, requiring eternal vigilance lest civilization itself be drowned in chaos. Even in peacetime, the war against disorder could never end. Peace meant continuing the war forever. Like most liberal internationalists of 1945, Eisenhower mixed Wilsonian language with an Augustinian geopolitical "realism." He rejected "idealism" and insisted on the need for continuing military power to protect the fragile order already attained.

Paradoxically, though, this mixture did give meaning to the war, for it strongly implied that there was nothing new or unprecedented about the war. If, as Eisenhower claimed, the line between good and evil had been more unmistakable than in any past war, the difference was only quantitative, not qualitative. The war had been a manifestation of an age-old struggle between selfishness and selflessness, he said, a struggle that would continue long into the future. In this context, there was nothing essentially disorienting about the war's chaos. For those raised in cultures pervaded by Christianity, it was a familiar and easily comprehensible part of the most basic structure of earthly life, the struggle between God and the Devil. This structure made peace at best the endpoint of a long arduous history leading to the apocalypse. In the worst case, peace would remain forever a partial state of affairs, an endless process of partial victories over selfishness that could lead only to new battles against this eternal enemy. In this sense peace would be a process of war without end. In either case, the war just past was rendered meaningful precisely by the claim that it was not really over, by the erasing of the distinction between war and peace.

## THE OFFICIAL STORY

Eisenhower's story of war and peace had an impressive degree of internal coherence. His understanding of peace, his warning of continued struggle, his call for international cooperation, and his support for UMT, service unification, and military preparedness all flowed from the same ideological—he would have called it spiritual—framework. This was the distinctive thread that bound together his military, political, and economic concerns, as it also bound together his roles as promoter of army interests and champion of liberal internationalism.

Since the military was the finest soil for nurturing self-restraint, in his opinion, it had a crucial role to play in the postwar world. UMT would give every one of the nation's young men the opportunity to practice selflessness by devoting a year to national service and being trained to return to that service immediately in an emergency. The unification of the services would bring down a "sledge hammer" on the bureaucratic "empire builders" in each service. It would force them to set aside their petty selfish rivalries and work together for the good of the nation, setting a valuable example for others.[30] Similarly, cooperation among the Allies both required and reflected a willingness to set aside selfish national desires for the sake of the United Nations and self-controlled freedom. The same self-sacrificing cooperation would be needed to keep the peace, he now asserted: "During the war, the sons and daughters of free nations have demonstrated a capacity for sacrifice of self and for uniting in a common cause that can now be turned into the more fruitful task that lies ahead."[31] In all these ways, Eisenhower proclaimed that the army, in partnership with liberal internationalism, could help to inaugurate a new world order.

On the other hand, insofar as disorder was endemic and permanent, there could be no guarantee that the forces of world order would prevail, at least in the foreseeable future. Since everything depended on the inward moral condition of the populace, every individual would have to choose, again and again, either to support or oppose the forces of order. Eisenhower's insistence that the war was still going on implied the need to choose. It also implied that those who chose the good would naturally ally themselves with liberal internationalism, and that they would want and need the protection of a powerful army.

Addressing the Freedom House, Eisenhower showed how skillfully he could interweave all the principle themes of his postwar rhetoric:

The demands of war and its after effects call for increased vigilance. We as citizens cannot shift our own responsibilities to the shoulders of representatives sitting around a conference table. . . . The seeds of war are found in each of us, in our selfishness, in our unwillingness to assume obligations that we hope others will bear for us. . . . We are living in a world of harsh realities and one of these is acknowledged weakness within ourselves. . . .

The solution, therefore, must obviate self-interest as well as idealism. As a first essential, our nation should have a responsible position in the matter of military readiness. . . . [This] involves time for technical and physical training and a definite drain upon the nation's purse. If the outpouring of all production should be too long or too frequently devoted to destructive processes, then, at least, fear and famine will stalk the earth and, as a cumulative effect, freedom will give way to the single effort to survive. Even when we have done this, we have not provided a cure for a world sickness that has reappeared through the ages with persistent frequency. . . .

No principal section of the earth should become so habitually impoverished that its inhabitants reach the stark conclusion that no catastrophe—even war—would represent a worsening of their situation. Everybody, everywhere, must come to feel that he has something to risk, something to lose, in a resort to war! If realization of this purpose requires from prosperous nations some reduction in expected profit—the cost can scarcely be so great as that imposed by international unrest and the threat of conflict! Certainly it will be far less than war itself! . . .

It is also to our own selfish interest, regardless of higher motives, to be nationally strong . . . to work with others in increasing prosperity of those that are denied even the necessities of life, and, with our partners in the great international enterprise now developing, to take timely steps to see that no man may, through fanaticism and bigotry, develop a dangerous military spirit.[32]

This speech summarized the typical themes of Eisenhower's public rhetorical exercises. Self-sacrificing teamwork—among the military services, among the Allies, and between the battlefront and the home front—had been the key to victory. But the war just past was only a chapter in an ongoing struggle. The same personal virtue that had won the war would now have to be mobilized to win the peace. The challenge now was to preserve the Allies' hard-won freedom against all future threats of totalitarianism. The immediate threat was that Europe might sink into the kind of economic and political chaos that breeds dictatorship and war. To prevent this, the United States would have to strengthen its military force and remain involved in international affairs. Only when European order was secured would the sacrifices of World War II be proven truly meaningful. The same rhetorical blend and the same image of the enemy linked the army's aims, the "great international enterprise" to shore up democratic capitalism, and the endless spiritual struggle. The enemy was, as always, the chaos born of selfishness. A continuing battle against that enemy was the recipe for, the only path to, and perhaps the very definition of, genuine peace.

Beneath this seemingly unified story, however, the contradictions among the various views of peace were never resolved in Eisenhower's discourse. This led to the ultimate paradox of his story. It was intended to reassure the world of an eternal order that even the horrors of World War II could not destroy. Its images of peace were all images of stability and order. But because those images were so different, drawn from conflicting traditions and conflicting meanings of peace, the story itself was built upon a constantly shifting foundation. At its deepest level it bespoke a disorder that could never be resolved. Therefore, its ultimate message was that the Wilsonian promise of world order had become merely a noble fiction. The world that had spawned that promise was gone forever. The reality now lay in the "realist" image of peace as a precarious order endlessly struggling to save itself from catastrophic chaos. In this sense, Eisenhower's story could not do what every postwar story is supposed to do. It could not give meaning by telling of a return to a peaceful order. It could only give meaning by telling of the endless struggle against disorder.

Perhaps, had he been asked in 1945, Eisenhower would have said that this was a temporary understanding of peace, crafted for a temporary situation. But little in his discourse encouraged the listener to look beyond this situation. So his understanding of peace at the war's end, when some story had to be told and it fell to him to be the teller, remained as the foundation of his discourse.

## CHAPTER 3

# Eisenhower and the Soviets, 1945–47

Historians have paid particular attention to one feature of Eisenhower's postwar role: his consistently positive attitude toward the Soviet Union. Whenever he spoke about U.S.–Soviet relations, his main theme was the possibility of friendship and cooperation. This seems surprising in light of the hardening anti-Soviet sentiment among U.S. leaders. As Blanche Wiesen Cook writes, "Eisenhower did not like being out of step. He was a team player."[1] In this case, though, he is remembered as resisting the trend toward cold war. This consensus among historians, however, may be based more on appearance than reality

It is important to recall that in the first postwar months his words of amity were right in the mainstream. The cold war mentality set in quite slowly. It took a year or more for the Truman administration to abandon, privately, its hope of good relations with the Stalin regime. It took even longer for that change of heart to become official public policy. The Truman Doctrine speech, usually seen as the first public proclamation of cold war from the U.S. side, came nearly two full years after V-E day. Still, most historians see Eisenhower lagging behind the trend: as the official discourse coming out of Washington transformed the Soviet Union from ally to mortal enemy, he continued to urge cooperation between the superpowers.

## THE LANGUAGE OF PEACE

The record of Eisenhower's public language seems to speak for itself. Shortly after the war ended, he traveled to Moscow and told journalists there, "I see nothing in the future that would prevent Russia and the United States from being the closest possible friends." He had found "the individual Russian one of the friendliest persons in the world," so there was no reason to think that the United States and the Soviet Union could not cooperate perfectly. On 28 August 1945, he wrote privately to Henry Wallace: "I am convinced that friendship—which means an honest desire on both sides to strive for mutual understanding—between Russia and the United States is absolutely essential to world tranquility. Moreover, I believe that most of the Russians I have met share this conviction."[2]

As Army Chief of Staff, he maintained the same public stance, telling a congressional committee: "There is not one thing, I believe, that guides the policy of Russia more today than to keep friendship with the United States." Throughout 1946 he urged Americans to extend a peaceful hand to the Soviets. He told a disabled veteran's group: "We must deal with those who do not well understand us, just as we do not fully understand them. We must work with those who view our motives with suspicion as we may sometimes be suspicious of their intent. . . . Discouragement must not paralyze your efforts." Addressing the Economics Club of New York, he said: "There is room in the world for different systems of government." At the University of Richmond, he told the audience: "We must learn in this world to accommodate ourselves so that we may live at peace with others whose basic philosophy may be different." Cautioning the Veterans of Foreign Wars not to give in to frustration, he said: "Our determination in this particular effort must be inexhaustible, because on its successful outcome depends the whole future of civilization, ours included."[3]

By the spring of 1947, after the Truman Doctrine had been announced, this message was becoming less prominent in Eisenhower's public speeches. But he would still tell the House Committee on Appropriations, on 5 June: "I believe that eventually we can work out a basis of friendly relations with Russia. I do not see how we can afford to do anything else." Three weeks later, at a hearing of the House Committee on Foreign Affairs, he told Rep. Helen Gahagan Douglas: "You cannot promote a family by excluding one member, and saying 'You are not fit to be spoken to, you are behind an iron curtain.'"[4]

Many historians and biographers have placed special emphasis on these conciliatory public words toward the Soviet Union, finding in them the early roots of President Eisenhower's supposed dedication to world peace. Stephen Ambrose, for example, says that friendship with the Soviet Union was "a theme he would repeat over and over, in speeches, at congressional hearings, in his private letters, in conversations. . . . He was most impressive in expressing his genuine desire for peace." Even the biographers who doubt this interpretation assume that in the immediate postwar months, he sincerely hoped to maintain the U.S–Soviet alliance. Piers Brendon, for example, agrees with this consensus: "Ike doggedly strove to prolong the brief era of good feelings between West and East. He scorned the notion that the Soviet Union was bent on world domination and pleaded for a continuation of wartime cooperation." Some historians do note that the unambiguous appeals for friendship were most frequent and emphatic in the first year after the war. But they conclude from this that Eisenhower was dragged unwillingly into the cold war, only slowly and reluctantly accepting the cold war consensus. Brendon, for example, says that Eisenhower only switched his tone when "it became impolitic at home to do anything else."[5]

Later in his life, Eisenhower himself cast doubt on this interpretation. In his book, *At Ease,* he praised James Forrestal for alerting him during World War II to the impending Soviet danger. "Since, from 1941 onward, I had, because of personal experience, become increasingly sure that the Soviets would not look upon the U.S. as anything other than a potential enemy, it was only natural that from the very beginning I had a high regard for Mr. Forrestal's opinion and for his foresight." When Forrestal died, Eisenhower noted in his diary: "He said— 'Be courteous & friendly in the effort to develop a satisfactory modus vivendi— but never believe we have changed their basic purpose, which is to destroy representative government.' He insisted they hated us—which I had good reason to believe myself."[6]

Eisenhower also claimed that in 1943 he had shared similar views with President Roosevelt, stressing the danger that the postwar chaos would be exploited by the Soviet Union. In his war memoir, *Crusade in Europe,* he claimed that he "had great sympathy" for Churchill's desire to get Allied troops into the Balkans to improve chances for "a stable post-hostilities world." (Churchill hoped that a U.S. and British military presence in eastern Europe would prevent Stalin from dominating that region.) In 1950 he told Secretary of Defense Louis Johnson that during World War II he had already foreseen that the postwar era would see "a long period of unsettled international relations," requiring the United States to maintain unprecedented military forces in peacetime, "and this had to be done without breaking our economy." A few months earlier he had told a group of journalists: "During the year of 1946 it became rather apparent that this beautiful dream [of permanent peace] that at least allowed us to drift along in something like indifferences [*sic*] was just a dream, wishful thinking. No more."[7]

Why, then, did he speak of the Soviets in such amicable terms through 1947? "We did not openly refer to the Soviets as a potential enemy in those days," he explained in *At Ease,* "because our political leaders were trying to develop workable agreements with them. But there was no doubt what we meant when we kept warning" of the need to keep a strong military in the face of an uneasy peace. This claim is usually written off as merely a convenient rewriting of history to conform to later cold war norms. Similarly, Blanche Wiesen Cook writes that by 1948, "enthusiastic adherence to the precepts of the Cold War was the only acceptable position for men in public life. Eisenhower would have to overcome his reputation as 'soft' on Russia." Having become the leader of the United States in an era of cold war, historians say, Eisenhower had to reinvent his past to allay any doubts about his credentials as a staunch cold warrior.[8]

Still, there is abundant evidence that he should be taken at his own word. His discourse reveals a striking disparity between his public words of amity and his private words, which were closer to the emerging cold war consensus. As Cook has perceptively observed, the tenor of his term as head of the occupation foreshadowed the "banner" of his presidency, endorsing "all anti-Communist activity, both possible and practical, short of war with the Soviet Union."[9]

## THE SOVIET THREAT

As early as May 1946, before the cold war consensus had taken hold in Washington, the general wrote in his diary that "democracy has arrived at its decade or quarter century of greatest crisis—any global war of the future will be ideological." It was a battle of individualism versus statism, he said. "Russia, completely statist, sees this and is so anxious to spread communism" that she uses propaganda, subversion, and even open force. "Our form of government is under deadly, persistent, and constant attack."[10] This point of view differs little from a diary entry of September 1947:[11]

> I believe that democracy has entered its decade (possibly quarter century) of greatest test. . . . The main issue is dictatorship versus a form of government only by the consent of the governed. . . . Russia is definitely out to communize the world—where it cannot gain complete control of territory . . . it promotes starvation, unrest, anarchy, in the certainty that these are breeding grounds for the growth of their damnable philosophy. . . . Now we face a battle to extinction between the two systems (although we declare that we can live with communism if it stays in its own areas and makes no attempt to interfere with us).

The final parenthetic remark is ambiguous. It is unclear whether Eisenhower was endorsing containment or marking it as a declaratory policy that he was forced to endorse publicly, yet privately viewed as unrealistic. As he continued the diary entry, he confirmed this ambiguity:

What are the problems? To prevent Russian expansion (1) by direct conquest and pressure; (2) by infiltration. Over the long term to win back areas that Russia has already overrun, and finally to produce a real accord among all nations that will prevent war. This must be preceded by a collapse of dictatorship everywhere, at least of all dictatorships that aggressively seek to dominate others.[12]

Should the Soviet system be allowed to remain intact, as long as it did not threaten others; i.e., as long as it was contained? Or would it have to be replaced with a liberal democracy? Eisenhower's answer remained unclear.

Both views are echoed in other writings as well. As Harry Truman was pronouncing his anticommunist doctrine, Eisenhower was telling a friend that he did not think "any other government has to have a form such as ours." But he immediately insisted that "significant portions of the world's population" must live within a capitalist system, if the U.S. system were to survive. In October 1947, he wrote to Henry Wilson that, despite Russia's "aggressive attitude," he could see "no better prescription, for the moment, than to be patient and conciliatory." He quickly added, however, that the Western alliance must keep up enough strength "so that conciliation and patience will not be mistaken for fear and weakness." The diary entries themselves indicate his clear opinion that this was "a battle to extinction" between two irreconcilable systems, and only one could prevail. So patience and conciliation were advisable only "for the moment."[13]

## POLICY IMPLICATIONS

Even before the war ended, Eisenhower's anticommunist and anti-Soviet feelings were helping to shape his policy decisions. As early as May 1944, he told Beetle Smith that he opposed giving the United States and Britain separate occupation zones after the war, because the Soviets would then play one side off against the other. He repeated this argument to Marshall in September. Writing to Marshall in October about postwar planning, he again urged the United States not to count on Allied cooperation:

As long as Europe is in a state of almost violent unrest, any American contingent left here should be a powerful one and capable of instantaneous and effective action in any direction, possibly even outside our own area. . . . A quite powerful bomber force would place the U.S. contingent on a substantial basis of equality, and this might conceivably be a most desirable state of affairs. . . . Frequent and prompt demonstrations of real strength might be a most economical way of enforcing our policies and regulations.[14]

The references to lack of Allied cooperation, attaining a basis of equality, and using force "outside our own area" obviously point to the Soviet Union and its occupying troops as the focus of concern.

Just a week after V-E day the general was already expressing concern that the Soviets, while not wanting war, were testing the West by pushing Yugoslav leader Tito to make territorial claims in Trieste. He warned that the Soviets might make more demands later; soon he feared that this tension might lead to another war.[15] In October 1945, he resisted pressure from the War Department to speed up demobilization by withdrawing U.S. troops from Czechoslovakia. The Czech leader, Benes, told him that only by keeping U.S. troops there could he "save the country as a strong democracy." The U.S. ambassador to Czechoslovakia, Laurence Steinhardt, wanted to "retain the U.S. troops as a stabilizing influence and to influence Czechoslovakian development in a manner sympathetic to the Western Democracies." Steinhardt reported that the Soviets "do intend to exploit the country's resources," and withdrawing the troops would ruin the chances for democracy. Eisenhower agreed, telling Marshall that as long as Soviet troops remained in Czechoslovakia, he wanted a U.S. contingent sufficiently large to make "a show of force." Diplomatic advisor Robert Murphy, on the other hand, urged withdrawing the troops, because the United States could not say publicly that it wanted a military presence to counter the Soviet presence.[16]

As chief of staff (C/S), Eisenhower often affirmed the assessment of his intelligence staff that the Soviets would not be interested in a war any time soon. At a White House conference on 11 June 1946, for example, he told President Truman that "they've gained about all they can assimilate" and would need a long economic and military buildup before initiating a war.[17] Although this has sometimes been put forth as evidence that he was a reluctant cold warrior, it was merely the common wisdom throughout the military. On occasion he was relatively dovish in his policy recommendations. He told the Joint Chiefs of Staff (JCS) that perhaps the United States should be willing to reduce its army more than the Soviets because the two armies had different peacetime missions. The JCS rejected this view. But they did accept the Army Chief of Staff's recommendation to take a more positive view of the United Nations Organization, since public doubts about its efficacy would become self-fulfilling prophecies and inevitably lead to the UNO's failure.[18]

In his official policy documents, though, Eisenhower was much more often in line with other policymakers. From the outset, he assumed the Soviet Union to be the only significant enemy. Near the beginning of his tenure as C/S, he approved a JCS document stating that the next war would pit the Soviet Union against either the United States or Great Britain. Indeed, in one policy document he referred to "peacetime" as "the period extending from the present until the assumed ideological war begins."[19]

As the army's chief military executive, he took his principal duty to be preparing for that war. He expected it to resemble, in some important respects, the war that had just ended. It would begin with a surprise attack on the United States. Catastrophe could strike at any time, in Eisenhower's view; he was determined that there would not be another Pearl Harbor and that mobilization would proceed more quickly next time. The war would again be global in scope, the entire nation would mobilize to fight, and it would last four to five years. This time, though, the United States would have to be prepared to fight without allies.[20]

Soon plans were being made to fight such a war. Because it would begin suddenly, the nation had to start planning for it now, coordinating the efforts of all public agencies and private industry with the military. The civilian and military sectors would have to be more closely linked than ever before, and civilians would have to be prepared for their role in "an emergency" (Eisenhower's most common euphemism for a war with the Soviet Union).

Eisenhower insisted that the battle itself would require extensive use of land troops. The army would not be rendered redundant even in the atomic age, if he had his way. It would hold a bridgehead in central Europe, while the brunt of the U.S. counterattack would come from the Middle East. This made it especially important to deny the Soviet Union access to Turkey; if Turkey fell, so would all of the Middle East.[21] Eisenhower became a strong proponent of plans for psychological warfare and "cover and deception" in the next war, as well as domestic public information programs to maintain popular support for the war effort.[22]

The fear of Soviet power also shaped his approach to military occupation policies. The C/S felt it his responsibility not only to prepare for all-out war but also to protect the national security against the threat of peacetime Soviet expansionism. He advised the JCS that foreign aid should not be allocated only on the basis of its value in the next war (as a staff report had suggested): "It would be wrong to assume that no substantial threats to U.S. security exist except in an ideological war [another euphemism for a war with the Soviet Union]." The United States should use peacetime foreign aid to block the spread of Soviet influence, "because of the high price of a continuous series of crises, and because the failure to prevent them will contribute to the continuation of international instability and expansionism."[23]

Urging the JCS to support more food aid for Austria, for example, he wrote: "Food is the main weapon used by the United States to maintain our position there." If no food were available it would lead to "riots and violence" that U.S. troops could not control, and the Austrians needed U.S. food aid to bolster their commitment to resisting Soviet expansion.[24] He made the same point more obliquely when he told Douglas MacArthur that civilian relief was needed in Korea and Japan to prevent "the disastrous effects that unrest and open defiance would have" on the occupation. Similarly, he argued that keeping the U.S. military in South Korea would save money in the long run because the cost of retreat was "far, far greater." There was no need to spell out the nature of the "cost," since everyone understood what was meant. Money given to the army to alleviate poverty was a sound investment, he was arguing, since it would obviate the need to spend more money quelling social disorder and, eventually, fighting the Russians.[25]

In a summary letter to Forrestal upon retiring as chief of staff in February 1948, he made the point more clearly than ever before. If the army lost any more funds or manpower, he insisted, it would mean that "the occupation is no longer possible and the areas involved would have to be abandoned to chaos and communism." Chaos would mean an invitation to communism. To prevent it, the army needed to not only keep order but also feed hungry people and rebuild the economy.[26]

In January 1946, he sent the JCS an intelligence estimate of the world in 1953, which forecast that the Soviet Union would not want war yet but would be supporting international expansion of its power. In November 1947, he was still urging Forrestal to initiate U.S. psychological warfare operations "to assist with the problem presented by the current campaign of the USSR in that field."[27]

He particularly feared Soviet inroads in Greece and Turkey and urged the use of U.S. troops to forestall it. A token U.S. force in Turkey would assure the Turks of greater support in case of a future war, and thus bolster Turkish resistance to Soviet political influence. Greece would need more aid, including U.S. field advisers, because economic aid now would be useless unless a noncommunist regime could first be assured. But as the U.S. government deliberated its response to the crisis in Greece, in February 1946, Eisenhower wanted the crisis to be seen in much broader terms. He urged a study of the needs of all prospective U.S. aid recipients, "so that one all-embracing assistance request could be submitted to Congress."[28] In thus anticipating the Marshall Plan, the general showed himself to be on the cutting edge of cold war planning. He worried constantly that Congress would cut foreign aid as well as military funds so much that the army would be unable to protect the nation against the enemy either in peacetime or in "an emergency." He treated all of these tasks as a single interrelated challenge.

## RHETORIC AS A TOOL OF POLICY

If Eisenhower was in fact a cold warrior from the beginning, how can his public calls for rapprochement and friendship with the Soviet Union be explained? First, it should be noted that many historians have exaggerated this part of his record. His calls for U.S.–Soviet cooperation were not too frequent even during the first year of the war. His major theme was the need for a peaceful world, to be achieved by universalizing U.S. values and the U.S. system. The war would not really be won until the millennial dream of eternal peace on earth was attained. Winning the war meant securing the peace—and vice versa; such a task would require international cooperation and understanding among all nations. The call for cooperation and understanding was a central theme in virtually every speech the C/S gave.[29] On occasion, as part of this larger theme, he invited the Soviet Union to join the effort.

Eisenhower never suggested, however, that the United States should make any substantial compromises to accommodate its rival. When he spoke of friendship, he was often careful to focus on friendship between the two peoples, not between their governments. When he said, "The peace lies, when you get down to it, with all the peoples of the world. . . . If all the peoples are friendly, we are going to have peace," he implied that the Russian people would gladly accept U.S. leadership if given a free voice; it was their government that prevented them from having that free voice.[30] From the outset he spoke often about the need for military strength to prevent a new dictator from seizing power in Europe. He must have known that many in his audiences would think immediately of Stalin, and he did little to contravene such obvious associations.

On some occasions he did clearly call for peaceful relations on the governmental level. But these calls did not contradict his strong anti-Soviet sentiments. Rather, they indicate that words can often serve to further the aims of policy objectives; the same words may have a different impact when used in another context. When Eisenhower suggested that the United States and USSR could get along politically, he had good practical reasons for doing so. In November 1945, he admitted as much when Rep. Chet Holifield asked him: "Do not you feel it is a great psychological hazard for this continued anti-Russian and anti-United States feeling to be developed in the newspapers and elsewhere?" Eisenhower replied cryptically: "Well, I can only say it does not help some of my problems, Congressman."[31]

Those problems were many, and some were quite practical. Eisenhower had started out as commander of the U.S. occupation forces in Germany, where he had to work out day-to-day problems in administering the occupation, many of which required some kind of cooperation with his Soviet counterparts. Alienating the Soviets would make his work that much more difficult. When he became chief of staff, he was still burdened with occupation problems, and the man he had left behind in his place to implement them, Lucius Clay, was a close personal friend (and bridge partner). He knew firsthand the kinds of problems Clay had to deal with, and he had some incentive to avoid putting unnecessary burdens on Clay's shoulders.

Another practical motivation for this message of peace grew from long-term military considerations. Eisenhower told his British wartime colleague, Field Marshal Bernard Montgomery, that he agreed with the latter's analysis of the long-term prospects. The Soviet Union, though now militarily weak, would eventually be strong. It would be to the advantage of the United States and Britain, facing a potentially powerful enemy, to "establish friendly relations and break down their suspicions."[32]

Other problems were more political. As head of the occupation in Germany, he had to defend the army against critics who accused it of delaying the institution of civilian government. To this end, he urged Marshall to mount a public relations campaign to deflect the criticism. Assurances of peaceful intent toward the Soviets, from the army's top man in Europe, would be a valuable aid in that campaign. While he tried to avoid any policy measures that might appear to contradict the verbal amity he was creating with the Soviet Union, he took few, if any, concrete policy steps to enhance this amity. His words were meant only to create symbolic images of cooperation, images that could be used to advance specific policy goals. Once Eisenhower became chief of staff, his main job was to foster public support for the army, its policies and, perhaps on a most urgent level, its budget. His speeches were meant to allay public fears that high peacetime military budgets would lead to excessive militarism. Had he expressed public doubts about getting along with the Soviets, he might have undermined this element in his rhetoric.

Army policy concerns also dictated pacific rhetoric. Whether or not Eisenhower accepted the Yalta axioms himself, he was obligated to give public endorsements of the official army view. As Stephen Ambrose says, "The feeling that as the head of the Army it was his duty to speak in its behalf dictated the theme of most of his speeches"; on most issues, "he followed the War Department line."[33]

As the prospects for a four-power consortium faded, public support for any kind of permanent international commitments began to decline. Eisenhower saw it as his task to help block that decline and keep the United States actively engaged around the world. So he argued on every occasion that international cooperation was the only route to a peaceful world order. Preaching this message was his duty as a leader, he believed. He also believed that every leader had to put on an optimistic face in public, regardless of his private feelings, if he wanted to succeed. "Any failure to appreciate the effect of buoyancy, optimism and enthusiasm in leadership is certain to react unfavorably whenever difficult problems are to be solved," he wrote to his friend Charles Portal in February 1947.[34] His calls for U.S.–Soviet cooperation were one important way to express public optimism about the chances for peace. Growing anti-Soviet sentiment would make it harder to keep these elements in his rhetoric.

Eisenhower was obligated to represent not only the army but also the Truman administration and its War Department. Throughout 1945 and most of 1946, the administration's official public stance still held out the possibility of cooperation, and the chief of staff was bound to endorse that policy in public. Years later, reminiscing with Winston Churchill, Eisenhower said that "he forgives anyone who was trying to make friends with Communists up to the time of the Berlin Airlift. He believes that anyone who was at least fairly friendly with the Communists from '33 to '46, should not be viewed with alarm. It was a policy of our government at that time to try to win over the Russians."[35] As 1946 went on, and administration officials split on incipient cold war issues, it was increasingly difficult for Eisenhower to know what policies were called for. In this sense, too, talk of U.S.–Soviet conflict caused problems for him.

As late as the fall of 1947, Secretary of War Robert Patterson told Eisenhower that the State Department was tacitly accepting Soviet violations of the Potsdam agreements, which created serious economic problems in Germany. "I cannot say that I blame them," Patterson added, "in view of the tremendous importance, in the interest of lasting peace, of coming to an understanding with Russia. Thus far, the progress of economic recovery in Germany has been sacrificed to the objective of One World." Eisenhower responded only that Patterson's comments were "applicable as well as clearly stated."[36]

Perhaps this was the terse comment of a frustrated man. In March 1946, Eisenhower told his friend Gen. Bradford Chynoweth that he was already frustrated in his position as C/S. It prevented him from speaking freely to the American people about their "tragic lack of understanding" of international relations and defense issues. What he most wanted the public to understand was the

Soviet threat. Perhaps Eisenhower alluded to this frustration once publicly when he told a press conference, "There is nothing that I can see that any great country in the world can gain by going to war." When a reporter asked, "Can we quote you?" the general replied enigmatically: "Relieve me from my position and I will give you my personal opinion."[37]

## "SOMETHING TOO HORRIBLE TO CONTEMPLATE"

There was one problem above all others that prevented Eisenhower from publicly expressing his private views: the threat of another war. As much as he feared Soviet expansionism, he feared World War III even more. On the broadest level, the problem of the postwar world, as he saw it, was to bring order to a chaotic world. He consistently offered the immense problems he faced in Germany as evidence that the Allies had to continue their struggle against disorder and dictatorship. He told a Kansas State College audience: "The way to durable peace is blocked by the ruin of shattered economies, by appalling human misery and by ideological strife that seems at times beyond composition. Unchecked, these foster anarchy, the fertile breeding ground for a malignant despotism." The Allies must remain strong and cooperate, he warned the Canadian Club in Ottawa, "lest new Hitlers rise to throw the world into a chaos more awful than the shattered countries of Europe present today."

In all his public speaking, however, he was careful to name these enemies only in the most abstract terms. He describes the nation's future foes as "hypothetical Hitlers of the future." Never did he explicitly identify these evils with the Soviet Union or any other specific nation. On the contrary, when he named the Soviet Union publicly it was almost always as a potential friend.[38] His ideological framework helps to explain why. Chaos was now the enemy and the next war would bring even more chaos than the last, he believed. Since war would inevitably bring chaos, and chaos would inevitably breed dictatorship (whether of the left or right), war would inevitably bring precisely the result it was designed to stave off. At all costs, then, another war must be prevented. "Few people have any real understanding of the grim potentialities of such a disaster, even if the outcome should be military victory," he told Cornelius Vanderbilt. He explained these grim potentialities in detail in a letter to his father-in-law, John Doud:

> We are traveling a long and rocky road toward a satisfactory world order but the big thing is that we never give up for an instant. No war can be anything else

but a great set-back in such progress. . . . We would be almost certain to lose that for which we fought—namely, the system of free enterprise and individual liberty, both of which are at the base of our system. Consequently, I raise my voice as loudly as I can in supporting every appropriate and logical program that seeks to promote the understanding among nations which will eventually eliminate war. . . . Our own self-interests can be served only by a long period of peace.[39]

The general saw war, and the instability that both caused and resulted from war, as greater enemies than the Soviet Union and communism. For this reason he encouraged his friend Beetle Smith, now the U.S. ambassador in Moscow, to keep working on U.S.–Soviet relations because "the alternative to progress has become something too horrible to contemplate."

Eisenhower voiced his fear of war publicly as well as privately. In a Fourth of July oration in 1947, in Mississippi, he warned: "Either the nations work together for the common good or one by one they will perish; slowly in withering decay; or quickly under the impact of total war, as is more likely the way of the future." Celebrating Veterans Day, 1946, in Lincoln, Nebraska, he explained that "even to the eventual winner [war] means bankruptcy, chaos and despair and destruction of thriving cities and farm communities." He brought this message to many audiences, including even a meat industry convention in September 1947, where he said that after the next war, civilized life "as we have known it will no longer be possible."[40]

Eisenhower's genuine fear of war was probably the main reason for his positive statements about U.S.–Soviet cooperation. He was hardly alone in seeing war with the Soviets as an imminent possibility; the idea was very much in the air. At that time, it seemed that the only alternative to rapprochement was a march, or at least a slide, toward another war. It seemed that everyone had to choose either one path or the other. The idea of a long-term cold war was not yet part of Eisenhower's discursive framework. Anyone who spoke openly about preparing for the next war could easily be understood, or misunderstood, as advocating war. So the C/S took great pains to scotch public discussion of any growing rift between the two powers. He forbade his staff to talk about "the next war," and when a reporter asked about such a possibility he became furious, insisting that the United States and the Soviet Union would remain on amicable terms. This passionate response seems to indicate that he believed war a real possibility and strongly hoped to avoid it.[41]

Therefore, his insistence on the possibility of friendship with the Soviets and his equally firm insistence on keeping the U.S. guard up were two symbolic ways

of saying that avoiding war was the wiser choice. He could be logically consistent in stressing amity with the Soviets yet still upholding his own wartime fear
of Soviet motives. He could call for U.S.–Soviet peace and cooperation, yet still
see the Soviets as the most likely enemy and insist on keeping up enough military strength to defeat them if war should break out. The expressed hopes for
peace were a necessary part of this larger strategy. Eisenhower voiced them so
often and so eloquently that he succeeded in misleading not only his contemporaries but generations of later historians, who have taken his public words as a
full and accurate indicator of his private views. It seems likely, however, that he
was already firmly committed to the anticommunist crusade when he returned
to Washington to become chief of staff.

# Part II

## CHIEF OF STAFF

CHAPTER 4

# Developing Ideology

$E$isenhower's years as chief of staff, from 1946–47, were years that brought significant changes to the United States. Anti-Soviet and anticommunist sentiment spread steadily and gradually became institutionalized. Military plans changed accordingly, as planners debated how to use the growing atomic arsenal against a presumed Soviet threat. There were intense public debates about demobilization, military budgets, Universal Military Training, and other military issues. The Truman administration began to institute a program to test the loyalty of its employees. A wave of strikes raised sweeping questions about relations between workers and employers. The major population shift to the suburbs began. The civil rights of black people became, for the first time in many decades, a matter of national public debate. Millions of women negotiated the complex transition from wartime workers to postwar housewives.

As problems grew and Truman's political stock weakened, sparking speculation about who would oppose him in 1948, many observers looked to Eisenhower. In light of his growing political prominence and the heightened political tensions, it might have been natural for the general's words to become much more politicized. This does not seem to have happened, however. In the surviving documentary record, at least, the C/S seems surprisingly detached from the turbulent events of the nation. Although he often addressed the issues of the day, his speeches did not usually focus on short-term policy debates.

Rather, his remarks were typically framed in a larger ideological context. His stated goal was usually to advance that ideology. He portrayed himself as above the political fray, offering a set of timeless truths that endured beyond all winds of change. In fact, both the substance and the specific language of his ideological discourse remained surprisingly constant those two years. This was true in his private as well as public discourse. Nor does his private discourse show much more interest than the public in the immediate battles raging in Washington.

Eisenhower was, if not above, then perhaps marginal to the political fray. He perceived the truly important part of his role to be overseeing and guiding the broadest possible principles. If that diverted his interest from the day-to-day policy struggles, others engaged in those struggles were probably quite content to have it that way.

This might have been a wise political move on his part. As chief of staff, Eisenhower continued to serve in a symbolic capacity as spokesman not only for the army but also for the liberal internationalist policy elite. He had to persuade the American public to give the army the resources he thought necessary to do its job. He also had to persuade the American public to support the program of pervasive long-term international involvement being developed by the U.S. government. Had he become entangled in short-term political conflicts, he might have undermined his influence in shaping long-term perceptions and policy directions. Moreover, he could not allow any suspicion that he might be promoting his own interests, or the interests of the army, in ways that were inimical to U.S. national interests.

So he insisted that his concerns and values, and those of the army, were exactly the same as the concerns and values of the United States. What was good for the army was good for the nation, and vice versa, he argued, because both army and nation should be guided by the eternal principles that he himself was articulating. Behind all of this lay another unspoken goal: to motivate the public to combat the Soviet challenge.

Eisenhower still aimed to achieve his goals primarily by telling a compelling story. Having returned home, however, he had to tell the story somewhat differently to appeal to the domestic audience. So, without changing any of the essentials, he reframed his story around a new central message: if Americans supported liberal internationalism and the army, they would not simply be doing other nations, or the army, a favor. The threat of the unnamed enemy reached beyond the war-torn lands of Europe and Asia to involve all Americans quite directly. Supporting the army and liberal internationalism was the best protection against that impending threat.

The general told all his audiences (either explicitly or implicitly) that American values and the American way of life epitomized all that was good, right, and desirable everywhere in the world. Upon this familiar premise he built an argument for the unity of civilization throughout the world. Then he asserted that, in one way or another, civilization was in danger throughout the world. The logical conclusion to this implicit syllogism was that America was in danger. His solution to this plight followed the same logic. Since America embodied the essence of civilization, Americanizing the world was the only way to rescue civilization. A strong, secure America meant a secure, peaceful world. World peace, in turn, was the prerequisite for peace and security at home. This, he proclaimed, was precisely what the army stood for and fought for, and he called on all Americans to stand and fight for the same goal.

An American audience that accepted this argument would have to feel responsible for, and therefore entwined in, the fate of the world. People imbued with a sense of global responsibility were more likely to support government policies aimed at whatever foes, named or unnamed, the government undertook to oppose. They were also more likely to support the army, especially when they heard its greatest hero assure them over and over again that the army's fondest wish was that it never have to fight again. To make this argument, the chief of staff had to develop his own public representation of American values, the U.S. system of government, and the meaning of peace. The speeches Eisenhower made as C/S were his first opportunity to develop this public representation, which Robert Griffith calls "the corporate commonwealth."[1]

## THE THEORETICAL FOUNDATIONS IN PUBLIC DISCOURSE

When fully laid out, the general's ideological views constituted a sort of primer in the popularized Lockean theory that underlay so much of the political discourse of his day. He offered an especially concise summary of his elementary civics lesson in a May 1947 speech to the Daughters of the American Revolution. Here, as Halford Ross Ryan says, "he stated his views on democracy for the first time in a cogent fashion."[2] His theory began with the claim that the United States was unique in its commitment to "the maximum of personal liberty." This value was not chosen arbitrarily: "Insistence upon individual freedom springs from unshakable conviction in the dignity of man, a belief—a religious belief—that through the possession of a soul he is endowed with certain rights" simply because he is a man. (In the ubiquitous male-oriented language of the day, of course, "man" meant human being.) "Further, if the individual is to be truly free, he must be provided opportunity to gain his livelihood through means of his own choosing." Free enterprise was essential for any real freedom; if the state owned all property, individuals "would necessarily respond only to the orders of the government."

But this raised the familiar Lockean dilemma. Man knows that "for certain of his basic needs he must depend upon concerted action of a group. . . . Thus have arisen organisms of collective political enterprise which have, so far, found their highest manifestation in what we call the nation." A nation needed "rules and laws to control relationships among individuals and measures to protect the whole against threat from without." This parallelism reflected another basic premise of all of Eisenhower's social thought: the inherent selfishness of individuals constituted an internal stress, always threatening to tear the group apart, which could be just as dangerous as threats from without. "The problem was to combine individual freedom with a linking together of the people of the thirteen colonies by bonds strong enough to keep the young nation intact and to enable it to carry on necessary central functions, including the basic one of security." The problem could be solved, now as then, "only so long as those individuals, by co-operative action, support and maintain the governmental mechanism." Cooperation meant voluntary restraint of the individual's selfish desires. "The obligations of the individual citizen to his central government are thus no less important in democracy than under dictatorship; the difference is that in democracy they are voluntarily undertaken—in the other case they are performed at the bayonet's point."

These were the themes on which Eisenhower built most of his speeches. "The thing we are defending is not territory and property, it is a way of life," he told the American Alumni Council. That way of life was based on "principles that we believe to be right—almost sacred." Chief among these principles was voluntary cooperation. Exhorting another audience to a "crusade [for] perpetuation of the fundamentals of the system that has made this country great," he declared: "I am a zealot for democracy, and I believe that democracy—if we have to define it in one word—must be grasped by the word 'co-operation.' Woodrow Wilson said, 'The highest form of efficiency is the spontaneous co-operation of a free people.' . . . It has been group effort, freely undertaken, that has produced . . . the American way of life."[3] Any reasonable person would see the need for self-restraint: "If any group of individuals seeks only its own immediate profit at the expense of others in a common enterprise, it inevitably lessens the efficiency of the whole and thus, eventually, defeats its own best interests." Thus, while democracy could tolerate diversity on secondary issues, it demanded "unity of purpose in fundamental issues, universality of cooperation and willing subordination of selfish ends to the common good." Any reasonable person would feel the power of such a Lockean argument, eschew selfishness, and subordinate all differences to the higher unity.[4]

But Eisenhower's own ideology cast strong doubt on the power of secular reasoning alone to produce cooperation. The underlying assumption in his social thought was that people are not always, nor perhaps often, reasonable. If they were, the tensions between individual and group would not arise in the first place: "None of us . . . can escape his responsibility for understanding that within him is a certain amount of greed, a certain amount of selfishness, a certain amount of prejudice. Those things are not going to be eradicated from our breasts within our time, but we can find ways to control them, to turn them to practical use, so we can get along together."[5] The human individual was not a Lockean tabula rasa, a free agent analyzing a range of options and choosing rationally among them. Rather, the individual was beset on every side by irrational impulses and had only two options—either controlling those impulses or yielding to them.

When Eisenhower projected this dualistic anthropology onto the societal level he created an implicit theory of political life. If the members of a group did not practice American-style voluntary self-restraint, they would end up in anarchy. This was "the fertile breeding ground for a malignant despotism," because selfish impulses would have to be restrained by some external compulsory force. And that force, typically the state, would inevitably abuse its power. In his political vocabulary, freedom was not primarily the ability to make rational choices, but the absence of external constraints, the freedom to control oneself. Since voluntary self-restraint was the essence of freedom as well as cooperation, there was not a conflict, but perfect synergy, between freedom and cooperation. Justice also meant being free from arbitrary external force. Thus every society was either "governed by justice or enslaved by force."[6] No third possibility could be admitted, and every society had to choose between the two. Here Lockean liberalism was pressed into the larger framework of the apocalyptic spiritual struggle.

If innate vice placed intrinsic limitations on the power of reason, however, how could people be motivated to choose freedom and justice? A crucial part of Eisenhower's answer lay in his concept of leadership. Drawing on his soldierly views, he explained to one audience that leadership was necessary to bind the unruly forces of human nature: "True leadership focuses and concentrates the discordant wills of many men into an effective union of strength, preserving them from dissolution into a futile mob. It is the essence of the democratic method, the antithesis of regimented compulsion." Eisenhower looked to educators as one source of leadership. Despite his frequent praise of education, however, the religious premise underlying his political philosophy gave little hope that training in careful thinking would win the spiritual victory. Therefore, he tried to blend his Lockean and apocalyptic views, urging educators to train young minds to make the right spiritual choices: "Our individual responsibilities and obligations cannot be ordered and enforced by central authority. . . . The meaning of America would be gone if human conscience should ever be replaced by the decree of government."[7]

On many other occasions, the general turned to religion itself for the solution. As he put it to the military Chaplains' Association, "religion has always been the most effective process of developing human character strong enough to forget the motivation of selfishness and to act on the larger concept of duty." Accepting the "Churchman Award," he argued that democracy required "some conviction of the value of this thing that we call the soul. . . . If there is not a soul that is related in some way to a religious Being, no matter what the faith, then I can see no reason why each of us should not exploit to the full any talent he may have vis-à-vis his fellow, vis-à-vis his neighbor, and take advantage if he possibly can." Previous generations of Americans had "recognized no bounds to their God-given ability to master themselves and their material world for the betterment of all men." In expounding such religious views, he was not only telling these audiences what they wanted to hear but also remaining consistent with views he expressed in many other settings. Leadership of any kind was good only if it evoked in the followers a commitment to voluntary self-restraint. Externally imposed restraints and mob rule were merely the two different faces of virtue's single enemy. This virtue, and the commitment to defeat its enemy, was the essence of religion, in Eisenhower's view—and the essence of true patriotism: "Love of country must inspire us to serve our own national interests by perfecting teamwork within [the nation]. . . . Patriotism is the expression of the will to sacrifice."[8]

This sense of patriotism was now "a virtue that cannot be confined within geographical limits." The true patriot cared about the whole world: "Personal ambitions and desires must now take second place to national need and solidarity. . . . Sheer national interest demands of us a unity of effort that must extend far beyond our national borders." The overriding aim of Eisenhower's public speeches was to increase U.S. public support for internationalism by identifying American values with the good of the entire world. He shared the view common among "realists" of his day that the world was now a geopolitical unity brought together by new technologies. He also shared their aspiration for what Richard A. Melanson calls the "global corporate commonwealth": a secure international system, built on America's liberal capitalist foundations.[9]

Eisenhower's internationalism was motivated by ideology as well as geopolitics. To remain logically consistent, he had to declare American values applicable throughout the world. His political theory was based on premises that would have to be universal if they were to be true. If voluntary cooperation was self-evidently the course that any reasonable person, or reasonable nation, would choose, then it would have to be equally self-evident everywhere. If human rights stemmed from a divine creator, then all humans would have the same claim to the same rights, no matter where they lived. And if selfishness were ultimately the barrier to receiving those rights, that barrier would be the same everywhere, since selfishness was an innate component of every human's nature. The basic problem of human society and its solution had to be universal. So the general had to say that the American way of life "is civilization as we know it." On another occasion, he proclaimed, "The rights and the dignity of the individual that have been traditionally at the roots of the English-speaking civilization . . . [are] in a class of the sacrosanct," and therefore formed the fulcrum of all values, the epitome of all true civilization. This was, self-evidently, the most reasonable way of life for everyone. Reason, freedom, and cooperation were the cornerstones of civilization.[10]

Since the true civilization was the rationality of the English-speaking peoples, now embodied in the American way of life, there could be no civilized alternative to it. The only alternative would be "a dismal, gray world where men are impelled, not by the higher civilized attributes . . . but solely by the stench of fear and the primordial instinct for survival. If man is not to live by reason and logic and right, the race will perish . . . The only thing that can prevent today's infant from living in the Golden Age of history is faulty teaching"—a failure to teach the values of English-speaking civilization.[11] This sort of rhetoric established the same kind of dualism that was so basic to the worldview of Eisenhower's sectarian Christian ancestors. The difference between right and wrong, between good and evil, was not only clear-cut but unbridgeable, allowing no middle ground. It was as vast as the distance separating the two roads of the Last Judgment, one leading to heaven and the other to hell. Although the C/S rarely spoke of those roads in specifically sectarian Christian terms, the hope for a heavenly Golden Age and the fear of dismal gray hell were always present, by implication, in his speeches.

Between the lines of this complex theoretical model, another message could be read quite easily, if anyone were looking for it: the United States now carried the banner of civilization against the forces of communism that threatened to undo civilization. Communism's collectivism, its statism, and its atheism all stemmed from the same root, in Eisenhower's theory. The root evil was denying the individual the right to practice the spiritual virtue of voluntary self-restraint. The C/S skillfully played his many variations on that single theme, implying that from every angle the U.S. system stood immutably opposed to the communist system. The foundation of his postwar story now explained clearly why chaos and communism were interrelated threats to the United States, so that those who wished to avoid chaos would have to avoid communism too. It might seem, then, that this entire theoretical edifice was an exercise in rhetorical manipulation. But such a judgment would be too hasty, for the same edifice was erected in Eisenhower's most private discourse as well.

## THE THEORETICAL FOUNDATIONS IN PRIVATE DISCOURSE

During his years as C/S, Eisenhower returned to frequent correspondence with friends and associates. In his letters he often addressed the same theoretical issues so central to the public speeches, and there was little apparent difference between public and private discursive frames. In a democracy "individualism rather than statism is the underlying concept of government," he wrote in his diary. "In free countries," he wrote to British Field Marshall Henry Wilson, "the unrestricted genius of all the people will in the long run be responsible for constructive development beyond that possible in a regimented and policed state." He linked free enterprise directly to individual liberty; these were "the base of our system," he wrote to his father-in-law. As he put it to his friend Al Browning: "To eliminate the profit motive would be to scuttle our form of government and our concepts of living; to these things I am fanatically devoted." Indeed the profit motive was absolutely necessary, given Eisenhower's view of human nature: "Human nature usually seeks avidly that which is difficult to get, whether it is money, position, or reputation," he wrote to James Forrestal. Without the incentives of special reward, "man's natural laziness and habits of self-indulgence" would surely prevail.[12]

To overcome the dangers inherent in competitive free enterprise, cooperation was "the single key," he wrote in his diary: "Moral regeneration, revival of patriotism, clear realization that progress in any great segment is not possible without progress for the whole; all these are necessary." To Eddie Rickenbacker he wrote that "cooperation for the good of the country is the only formula for permanent advancement of individual good." He told his brother Milton of "the one underlying principle that I have always believed to be binding on every American. That principle is that every citizen is required to do his duty for the country no matter what it may be." True patriotism meant self-restraint. This equation shaped his approach to policy matters on some occasions. Asked to decide whether the army should censor a military newspaper, he said the paper "should be free but it should be in the hands of people who are completely patriotic, and not irresponsible individuals."[13]

The upshot of all this was what Eisenhower loved to call "the middle way" between individualism and cooperation. As his friend William Robinson described it (summarizing numerous conversations with the C/S), "it was not rugged individualism in the old-fashioned Republican sense of the word; but was freedom and independence for the individual with its collateral responsibility for cooperation." Every individual "owed a part of himself to the welfare of the community and the nation"; that debt would be paid not only by sacrificing for the common good but by "qualifying himself for some function in the life of the community."

"He doesn't want to make public statements on politics," Robinson noted, echoing Eisenhower's own frequent reminders that soldiers ought not to speak politically. This reticence may also have been calculated to keep the potential candidate above the political fray. But in his private conversations with this friend he was apparently more willing to link the broad abstractions of political theory to the specific issues of the day. He criticized the Democratic Party for promoting a New Deal that "sought to substitute SECURITY for OPPORTUNITY." He told Robinson, "The unlimited growth of bureaucracy in Washington as a result of the New Deal policies is a national disgrace. . . . Unless this is cleaned up completely and thoroughly, our Federal Government in any hands faces a doubtful future." He also expressed concern that organized labor was "forever seeking laws to hamstring Management," rather than taking responsibility for more efficient production, though he also wanted management to offer "fair and decent treatment of its workers." All in all, he told his friend, he was "a Liberal Republican" in the "sound responsible middle-of-the-road."[14]

Generally, though, when he enumerated his principles in private as well as in public, Eisenhower gave much more attention to their religious basis than their political application. He wrote to his close boyhood friend, Swede Hazlett: "I believe fanatically in the American form of democracy—a system that recognizes and protects the rights of the individual and that ascribes to the individual a dignity accruing to him because of his being created in the image of a supreme being and which rests upon the conviction that only through a system of free enterprise can this type of democracy by preserved." Similarly, in his private diary he wrote of the need for "complete devotion to democracy, which means a faith in men as men (essentially religious concept) and practice of free enterprise."[15]

As always, Eisenhower linked cooperation with the religious virtues of self-discipline and self-sacrifice. When people were selfish rather than cooperative, it was evidence of "man's stupidity." Education was one antidote. He urged his brother Milton, an educator, to teach young people about "the history of sacrifices made since 1215 to establish the equality of citizens before the law." Beyond education, however, democracy needed a spiritual virtue, a voluntary control of the will, to control "man's natural laziness and habits of self-indulgence."[16]

Eisenhower was careful to locate the solution to all human problems in a generic concept of religion, "no matter what the faith." Although he assumed that all people had some taint of sin, he also assumed that anyone could choose to overcome the power of sin through education and a strenuous effort of the will.

In this sense Eisenhower may be numbered among the "ministers of reform" who combined Christianity and Progressivism in their political leadership (and perhaps as the last of these to inhabit the White House).[17]

Eisenhower claimed not only to preach but to practice self-willed virtue. In 1948 he decided not to run for president that year. He told a friend that he "tried very hard to keep personal desire and convenience out of my mental process." A few days earlier he had written Leonard Finder, publisher of the *Manchester Union Leader,* that his decision not to run perfectly suited his own personal desire. "When this is the case a man should scrutinize his own analysis with a jaundiced eye," he added, in classical Kantian tones; only decisions made against one's desires were genuine evidence of doing one's duty. Too few people put the good of the whole nation above personal or partisan concerns, he complained to Beetle Smith: "I should like to be numbered among this disinterested group." He wrote to Swede Hazlett, "I am talking or working for all, not for any political party or for any political ambition. This is the attitude I hope that I can preserve to the end of my days." Voluntary cooperation among free, self-restrained, rational individuals was the heart of his private as well as his public notion of moral and religious virtue.[18]

Eisenhower told Smith that he did so much speaking "due to my very great desire to promote a few simple ideas in which I so earnestly believe." In his diary, after complaining of the unexpected number of speaking engagements, he explained: "Some of them are difficult to refuse. I so firmly believe we should all do our part to reawaken in our country a realization of our own blessings and what we have to do to protect them (this protection involving also spreading them) that when any organization that has a similar purpose asks me to appear, I feel a sense of guilt when I decline." Telling the official story was one crucial way of protecting and spreading "the American way."[19]

When any political figure claims to "earnestly believe" in his rhetoric, there is a natural tendency for historians to be skeptical. Many might find more truth in Eisenhower's admission to Gen. Jonathan Wainwright that he accepted speaking engagements "only where the Staff insists that the welfare of the Army is involved."[20] Perhaps Eisenhower was stressing this principle because it would eventually give him a justification for running for president, as some biographers claim. Indeed the same might be said of many other private correspondences: perhaps he was creating a distinct impression of himself and his principles in the minds of people who could help his political fortunes. But historians who pursue this line of interpretation must confront the total absence of any confirming evidence. If his most private letters were purely for public consumption—if his true thoughts were different—then there is simply no evidence for those true thoughts. Indeed, it would be striking that he could voice these ideas so often in private as well as public, to so many different people, and with such consistency, while so completely hiding his true private thoughts.

It is important to recall, too, that he had articulated many of these views just as clearly and forcefully in his wartime letters to his most intimate correspondents, before his name had ever been mentioned as a presidential candidate. Whatever new ideas he was developing flowed logically from those that were already well established. On the whole, his private writings espoused views he had expressed before becoming C/S and would express long after he left that office. If Eisenhower was sometimes telling others what they wanted to hear, in order to establish his reputation, he was at least speaking consistently and without risk of contradicting himself. What he really thought, no historian shall ever know. The one thing the historian can say with some certainty is that the private discourse of the C/S was strikingly congruent with his public discourse on every major issue in his theoretical framework—except one, the issue of peace.

## THE MEANING OF PEACE

*Peace* has always been a key word of U.S. political speech. Eisenhower, however, elevated it to a central place in his public discourse, drawing heavily on the discursive legacy of Woodrow Wilson, so deeply steeped in Christian traditions. He did so for good practical reasons. He faced a dilemma much like Wilson's: trying to stimulate support for liberal internationalism in a postwar era, when the public tended to equate peace with avoiding foreign entanglements. As Army Chief of Staff, of course, he had the additional problem of seeking support for military spending in a postwar era, when the public wanted drastic cuts in that spending. He had to convince the public that neither the army nor the government wanted war, that foreign entanglements need not mean war, and that just such foreign entanglements were the only way to avoid war and attain lasting peace.

Like Wilson, Eisenhower pursued these aims by constructing, in his public language, the meaning of peace, the context in which it could be pursued, and the process by which it could be attained. The meaning and context of peace were constructed out of his entire discursive framework, so the process was naturally congruent with that framework. Peace, and the path to it, became symbolic expressions of the whole complex of his values, extended on a worldwide scale. Therefore Eisenhower could elaborate a rich view of peace, articulate it consistently, and support it sincerely.

To understand peace one had to understand the causes of war, which were "evils entrenched in the structure of human relations." He said, "When you come down to it, the seeds of war are in the breast of each of us." Controlling the selfishness innate in human nature was the key to peace in Eisenhower's discourse. When he offered "my definition of pacifism: Every practical decent and proper step that will prevent the outbreak of war," he was careful not to reduce peace merely to the absence of war. Peace meant an absence of war achieved by following "decent and proper" values.[21]

When it came to defining peace, the values were even more important than the avoidance of war. To attain peace meant "to substitute the council table for the battlefield," "to substitute mutual confidence for mutual suspicion and rule by law for rule by the sword," to make the "transition from war to peace, from destructive chaos toward orderly procedures." At another time he said, "We live by the axiom that arbitration is a more effective means of settling disputes than is war." The international machinery of peace would "remove from nations any reason for, or any desire to, attack." At the council table, where rules prevailed, life was orderly precisely because people restrained their impulses. Only "orderly, legal procedures," not state force, could "give civilization a firm foundation." A "firm foundation" meant a civilization with enduring mechanisms to institutionalize the practice of self-restraint. Mutual confidence in a dependable social order based on law was essential to prevent the disruptions of conflict and war that were caused by selfishness.[22]

Eisenhower, however, was not a legalist; law and institutions alone were not enough. There had to be some assurance that people would freely respect laws and institutions. When he wrote, in his war memoir, that "no binding regulation, law, or custom" can hold together a wartime alliance, but "only a highly developed sense of mutual confidence," he went out of his way to add: "Possibly this truth has equal applicability in peace." He often insisted that clear logical thinking was the path to mutual confidence and peace. To take any other path would be irrational. As a soldier recently returned from battle, he told his audiences that he was acutely aware of "the ignorance, the intolerance, the stupidity that have led nations to aggressive use of force"; and "As the fruits of education are widely spread, the cleansing spring of knowledge, logic and reason is made to flow over the dark ground of prejudice, fear, hysteria—the soil in which the evil seeds of war forever flourish." When reason and understanding ruled, all people would be civilized, accepting limits to their greed and compromising their differences through arbitration. "In the end, it will be the citizens of all countries who must outlaw war. Until the people of the world understand and respect the interest of their neighbors, the victory will elude us."[23]

In Eisenhower's discourse, war was identified with chaos, unreason, and force, which was in turn identified with external compulsion of all kinds, and hence with injustice. In one speech he equated "our hatred of war" with "our repudiation of rule by force which means enslavement." Peace was identified with order, rationality, mutual understanding, and justice. Because these were the hallmarks of democracy, democracies were inherently peaceable. It was logical to conclude that only totalitarian systems, not democracies, would begin wars: "Every effort aimed at . . . the liberation of our world from war and the fear of war is a natural extension of the democratic ideal"; and "In adherence to the philosophies of individual liberty and free enterprise lies the surest way to peace and happiness."[24]

Since this understanding of peace was grounded in his universalizing political philosophy it, too, had to be valid everywhere. The C/S treated nations as individuals; some were selfish and others self-disciplined. Selfishness in any one land, however, would inevitably encroach on all others: "There can be no peace for any one nation in this world unless there is peace for all"; "The peace we fought for must be universal in its scope, embracing all nations. . . . Rights and obligations, universally recognized, are the essence of peace; and so to attain peace, there must be found a way to protect the rights and enforce the obligations"; and "The glowing future of peace, confidence, and freedom that we visualize for every individual within our borders will not be completely attained until other nations can, in some degree, achieve comparable goals."[25]

Peace, then, required universal adherence to a basic core of principles, which just happened to be the core values of the American system. An enduringly peaceable society had been built on such principles in this nation, which was proof that the world could learn to live in peace: "If it has been done among 140 million [in the United States], it can be done among twice or twenty times that number." Only when the principles of the American way became the operative principle of the international community would there be genuine peace. "The glowing future of peace, confidence and freedom that we visualize for every individual within our borders will not be completely attained until other nations can, in some degree, achieve comparable goals." In effect, peace meant the stability and security of the corporate commonwealth, made permanently inviolable because it had been made universal. In all his speeches he took it for granted, and assumed his audience would agree, that individual freedom, free enterprise (and the abundance it produced), and peace were interwoven values that everyone in the world would prize: "All of us firmly believe that humanity wants peace and if given full voice the majority will demand peace. This is the inspiration for our support of majority rule"; and "Many peoples throughout the world desire to march shoulder to shoulder with us toward freedom and justice—toward peace. . . . Progress along this path cannot be unilateral." Given the premises of his public discourse, a desire to emulate "the American way" was the only conclusion that clear-thinking people could reach.[26]

Was it reasonable to place such great faith in the power of human reason to achieve it? The social order and mutual understanding at the heart of peace required acts of free will—spiritual acts. Without them, the absence of a shooting war would mark only an interlude in which the seeds of the next war would flourish. Yet the general's Augustinian "realism" cast a long shadow of doubt on the possibility of lasting peace. He sometimes admitted that war might never be eliminated altogether. The struggle between peace and war would go on forever, he told a group of chaplains: "Your struggle is an endless one. The inner peace of a well integrated life is something that must be continually achieved; the outer peace of a world in which nations live together in a spirit of brotherhood is something that must be continually earned." This was a logical inference from his premise that war was caused by vices innate in every human being. The best to hope for was not elimination, but merely containment of the threat of war. To the National Board of Fire Underwriters he proposed a parallel between war and fire. Both were dangers that humans would always have to face but could learn to control ever more proficiently. Therefore, he called for "individual, community, and national attitudes that will remove war from the category of the inevitable into its proper position as an evil subject to prevention, or at least control. . . . War may happen—but it will cease to be an institution, a characteristic of human society."[27]

More often, though, when the general spoke of peace as a spiritual virtue he held out a vision of a permanent universal peace: "the millennium when arbitration and reason will entirely replace force." At Gettysburg, he said that the eternal flame of the town's battlefield, which "symbolizes permanent accord among ourselves, can be the prototype of another light symbolizing universal peace. . . . What has been won for the peoples of this continent, you can preserve here and help win for all the world!" He told one audience that the United States and its allies must "marshal our forces into one mighty effort . . . toward the goal of permanent peace . . . this glorious, universal crusade." He called on another audience to join a "great crusade" marching "toward peace and, finally, total and universal disarmament. . . . When, but only when, we have the certainty of universal peace we could at last enter the world of total disarmament." The relationship might also work in reverse; the Baruch plan for nuclear disarmament, he told journalists, "might mean the outlawing of war." In any event, the goal he held out was total disarmament, perfect peace, and universal security—"the world's salvation" and "the peace that man has hoped for through the centuries, the peace that has no end."[28]

Eisenhower knew that his audiences expected to hear such eschatological promises of a more perfect world coming soon, in order to legitimate the sacrifices they had made during the war. War inevitably generates a sense of apocalyptic expectation, particularly in cultures shaped by the biblical tradition. The drive for unconditional surrender and total victory had heightened the apocalypticism of World War II. The public was primed to expect a fundamental transformation, a permanent eradication of evil and triumph of good. The war's most famous general was eager to tell them that their hopes would be fulfilled.

Certainly he knew, too, that such dramatic religious rhetoric would move his audiences more than dry political analyses. The general could have offered sustained logical expositions of his ideological views. In his public discourse, he was constructing the meaning of peace as a principal support for his ideological vision of the meaning and role of the United States in world history. As he constructed that vision, he was also constructing and supporting a particular meaning of peace. The theoretical edifice was, in its overall structure, a logically consistent unity. In this construction, democracy, capitalism, and religious faith, as well as peace, were the necessary institutions of a self-restrained people. Each implied all the others, so that all stood or fell together. But Eisenhower was asking his audiences to accept government and army policies that reason alone might well hesitate to approve. Arguments on the basis of logic alone would be open to counter-argument, and perhaps to refutation. Careful analyses of his speeches would certainly reveal their conceptual confusion. As in his months in Europe, heading the occupation, he was drawing on Augustinian, apocalyptic, and Wilsonian language, blending these very different ideological systems without regard to their contradictions.

This issue was largely irrelevant, though, because the chief of staff was striving to persuade, not logically but emotionally. To achieve the desired emotional effect, he replaced sustained logical argumentation with sermonic exhortation. He strung together selected small pieces of his overall ideological framework, each featuring one or more treasured key words of the American political lexicon. Each key word became a symbol of the entirety of the American faith, as he interpreted it; each functioned synecdochically to represent the whole ideological framework. These synecdochical links, not the logical links, served to communicate internal consistency and coherence of the whole ensemble. This ensemble was held out as the highest ideal toward which any society could strive. Eisenhower was painting verbal pictures, often quite powerful pictures, of the given and the possible. He clearly implied that the policies currently promoted by the army and the government could turn possibility into reality, if they were wholeheartedly supported by a self-disciplined public truly committed to the American faith.

Curiously, though, this apparently burning desire for peace was rarely reflected in his many private letters. A reader of the published private papers from his tenure as C/S, which fill three sizable volumes, would have little (if any) idea that Eisenhower cared deeply about peace as an abstract ideal. This is the one area in which his publicly and privately expressed theoretical principles diverged. The private did not contradict the public; it merely gave the subject of peace little attention.[29] He could easily have woven a concept of peace into his private discourse. The premises of the public and private were virtually identical, as were the conclusions on nearly every subject except peace. For the most part, however, the theme of peace was absent from the private writings. The explanation of this anomaly will emerge from a look at Eisenhower's public and private stories of war and peace in the postwar world. Those stories affirmed that the nation's hopes for peace could not yet be fulfilled. His discursive framework, as well as practical considerations of the army's needs, required that he also stress the unfinished business of the war.

## CHAPTER 5

# The Story of the Postwar World

B uilding on his theoretical foundation, Eisenhower reconstructed for domestic audiences the story he had developed about World War II and the return to peacetime. His political/religious understanding of "the American way" was the new thread upon which he could string all the elements of that story. He hoped to persuade the U.S. public that it could not turn its back on the rest of the world, for whatever dangers threatened abroad also threatened at home, including the great, unnamed Soviet menace.

## THE POSTWAR WORLD IN PUBLIC DISCOURSE

The ultimate source of the war, he explained, had been the same moral shortcomings that cause every war: the "indifference, the blind complacency, the sheer selfish laziness that more than once have permitted war to burst upon us." He found a pattern in history: "We found in 1914 and again in 1939 that abuse of power, lack of restraint in its exercise, lust for its increase, breed war. . . . Local passions, misguided fanatics and age-old prejudices can all bring about crises of the gravest kind." The United States had fought not only to protect itself, but to protect its values wherever they might be practiced—"to maintain the line for the freedom of man. Had you failed we and no other nation could have continued to live as a free people."[1]

With these kinds of words, Eisenhower sought to reshape his audiences' understanding of the war. It had not been a battle against the singular evil of Germany or Japan, he implied; indeed he rarely singled out the Axis nations for opprobrium. Instead he framed the war in the terms he had first developed privately during the war itself, as a battle between abstract virtues and abstract vices. Above all the war had been caused by a lack of, and fought to restore, the true American values of reason, self-discipline, and cooperation. Within this framework, Eisenhower could use the memory of the recent past to shape perceptions of the present. Though he seemed to be speaking about the "hot" war past, he was actually establishing principles for setting national priorities in the present.

Thus he argued that World War II had been fought not only to destroy the Axis powers, but "to undertake with our Allies a long-range system of international co-operation that would minimize if not eliminate the danger of future conflicts." The war had "accomplished the first phase of the purposes for which our country went to war. But this, as all of us *now* know, did not mean that complete victory had been won." Likewise, he said, "Peace did not descend upon Central Europe with the cessation of hostilities. [The cessation of hostilities] marked the end of killing and it provided an opportunity to begin the laborious business of restoring order from chaos." His months as head of the occupation, he told Congress, had been devoted to "bringing order out of chaos." The remaining task, being carried out by the army in occupied countries, was *the maintenance of law and order amid conditions of hardship and near starvation.* The implicit argument here was clear enough: war is always a struggle of order against chaos; the United States has always stood for order, which is clearly the higher virtue; wherever chaos threatened, the United States would have as its highest priority the maintenance or restoration of order.[2]

To fit the present as well as the past into his ideological mold, the C/S had to depict the present as a threatening chaos. Then he could present the U.S. mission to restore order as the urgent need of the day. The news from Europe, however, might have suggested a different interpretation. During 1946 most European nations outside the Soviet orbit were making a surprisingly rapid economic recovery.[3] But Eisenhower's audiences heard a very different story. He had hoped that "the occupied peoples would remain tractable," he told them. But the chaos born of war made it impossible, at present, to achieve this goal. He made this clear on several different occasions: "The liberated areas of Europe were left without the ability to produce adequate coal, without transportation, without their own skilled labor, with their currencies unsettled, without foreign exchange and without the raw materials to revive industry"; "In an atmosphere of confusion and fear, and where great portions of the earth's population seethe in misery and in hunger, efforts to substitute mutual confidence for mutual suspicion, and rule by law for rule by the sword cannot prosper"; and "Our own conception of democracy . . . is of little importance to men whose immediate concern is the preservation of physical life. With famine and starvation the lot of half the world, food is of far more current importance to them than are political ideas." He put the message most dramatically to the American Legion: "Our nation is faced today with problems . . . almost beyond precedent. . . . Are we expected to sit idly by, doing nothing, while hunger and hopelessness inexorably push the shadow of enslavement ever and ever closer to our own shores? . . . World chaos is the enemy of our security."[4]

Eisenhower had a simple theory to link world hunger and poverty to U.S. security: hunger and poverty fostered the dictators who forced the United States into war. "A hungry world is a restless and disturbed arena in which the agitator and political charlatan find ready followers, for men will sacrifice principle and peace to win food for their families," he warned. "The way to durable peace is blocked by the ruin of shattered economies, by appalling human misery and by ideological strife that seems at times beyond composition. Unchecked, these foster anarchy, the fertile breeding ground for a malignant despotism." This was just what had caused the recent war, he argued.[5]

If the United States did not play a full international role, "into the vacuum will rush the same evil elements which nullified democracy's triumph in the First World War," and history would repeat itself. "New Hitlers [would] rise to throw the world into a chaos more awful than the shattered countries of Europe present today." The United States had to bring order out of the present chaos, above all, in order to forestall the rise of "this hypothetical Hitler of the future."[6]

Privately, of course, the general said quite plainly that the "new Hitlers" would come from the Soviet Union. In policy papers, he urged food and other forms of aid to war-torn areas. Without the aid, he argued, the continuing chaos would allow the Soviets to expand their influence, and perhaps get control of contested nations such as Austria, Greece, and Korea. He never acknowledged that the contests in such nations were largely civil wars. He assumed that local insurgents were merely proxies for the worldwide conspiracy directed from Moscow. In public, though, he was still careful never to mention the Soviet Union or any other nation or group by name.[7]

## THE DANGER TO CIVILIZATION

The public Eisenhower portrayed the postwar world in the same abstract categories he used to interpret the war. His favorite categories were chaos and civilization, now pitted against each other in the ultimate battle. Victory for civilization would bring "universal peace," "the millennium." The alternative was almost too horrible to contemplate. But as he sought to rally public support for the army, internationalism, and the anticommunist struggle, he was quick to invoke this most frightening specter. The C/S had lived out his whole military career during the three decades when U.S. leaders attempted to uphold their system against internal stresses (World War I, industrial strife, global depression) and the external threats posed by alternative systems (communism and fascism). In spite of the victory of World War II, the future of the global corporate commonwealth still seemed tremendously precarious. If civilization collapsed in some places, it would not be safe in any place, for the destiny of every nation was now interwoven with all others.

In Eisenhower's discourse, every specific danger led back directly to this ultimate danger—the end of civilization. Two and a half years after the war's end, he was still describing civilization as "paralyzed and wasted by dissension." Such imagery was rather benign, however, compared to the terrors he foresaw in the future: "Our civilization has reached a brink from which the prospect—if we turn not into sure paths of peace—is a thousand times more terrifying than anything yet witnessed. . . . I urge that we do not delay—that we do not complacently assume the absence of mortal danger"; "I am convinced that the alternative to making that victory [of WW II] secure is the a nightmare of death, horror, and black ruin such as no man has ever dreamed of." "Civilization as we know it" and "humanity's existence" were at stake, he warned time and again: "The earth may become a flowering garden or a sterile desert"; "Mutual understanding between nations . . . will build a constantly easier road toward the ultimate goal" of peace, but "its lack will surely bring us finally to disaster, if not extinction"; "Should we falter in our forward march or shirk our duty, we jeopardize not only world peace but our very existence"; and "The future of civilization, so far as we can see, depends on the outcome of world co-operation."[8]

The choice was now between peace and extinction, because of the unprecedented destructiveness of war: "Either the nations work together for the common good or one by one they will perish; slowly in withering decay; or quickly under the impact of total war, as is more likely the way of the future. Industrial development and atomic science have left no limits to global conflict, either in scope or destructive results"; "Every intelligent man in the world knows that civilization cannot stand another war." It would mean "another world cataclysm, whose disastrous effects would dwarf any that civilization has yet endured." After the next war, "civilized life as we have known it will no longer be possible and the sacrifices particularly of the English-speaking races back to 1215 will all have been in vain."[9]

Eisenhower stressed the difficulties and dangers, for he wanted to persuade Americans that, without the concerted effort of their nation and its army, the world could again plunge into depression and social chaos. By equating civilization with the American way of life and crying the warning that the former was threatened, he was saying (sometimes explicitly and sometimes implicitly) that the latter itself was at stake. Thus he made it seem impossible for Americans to avoid involvement in the global crisis. If the postwar conditions degenerated into anarchy and then despotism, they could "end all freedom and destroy every democracy." Likewise, "Democracy has entered its decade of greatest crisis. . . . Personal ambitions and desires must now take second place to national need and solidarity."[10]

Americans seeking to forget the traumatic horrors of the Depression and World War II might have been stunned to hear that the decade of greatest crisis was just beginning. But their belief that the worst was past was just the kind of complacency Eisenhower assailed: "Complacency, greed, inertia, weakness, hysterical fear—any of these could destroy us; together they would surely do so. . . . [and] we shall not salvage our civilization from the ruin of war." Toward the end of his term, the chief of staff put increasing stress on such internal threats to civilization: "Liberty can find destruction in either of two extremes—license on the one hand, neglect on the other"; "No other person can assume your responsibility—else democracy will cease to exist"; and "No one can defeat us unless we first defeat ourselves."[11]

With words like these Eisenhower fused internal and external dangers into one indivisible threat of doom. The two dangers had to be fused, in the logic of his discourse; restraint, if not freely given, would have to be imposed externally, which would eventually lead to war. This was the essence of the global crisis: "All must work together—or eventually we will work under the whip!"; "The world is in a fluid, turbulent period, and unless we continue to do our utmost to make it a better place to live, the problem will likely be how to preserve it as a place in which we can live!" A newspaper headline summed up his message succinctly: "Eisenhower Sees Peace or Cave Life."[12]

This dichotomy was rooted in his religiously based worldview and, more specifically, in the apocalyptic tradition on which generations of Christians had been raised—including Eisenhower himself. The choice was between the millennium and damnation. No middle ground was possible. Occasionally he used overtly religious language to make the point, especially on ritual occasions. At a D day commemoration in 1947, he spoke of the future time when "universal security is attained and firmly grasped," calling it "the world's salvation." He urged his audience to follow the path to this salvation, for the alternative was "chaos among hundreds of millions" and "the collapse of the civilized structure."[13]

His public rhetoric broke with his religious training, though, because the rhetoric offered no guarantee that the utopian outcome would inevitably, by divine decree, come to pass. The question was still salvation or doom, but the outcome depended entirely on human choice. Self-discipline, education, and cooperative politics—good works, not grace—was the answer. This was something of a theological innovation, one that Christian thought would find rather contradictory. He was defining the postwar problem, and indeed the human condition, in largely Augustinian terms, but the solution he offered was that championed by Augustine's theological archrival, Pelagius. Of course Eisenhower was heedless of the theological background or implications of his words. He knew only that he wanted to rouse the public to action.

## CONTINUING THE WAR

When Eisenhower spoke of the action needed to combat postwar chaos, he used the language most natural to him after three decades in the military. The only way to achieve peace and avoid doom, he insisted, was to continue the war. After so much talk of the choice between peace and doom, this may have struck some as a paradoxical conclusion. But the logic of his story of war and peace, as well as the story's policy aims, led inexorably to this conclusion. If the war had been a struggle to preserve American values and build global peace upon them, it was only logical that the war could not really end until the U.S. system and the global corporate commonwealth were permanently secure. This left him with no logical option but to declare that the work of the war remained unfinished. Also, of course, his practical aim was to enlist public support for the policies he thought essential to protect the U.S. system. The war had kindled a surprisingly immense outburst of national unity and energy. There was no better way to maintain that unity and energy than to declare the war still unfinished. This was both the most logical and the most practical moral to the general's story, and he preached it at every opportunity.

The Allies had entered into the last war with a twofold pledge, he said: "to rid the world of tyranny" and "tirelessly to seek a lasting peace." Since only the first pledge had been redeemed, the war had to go on: "The campaign that engages us now is the closing action of the war"; "Conflict does not necessarily end when the shells and bombs stop falling"; "The victory is an empty one if it does not lead to a just and lasting peace"; and "We are still pursuing the purposes for which we went to war."[14]

As he spoke of continuing the war, military metaphors came naturally to the general. Although the victory had been glorious, he said, "now the winners have set themselves a new and even greater task—to work out a formula and a practical procedure intended to smooth international frictions, to find a way to banish war forever from the world. Just as each was necessary to victory, all must march together toward peace. Attack, not defense, is indicated!" He called on veterans to be leaders in the fight for peace and to "bring under your banner a constantly increasing army determined, with you, to win the peace." Victory, he told a college audience, would mean "an entire world—peaceful, tranquil, prosperous! The alternative will not wait, the time to attack is now." He told graduating cadets: "If today I were compelled to send you as leaders of platoons into battle I would say to you—you understand the essentials of the task assigned you. Success is yours for the winning! I can think of no better message to give you as you go out to lead your fellows in the winning of international co-operation and enduring peace!"[15]

Certainly, many in Eisenhower's audiences were amazed and dismayed to hear that World War II had not brought real victory at all, that they were not at peace, and that the war had to go on. World War II had ended. Was it not necessary to describe the present as, in some sense, already a period of peacetime? Occasionally the C/S did speak in such terms. In early 1946, he told Congress that the army was struggling to complete a three-stage mission: winning the war, securing the peace, and preserving the peace. He used this image to oppose the public clamor for rapid demobilization, urging Congress to slow down the process and help the army complete all three stages. On another occasion he called on the United States to "help protect the peace, our own peace and that of others that look to us for leadership," and "to control any world gangsters who may threaten world peace." When he spoke of peace in such terms, he was implicitly defining it as merely the absence of a shooting war. In a Christmas message to his troops he made this point clear: "All of you are guardians of peace. . . . Your basic purpose must always be [war's] prevention rather than its waging."[16]

It is clear, however, that Eisenhower meant to speak of peace as something much more than just the absence of war. The goal was a global corporate commonwealth so secure it would never have to fight again; the perilous, chaotic present he described, so far from that goal, could hardly be called peaceful. His public discourse could call the nation to continued war only because it promised perfect peace. Precisely because of this utopian promise, which appeared as an immensely distant hope, he had to call the nation to continue the apocalyptic war. So the C/S rarely spoke of the existing peace as a fully achieved state, the antithesis of war. That full peace was almost always proposed as a millennial goal still to be attained. When he spoke of "this peace we have won at such tremendous cost," for example, he urged his audience to ensure that it would be "a lasting, an enduring peace; not an uneasy cessation of hostilities such as we so bitterly experienced between the two World Wars."[17]

He moved toward some resolution of the tension between present and future peace by portraying peace as a process: "Neither will the day of international order, nor that of complete spiritual regeneration, come suddenly and instantly. . . . Progress toward such peace will be slow." He made it clear that "The path to peace will be a long and rocky climb. We are only beginning." The present time was "the current state of world transition from war to peace, from destructive chaos toward orderly procedures." Educated youth had a special responsibility to "lead us, in safe stages, toward our goal to win the peace." The notion of peace as a global corporate commonwealth and as a process toward that goal combined to further blur, and perhaps erase, the difference between peace and war. Peace as a process was a struggle against the same forces that had engendered the war. There was no fundamental break between wartime and peacetime.[18]

The C/S built this view upon his Augustinian foundations. He assumed that war would always be caused by irrational aggressors breaking through the boundaries of orderly civilization. The aggressors would always be there, just over the border, awaiting their chance; periodically, when they saw a chance of victory, they would attack. If they failed and were repulsed, they would refortify themselves and await their next opportunity. There could be no end to the threat. But his vision of eternal peace reflected the very different apocalyptic view, which promised to put an end to this danger once and for all. As a struggle against absolute evil, this war allowed no compromise; it had to be waged to the bitter end.

Unlike the biblical millennium, though, the universal peace he foresaw would not come in the twinkling of an eye. In effect, he was projecting the Augustinian image of war and peace onto an apocalyptic scale: each cycle of incursion and repulsion was one more battle in the same gradually unfolding apocalyptic war. The apocalypse was now a gradual process, a long series of incursions and repulsions. In one sense the victory had already been won and peace already attained; in another sense victory remained a far distant goal. This was the traditional Christian affirmation that the world was already redeemed but not yet redeemed, now pressed into the modern vision of progress. The only way to reach the final redemption—the secular analogue to the Second Coming—was to continue resisting the aggressors, to continue the war.[19]

Apparently the general realized that his call to participate in an ongoing war might be confusing. At least once he felt compelled to make it clear that he was not talking about using a shooting war to get peace: "If the world is going to struggle for peace, we can't state in advance that we must fight another war. This business of fighting for peace is getting tiresome to the world."[20] Nevertheless, he went on using the martial imagery. Perhaps he took it for granted that his many public warnings about the unthinkable evil of another "hot" war would make the point clear. A careful reader of or listener to his words would find the point quite clear. A "hot" war could no longer be a way to peace. But the absence of peace meant that there had to be continuing war. The only possible solution was to wage a "cold" war, and this is what the C/S was calling for (although he did not yet use the term). On either side of that "middle way," whether fighting too physically or not at all, lay the ultimate peril. The cold war as a gradual apocalypse demanded constant vigilance against both faces of that peril.

## MILITARY STRENGTH IN PUBLIC DISCOURSE

As one of the three highest-ranking military men in the nation, Eisenhower was bound to allot a major portion of his public rhetoric to explaining and defending the military's role. The postwar pressure was still strong for dramatic cuts in military spending. The debates about a peacetime draft and Universal Military Training raged on, with no end in sight. The Army Chief of Staff had to frame his story, in large part, to justify the military's manpower and budgetary demands. In all his speeches, he remained acutely aware that he was not representing himself but rather the army and the military establishment. Still, Stephen Ambrose's comment that, on most issues, "he had nothing original to say; rather, he followed the War Department line,"[21] is somewhat misleading. Eisenhower never contradicted the War Department line, and he had little, if anything, original to say on policy issues. His public speeches, however, rarely focused on the specific policy debates of the day. Rather, he spoke in broad terms about the role of the army, placing it within his own ideological and rhetorical wrappings. Those wrappings were equally evident in the private discourse. Yet on this issue, too, the similarities and differences between public and private discourse, set side by side, prove most revealing.

His main public point was to assure audiences that there was no contradiction between the army's best interests and the nation's best interests. Both shared the same problems, the same hopes, and the same values. The military had no desire to perpetuate itself or militarize the nation. The soldier wanted to end war just as much as the civilian. Indeed, having experienced war's horrors firsthand, the soldier was "the world's greatest and most realistic pacifist—he insists that his military victory be followed up with the strength of this nation as it takes the lead in devising orderly processes for elimination of war." Toward the end of his tenure as chief of staff, he drafted a public statement justifying the army's continuing occupation of defeated Axis nations in just these terms. The army was needed to ensure stability, law, and order, he asserted. Generalizing from the occupied lands to the whole world, he called military preparation a "great stabilizing influence" because it would promote "orderly settlement of the world's difficulties" and deter others from initiating war.[22]

In Eisenhower's discourse it was logical, not paradoxical, to assert that a powerful military was "the first essential to lasting peace." If peace would come only when the war had been brought to its ultimate conclusion, the United States still had to fight the closing action of the war: "It is just as essential now to provide the necessary military strength and to distribute those forces properly as it was during the critical days of the shooting war." But he did not rely on this argument alone. Striving to prove that military strength would promote peace, not war, he made the point in every way he could conceive. The military, he argued, was the finest soil for nurturing the essential prerequisites of peaceful order: teamwork, self-discipline, devotion to duty. Now posted around the world, U.S. military personnel were spreading those values throughout the world.[23]

Above all, the chief of staff proclaimed again and again the traditional view that nations achieve peace only through strength. The idea of "peace through strength" was not a conclusion drawn from analysis of empirical evidence. Rather, it was a convenient slogan to represent a complex discursive construction. This construction was rooted in, and demanded by, the strongly Augustinian cast of Eisenhower's ideology. In this construction history was an endless struggle by potentially victimized nations to ward off potential aggressors; every nation was either a victim or an aggressor. History would inevitably bring another Hitler marching in the footsteps of the most recent foe, ready to attack whenever victory seemed attainable. Peace required, and was essentially identical with, an ensemble of potential victims maintaining a force strong enough to keep all potential aggressors on the other side of the border, to prevent them from impinging on "civilization": "If we are strong—there will be given this hypothetical Hitler of the future no advantage in singling us out first for attack. . . . To be strong nationally is not a sin, it is a necessity! . . . A weakling . . . is apt to invite contempt; but the same plea from the strong is listened to most respectfully."[24] Here was a simple notion of deterrent force: weapons would be used as symbolic messages, communicating images of strength so compelling that the weapons would never actually be used.

Eisenhower could not press the Augustinian argument consistently, though, since it allowed no end to the aggressor's threat. To sustain his promise of permanent peace, he had to adapt the argument to his image of peace as a process of gradual apocalypse. Over and over again, therefore, he distinguished between the genuine peace at the end of the road and the interim security that came from mere military strength. Even the great victory just past "could not delude our people into believing that armies should be trusted above friendship for security, that reliance upon military power can give civilization as firm a foundation as can orderly legal procedures." The military could give only relative security, he said: "Only through success in international co-operation is there any absolute security for us and for all nations." Having made this clear, he could tell a group of officers that "our aim is to maintain an interim Army" just long enough to achieve "a lasting peace. You, at least, will not be subject to the accusation that you strive for aggrandizement of the army." Indeed, he voiced the hope that educators would eventually put him and all other military leaders out of a job. Within this dual framework he could claim that Augustinian "peace through strength" was merely a temporary necessity: "Weakness and nakedness cannot serve us now. We must rely on the war system of providing the necessary strength until the problems of the war have been solved."[25]

There was no way to predict how long this temporary situation would last, however. So the promise of eventual peace did not make "peace through strength" any less necessary. Only behind a secure shield, Eisenhower argued, could the United States make and implement the sound decisions that would lead to lasting peace. Halford Ross Ryan explains that Eisenhower's public rhetoric rested on an implicit syllogism: peace must be maintained, security maintains peace, therefore security must be maintained. On some occasions, though, he made the syllogism more complex by introducing fear as a middle term: "Until the world is ready completely to repudiate force as a means of settling international difficulty, our country must be strong in those processes by which force is represented. We must feel secure, else fear will warp our own judgment and, externally, reduce our influence to futility"; "Unless we have that amount of strength against external forces that give us a certain feeling of security, we will make foolish decisions." Hysterical fear would lead to decisions either for appeasement or aggression, but "the strong man can go down the middle of the road" because he is not afraid.[26]

Eisenhower told many audiences that he did not expect to have to fight a shooting war any time soon. This view was shared by nearly all top leaders in the Pentagon and the Truman administration. But he shaped the message to fit his own ideological framework: "I do not want to be understood as seeing a global war as an immediate threat. It is fully as important to prevent blind fear and hysteria from influencing us as it is to look facts soberly in the face . . . No great nation is today in position deliberately to provoke a long and exhausting conflict with any hope of gain." "Hysteria" was his code word for what he took to be excessive fear of communist aggression or subversion. His public stance as an opponent of hysteria was part of his effort to exclude all talk of war and thereby avoid war. He urged greater military preparedness as a way to make the nation feel secure and thus avoid hysteria and, ultimately, war.[27]

Eisenhower was careful not to present the military's effort as altruism. "The true soldier of America, therefore, is a leader for world co-operation, knowing that to serve best the security of his country he must work for the cause of peace." His ideology, however, allowed no contradiction between protecting U.S. interests and promoting the world's interests, since the two were identical. The world needed U.S. strength: "Either the United States maintains its own security establishment or the world will lose its last barrier against chaos." Conversely, the United States would be strongest when the entire world was secure against aggression. Thus Eisenhower's rhetoric made "peace through strength" seem just as necessary for internationalists as for isolationists, for Wilsonians as for "realist" Augustinians. Peace might mean a global arrangement to end all war, or merely an arrangement to keep the United States free from disturbance for a good long time. The C/S was perfectly willing to let the ambiguity stand, so that his words might mean all things to all people; this gave everyone a reason to support the military.[28]

Members of the news media were keen to broadcast, and put their own spin on, the general's message. At the outset of his public speaking career, his speech at the Guildhall in London received extensive coverage. Both *Time* and *Newsweek* reported on his peace-affirming rhetoric, but both chose to quote only one line, the same line, from that speech: "Neither London nor Abilene, sisters under the skin, will sell her birthright for physical safety, her liberty for mere existence." It was the willingness to fight again, if need be, that the newsweeklies wanted to proclaim most loudly at home. When he returned home the following week for a brief, triumphant visit, *Time* reported that he "warned against national weakness," quoting his line, "Only strength can cooperate." Once Eisenhower returned home to stay, the same newsweeklies gave his rhetoric little coverage. (They were much more interested in his presidential prospects.) The *New York Times* did report his speeches quite often, and the headlines (particularly in his first year as C/S) usually put his calls for military strength alongside his praise of peace, clearly implying that the former was the path to the latter. The implication here was clearly that higher military budgets were in order, and that citizens would be well advised to pay, whatever the cost.[29]

## "WE MUST LEAD THE WORLD"

Eisenhower wanted the citizenry to do more than pay their taxes. He set military strength in a wider context that involved every American. Military strength depended on the nation's "productive capacity, which in turn . . . is shaped by the unified purposes of our people. National solidarity is a requisite of national security." On other occasions, he said: "Our strength is represented in the uninterrupted productiveness of our mines and farms and factories"; and "Hunger and want are the deadliest fears of peace. If the productiveness of our farms and of our factories can roll off to ourselves and to the people across the world, the path of permanent peace will be much easier."[30]

Because military and economic strength were indivisible, there was no longer any clear distinction between the soldier and the civilian. His public comments on several occasions made this point clear: "War is no longer the concern of the soldier alone . . . security against war is a function of citizenship"; "In the so-called future push-button war . . . everybody in the United States is going to be a target . . . those that are in critical places in the U.S"; "Just as a whole nation is the potential objective, so is the whole nation and everything and person in it the only organism by which successful war can be waged"; "Our armies, our navies, our air forces, in fact our whole citizenry, must be always ready to uphold against any apparent threat principles that we believe to be right—almost sacred"; and "The integration of our national economy into an effective security machine must be accomplished—in thought and in plans—before an emergency occurs. The responsibility for achieving this purpose rests with all of us." In other words, the whole nation had to be integrated into what he would later famously warn against: a military-industrial complex.[31]

In this war, as in every war, success depended above all on the self-discipline of the troops. Every American was now called upon to "fight the indifference, the blind complacency, the selfish inertia that more than once have let us drift into a war that might have been prevented." The struggle for peace required "an awareness by every American that he, personally, and the democracy of which he is a part, is living in a decade of test before the world. The contribution of every individual is necessary to the teamwork which alone can produce an America of greatest influence in the search for peace. Every co-operative effort in the community, the nation, the world, demands sacrifice of some sort from every individual."[32]

In Eisenhower's discourse, the cold war, like every war, was essentially a test of individual moral purity. The true battlefront lay not in eastern Europe but within the soul of every individual. "What this world needs more than anything else is moral regeneration," he told a Christian audience. He spoke to a Jewish group of "the moral regeneration needed to banish from the world these evils that have darkened the way to peace among men." The general offered such sentiments to secular audiences as well. "The solution of problems deep-rooted in human nature . . . [would be] necessary to build a world co-operating for peace," he told a group of newspaper advertising executives. Even when he spoke of the apocalyptic implications of the atomic bomb, he prescribed strenuous spiritual exertion as the only remedy: "The only hope for the world as we know it will be complete spiritual regeneration, a strengthening of moral fiber that will place upon all men a self-imposed determination to respect the rights of others."[33]

If the cold war was a spiritual test for all humanity, a special burden was laid upon the citizens of the United States. Eisenhower's public discourse assumed that this war would finally be won only when the United States had become the model for the world. Selfless leadership (the kind that the military produced), setting an example for the world, was "more needed than ever before; lacking it, this country—the world—faces disaster." If the United States were to lead the world to peace, every citizen would have to cultivate the military virtue of selflessness, the essence of leadership. The United States was "either going to take, or fail to take, our natural position in the world as a rallying point for those who yearn for the way of life you and the nation fought for in this past war. Myriads of hopeful but fear-ridden eyes are watching us." The fear was wholly appropriate, in the general's view: "Anxious eyes . . . will watch us fearfully but hopefully during these chaotic years. We must lead the world toward democracy, or it will lead us to ruin." Under the headline, "Eisenhower Bids US Stabilize World," the *New York Times* reported his declaration: "Without the United States, civilization, as we know it, will perish." He told a Fourth of July audience that "Unless the United States helps plan and build a world structure for peace, humanity may suffer the Golgotha of a third world war." [34]

At times he suggested that the United States needed only to set its own house in virtuous order. "The world is uneasy; the world is bewildered; and the world is in fear," he admitted to a press conference, "but what can be done about it other than to pursue our own path of moral rectitude . . . I don't know." The Lockean side of his ideology dictated that any reasonable nation, seeking the best for itself, would emulate the U.S. example. But the Augustinian side taught that nations, like individuals, did not always follow their own rational best interests. So they had to be shown the way: "We need to tell the people of the world the advantages of our system," he urged a congressional committee, to say that, "if followed, it will lead to peace and security."[35]

In these rhetorical appeals, the general skillfully blended two conceptually distinct cultural traditions: the United States as an example ("we shall be as a City upon a Hill; the eyes of all people are upon us") and as an emissary, actively going abroad to reshape the world. To be an effective example, he claimed, the United States also had to be a leader, and vice versa. The premise linking the two traditions was simple: what happened to the United States would, necessarily, happen to the whole world. So Americans should be striving to produce "a stable and strong America and therefore a peaceful and orderly world." On another occasion, "If the United States of America is to retain and enhance the effectiveness of its leadership in the new venture toward international harmony, we must, first of all, stand before the world as a shining example of the superior advantages of self-government."[36]

Eisenhower did occasionally acknowledge that there was some self-interest in U.S. efforts to lead the "free world": "If we have any great war again, it will be between governmental systems; if we want to use a bigger word, ideologies. It is, therefore, to our benefit to get the greatest possible number of people in the world to believing [sic] in our ideology, our system." At the same time he insisted that U.S. leadership had nothing to do with imposing itself upon others: "I do not mean the swashbuckling, arrogant strength of the bully [but] a thoroughgoing practice of the co-operative methods that are implicit in the system of free enterprise." In congressional testimony he referred to imperialist ventures in the U.S. past but insisted, "That was a long time ago. We have reformed. We don't do those things any more. We do honestly believe in the purity of our motives today." Here was a classic example of another perennial national tradition: the American Adam, setting out with the innocence of the garden to remake the world.[37]

The purity and innocence of America was a fundamental premise of Eisenhower's discourse; it legitimated every American policy and maneuver in the incipient cold war. He could allow no contradiction between innocence and "peace through strength." Indeed, he managed to make innocence and military strength logical partners. Purity, in his discourse, meant not an absence of sin but a voluntary refusal to act upon sinful impulses. Eisenhower held up the military as the prime example of such purity. He couched his calls for higher military spending (like his calls to win World War II) as opportunities to overcome the cardinal sin of selfishness. So the buildup of the military-industrial complex and the integration of all citizens into a national security state became ways for the nation to demonstrate, and rededicate itself to, its purity and innocence. The military buildup became the most tangible and visible symbol of the nation's unique moral status and its unique role in the global spiritual civil war. The military was linked logically not only to virtue, but to political freedom, economic abundance, and the leadership that would bring world peace. Everything good and desirable in human life was embodied in the symbol of military strength.

The claim of American innocence still left logical problems, however. If U.S. motives were selfless, why the need for so many exhortations to selflessness? Could a nation be pure if so many of its citizens were less than pure? Eisenhower never addressed this issue directly. But when he spoke of the purity of "our" motives, he was describing the policies of the Truman administration. This statement, juxtaposed with the continuing calls for more virtue from the average citizen, implied a clear message: "we"—the leaders, the political elite—act selflessly, for the good of all; "you"—the masses—ought to follow "our" example. In light of Eisenhower's theory of military leadership, this was a perfectly logical train of thought. He was simply exhorting the troops to emulate the generals. Perhaps, too, he was unwittingly perpetuating the tradition of the American jeremiad, measuring the supposed shortcomings of the actual nation against the perfect virtue of an ideal "America," the nation as it was intended to be. He never went so far as to say explicitly that America was God's chosen nation, with a special role to play in a divine plan of history. But it was not hard to hear that claim between the lines.[38]

The appeal to American innocence raised another problem too. Drawing on the tradition of American exceptionalism, it granted the United States a unique status as a nation that had become inherently incapable of aggression. (Eisenhower made this point explicitly any number of times.) In a world of conflict driven by original sin, the United States, though peopled by ordinary humans with ordinary human desires, was somehow untainted by those desires when it acted upon the world stage. In the Augustinian worldview, however, every nation had to be either an aggressor or a potential victim. If the United States could never be an aggressor, it had to be a permanent potential victim. It could never escape its vulnerability. The only logical policy for the United States was to maintain a permanently formidable level of military preparedness, regardless of whatever geopolitical changes history might bring. But no amount of military strength could ever free the nation from its vulnerability, nor from the fear that vulnerability brings. Military strength would always be a symbol of all that was alarming, as well as all that was virtuous—and the virtuous leader would always have to be an alarmist.

Eisenhower's cries of alarm, his clarion calls to battle, and his plea for peace through strength were weapons aimed at the American people, trying to persuade them that they stood at the crossroads of history. If they continued the war, supporting liberal internationalism and military strength, they would lead the world to an era of utopian peace. If they turned their back on the rest of the world and let down their military guard, their way of life was doomed. The choice was ultimately a spiritual decision between absolute good and absolute evil. Within the apocalyptic framework of Eisenhower's public rhetoric, no third option was possible. His rhetoric proclaimed that its primary purpose was to persuade the nation to turn from evil and choose the good. His private discourse, however, was another matter.

## THE POSTWAR WORLD IN PRIVATE DISCOURSE

"Alarmist Ike" recorded in his private diary that his travels around the world could be summarized in two words: "Trouble everywhere." In another diary entry he wrote, "Abroad there are so many nations needing our help that the whole job seems appalling." He wrote to Gen. Ike Eichelberger, "The world situation presents nothing that can be classed as improvement, in fact in some areas things seem to be becoming almost alarming." "The world situation is chaotic," he told his father-in-law in the summer of 1946. A week later he told Beetle Smith that "each day brings a succession of troubling and worrisome problems. There never seems to be a piece of good news." "Every day brings fresh evidence of world unrest and tension," he wrote to his son John.[39]

This tension was particularly disturbing to Eisenhower because he spent so much time making plans for a war such as World War II, which would start with a bolt out of the blue. Catastrophe lurked behind every form of chaos. To Louis Marx he explained the spiritual root of the problem; it was "a world of turmoil pervaded by 'isms' of all kinds and with temptations of immediate self-interest beclouding the clarity of principles that are almost sacred—at least to us."[40]

The C/S saw even more disturbing signs of spiritual decay at home. "International reactions are bad enough, but they are insignificant compared to domestic issues," he wrote with typical overstatement. The problem at home, even more than abroad, was neglect of sacred principles. Shortly after taking office he noted in his diary: "Although everyone believes in cooperation (the single key) as a principle, no one is ready to abandon immediate advantage or position in practicing cooperation." He wrote in a similar vein to his son: "The most noticeable thing here at home is the great confusion, doubt and haziness that seems to prevail in all circles." A year and a half later, he was still complaining (here to Beetle Smith) of "the smoldering doubts and fears that are plaguing this country if not the whole world today."[41]

Eisenhower occasionally seemed philosophically resigned to this situation. "In the aftermath of major conflicts," he told one audience, "there is invariably and inescapably experienced throughout the world a feeling of confusion, uneasiness, doubt and indecision. These create unrest in many fields." On another occasion he reflected that "the indifference, the blind complacency, the selfish inertia that more than once have let us drift into a war [are] recurrent—they appear to be mastered but crop up again in new form." So there would inevitably be "new problems and emergencies in the world of today and of tomorrow—that is the nature of this life." Such remarks underscored the Augustinian side of Eisenhower's discourse and made peace seem a far distant possibility, at best.[42]

Yet he may very well have seen such reflections not as signs of pessimism but as gestures of reassurance. "You shouldn't worry too much, I think, about occasional fits of depression and despondency," he told John, "The world is running true to form in going through a stage that might be called mass hysteria—the aftermath of all big wars. . . . Chaotic conditions constantly give evidence of man's stupidity. An individual must always be careful not to take on his own shoulders the burdens of the world, particularly in those instances where there is nothing that he can do about it." Perhaps he was trying to reassure not only his public audiences and his son, but also himself, as he told Beetle Smith: "Such of these matters as are inescapable and inherent in current chaotic conditions, I can take in my stride." Perhaps, too, he wanted to legitimate in his own mind the uncertainty of U.S. policy, the continuing uncertainties and debates over army policy, and his own inability to shape effective policies.[43]

This tone of reassurance through resignation was more than offset in the private writings by warnings of doom. The general's public jeremiads were not merely rhetorical devices to motivate the public. His private discourse was even more alarmist, with the emphasis even more strongly on internal threats to U.S. society. Trying to convince Bernard Baruch to support Universal Military Training, he wrote: "What plans we make must be made now before our forces have completely disintegrated and before we become paralyzed by that public apathy which seems inevitable in times of relative peace." Labor conflicts were a source of stress that particularly disturbed him. "Internal 'Munichs' can, in the long run, be as bad as they are in the international field," he fretted in his diary, "If we have to break up in a real industrial conflict with 'public be damned' the watchword, then our prospects for bringing about world order are slim indeed." In another diary entry he wrote, "Capital and labor would easily solve their difficulties if both knew their very existence depended upon accord."[44] For Eisenhower, every major strike imperiled the nation's very existence.

THE STORY OF THE POSTWAR WORLD          117

As during World War II, the general saw the internal and external dangers interwoven in peacetime. Only an internally strong United States could prevent the international crisis from exploding and destroying civilization: "I most earnestly believe that unless those that now live in freedom begin, en masse, to look this world in the face, and begin voluntarily and energetically to meet the issues placed before us, then we are doomed—rather, the system, as we know it, is doomed"; "The important thing is that democracy has arrived at its decade or quarter century of greatest crisis. . . . The next two years should establish the pattern; if it unfavorable to us it will be partly our own fault, but it will be wholly black in its implications for the future." As during World War II, he placed himself among the unselfish few who saw the impending catastrophe and sounded the alarm: "America is facing national and international problems of such grave import that little room is left for political maneuvering," he told a trusted friend. But "there are few people outside the armed services and the higher echelons of the State Department that are giving their full attention to American interests as a whole and refusing to color their conclusions and convictions with the interest of party politics." Clearly, he continued to portray himself as one of the chosen few who were able, and therefore obliged, to serve American interests as a whole.[45]

## MILITARY STRENGTH IN PRIVATE DISCOURSE

As chief of staff, Eisenhower argued continually that American interests required a high level of military preparedness. His occasional private reflections on military strength differed from the public language because they contained no explicit images of a continuing war. The idea of a continuing war was clearly implied in these reflections, however, and the private language, unlike the public, included expectations that the war might eventually have to be fought with guns and bombs, including nuclear bombs.

The C/S wanted the nation to start planning immediately for the next war, coordinating the efforts of all public agencies and private industry with the military. The civilian and military sectors would have to be more closely tied than ever before, and civilians would have to be prepared for their role in war. To Thomas Hargrave, author of a plan for war industrialization, he wrote that because the next war would begin so suddenly, peacetime planning for the war was "necessitated by the basic impulse of survival." Similarly, he wrote to Sen. Walter Judd that in the next war, "the existence or nonexistence of our nation" would depend on a well-organized civilian component in the army; only a well-trained citizenry could prevent total defeat. In the next war, he wrote to Rep. Walter Andrews, "everybody in this country would serve under some form of call to duty."[46]

In private, Eisenhower had no reason to avoid naming the enemy he was preparing to fight. "Russia has a healthy respect for the power this nation can generate," he wrote to Beetle Smith, "Unless they had such a respect they would go right ahead and do as they please in Europe."[47] But in a diary entry two months earlier he had indicated that the issue was more complicated.[48] After asserting that "we face a battle to extinction between the two systems," he continued: "What are the problems? To prevent Russian expansion (1) by direct conquest and pressure; (2) by infiltration. Over the long term to win back areas that Russia has already overrun, and finally to produce a real accord among all nations that will prevent war. This must be preceded by a collapse of dictatorship everywhere, at least of all dictatorships that aggressively seek to dominate others."

He then reflected on how to stave off the two types of Russian expansion. Referring to the threat of direct conquest, he continued: "(1) This is the problem that can be solved only by the maintenance of adequate American military strength. . . . Anything less will mean only a succession of new Munichs, finally war under conditions least favorable to us." The threat of Russian infiltration, on the other hand, demanded "independent, friendly nations with which to trade. . . . Unless broken economies are restored they will almost certainly fall prey to communism." The United States would end up an "isolated democracy," and "the result is clear."

This diary entry is particularly telling in two respects. First, it shows the inseparable link between military and economic strength in the private discourse. Of course throughout the private writings these two were intertwined with moral and spiritual strength, and U.S. leadership as well. Another diary entry (written much earlier in his tenure as C/S) offered the full picture:

> The underlying, important thing, therefore, is our national lack of understanding that we (our form of government) is under deadly, persistent, and constant attack. To lead others to democracy we must help actively, but more than this we must be an example of the worth of democracy. Industrial power must be achieved, and increased productivity must follow or we are cutting our own throats. Our strength is a combination of (1) complete devotion to democracy, which means a faith in men as men (essentially religious concept) and practice of free enterprise . . . (2) industrial and economic strength; (3) more probity in all dealings; (4) necessary military strength.[49]

This was a succinct summary of the general's theoretical framework, equating the totality of that framework with his notion of "strength." Since military strength was directly connected to all other types of strength, it could serve as the most tangible symbolic representation of the full panoply of strengths needed to stave off all the intertwined forms of threat.

The diary reflection on preventing Russian expansion was also significant because it showed the clear link between U.S. strength and the notion of peace in the private discourse. On the rare occasions that any vision of peace was privately expressed, it was always linked directly with notions of U.S. strength, as when he told Cornelius Vanderbilt, Jr.: "Moral, industrial, and political strength, properly buttressed by a sensible military structure, represents our best hope of maintaining our security now, and of progressing toward worthwhile agreements involving world stability and disarmament."[50]

Two letters to Swede Hazlett in the summer of 1947 made the link equally clear: "I believe that world order can only be established by the practice of true cooperation among the sovereign nations and that American leadership toward this goal depends upon her strength—her strength of will, her moral, social and economic strength and, until an effective world order is achieved, upon her military strength." In the other letter he wrote: "My own deepest concern involves America's situation in the world today. Her security position and her international leadership I regard as matters of the gravest concern to all of us and to our national future. Allied to these questions of course is that of internal health, particularly maximum productivity." These passages echo the prevailing themes of the public statements. Peace meant a stable order, which meant a global system of voluntary cooperation. By the logic of Eisenhower's discourse, this would require the universalizing of the U.S. liberal democratic system, or at least the protection of all liberal democracies against totalitarian threats. In these private letters, U.S. strength became the pivotal symbolic term linking leadership, peace, and victory in the spiritual civil war. As in the public discourse, strength became a crucial step on the way to peace, though the private words, naming the Soviets as the threat to peace, explained more clearly why that step was so necessary.[51]

Again, though, these references to progress toward genuine peace or world order—what Eisenhower called absolute security—were rare in the private discourse. They were also ambiguous. Only the letter to Hazlett set "true cooperation" among all nations as a goal. The letter to Vanderbilt spoke merely of "worthwhile agreements involving world stability," which could mean no more than assured containment of destabilizing threats. The diary entry set the prevention of war as the highest goal, and it required as a prerequisite "the collapse of dictatorship everywhere, at least of all dictatorships that aggressively seek to dominate others." The "at least" implied that the global corporate commonwealth would not have to include all nations. Dictators could remain outside it as long as they were permanently contained, which would be enough to prevent war. This might well be the most that one could aspire to. (The "at least" also legitimated right-wing dictatorships within the global corporate commonwealth.)

On the whole, the message that emerged from the private discourse was the desperate need to stave off impending doom by awakening the public to the danger of chaos and communism. In this context, the repeated calls for adequate military strength appear as cries of alarm, pleas for an adequate measure of prevention. That measure would be more than an ounce, to be sure, but without it there would be no cure—not ever, the C/S warned. With the world and the nation in such dire straits, it would be premature to give serious attention to the distant goal of genuine world peace. It would be equally premature to talk of the ideological correlate to world peace—the globalizing of "the American way." When Eisenhower wrote in his diary of the need "to reawaken in our country a realization of our own blessings and what we have to do to protect them (this protection involving also spreading them),"[52] he gave a clear indication of his priorities. The overriding task was to protect the U.S. system; only parenthetically did he think of spreading it.

A unified, peaceful world order might be at best an eschatological concept in the strict sense: a distant horizon-concept that was logically necessary for the discursive system to cohere, but was invisible from the perspective of the present. It had no relevance to the present or the foreseeable future, and thus no relevance to any of the policy debates of the day. The best to hope for, for the foreseeable future, was adequate strength to ensure that disaster could be prevented. The name for this adequate strength, in the emerging postwar discourse, was "stability." Clearly this was the best that Eisenhower's private discourse could really hope for. He made the point succinctly to his British friend and colleague Freddie Morgan: "The only worthy ambition for people as old as you and I are is to struggle toward stabilizing conditions so as to give our youngsters a chance to work out world improvements."[53]

But what chance did the youngsters have? The private discourse left this unclear, for its pessimism was built upon a deep foundation of Augustinian skepticism. It could offer no certainty, nor even likelihood, that the processes of human history would ever bring lasting global peace. In this construction, innocent nations would always have to keep up their strength simply to defend themselves against endless threats. Since Eisenhower constructed an image of the United States as uniquely innocent and therefore uniquely and permanently vulnerable in his private as well as his public discourse, he United States was especially obligated to maintain military strength in perpetuity. The private discourse neither required nor offered any image of world peace as a meaningful concept that would offset this permanent obligation. What Eisenhower called relative security was the highest goal a "realist" could reasonably hope for, and the highest goal toward which policymaking could aim. It was no small goal. In the logic of the private as well as public discourse, protecting the United States through adequate strength entailed protecting the entire "free world," and vice versa.

One document summed up this Augustinian vision particularly well and showed how it was carried directly into policy decisions. In a memo to the other chiefs of staff, urging more foreign aid, the C/S wrote: "It would be wrong to assume that no substantial threats to U.S. security exist except in an ideological war. In peacetime, during the period extending from the present until the assumed ideological war begins, there are requirements for U.S. aid which must be met in order to oppose expansionist efforts which would otherwise progressively impair U.S. security."[54] This did not mean that Eisenhower thought World War III inevitable. It did mean that he saw no clear difference between peacetime and wartime. Peace was the time in which nations fought by "cold" means and prepared for the next "hot" war. Of course any chief of staff would be obligated to see peace this way when acting in his professional capacity as a military planner. But this C/S was also inclined to see things this way when surveying the world from within his private discursive framework, where the best to hope for was to keep the war cold.

Here was essentially a doctrine of peace as containment: containing all forms of chaos, by mitigating the disastrous effects of the last war and staving off both another war and communist expansion, thereby saving civilization. It might well seem enough. But it was still only relative security. It left no place for the grander vision of peace as genuine harmony and cooperation, the vision offered in his public rhetoric. Military strength thus became a symbolic marker representing stability as the highest goal worth pursuing. The pursuit of that goal would require all the same kinds of strength, including military, that Eisenhower's public rhetoric identified as keys to winning the ongoing war.

As military strength played this symbolic role, though, it would also be a vivid reminder of the threats to civilization. Portrayed as a wall protecting civilization from its foes, it would symbolize the absolute gulf between the two. So the language of peace through strength reinforced the pervasive dualism of Eisenhower's language, demarcating the United States, as bearer of civilized values, from all those forces that would destroy civilization, if given a chance.

CHAPTER 6

# The Uses of Symbolism

$A$s Eisenhower wielded words about weaponry for their symbolic value, he knew that his weapons might some day be used for their traditional purpose as well. He was obliged to plan for that possibility. But even in making war plans, he showed that he valued military strength mostly for its symbolic value. This was clearly evident in his discourse about the atomic bomb.

### DISARMAMENT

Eisenhower often expressed his concern about the threat of atomic war and his commitment to disarmament, in policy documents as well as public pronouncements. Some historians cite such statements as supposed evidence of his pacific intent. In the early postwar period, however, he actually showed little real commitment to disarmament.

During his term as chief of staff, all discussion of disarmament revolved around a plan proposed to the United Nations, on behalf of the Truman administration, by Bernard Baruch. Early in 1946, Truman appointed committees, chaired by Undersecretary of State Dean Acheson and Atomic Energy Commission head David Lilienthal, to develop a disarmament proposal. Baruch, however, was given virtual carte blanche to revise the Acheson-Lilienthal plan before offering it to the UN. Baruch arranged to meet with Eisenhower, to find out the military's views on disarmament. Just three days before the meeting, the General Staff's Plans and Operations Division (P&O) prepared the C/S for it with a briefing memo. P&O knew that Baruch was considering tightening the Acheson-Lilienthal proposals by demanding that the Soviets agree to open inspection of their atomic facilities and international control of uranium supplies. The memo warned that acceptance of these conditions would require "a profound revolution in present Russian policy," which experts in both the State and War Departments viewed as "almost unthinkable." Soviet acceptance would be for "only superficial cooperation." P&O advised the C/S to tell Baruch that the United States had to keep its atomic weapons in order to keep peace, because the U.S. military was the world's "only effective police power." P&O also noted that Baruch had already talked extensively with Gen. Leslie Groves; Groves, who had headed the military side of the Manhattan Project, was well known as an extreme anticommunist and an ardent proponent of a massive nuclear buildup.[1]

On 15 April 1946, Baruch came to Eisenhower's office, along with Groves and others. The consensus of the meeting was that the Acheson-Lilienthal plan was good theoretically, but it would have to depend on the Soviets agreeing to open inspection of their atomic facilities and international control of uranium supplies. The participants also agreed that the United States should not stop making atomic weapons before the Soviets agreed to these conditions. These stipulations would be the crucial innovations in Baruch's iteration of the proposal and the crucial sticking points that blocked its acceptance by the Soviets. Eisenhower raised no objection, though he was well aware of the likelihood of Soviet rejection. At the meeting's end, Eisenhower suggested Groves as Baruch's liaison with the military. The C/S was clearly supporting Baruch's hard-line approach.[2]

The following month, when Baruch formally requested Eisenhower's advice in writing, the latter responded that each of the Joint Chiefs of Staff should give their own independent advice, though he was confident that they all agreed on "the basics." P&O prepared Eisenhower's own response, which was sent on 14 June. This letter had no direct influence on Baruch's formulation, since that very day he offered his proposal to the UN. It was merely a statement for the record, but it bears careful analysis, since it has been cited by historians as evidence for Eisenhower's purported desire for disarmament. In fact, it reflects the hard-line approach on which Eisenhower and Baruch had already agreed.

Eisenhower declared himself pleased with Baruch's work: "Only through effective international control of atomic energy can we hope to prevent atomic war." [3] He immediately endorsed Baruch's view that "effective" control required "a system of free and complete inspection." Just a week earlier Eisenhower had told a House committee that he was "very, very fixed" on assurance of full free inspection before "giving away any secret of the United States." Thereafter, whenever he supported disarmament, privately or publicly, he always added the proviso, "verification is essential." In light of warning from his staff that such an agreement was "almost unthinkable," Eisenhower's qualified support for disarmament may actually be read as a veiled rejection.[4]

The rest of the letter to Baruch, rather than supporting disarmament proposals, only detailed the dangers inherent in the idea. The C/S feared that even a fully verifiable agreement might provoke the Soviets into a first strike while leaving the United States more vulnerable than before. In addition, the U.S. public might not support the stern punitive measures needed to enforce an agreement if the Soviets broke it: "In the face of threats of unmistakable import and seriousness, our practice has been to indulge in wishful thinking rather than to undertake decisive action." Here again, Eisenhower depicted himself as one of the few who would recognize and respond adequately to an impending danger.

Perhaps the most disturbing danger was that "biological, chemical, and other as yet unforeseen weapons may prove no less effective than the atomic bomb, and even less susceptible to control. Another major war may see the use of such destructive weapons," even by a nation that was party to a nuclear abolition agreement. So "the problem of controlling, and finally preventing, the use of atomic bombs (and other decisive weapons) thus becomes the problem of preventing war itself."[5] This kind of melodramatic cry of alarm was typical of Eisenhower's apocalyptic language. The utopian goal, equally typical of apocalypticism, may have been intended as a barrier to practical action. By implying that the only goal worth striving for was "preventing war itself," he was in effect saying that it was hardly worthwhile making any effort at all. In fact, Eisenhower gave little practical attention to concrete disarmament plans. As McGeorge Bundy says, he watched Baruch's efforts "with sympathy but not with close attention." He rarely mentioned the subject again, confirming that it did not rank high among his concerns.[6]

Eisenhower's main concern was never to avoid the dangers attendant on using the bomb. It was, rather, how to use the bomb effectively in formulating policies to ward off other dangers. He concluded his memo to Baruch with a firm statement on how the bomb could be used. The surest way to prevent a future war was not the path of negotiation, he said, but massive U.S. military strength, including atomic strength: "The existence of the atomic bomb in our hands is a deterrent, in fact, to aggression in the world. We cannot at this time limit our capability to produce or use this weapon." Indeed, when Lauris Norstad, head of P&O, analyzed the differences between this letter and Baruch's actual proposal, he found Eisenhower putting more emphasis on the need for nuclear weapons for "effective retaliation" and for a promise of "automatic retaliation" against Soviet attack. Eisenhower was even "more emphatic in requiring tested and proven control arrangements," which were likely to scuttle all efforts at disarmament.[7]

Another way to avoid disarmament while seeming to endorse it was to insist that it must come in one all-encompassing fell swoop. In a step by step disarmament process, the C/S told Norstad, the United States could get "shoved off one defensive position after another until we are likely to find ourselves naked and disarmed before the world," while the Soviet Union has not disarmed at all. On the other hand, he continued, "if every kind of armament were abolished in the world, the United States would be by far relatively the strongest" and the United States could not possibly suffer—as long as there was a foolproof verification scheme. Here once again was Eisenhower's penchant for framing issues in absolutes. The only alternative he could see to total global disarmament was a United States totally "naked and disarmed"; no middle ground was possible. Since success had to be absolute, failure had to be equally absolute, and absolutism led to exaggerated fears. It was hardly realistic to imagine that the United States, by far the world's greatest military power, could ever end up "naked and disarmed." But such fear-laden expressions came quite naturally to "Alarmist Ike."

Shortly after Baruch made his proposals, P&O advised Eisenhower that the State Department wanted the United States to agree to the eventual elimination of all nuclear weapons for "political and propaganda considerations." Eventually the C/S did formally suggest to his JCS colleagues that they should endorse the eventual elimination of all nuclear weapons if the Soviets accepted all the conditions of the Baruch plan. This was an issue that was dividing the military leadership. Eisenhower, along with others, was signaling his appreciation of diplomatic concerns, but not any serious intention to relinquish what Truman had called "the hammer." Publicly, he justified this position when he told a Senate committee that he hoped nuclear weapons would be totally abolished, "if for no other reason— we know so little about it—than the possibility finally that the nation using it would destroy itself also. It might be a self-destroying weapon in the long run." Here again was the tendency to view the issue in absolutes: either nations should abolish the weapons, or the weapons would abolish the nations that possessed them. This comment exemplified his whole approach to deterrence and disarmament. Foreseeing only the most extreme possibilities of good and evil, it remained in the realm of pure abstraction. It was not linked with any practical suggestions for steps to alleviate the threat. It reflected not the logic of pragmatic military planning, but the hopes and fears of apocalyptic imagination.[9]

At the same time, Eisenhower hoped to take the offensive in the public relations battle surrounding disarmament. He promoted a report by Gen. Matthew Ridgway, claiming that Soviet efforts at disarmament were part of "an integrated plan to bring about unilateral disarmament by the United States." He wanted the government to develop a public relations campaign to publicize this idea. When the proposed campaign was endorsed by Secretary of State George Marshall, Eisenhower was (Norstad told Ridgway) "greatly pleased."[10]

Eisenhower's views on disarmament, like all his policy views, suggest a staunch anti-Soviet stance. If others were even more staunch, this should not be taken as evidence that his policy recommendations were aimed at easing cold war tension. There is little in the record to suggest that he tried to steer the military in a more dovish direction, even when he had the opportunity.[11]

## A SLIGHT INTEREST IN DETERRENCE

Early in Eisenhower's term, he read an insightful book by Bernard Brodie called *The Absolute Weapon*.[12] The bomb had abolished the military's traditional purpose of winning wars, Brodie argued: "From now on its chief purpose must be to avert them. It can have almost no other useful purpose." Brodie foresaw what would eventually become common cold war wisdom. Military forces now had a new purpose. Rather than directly killing with them, the government would use them in the same way it used words: as symbolic tokens. They would represent the whole ensemble of strengths that would evoke feelings of security at home, while gaining "respect" from enemies and allies abroad. Military strength as a symbol would thus guarantee the U.S. world leadership and contain the communist threat. It would proclaim U.S. commitment to moving the world toward peace, or at least enduring stability. It would be one more emblem of all that was good in the U.S. system, hence an emblem of civilization itself. The idea of a cold war endowed this symbolic meaning of military strength with practical effect. Brodie argued, in effect, that the bomb should be used only as a symbol, relying on its unprecedented power for deterrence. This was the mission that Eisenhower had assigned to all military forces in his public rhetoric. Although he read Brodie's classic when it was first published, he showed surprisingly little interest or faith in the bomb as a symbolic signifier that would deter war.

When columnist Dorothy Thompson called for safety through a U.S. atomic monopoly, Eisenhower responded to her that the bomb would not give one nation dominance over others, at least in the short run. Some nations were "peculiarly allergic to threat," he argued, and the bomb was not necessarily a decisive weapon in any event. But he closed his letter to Thompson with an intriguing foreshadowing of a later approach to nuclear deterrence: "Incidentally, you will be interested in the following quotation from another letter I have just read from a scientific friend: 'Bigger and better atomic bombs should be built and their use recognized as legitimate. . . . We should never see another war . . . The very fearsomeness of the atomic bomb should be a real insurance to the peace of the world.'" Perhaps he was speculating here that deterrence would not be an effective policy tool until bombs became powerful enough to be decisive. In any event, there is no indication that he embraced this approach to deterrence during his tenure as C/S.[13]

On 29 June 1946, Eisenhower did make a rare early reference to nuclear deterrence. He publicly justified the atomic bomb tests at Bikini atoll with the claim that "moral nations must remain forever strong" and ensure that another war would be impossible.[14] This was apparently an effort to legitimate the tests at a time when the morality of the bomb was still a hotly debated issue. It was also another opportunity to expound his favorite theme of peace through strength, which assumed the deterrent power of all U.S. weapons. But as the question of the bomb's morality faded from the public spotlight, and he no longer had to defend the legitimacy of the bomb, his interest in specifically nuclear deterrence faded too.

His real concern was deterring not war, but Soviet expansion. That was the ultimate goal of all his military planning. To achieve that goal, he warned, it would be better not to tout the bomb as a deterrent. He feared that too much trust in deterrence would weaken public support for military preparedness: "Above all we cannot permit complacency or an 'atomic bomb mentality'—a possible modern counterpart of the 'Maginot Line mentality'—to lull us into another postwar apathy."[15] The danger was that the public would give too much, not too little, support for atomic weaponry, which might mean correspondingly less support for the army and its predominantly non-nuclear programs.

On the other hand, he warned the JCS privately against excessive military mobilization. He made this point as he cautioned his colleagues against assuming that the Soviets would soon initiate war. To act on that assumption and spend too much on the military would weaken the nation's economy; and economic strength might be even more important than military strength in containing communist expansionism. So military planners should emphasize "strengthening the economic and social dikes against Soviet communism."[16] It was building that dike, not preventing war, that preoccupied the chief of staff.

## THE USES OF THE BOMB

Although Eisenhower was reticent about praising the bomb publicly as a deterrent, he was enthusiastic in private about the possibilities it opened up. Indeed, his primary concern was to develop plans for its effective use. Whether those plans led to deterring or winning a future war seemed a distinctly secondary issue, because he articulated no essential difference between using a weapon to deter war and using it to win a war. In his discourse, the capability to win a war was itself the only meaningful deterrent. Brodie argued that the bomb could be used as a symbolic signifier to prevent war, but not as a meaningful weapon for winning a war. Eisenhower seemed to assume, on the contrary, that the bomb could be used as a symbolic signifier only if it were also made a war-winning weapon. Therefore, while he told the nation that its military was dedicated to deterring the next war and reducing armaments, as a policy planner he seemed much more concerned about using armaments to win the next war. He had no doubt that "new weapons" would play a crucial role in that war.

But what would the bomb's role be? During Eisenhower's years as chief of staff, military leaders were perplexed by that question and debated it heatedly. Air force officers such as Gen. Leslie Groves led a campaign for a radical shift to a fully air-atomic strategy. They argued that the immense power of the new weapon made all previous military technology virtually obsolete. The next war would be won by atomic bombs and atomic bombs alone. Army and navy officers naturally resisted this view, fearing that in its most radical form it would make their services wholly irrelevant. Eisenhower's views were not as radical as the air force officers', but he was surprisingly enthusiastic about the possibilities of the air-atomic approach. Despite his well-known qualms about the bombing of Hiroshima and Nagasaki,[17] he had no principled hesitation about actually using the bomb in a future war. He insisted early on that it would and should be used, at a time when most of his colleagues in the army hesitated to draw that conclusion. One of his first actions as chief of staff was to sign a memorandum on the "Overall Effect of the Atomic Bomb on Warfare and Military Organization." This memorandum embodied, according to Geoffrey Perret, "Eisenhower's view of the future—an America guarded by missiles carrying atomic warheads over huge distances. He foresaw the blunt instrument of containment before Kennan even wrote a line about containment."[18]

The chief of staff circulated to the JCS a memo by Groves advocating an air-atomic strategy, commenting: "There is much that is good in this . . . while perhaps extreme in some aspects, it might be helpful." As Gregg Herken notes, even such a qualified endorsement "could hardly have displeased the air-atomic advocates." When Eisenhower came to a passage in the memo that read, "If used in sufficient numbers, [the atomic bomb] can completely destroy the densely populated centers of any nation," he double-underlined the word *sufficient*. He also underlined Groves's warning that "the entire nation must be disciplined to withstand cataclysmic destruction of key cities at home and still be able to win the war." Clearly, he viewed the bomb as an instrument that had the potential to fight and win wars.[19]

In this respect, Eisenhower's approach to the bomb prefigured the view that became typical of the whole military establishment. As Steven Ross concludes, "the

JCS maintained the conviction that a war between the US and the USSR would resemble the course and outcome of World War II. The grand strategy of World War III would also follow the pattern of the Second World War. . . . The JCS regarded the atomic bomb primarily as a more effective iron bomb. Atomic missions resembled the kind of strikes flown in World War II."[20] Eisenhower seems to have shared this premise from the outset of the postwar era. Neither he nor his military colleagues accepted the idea that there would be no winner in the next war, that the atomic bomb had made the idea of "winning" a war meaningless.

As an army man, Eisenhower could not embrace visions of air-atomic redemption completely, since they left little, if any, role for the army's ground troops. Yet after his experience as supreme commander of the European theater he was no longer so much an army man as an apostle of unified military command. He continued to hope for increasing unity in the armed forces, which had been so successful in World War II, despite the bitter struggle between the advocates of an air-atomic strategy and the more traditional views of the army and navy. One way to move toward a unified policy was to cast the bomb as "a decisive weapon but not the decisive weapon in a general war."[21] This could be seen as a significant shift toward an air-atomic strategy, while never endorsing that strategy completely. Understandably, the idea of a weapon that was decisive yet not decisive left some confusion about the proper role of the bomb.

This was only a part of the confusion marking Eisenhower's stated views on the use of the bomb. Though he insisted that it should be used in a future war, he was never quite sure how or why it should be used. The earliest memos he prepared for JCS deliberations on atomic policy simply indicated that the problem of the bomb's use needed further study. The primary goal of these early memos was to create favorable congressional and public opinion on the military's long-range preparedness goals, not to develop a clear idea of the bomb's appropriate strategic use. His memo of early 1946, for example, voiced his fear that giving the bomb too big a role might create a public vision of a revolution in warfare, which would undermine support for the military's present structure.[22] By March 1947, at the latest, Eisenhower had concluded that the atomic bomb would be used in any war with the Soviet Union. He then urged the JCS to include atomic bombing in their war plans, without articulating any specific mission for it.[23]

Eisenhower was hardly unusual in wanting to give the bomb a primary role in U.S. war plans without knowing exactly what that role should be. Samuel Williamson and Steven Rearden have shown that most military leaders were confused about the atomic bomb's practical uses. The growing importance of the bomb did not stem from any compelling analysis of its strategic value. Rather, it arose out of "overriding concerns for other problems" that arose as military planners tried to figure out how to be better prepared for a rerun of the last war. The bomb was "the logical way to make up expected weaknesses and shortcomings in the defense posture. . . . [It] could obscure but not resolve the gaps in an ambivalent strategic policy."[24]

One of the bomb's greatest appeals would later be summed up in the popular slogan, "More bang for the buck." As in every postwar era, the public demanded a smaller and cheaper military. Yet to satisfy itself as well as the public, the military had to proffer believable claims that it could still win whatever war might arise. It had to persuade the public that it could spend less money without losing its potency. Before the first atomic bomb had been tested, Eisenhower had already proclaimed his allegiance to the general principle by which he would solve this problem of public perception: "When a bomb can do the work, let us not spend an unnecessary American life for it"—nor, he might have added, an unnecessary American dollar. For lack of any viable alternative, Eisenhower and his colleagues used the atomic bomb to deliver this symbolic message. In order for the message to be credible, however, the bomb had to be portrayed as decisive in some sense. Although military leaders had no specific analysis of the bomb's strategic role, but simply wanted to use it to "fill the gaps," they had to believe that it would be decisive, though they could not define exactly how.[25]

This helps to explain why the general's views on nuclear strategy, and his arguments for increasing the nuclear arsenal, reveal such confusion. At times he treated the bomb as one more weapon in the arsenal, bigger but not essentially different from other weapons. At other times he invested it with extraordinary power, assuming that it could somehow perform wondrous feats, though he could not say just what or how. But the record shows that he felt no special urgency to resolve that confusion. Certainly his references to the new weapon show little sense of an immediate or total revolution in warfare requiring a whole new set of strategic principles. He treated the question of the bomb's proper role as one among many pieces in the puzzle of administrative and strategic planning to prepare for another war. The puzzle was resisting any clear solution, but Eisenhower did not seem too disturbed about that.

## THE BOMB AS A SYMBOL

Eisenhower's early interest in the air-atomic strategy holds a clue to his relatively untroubled attitude. Michael Sherry has shown that the first advocates of an air-atomic strategy had little persuasive evidence, or precise understanding, of its strategic value and no clear idea of the strategic role of the bomb. This left them free to bestow on the bomb virtually any meaning they chose, with little empirical reality to place a check on the creativity of the symbolic imagination. So they relied on aerial bombardment, as they had in World War II, because of its rich symbolic appeal. They viewed the bomb as an almost magical weapon that would "smite the enemy and reorder the affairs of man . . . for the good of all."[26]

Apocalyptic images of world destruction and world salvation were rooted in a long pre-atomic tradition of the symbolic meanings of aerial bombardment. These images lay at the heart of the air-atomic advocates' passionate vision. This tradition, rooted in religious images, was directly related to the hope that the righteous would win wars with minimal loss of life on their own side, a hope that Eisenhower surely shared. So it seems likely that he, too, advocated extensive reliance on the bomb, without knowing or worrying much about what strategic role it should play. He did this not only for military-political reasons, but because he was swayed by the symbolic messages it could send—not only to an enemy to deter war, but (perhaps more important) also to Americans, which included him. He dealt with the new weapon not so much by probing its strategic challenge as by integrating it into the symbolic construct of his apocalypticism.

The absolutism of a decisive weapon with unprecedented power reinforced the absolutism that already pervaded Eisenhower's discourse. Viewing the bomb as one weapon in a much larger arsenal, composed principally of ground forces, may have tempered the intensity of Eisenhower's apocalyptic image of the bomb. But the integration of "a decisive weapon" into the overall mix of weaponry intensified his propensity to view all war in apocalyptic terms. So the vision of an absolute weapon wedded him more firmly to his apocalyptic view of war as a struggle between absolute good and absolute evil. Conversely, his absolutist vision of war made him more susceptible to the symbolic appeal of a decisive weapon. He was already committed to the view that another world war would probably destroy civilization even if fought only with conventional weapons. He could view the bomb as a decisive weapon but not *the* decisive weapon because he foresaw no great increase in destruction merely from crossing the atomic threshold. Holding such an apocalyptic vision of war, he could be swayed by the bomb's quasi-religious symbolism earlier and more strongly than other army leaders.

Of course the bomb also made it more dangerous than ever to contemplate the traditional apocalyptic solution to the apocalyptic problem: a final battle at Armageddon. This meant that the only possible goal could be absolute containment; such an absolute goal justified, and indeed morally required, every available means. With its apparent promise of absolute power, the bomb offered the perfect symbolic tool to express absolute and total resistance to the threat of externally imposed restraint. To express that meaning, the bomb did not have to be charged with any specific military or strategic task. Its role could remain as vaguely and symbolically defined as the project of containment itself.

In fact, the unwavering commitment to containment could be fully manifest simply by planning for atomic war. In the logic of Eisenhower's discourse, the only way to contain all impending forms of chaos was for Americans to have sufficient spiritual virtue. Spiritual virtue was the one area, above all, in which one could not compromise. It had to be an absolute, like the absolute weapon. If the essence of such virtue was self-discipline, how better to demonstrate it than to make the sacrifices necessary to build the most powerful modern arsenal that money could buy? In this way the bomb could function, better than any other tangible reality, as a symbol of enduring resolute containment, a national strength massive enough to contain every threat. If containment failed, of course, Eisenhower and the other air-atomic strategists assumed that the bomb would provide the strength to win the next, the ultimately apocalyptic, war. No matter how effective it was as a symbol of containment, the bomb could never be severed from its profoundly apocalyptic symbolism.[27]

The bomb, therefore, became the very material meeting point for the two foci of Eisenhower's discourse. As the great symbol of containment, it announced that the threat of chaos would continue to exist so formidably that an absolute weapon would be needed to keep it forever at bay. As the great symbol of apocalyptic victory, it announced that the threat of chaos, although absolute, might some day be ended by the absolute weapon wielded in righteous hands. The bomb thus became a symbol of both the unending vicissitudes of history and the promise of some day transcending history.[28] By playing skillfully on this symbolism, Eisenhower was able to combine these two major strands in his rhetoric and obscure the contradictions between the two approaches. He aimed to use the weapons themselves as a principal means of curbing their threat. He could be seen, quite accurately, as a dedicated soldier, stoutly committed to containment and a growing nuclear arsenal as the primary weapon of containment. He could also be seen, quite justly, as a soldier dedicated to winning the next war, should containment fail.

The same combination of symbolism shaped his policymaking. He said in many ways that the only effective deterrent to war was effective planning for war. Absolute containment depended on credible plans for absolute victory; containment depended on apocalypticism. At times he treated the bomb as part of the ordinary material of familiar military history. At other times he treated it as an extraordinary power that qualitatively transcended everything previously known. This ambiguity did not seem to disturb him, perhaps because it made the bomb a rare tangible symbol of a connection between the ordinary and the transcendent. There was no contradiction among these views and policies because all flowed logically from the general's basic premises.

All of these symbolic meanings met in the "new weapons." As long as the bomb was given a central place in planning for the next war, there was little need to worry whether those plans were strategically cogent, or just what would happen if ever they were implemented. Precise estimates of empirical reality were rather less important than constructing a satisfying symbolic reality, which would at the same time meet the military's most pressing political needs. So it was easy for Eisenhower simply to assume that the bomb would have to play some significant role in defending civilization, without ever defining that role. As long as the United States possessed the bomb and had some kind of plan to use it, it would fulfill its most important role—sending a message.

## THE COLD WAR CONSENSUS

During late 1946 and 1947, as the cold war consensus settled upon Washington, Eisenhower's public and private discourse gradually drew closer together. His references to the dangers of communism grew more frequent, more pointed, and more elaborate. As Peter Lyon says, "he inched closer to a consentient and respectable political position in regard to the Soviet Union."[29] Still, it would be wrong to suggest (as Lyon and so many others do) that the new cold war consensus forced him to change his views and his rhetoric. Rather, the new consensus allowed him to offer rhetoric that matched his private policy views. He was no longer so tightly constrained by an official policy of rapprochement. He no longer had to fear sounding too belligerent. Rather, he had to fear sounding too Pollyannish and unrealistic, which would render his speaking politically ineffective.

At the same time, though, the chief of staff was still determined to help steer the nation away from another war. He saw skillful words as the key to this task. In a cold war, verbal messages—including messages about military force—would have to be the decisive weapons. The most crucial words, in Eisenhower's view, were those directed to the folks at home, to rouse them to enlist in the crusade against the foe.[30] Of course it was forbidden to aim words explicitly against the enemy. In fact, constraints of policy and prudence led him to call publicly for cooperation with the Soviets. The result was a complex new discursive framework in which continuing expressions of a hope for peace were offset by expectations of conflict, criticisms of the Soviet Union, and calls for U.S. dominance.

In an April 1946 speech the C/S said the following:

> We can be firm without being offensive in support of principles that are sacred to us. We must remember that good humor, patience and tolerance are as important internationally as they are individually. . . . Two houses differently constructed can exist on the same street. Good neighbors do not pry into the domestic life of each other's families even while they observe common standards of conduct in their daily association. A people whose entire history is steeped in different doctrine may give to such words as democracy and freedom a totally different meaning than we do.[31]

This passage illustrates a pattern that would become increasingly common in the general's rhetoric. He used his seeming tolerance as a way to create a binary opposition between the U.S. and Soviet systems. Assuming that the United States unquestionably upheld "common standards" of freedom, tolerance, and mutual respect, he could offer a thinly veiled indictment of the Soviet effort to impose its way on others, yet never identify the enemy by name.

In November 1946, when he said that "there is room in the world for different systems of government," he immediately added: "provided, always, and provided necessarily, that no single one of those governments attempts to impose its system on any other, no matter what the means they may use."[32] The audience would have understood quite clearly which one of those governments the speaker had in mind.

The United States must not be "flaunted and ridiculed as it labors to promote world order," he told a veterans group. "When we believe that courtesy is met with rudeness, generosity with arrogance, patience wears thin." The rudeness was especially frustrating, he implied, because the United States was only trying to lead the world on the path to peace and mutual understanding:

> Yet our determination in this particular effort must be inexhaustible, because on its successful outcome depends the whole future of civilization, ours included. Moreover, it is only through patient study and exploration that we can discover the basic reasons why any other should seemingly obstruct progress toward a goal that holds out such promise to all mankind. . . . Every leader recognizes that in welding together a group for a common purpose some of his followers fall into line easily, others are difficult. . . . He strives to discover and eliminate the reasons that

inspire the recalcitrant members of the team. In the same way, if our nation is to be a successful leader of the world toward peace, it must exercise . . . patience and determination in winning over any that through fear, hope for revenge or any self- ish purpose, are blinded to their own national, as well as the world's, best interests.

By stressing U.S. patience and understanding, Eisenhower seemed to exemplify his premise that "the American way" was the only way to peace. This made it perfectly logical to see the Soviet Union as a "recalcitrant member of the team" blinded to its own best interests.[33]

At times the general made it clear that he saw no difference between the best interests of the United States and the best interests of the world, including the Soviet Union. Testifying to the House Committee on Foreign Affairs hearing, in June 1947, he was asked a question about Latin America. But he volunteered an answer directed toward U.S. relations with nations behind "an iron curtain":

> I think the world experience shows today you cannot promote a family by excluding one member, and saying "You are not fit to be spoken to, you are behind an iron curtain." I do not say there must be equal treatment, but we must get them behind a conference table and get them to stay there. They must under- stand our common problems, what our common risks are, and the common dan- gers, and the things we can do to keep ourselves out of that. I agree with you thoroughly that the thing we are defending is not territory and property, it is a way of life. That is what we are trying to defend, and we are never going to get those countries to go with us if they want to go some other way, by excluding them and telling them they are the prodigal sons and telling them we will have nothing to do with them. We must get them to come along with us some part of the way. It is going to be a slow and tedious process. I do not think there is any panacea for making people adopt, suddenly, things we believe to be almost sanc- tified, as far as our own feelings are concerned.[34]

Here he moved effortlessly from the goal of peace through mutual under- standing to the goal of protecting the U.S. system, suggesting that he saw no dif- ference between the two. He underscored this point by assuming that risks to the U.S. system were risks shared in common with the Soviets. Again, this made it seem plausible, and indeed necessary, to persuade the Soviets to "come along with us" by adopting U.S. values and the U.S. way of life, "things we believe to be almost sanctified." In Eisenhower's discourse this was the only way to peace, and it appeared wholly benign, since it was done in the name of peace.[35]

Describing his efforts to develop U.S.–Soviet friendship, he urged a congressional committee to understand the deep-seated fears in the Soviet Union. To illustrate the point, he told an anecdote about a Russian officer whom he considered a friend. The Russian had said to him, "For 25 years we have been surrounded by enemies, we had no friends," to which he had replied: "We don't like your darned system and that is that."[36] The general saw nothing in this exchange incompatible with his call for greater friendship and understanding. He did not see (or pretended not to see) how his blunt views would confirm the Soviet sense of being surrounded by enemies, nor how they might be a barrier to mutual understanding.

As 1947 went on, Eisenhower's public discourse was increasingly marked by the anti-Soviet sentiment so clear in his private discourse. By the late summer he had accepted "a two-world concept when we have been working for a one-world plan,"[37] and he plaintively asked an American Legion convention:

Are we expected to sit idly by, doing nothing, while hunger and hopelessness inexorably push the shadow of enslavement ever and ever closer to our own shores? . . . The friends of freedom must stand staunchly in its support or its foes will eliminate freedom from the earth. . . . The world comprises two great camps, grouped on the one side around dictatorships which subject the individual to absolute control and, on the other, democracy which provides him a free and unlimited horizon. In my view, conflicting political theories can exist peacefully in the same world provided there is no deliberate effort on the part of either to engage in unjust coercion or unwarranted interference against the other. But as long as aggression against the right of free men and the existence of free governments may be a part of the international picture, we must be prepared for whatever this may finally mean to us.[38]

Certainly by this time neither the Legionnaires nor anyone else could have doubted who the aggressor was, in the speaker's mind. Yet he continued to refrain from identifying the Soviet Union publicly by name.

He also refrained, quite scrupulously, from condemning the Soviets. Eisenhower rarely spoke in harsh or angry tones during this period.[39] It was all a matter of misunderstanding, he suggested. Good will on both sides—the kind of good will self-evidently ascribed to the United States—would have solved every problem. He might say, "we dwell today in a world where force and the threat of its employment make most difficult, and even impossible in certain areas, the realization of our dream of peace among men." But his rhetorical tone suggested that this was an unfortunate temporary situation, a cause not for anger but for sadness and regret; of course he took it for granted that the Soviet Union was wholly to blame. The image of an innocent United States, patiently pursuing peace, was most clearly etched when so strongly contrasted, in tone as well as text, to the supposedly very different attitude of the other side.

## "REALISM" AND "IDEALISM"

Eisenhower's continued expressions of peaceful intent persuaded many of his contemporaries, and many later historians, that he was only reluctantly forced to become a cold warrior. Such a misunderstanding was easy enough to come by when his rhetoric was accepted at face value. But his private writings and policy documents indicate clearly that the rhetoric should not be taken at face value. It was well-crafted, highly self-conscious discourse employed for specific goals. The general was never talking about the Soviet Union in literal, empirical terms, nor was it treated in any detail on its own terms. It remained a symbolic image, a discursive construction that gained meaning only by being incorporated into his larger discursive framework. Simultaneously, every implicit reference to the Soviets served to legitimate that framework. This enabled him to employ the symbolism of the Soviet Union in different ways to fit the changing needs of policy.

When it was useful, he drew on the "idealism" of Wilsonian liberal internationalism to depict World War II as one stage in the long, gradual progress toward a world of perfect peace and harmony. Within Eisenhower's discursive framework, the emerging cold war had to be treated as a temporary situation. He consistently endorsed the liberal internationalist view that peace was indivisible. The United States was the only nation willing and able to lead the world to peace; to do so, it would have to forge a unified world order founded on liberal internationalist values. The Soviet Union, standing outside the liberal internationalist order, was the obstacle to world peace. One way or another, it would eventually have to join, or at least accept, the U.S.-led world order. Eisenhower never differed with other U.S. leaders on that basic assumption; the only debatable question was the best way to achieve that goal. Proponents of the Riga axioms held that it would require force. As a supporter of the Yalta axioms, the Army Chief of Staff still hoped that it could be accomplished through persuasion and cooperation. From this perspective, friendship with the Soviet Union was a way to bring the gradual apocalypse to an end in a very unapocalyptic manner—by evil voluntary capitulating and joining the good in a single cooperative world system. Therefore, its evil had to be seen as a temporary, redeemable state.

But Eisenhower's private skepticism about Soviet cooperation, which increasingly shaped his public rhetoric, reflected his Augustinian bent and its geopolitical correlate, the "realism" that prevailed in policymaking discourse. For "realists," the real meaning of the war was a major realignment of world power. Four great powers had been destroyed or reduced to a second rank, leaving the United States and the Soviet Union as the only major powers able to compete for dominance. By the rules of this "realism," they would inevitably have to compete. The enemy's forces would always be gathering their strength on the other side of the border, eager to aggress whenever they were strong enough. Peace would always be, at best, a matter of staying strong and vigilant enough to ward off the endless threat of chaos. From this perspective, the Soviet Union became the mid-twentieth-century embodiment of sin. In principle, it could never be enfolded into the global corporate commonwealth.

By the end of Eisenhower's tenure as C/S, conflicting policy imperatives had led him to a unique mix of "realism" and "idealism." As he preached his message of world peace, he blended these two distinct visions of peace in his rhetoric, drawing on each as needed for specific policy needs. The blend was so successful because both types of discourse rested on and promoted the same principle, which was the basic theme of all his speeches: chaos—whether in the form of anarchy, communism, economic collapse, or world war—must be fought and overcome, or at least contained. Unlike so many others, he did not revise his worldview to make all forms of disorder subsets of "the communist threat." He did not cast Soviet communism as the one and only villain in the world historical drama. He continued to place the Soviet Union within his larger discursive framework. His "realist" language treated it as a subset (albeit the largest and most important subset) of the larger category of world chaos.

Although his "idealist" language portrayed the Soviets as a potential partner in the struggle against chaos, it actually accomplished the same purpose as the "realist" language, in a more subtle way. Refusing to name the enemy explicitly underscored the apparent U.S. desire for and confidence in a peaceful future. The language of peace thus served to cast into stark relief the difference between U.S. and Soviet aims. It said, more loudly than explicit condemnations, that the Soviet Union was the single barrier to peace, and that this was its biggest sin.

The language of peace also became a way to encapsulate the many vast differences he saw between the two antagonists. "Idealism" served even better than "realism" to proclaim that a peaceful world order would have to be built on the principles of liberal democratic capitalism. Eisenhower could use the language of peace to say clearly (albeit implicitly) that the Soviet Union, with its very different principles, posed a threat not only to the United States, but to all of Western civilization and its values. There was no need to name the "foes of freedom," the nation practicing "deliberate aggression against the rights of free men," for his audiences knew perfectly well which nation was being targeted. To pursue peace meant to save civilization from "chaos and communism." Eisenhower could say all this most persuasively by using the language of hope for a peaceful world order, built on the principles of liberal democratic capitalism. So he depended primarily on the abstract language of enduring peace and fear of chaos, rather than the concrete geopolitical language of fear of the Soviet Union, to legitimate and promote the interests of the army and liberal internationalism.

It was a testimony to the skill of his rhetoric that he could so easily use his calls for increased military strength to pursue precisely the same purpose. There was no contradiction between his hopes for peace and his call for more money for the army and the other services. Both served to mark the same unbridgeable discursive chasm between civilization and its enemies, and both flowed logically from the same discursive framework. Eisenhower's image of peace as a process, unfolding in stages, made it seem logical to speak of the Soviets as both enemy and friend: enemy in the immediate present, friend in the long-term future.

The same image of peace as process legitimated military strength, including nuclear strength, as necessary guardian of the process. The bomb epitomized the role of all military strength; it would guard the way to peace precisely because it would be used only as a symbol, not as a real instrument for killing. It would be a symbol both of the "idealist" hope for a perfect world order, free of all chaos, and the "realist" hope for the permanent containment of chaos. In Eisenhower's rhetoric, of course, the Soviet Union came to play just the same dual symbolic role.

The bomb would also be the primary symbol of the third element in Eisenhower's discourse, the penchant for expressing both "realist" and "idealist" views in an apocalyptic key. "Idealism" was no longer merely a matter of human progress, the historical triumph of Western Enlightenment values. It was a triumph of the spiritual side of human nature over its eternal enemy. "Realism" was no longer merely a secular force of order preserving itself against its secular opposite. It was the force of the spirit staving off the eternal threat of absolute evil. Through apocalypticism, the difference between "realism" and "idealism" was further obscured, as both were pressed into the service of the same religiously based worldview. In that worldview, history itself was an endless movement toward absolute peace, which was simultaneously an endless spiritual war.

In this way, Eisenhower ended up using the language of peace and the language of war to communicate the same ambiguous, though seemingly consistent, message. He could speak of his hopes for peace and preparations for war without acknowledging any conflict between the two. The difference between peace and war, apparently so central to his discourse, actually approached the vanishing point. The vivid contrast between peace and war, which raised such powerful hopes for the former and fears of the latter, served to erase the difference between the two. If pursuing peace and preparing for war were now the same activity, then that activity was the only one the nation could pursue. There was no alternative to it. No one could escape it. And its name was "the cold war."

## OPTIMISM

Eisenhower had another important reason for his public emphasis on U.S.–Soviet rapprochement. He presented himself as a military commander, fighting the most crucial of all wars and calling all Americans to enlist as troops, to rally around the same flag of virtue for which his GIs had fought and died. Every military commander, he had written during the war, had to instill his troops with a full understanding of the seriousness of the battle and the danger of the enemy. His warnings about the possible demise of civilization certainly did that. But in this war he had to refrain from publicly calling the enemy by its true name, and not only for tactical reasons or fear of open war. He refrained from such finger-pointing in large part because of his conviction that a leader had to offer hope that there would be a final end to the war, a genuine lasting peace between the superpowers—even if the leader himself was unsure that such a victory could ever be obtained. In Eisenhower's view of military command, arousing fear was as dangerous as it was necessary. The cries of alarm had to be offset by reassuring words of optimism and promises of peace.

The United States, as leader of the "free world," was obliged to demonstrate national optimism, the C/S said: "Our vigor and optimism . . . must revive and nourish the hopes of millions." So he criticized "those who speak of inevitable war. . . . If world order is worth struggling for, we do not advance the cause by predicting failure in advance. . . . There is no corner of the world where is not felt a desperate need for peace. . . . These things give hope and heart to those who work earnestly for lasting peace." On some occasions the general could sound buoyantly optimistic: "No matter what the pessimists may say, there has never been a time in the world's history that so many men of so many nations of such diverse cultures and traditions have been willing to seek in confidence a solution to international problems"; "Be of good heart and confidence. . . . Your faith in the cause for which you struggle will carry you through every trial"; and "The task is formidable but it can be mastered." Citing a typical example ("We cannot face the future with bland despair and by stewing in pessimism"), Ambrose comments sardonically on the banality of such clichés: "So welcome was this sage advice that the *New York Times* featured it the next day." Apparently, though, the *Times* did not think it banal.[40]

Even in these public words of optimism, the private ideology could often be seen. On one occasion, when he affirmed, "I am on the optimistic side," he explained his grounds for optimism with the rather minimal claim that the prospect of staying out of war "is not hopeless." Another speech was reported under the headline: "Eisenhower Sees World of Peace; Not Impossible, He Says, But Warns Security Is the First Concern of Prudent Nation." This headline typified his usual pattern: expressions of hope followed by a cautionary "however," leading into the paramount theme of dangers yet to be overcome. Sometimes he suggested that hope depended on fear of disaster, as when he insisted that peace and mutual understanding among nations "*can* be achieved, if every nation realizes that its very survival may depend on its earnest co-operation in the peaceful settlement of disputes." Throughout Eisenhower's public rhetoric, words of assurance were subordinated to words of warning. This was perhaps inevitable. His principal task was not to calm fears but to arouse a country that was, he believed, falling into dangerous complacency. Moreover, his discourse offered little reason to trust in the eventual victory of self-restraint.[41]

It was precisely his commitment to self-restraint, however, that brought about his gestures of optimism. As a commander, he felt obliged to set an example by restraining and masking his own fears as much as possible. Of course he could not admit publicly what he was doing. Privately, though, he explained his optimism and urged others to follow his example. In a speech to his staff shortly after taking office, he began by acknowledging how many difficulties they all faced and then immediately added: "Now there is one thing in any situation that I believe is always applicable, and that is optimism and a grin. . . . Just as in war, we have to keep our heads up, keep grinning, and keep plugging."[42]

The antidote to despair was optimism, he told many private correspondents, even if it had to be consciously cultivated:

> All of us, during the war, clearly understood that a period of bewilderment, misunderstanding, and probably some bungling would follow upon the conclusion of hostilities. However, I doubt that any of us could have foreseen the degree to which the world would surrender itself to pessimism and gloom, which . . . seem to prevail in every single spot of the earth's surface and in many instances

grow worse instead of better, month by month. I am not one who believes that by insisting there is nothing wrong I can cure a broken leg but I think that any failure to appreciate the effect of buoyancy, optimism and enthusiasm in leadership is certain to react unfavorably whenever difficult problems are to be solved. No one seems to get any fun any more just out of sheer work—I confess to feeling the effect myself.[43]

The longer he held the post of C/S, the more preoccupied he became with the struggle between fear and confidence. During the last week of October 1947, he referred to it in five separate letters. He told a friend (only half in jest) that one reason for his planned retirement from active duty was to escape being "constantly frightened by lugubrious staff officers." He told Beetle Smith that "it would indeed be a blessing if the country could regain a bit of serenity and peace." And he wrote to a British friend: "It seems a great pity that the world cannot regain some peace of mind . . . to relieve ourselves of the fears and hatreds that are generating among us all a near hysteria."[44]

This spate of concern about fear and its consequences may have been occasioned by two recent experiences. Returning from a brief visit to Kansas, he wrote to Swede Hazlett that Abilene struck him as unaffected by change: "[It] seems to drift along in the even tenor of its ways, and its people are the happier for it." In the same week, he read a speech by Harvard University president James B. Conant, warning that the Soviets would soon have the atomic bomb. He confessed to Conant: "Sometimes I become fearful." He sympathized with those who longed for the good old days before technology had wrought such new marvels (an era still alive in Abilene, apparently). But the proper response to these disturbing fears and nostalgias, he told Conant, was patience, study, and "at least a modicum of optimism."[45]

At times Eisenhower tried to deceive himself into believing in his own hopeful words: "You know me to be an incurable optimist," he wrote to Beetle Smith. "No one thinks clearly when he's scared," and the United States should not be scared, despite "the enormity of the problem." To the photographer Yousef Karsh he wrote of "my belief that through universal widening of understanding and knowledge there is some hope that order and logic can gradually replace chaos and hysteria in the world." Writing to wartime British colleagues, he used the war itself as a reason for at least a bit of optimism: "We often overemphasize difficulties and obstacles. We forget the tremendous nature and size of the forces that work for decency, for stability and for a brighter future. It is often the same in battle"; "I refuse to give up hope of progress along the lines of promoting a mutual understanding that we so often discussed during the war. The reason for my optimism is a simple one. . . . The United States and the British Empire, working together, did a job that looked almost impossible at the time it was undertaken."[46]

In all these letters Eisenhower was clearly evincing the battle within himself. He preached that the duties of a selfless leader overrode all other concerns. If "a modicum of optimism" was essential to fulfill those duties, he wanted to exhibit that optimism, even if he could not genuinely feel it, so that he could legitimately exhort others to do the same. He was struggling to deal with his own fear and keep up the grin that he expected from his subordinates. This was essential, he claimed, if there was to be any hope for a more stable future. For Eisenhower, hope—the product of self-discipline—was itself a crucial form of stability. In the term *stability,* political and personal moral virtues were blended into a single value that was, he asserted, the key to a brighter future.

But his private expressions of hope were relatively few and guarded. In private as in public, he rarely sounded a wholly optimistic note. His discourse was filled with sounds of alarm and calls to meet immense challenges. There was in fact little of the confidence, the assurance of success, toward which he exhorted himself and his friends privately. When he complained of lugubrious officers who overemphasized obstacles, he was certainly (if unconsciously) describing himself.

This internal struggle was reflected in his approach to the atomic bomb. He used atomic fear publicly as a way to underscore the urgency of his hope for peace. He often put images of atomic danger in a larger context to advise calming and transcending it: "I think war will become more of a struggle in basic destruction and endurance! . . . That is when I believe that discipline among the whole population will be so important. Because it will take tremendous fortitude and tremendous control to keep from yelling 'uncle' right that second [when attacked]."[47] As his letter to Conant showed, Eisenhower made a conscious effort to put the uniquely apocalyptic implications of the new weapons out of mind, and he urged others to do the same. He avoided considering the bomb as a new reality in and of itself.

Despite the new weapon's power, he found his guiding principle just as true in the nuclear age as it had been before: civilization depended upon calm self-controlled rationality, clear understanding, and at least a modicum of optimism. The bomb was now the prime public symbol of the possibility of destroying a whole civilization and all its forms of social control. Therefore, it was especially important to turn it into a symbol of controlling anxiety voluntarily. Consciously repressing nuclear fear and its effects, while continuing the nuclear buildup, would be both a sign and a result of the requisite self-control. Of course it would also help to repress any antinuclear sentiments that might challenge the military's growing reliance on the bomb. Once again, pragmatic military/political concerns and discursive motives were mutually reinforcing.

(On occasion, though, "Alarmist Ike" could not help phrasing his message of reassuring optimism in a way that would raise fears. At a 1945 congressional hearing he agreed that Universal Military Training would prepare citizens to withstand and fight a nuclear war. But he made his point with a macabre apocalyptic image: "If we have the discipline and moral fiber to stand up until we can mass our defenses, no single blow can destroy us until the destructive effects become so great that all of us would disappear in thin air.")[48]

Optimism, as a form of self-restraint, was fundamentally a spiritual value for Eisenhower. Naturally he stressed this theme when speaking to military chaplains. He told them they had a special role to play in the postwar era, "a cataclysmic period of doubt and fear and mutual suspicion. Through this we can travel only by clinging to the eternal truths." Since religious values were at stake, there could be no middle ground; the right had either to prevail or perish: "Except in a moral regeneration throughout the world, there is no hope for us and we are all going to disappear one day in the dust of an atomic explosion." But he also told a secular university audience, "We hope to cast the light of mutual understanding upon the dark shadows of envy and suspicion and hate in which mankind has groped its way perilously close to destruction." And he reminded the Economic Club of New York, hardly a religiously oriented audience, that "Christianity did not spread without crusaders. There were apostles, there were men who carried the faith. . . . You have not discharged your duty until . . . you become crusaders to spread the truth."[49]

The absolute spiritual dualism of the crusader was fundamental to both the private and the public discourse. Optimism formed an important link between the two. In the private discourse, the absent dualism of aggressive force versus ideal peace was replaced by two analogous and equally stark dualisms: the collapse of civilization versus saving civilization, and despair versus optimism. All three forms of dualism were interconnected. Since Eisenhower defined the problems he faced, both publicly and privately, in such apocalyptic terms, he articulated his personal response to those problems in the equally stark alternatives of buoyant optimism and total despair. He argued that optimism was a necessary part of the leadership that would save civilization, and it seems plausible to conclude, from the private writings, that he really was struggling to maintain a sense of hope in the face of a powerful foreboding of doom. To keep up this struggle, he could not afford to let himself acknowledge the overpoweringly frightening implications of his apocalyptic imagery. Public optimism was necessary to prevent a private disaster. Like powerful weapons and skillful words, optimism was a tool to contain the forces of chaos—in this case, psychological as well as social chaos—perhaps forever.

It is not surprising, then, that optimism had an impact on the private as well as the public understanding of peace. The orator who could so convincingly point his audiences to the coming day of salvation could hardly be totally immune from that vision in his private life. His public oratory would not have been so convincing if there had not been some modicum of private commitment behind it. This private optimism was necessary to prevent a public disaster; i.e., a public admission of pessimism. Eisenhower's occasional private references to world peace as a goal showed evidence of optimism. More common was a certain kind of hope expressed in his seemingly pessimistic vision of the future. Even if the best to hope for was containing chaos and communism, within a dualistic framework that containment had to function as the polar opposite of disaster. So Eisenhower spoke, and perhaps had to speak, in optimistic terms of a coming era of stability, a time when all threats would be dependably and permanently contained. The optimism of this vision, while certainly minimal, served the same structural role in the private language as the millennial visions played in the public language. But it could not promise an end to peril and war.

CHAPTER 7

# Chief of Staff: Conclusions

E arlier in this examination of Eisenhower's tenure as chief of staff, the question was posed: Why did he offer such a rich promise of perfect peace in his
public discourse, but not in his private? That way of putting the question
assumed a strict line, perhaps an overly and artificially strict line, between the
two types of discourse. This is useful for the sake of analysis, but as the discussion of optimism showed, the two types overlapped and influenced each other in
significant ways. So it is possible, and fruitful, to examine the totality of
Eisenhower's discourse as a single ensemble. That unified view will afford the
fullest possible answer to the question that was posed.

## THE DISCOURSE AS A WHOLE

The two modes of discourse shared many important elements. Both were built
on strict dualisms, particularly the dualism of civilized order versus chaos, and
both made the establishment and maintenance of order the highest goal. Both
used the same apocalyptic images of impending chaos and the demise of the U.S.
system. Both called for continuing spiritual, economic, and military strength to
combat these threats while preventing war. In both, visions of catastrophe and
the prospect of continuing war were intertwined with the notion of peace. Both
made peace a process dependent on U.S. leadership. Both agreed that the United
States alone had the ability, and thus the responsibility, to save the "free world"
and civilization. Both made peace a process that depended on effective deploy-
ment of U.S. strength, so that the difference between war and peace was blurred
almost to the point of disappearing.

But a body of discourse is held together by more than its common themes.
It is equally unified by the interplay among its different constituent elements.
The differences between Eisenhower's public and private discourses, and the

dynamic interactions generated by those differences, are crucial to understanding his discourse in its totality. The contrasting use of peace language in the two bodies of discourse gave quite different contexts, and thus quite different meanings, to their warnings of Armageddon.

In his private discourse, Eisenhower cast the specific problems of the postwar era as threats to the U.S. way of life and therefore to civilization itself. He called for global expansion of the U.S. way of life, not as a confident optimistic expression of any "manifest destiny," but as a means to contain chaos and communism, in order to defend "the American way." This was the only realistic goal within his field of vision. Protection through eternal containment became his effective definition of peace. Every threat to civilization was a threat to this peace. Since the threats were endless, though, the only way to protect civilization was to continue waging the cold war. Civilization had to keep on waging war to keep the peace; keeping the peace meant waging war.

This seeming paradox had a meaningful inner logic only because the war was now a cold war. It was essentially the same war Eisenhower had claimed to fight during World War II: the spiritual civil war between the forces of selfishness and the forces of self-restraint. Waging the war was a way to ensure the permanent rule of self-restraint in the future by embodying that value in the present. The essence of peace was the triumph of self-restraint. As in World War II, however, that triumph came more in the process of fighting the war than after its conclusion. So once again there could be no clear difference between war and peace.

Because the war had to remain cold, its primary weapons would be military force, used as symbolic images, and, most important, words. The words were woven into a public story about the United States as the principal bearer of civilized values. In that story peace meant the universalizing of the U.S. system, the permanent triumph of civilization. This was an eschatological state, the final victory of self-restraint over selfishness. But, the story continued, that victory was still far from assured. Only U.S. leadership of the world could save civilization. This crisis demanded a total national effort to continue the apocalyptic war and move gradually toward genuine peace.

This story had the same skeletal structure as the story Eisenhower had told to Europeans during the occupation. He was still presenting World War II and the postwar struggle as two parts of the same familiar spiritual "struggle of the ages." It was precisely the lack of closure—the continuing war—that gave meaning to war just ended and the many lives it had claimed. There were important differences, however, between the contexts of the occupation story and the C/S story. The most obvious differences revolved around the fact that they were addressed to different audiences and had different aims. The C/S version, developed more slowly in many more speaking engagements, was more elaborate and detailed.

Perhaps most important, in the summer and fall of 1945, Eisenhower could still speak as if the postwar chaos might be a brief prelude to a new world order.[1] He was most concerned with looking back to World War II and ahead to the new order, setting the present as a disturbing but hopefully brief interlude between them. During 1946 and 1947, he gradually came to base his discourse on the premise that chaos, or at least the threat of chaos, might well continue indefinitely because of continuing Soviet intransigence. He felt a growing need to sound a public alarm, though he still felt bound to do it indirectly. So his story began to focus more on the present. Superficially, it still seemed to be in part a story about World War II, proclaiming that war is meaningful only as a crusade ending in the unconditional surrender of absolute evil. On a different level, it seemed to be a story about the promise of absolute peace in the long-term future. In fact, though, its primary goal was to respond to the perceived threat of the present. Precisely because his story promised a peace that seemed so distant, it had to demand a continuing war.

Of course Eisenhower would rarely talk directly about the cold war, and even less about the unconditional surrender of the enemy. He had to find indirect ways to motivate the public to fight the cold war successfully while avoiding a "hot" war. This was the principal purpose for which he created his images and rhetoric of peace. His words about peace, like all his other words, were constructed as weapons for this new kind of war. The public discourse could call the nation to continued war only because it promised the light of peace at the end of the tunnel. How could masses of people be motivated to make the sacrifices necessary for a continuing war unless they were promised a total victory as their reward? But if that victory could not be described explicitly as the unconditional surrender of the Soviet Union, it had to be depicted in some immensely appealing way. The good officer, having stirred up his troops with fears of the enemy, had to offer them optimistic visions of total victory and encourage them to believe that they could achieve it. World peace was the answer. He highlighted the bright future of world peace because it was a necessary conclusion to the story. When Eisenhower spoke publicly about world peace, it was obvious to the careful listener that his vision entailed the unconditional surrender of the Soviet system to the U.S. system.

The skeptical historian might discount the content and internal logic of the public rhetoric, seeing it as merely skillful subterfuge, a veiled way to promote the cold war and enrich the army's budget. The skeptical historian could support this interpretation by pointing out that neither the promise of peace nor the talk of an unfinished war are to be found in the private writings. Although the words of war and peace seem to be a unified construct designed only for public consumption, the complex interactions between public and private language make such a skeptical view untenable.

The private discourse did not need the vision of millennial peace because it was directed to people who already shared Eisenhower's assumptions, people who were already prepared to enlist for the duration, with no expectation of a salvific end. It did, however, contain an element of optimism in its vision of peace as endless containment. This, too, required a continuing war, though that specific language was avoided—perhaps because it was a war without end. Perhaps the C/S dared not admit this to anyone, not even to himself, because there was no light of global peace ahead. Permanent containment as the highest goal left open the real possibility of a permanent cold war. If that was not the only imaginable goal, it was the only goal possible for the foreseeable future and thus the only goal relevant to policy decisions. In the private discourse, containment was the essential meaning of peace.

Eisenhower's firm hopes for friendship with the Soviets and his equally firm insistence on keeping the U.S. guard up were two public ways of promoting his private goal of containment. He could be logically consistent in publicly stressing amity with the Soviets yet maintaining his private mistrust of Soviet motives. He could call for U.S-Soviet peace and cooperation, yet still see the Soviets as the most likely enemy and insist on keeping up enough military strength to deter war—and to win a war if deterrence should fail, which he treated as a very real possibility. Moreover, in the private discourse there was no foreseeable end to the possibility that war might erupt at any moment; as the Soviets recouped their military strength, war would become more likely, military planners agreed. Likewise, if the war remained cold—fought without ever actually using guns or bombs—it was more likely to continue far into the future. So Eisenhower stressed the need to avoid war precisely because he saw, in private, so little hope of the genuine peace he championed in public.

If Eisenhower's private pessimism demanded public optimism, it also infected the public rhetoric with its doubts, in the form of copious images of impending disaster and adjurations to contain them. This created a tension, in both public and private, between peace as an eschatological goal and peace as merely the immediate prevention of disaster. The images of peace as a gradual apocalypse and peace as endless containment mitigated that tension, but they could not remove it completely. At the same time that image blurred, and perhaps erased, the central dualism of war and peace. Eisenhower had to make the forces of war central to the process of peace, not only for pragmatic reasons, but also because his eschatological promise of peace made that process a form of war. In private, he blurred the same line because he held out so little hope for eschatological peace.

In the interaction between public and private discourse, all the tangled dualisms of Eisenhower's discourse met. He was using the dualism of the chaos of history versus millennial peace to motivate the public to support the U.S. system against its radical opposite. He needed an optimistic vision to fend off despair (the public's and his own), as he enlisted civilians for a battle between civilization and chaos that had no end in sight. The public language of peace served that optimistic role.

## THE IRONIES OF STABLE ORDER

In order to make his public rhetoric effective, Eisenhower had to construct specific meanings for both peace and the U.S. system, and each meaning had to entail the other. Therefore, each had to construct the other. There was a natural affinity between the two sets of meanings, because both were ultimately intended to aid the nation in fending off chaos and achieving a stable postwar order. Eisenhower understood stability in geopolitical, economic, and spiritual terms. Since he saw all these forms as interwoven, it seems likely that he was quite conscious of the uses of language in pursuing the ensemble they formed.

It seems unlikely, though, that he recognized the ways in which language itself is a form of stability. The story that a society tells itself to give meaning to its experience is not merely a means to other ends. It has often been argued that every society needs, or at least wants, a stable set of stories as an end in itself. According to this argument, the meaning provided by the stories does not come as much from their content as from their perceived stability. Although the stories may in fact be constantly changing, the society develops mechanisms to deny that change. The most powerful mechanism may be simply the constantly repeated claim that the group has always said, or done, or believed this.[2] Does every society indeed need, or want, such a perception of stability in its shared public stories? The topic is widely debated and may never be resolved.[3]

It would be safe to say, however, that large numbers of people in the United States, particularly the white middle-class audiences to whom Eisenhower addressed himself, did value stability in their stories, and in their meaning structures, as an end in itself. There is a long-standing tradition in this country of using language about the nation, its future, and its role in the world as a mechanism for creating and maintaining a relatively stable sense of identity. To be sure, the language has usually been created by a white male elite, but it has often been used by many others (principally, though not solely, white people) to shore up their own sense of identity.[4] From this perspective, Eisenhower's public discourse was playing a role that was larger than even he understood. It was part of an effort by the postwar elite to create a relatively fixed meaning structure that would be acceptable to large numbers of Americans, at a time when stability seemed to be a scarce commodity indeed. Peace was a central symbolic term in that structure.

There is a classic irony in the language the United States has used to pursue stability. Because it has focused so much on the nation's special role in world history, it has built its images of stability on the same kind of dualism so pervasive in Eisenhower's language. The United States would appear stable, and a unique agent of world stability, only if juxtaposed with some less stable reality. And the sharper the juxtaposition, the more certain the U.S. stability became. Therefore, most stories about stability came to hinge on a radical opposition between the United States and the forces of chaos that threatened to destabilize it. There could be no stability without a threatening enemy. With the enemy at the gates, though, who could really feel stable? Eisenhower's discourse was a classic example of this irony. The more he spoke of peace, the more he undermined the nation's chances of feeling stable or at peace. His public and private frameworks came together to produce this paradoxical dynamic and make it inescapable.[5]

One source of instability was internal confusion within the discourse itself. When the general spoke of peace, it was never clear exactly what he meant. He still used all the various meanings of the word that had informed his public story as head of the European occupation: a present state, an imminent eschaton, a state of perpetual containment, a temporary hiatus before the next war, the end point of a long, gradual apocalypse. He was still blending Wilsonian, Augustinian, and apocalyptic language to create several different images of peace, each of which promised some kind of future order and stability. Because his story as C/S was more detailed and complex, all of his images of peace were spelled out in more detail, which made their mutually contradictory elements stand out more vividly. As he constructed his many-sided notion of peace, he was also constructing a sense of national identity. So the latter was confused too. Yet that sense of national identity required a much more elaborate ideological structure as the context for his images of peace. The structure gave a rhetorical impression of logical consistency. But this impression masked the continuing contradictions among the images of peace and the traditions on which they drew. Going unnoticed because they were so well masked, those contradictions created an even greater disorder within his own discourse. Despite its superficial consistency, his story could not really communicate a sense of postwar stability because the foundational assumptions and guiding goals of the story were so unstable.

Although Eisenhower had a relatively more consistent view of peace in private, this discourse also showed signs of internal contradiction. Apart from his occasional hints of working for a global corporate commonwealth, it remained unclear whether he wanted the United States to begin long-term planning for permanent containment or only to take emergency steps to fend off immediate disaster. If the former, was there any hope that all forms of chaos could eventually be contained, and if so, how? If the latter, did it make any sense to talk of peace at all? These questions had no clear answer, and the contradictions in the private discourse created greater contradictions in the public. The general knew that a leader, sending troops into battle, should give them a definite goal and a clearly articulated motivation. His private discourse did not offer this. So he gave the public eschatological images of future peace (and occasionally images of an already existing peace) to cover the gap. In the immediacy of the rhetorical moment these images concealed the confusion in goals and motives. Peace became a rhetorical marker denoting all of the goals that Eisenhower held out for the nation and the world. Thus it served as a thread connecting all those goals; it gave the discourse a superficial appearance of unity.

In the long run, though, the many meanings of peace only amplified the discursive confusion and made it inescapable. A nation just emerged from the chaos of war might have looked to its favorite hero for clarity of meaning and purpose. But in Eisenhower they found only a superficial clarity. Beneath the surface, the public's desire was being frustrated, and therefore stimulated. If the cold war in the United States was in some measure produced by a frustrated longing for postwar clarity,[6] Eisenhower's public discourse moved the nation one step closer to a total commitment to cold war. This commitment may well have been his intention (if the private discourse is taken as a guide to his intention), but this was not his consciously chosen way of achieving it. Apparently, it simply happened that way.

Yet, in a curious way, this process was an inevitable product of theological history. With his immense talent for public relations, Eisenhower was telling the public what it wanted to hear. He had to speak in a language that was familiar and comfortable to his audiences. He could do that so well because he was so familiar and comfortable with the same language. It was an ostensibly secular language, and yet it contained the sediment of centuries of Christendom. So it might be more accurate to see it as a language still in the process of being secularized. Its constituent theological traditions were receding at different rates. For example, Augustine's rejection of salvation through works had already largely vanished in favor of the Pelagian reliance on human action. But Augustine's view of human nature as inevitably flawed was disappearing rather more slowly. It no longer had the immense power of previous eras, but it was still quite influential.

The public Eisenhower could play effectively on the paradox of a Pelagian solution for an Augustinian problem, because his private language had such a similar foundation. His private discourse showed that he could see no possible answer that did not involve strenuous human effort, but it also betrayed deep skepticism about whether many humans would choose to make that effort. Its Augustinian strain made it seem unlikely that human effort would bring salvation, at least in the foreseeable future. Yet it showed no hint at all of the Augustinian solution to the problem, which was divine grace. Neither works nor grace could offer any escape from the vicissitudes of history. The only problem worth addressing, in the private discourse, was the classic Augustinian problem of preventing greater disorder in history. Yet the problem of history was not really defined in Augustinian terms, for the great theologian had imagined history as an endless waxing and waning of relative degrees of disorder. The apocalyptic denouement would begin only when history had come to an end. For Eisenhower, the problem was a looming threat of absolute disorder being played out in history. He portrayed history in precisely the apocalyptic terms that Augustine eschewed.[7] Of course an apocalyptic solution—a single, decisive battle—was no longer allowed, since that would only magnify the disorder. So the Augustinian solution of peace through strength—containing chaos with bulwarks of superior force—would have to suffice.

Eisenhower was apparently unaware of the theological background of his language. Although he never brought conscious theological considerations into his discourse, a theological interpretation is illuminating. Augustine and Pelagius both grappled with the fundamental questions of human nature and human history, the same questions that informed Eisenhower's discourse. The two theologians became classic rivals because each offered a consistent set of answers; between them they covered virtually all the options available within the Western cultural tradition. But Eisenhower's words sided with neither. Those words promiscuously reflected pieces of the answers offered by both, without embracing either position completely (nor did they embrace the classic "semi-Pelagian" compromise position). He was offering no consistent set of answers to the problems of humanity. He was offering only a grab bag of conflicting and sometimes mutually contradictory partial answers, which seemed to serve his immediate purposes.

## THE DIALECTIC OF HOPE AND FEAR

Underlying those various purposes was a consistent desire to shape public attitudes, which meant in the first instance stirring up a shared sense of threat. This desire, along with Eisenhower's discursive bent, generated a consistent tendency to frame issues in starkly dualistic terms. Yet these consistencies did not, in the end, offset the effects of a confused discourse of peace. They did not move the public any closer to a clear sense of national meaning. On the contrary, they only compounded the sense of instability and its attendant fears.

Both the public and private frameworks called for a war against chaos and communism and promised some form of victory. In each arena, however, that promise magnified the image of the enemy and its threat. Thus optimistic visions actually heightened the fear they were meant to contain, and there was no way to avoid this effect. As in any dualistic system, each terminus needed the other to give the system meaning. The pervasive fear required hope, not only to make the fear endurable but to make it meaningful in the discursive system. It might be hope for an imminent millennial peace, a distant peace (in "our children's" generation, a quarter century on), or only a dependable ongoing containment. But the hope had to be there to sustain the dualism of the discourse. Conversely, the hope, in order to be hope, required an element of fear to make the hope meaningful and to sustain the system. The fear of a "hypothetical Hitler" and another war was logically (as well as pragmatically) necessary to the dualistic discourse. If it had not been "the red menace," it would have been some other threat; if the Soviet Union had not existed, Eisenhower would have had to invent it—or radically alter the fundamental structure of his discourse.

This dilemma is unavoidable in any discourse built on Augustinian premises. The hope for enduring order is meaningful only when set against the chaos that threatens from beyond the borders of order. Order is the process of forestalling or repelling chaos. Order can endure as a meaningful category only as long as the threat of chaos exists—hence the assumption of an eternal threat. In more contemporary terms, the world must remain divided into spheres of influence, one controlled by the forces of order and another by the forces of chaos. Since war is understood as the incursion of an unprovoked aggressor into order's sphere, the possibility of war must be equally eternal. In Augustinian language, of course, the forces of order are only relatively superior to their enemies; all harbor tendencies toward chaos within them.

Eisenhower's public discourse blurred the theological genres by projecting the Augustinian paradigm onto an apocalyptic canvas. This allowed him to speak the language of Wilsonian "idealism" and offer hope of a final victory over chaos. To do so, he had to violate the basic premise of Augustinian "realism" and talk of a perfect universal order achieved through the processes of history. In practical terms, this meant a promise of global preeminence for the American way. If the goal were perfection, though, every obstacle toward that goal became an enemy of absolute good, hence an absolute evil. With one pole of the duality absolutized, the other had to be framed in equally absolute terms. The public hope for peace thus required not merely an enemy, but one that threatened to use the historical process to put an end to history. In practical terms, Eisenhower had to posit that the only alternative to global preeminence for the American way was a total loss of the American way. So talk of perfect millennial peace or permanent total containment heightened fears of the end of civilization. The only reasonable response was to become absolutely defensive.

The interaction between public and private discourse intensified this absolutizing dynamic. Because Eisenhower's private language required optimism as its equivalent of hope, he felt bound to speak in publicly optimistic tones, which led him to magnify the "idealist" hope for peace in his public rhetoric. He was free to paint his hopes for peace in the most utopian colors because he did not hold those views in private. They would not intrude on his policymaking decisions; there was no reality to check them. Yet his extreme language in public fit easily with, and reinforced, his predilection for absolute language in private; the stronger his private fears, the stronger his determination to sound hopeful in public. The more absolute each pole of the dualism became, the more absolute grew the other. Optimism had to bring greater fear, in both the public and private discourse.

As fear grew, of course, it became harder and harder to hold on to any sense of or hope for an enduring stable order. Yet it was precisely because perfect order was so ardently desired that leaders such as Eisenhower praised it, promoted it, and promised it. These leaders had to tell the public some substantial part of what it wanted to hear, in order for that same public to listen to what they wanted it to hear. This method merely locked the nation into the cycle of apocalyptic rhetoric. As eschatological promises of peace raised apocalyptic fears, they pushed any sense of lasting order ever further from the nation's grasp.

This dynamic gave the discourse a curiously utopian air of unreality, despite its Augustinian underpinnings. The unreality was most apparent in the public discourse, but in a more subtle way it marked the private discourse as well. Speaking in terms of ideal solutions (whether millennial peace or permanent containment), the general was less likely to focus on specific, achievable, near-term goals. Despite the apparently conciliatory words directed toward the Soviets, the absolute dualism militated against making any genuine effort in this direction. If the language admitted no middle ground, there was no way to think seriously about searching for any middle ground. In fact the public discourse could not really articulate any meaningful goals since those, as defined by the private discourse, centered on specific steps to contain the Soviet Union.

With such an air of unreality, the general's discourse was unlikely to help move the nation toward the kind of utopian solutions he publicly prized. It was unlikely even to palliate the atmosphere of threat that it so vividly represented. The best it could hope for was not to eliminate, but to contain, both the nation's fear and the objects of its fear. And every step toward containment, legitimated in such apocalyptic terms, only locked the discourse more firmly into the dialectic of spiraling hope and fear.

This dilemma was most evident in Eisenhower's use of the Soviets and the bomb as symbols. Both could be employed either as symbols of "idealism" or "realism," of hope or fear, depending on the immediate needs and purposes of the hour. Precisely because of their ambivalent meanings, each one encapsulated the dialectic of hope and fear; and because the two together were the twin pivots of all cold war discourse, there was no way for Eisenhower's discourse to escape the dialectic. Each one, when turned into a symbol of hope for perfect peace, inevitably became a symbol of apocalyptic threat as well.

The bomb's symbolism as a threat was perhaps inescapable. Certainly it was for Eisenhower, who stressed the dangers of World War III even more in private than in public. He did not, however, have to present the Soviet Union as a threat of similar magnitude. He could have portrayed it in classic "realist" terms as simply a rival for power, a nation like the United States; he could have portrayed it in moderate liberal internationalist terms as an ideological rival of modest and manageable proportions. These approaches, though, would not work in his framework of absolute dualism. In order to present the United States as the epitome of civilization, he needed some entity to serve as the antithesis—the symbol of all threats to orderly life. So the abstract language he used to voice a hope for lasting peace inevitably heightened cold war fears and made the cold war enemy appear uniquely frightening.

When the bomb and the Soviets were brought together, each amplified the fears inherent in the other. Eisenhower's fears of Soviet deceit prevented him from giving substantial support to disarmament plans; on the contrary, those fears encouraged him to view the bomb solely as a weapon of war. And the longer he planned for a war of apocalyptic magnitude, the more he had to view the Soviets as well as the bomb as absolute threats. This dynamic made it increasingly more imperative to speak optimistic words of world peace. Whenever the general spoke of peace, whether cooperation with the Soviets or peace through military strength in a nuclear age, he intended to calm fears. But his words, motivated by private fears, only raised the same fears in the public. All of Eisenhower's public visions of millennial peace could not mask the overriding theme of his private discourse—the pervasive fear of disaster. The more he spoke of optimism and hope, the more he revealed that he was still "Alarmist Ike." Every time he spoke about the Soviets or the bomb he impaled himself more firmly on both horns of this destabilizing discursive dilemma.

# Part III

## PRESIDENT OF COLUMBIA

## CHAPTER 8

# The Private Discourse

On 7 February 1948, Eisenhower retired as chief of staff of the army and left active military duty for the first time in thirty-seven years. Throughout his term as C/S, he had used the language of continuing war almost exclusively in his public, not his private, words. Had he now decided, privately, that he no longer wished to be a professional warrior? Not at all. In fact he used the language of continuing war, privately as well as publicly, to explain his decision to leave active duty and take the presidency of Columbia University. He was not changing his essential occupation, he contended on several different occasions: "Going to Columbia is merely to change the location of my headquarters. . . . I am changing the method by which I will continue to strive for the same goal"; "I will never truly leave the Army"; and "The average soldier thought he was fighting to save his type of nation . . . It is this that I am trying to continue to do, but in a different field."[1]

There is good reason to think that Eisenhower should be taken at his word. Throughout 1948 he kept up informal contacts with top military officials in Washington. In 1949 he took on a formal role, first as an advisor to, and then as temporary chairman of, the Joint Chiefs of Staff. The majority of his diary entries for this period dealt with military matters, especially the military budget.

## MILITARY PREPAREDNESS

During his brief hiatus between the Pentagon and Columbia, Eisenhower was called to testify to the Senate Committee on Armed Services. There was no longer any hope that the Soviet Union would provide a way for the opposing geopolitical camps to get along, he asserted. The Soviets wanted only to destroy democracy. In the face of such a threat, national security now meant preserving the United States "under such a way [of life] and with so much confidence that we probably will not get into war." To achieve this, the United States needed sufficient military forces and dependable allies. Without allies, the nation would have to "live as an island of democracy in a surrounding sea of dictatorship." These were essentially the same premises that had shaped his private discourse as C/S.[2]

In early 1949, when he set down in his diary "the main facts of our present existence," Eisenhower held to quite similar views. The first and overriding fact was that "the free world is under threat by the monolithic mass of Communistic Imperialism." The world's prospects were "darker than ever," he told Secretary of Defense James Forrestal in the fall of 1948. There had been no good news for three years. It was time to think about preparations for war, by which he meant full industrial production, even though a war would "leave civilization in an almost chaotic state." Diplomacy would no longer avail. The United States had already made too many concessions to the Soviets who, he was convinced, had no desire for a diplomatic settlement. ("I shall never understand the Russkys," he lamented.) This left him with no idea how to fulfill his vision of an integrated Europe, he confessed, "short of a collapse in the East or going communistic in the West." Only the most extreme solutions seemed realistic to him.[3]

On one occasion Eisenhower shared his pessimistic assessment with the Council on Foreign Relations study group on aid to Europe, which he chaired. He "shocked his audience by stating that if western Europe were overrun by the Soviets, the United States would be on its way to extinction. The general proposed, in a rough outline of the domino theory, that, without western European nations as allies, the United States could eventually be surrounded by enemies. He continued his analogy by arguing that if western Europe were to go, Africa would be in danger and so would South America. He further noted that he believed that Asia was already lost or in jeopardy." A few months later he underscored his despair about Asia in his diary: "I wonder how long the few remaining areas in S.W. Pacific can hold out!! Our leadership is too intermittent; Communism is on the job every minute of every day. . . . What do our bosses think that the Chinese commies are now going to do? I believe Asia is lost with *Japan, P.I, N.E.I., and even Australia under threat*. India itself is *not* safe!" This may have been a response to the communist victory in China. But the entry is strikingly similar to the note that he had made to himself more than eight years earlier, when planning the defense of that area against the Japanese. Now, as then, he prided himself on seeing dangers to which his superiors, and most Americans, were still blind.[4]

Eisenhower, however, did not expect a Soviet attack in the near future. Shortly after he ended his tour as C/S, his successor in the Berlin command, Gen. Lucius Clay, warned President Truman that war "may come with dramatic suddenness."

Within a few days, a communist government came to power in Czechoslovakia. Eisenhower could no longer complain that the "red menace" was being ignored by the public. Throughout the land there were voices proclaiming a clear and present danger. The country was filled with talk of imminent war. A few months later, the Berlin blockade brought renewed talk at the highest governmental levels of launching a preventive war against the Soviet Union. Now he had to worry that his cries of alarm had been heeded too well; a rush to war was not at all what Eisenhower had in mind. He tried to cool things off by telling journalists that "no great nation would deliberately provoke global war at this time. Wars are stupid and they start stupidly. There could be many situations from which our nation as well as others would find it difficult to back away from [sic]." Over the next two years he took great pains to repeat this statement frequently, with minor variations, almost as a mantra.[5]

Both parts of the carefully worded statement were equally important. It was meant to downplay visions of a Soviet "bolt out of the blue" that fueled talk of preventive war, while sustaining fears that a local conflict might inadvertently lead to war. The way to prevent such a war, Eisenhower and other military leaders argued, was to restrain and contain Soviet behavior with displays of overwhelming force, to make it clear that there would be no appeasement. Berlin 1948 combined with Munich 1938 to form the operative paradigm. This led directly to another "main fact of our present existence" that the general inscribed in his diary: "The U.S. must wake up & prepare a position of strength . . . without bankrupting ourselves."[6]

## THE BATTLE OF THE BUDGET

As chief of staff, Eisenhower had occasionally mentioned the danger of spending too much on the military. In his years at Columbia this became an increasing concern. He still wanted to see the military budget grow, and it was obvious that stirring up fears of war was one route, perhaps the only route, to success in the face of a budget-cutting Congress. Gregg Herken points out that Lucius Clay's "remarkable message—like that of his air force counterpart during the previous year—probably had its origins more in a concern for a share of upcoming defense appropriations than in any new or better perception of the Soviet threat."[7] But Eisenhower consistently declined to use talk of imminent war in this way.

This made the budget problem more difficult. If war were imminent, there would be no limit on military spending. But with war always a vague or distant possibility, it was necessary to budget not for a crisis but for "a period of indeterminate length." Eisenhower may have taken this approach to keep military spending down for economic reasons, as some would later argue about his policies as president. Still, the spending levels he proposed were higher than Truman's target ceilings, and far higher than the levels proposed by conservatives such as Sen. Robert Taft. Perhaps Eisenhower was also using this as an opportunity to reinforce his message that no one should expect imminent war. He wanted the government to plan for what he would later call "the long haul."[8]

He had to assume, too, that the enemies of freedom would always have the advantage of surprise. For Eisenhower, every possible war scenario boiled down to some variant of the same essential paradigm: an innocent democracy forced to defend itself against invasion (probably a surprise attack) by an aggressive dictatorship. This paradigm lay at the heart of the budgeting dilemma, he claimed. The United States, bound to be a defender in war, could never know just what to expect at the outset of a war. For this reason each military service had good reason to ask for everything it might possibly need. Such a scenario, though, was unaffordable; efforts to attain a perfect defense would spell "National Bankruptcy."

In his very first week in New York he told the state's Chamber of Commerce that the military was defending "a way of life," and that if military spending were not controlled "eventually we will destroy ourselves through expenditures we cannot afford." This theme became increasingly common over the next two years: "A democracy will always have an obvious deficit in the desirable strength of its security establishment. . . . Some middle line must be determined between desirable strength and unbearable cost." He warned that the United States as well as the world faced the possibility of either bankruptcy or war if too much money was spent on armaments. An excessive U.S. defense budget "cannot fail to be playing exactly into the hands of the enemy." At another time, he stated, "If we are then trying to defend a way of living, freedom which is tied up with free competitive enterprise, we cannot bankrupt the system at home by pretending to mobilize forces that are going to protect it. . . . Obviously, a senseless proceeding."[9]

The great question that plagued Eisenhower and his colleagues was how to pay for both the "new weapons" and a larger panoply of conventional weapons. All military leaders agreed on the need for more resources, but they disagreed on how to allocate those resources. The struggle over the military budget was bitter and seemingly endless. Eisenhower objected strongly to the unseemly public squabbles among the Joint Chiefs of Staff. They were violating the prime directive of military leadership—teamwork. The military was usually the most selfless of all institutions, he told Swede Hazlett, which made it particularly distressing to watch the public spectacle. If the president did not act forcefully to end the interservice battle, "we are going to have a blowup." He used appearances before congressional committees to try to mend fences and urge more cooperation. On one such occasion the *New York Times* reported that "the appearance of disagreement was soft-pedaled throughout the general's testimony." A *Times* headline on another occasion summed up his message: "Eisenhower Urges An End to Feuding; Emphasizes Unity; Holds Unified U.S. 'Can Whip World.'" At Columbia as at the Pentagon, his recipe for whipping the world was unity in ideology plus superiority in weaponry.[10]

## THE BOMB

Superior weaponry meant technologically advanced conventional weapons, but on the most important level it meant maintaining the U.S. nuclear advantage. The general had no doubt that the atomic bomb and the proposed hydrogen bomb would be essential elements in the position of strength he was helping to build. But what precise strategic role would they play? The question seems to have held no special urgency for Eisenhower. Certainly his references to these "new weapons" showed little sense of an immediate or total revolution in warfare requiring a whole new set of strategic principles. He treated the bomb as one among many pieces in the puzzle of administrative and strategic planning to prepare for another war. Historian Gregg Herken notes that by 1948, the JCS still had not approved any war plan as an operational plan. This shows, in his view, that they also lacked a sense of urgency regarding the continuing contradictions in strategy.[11]

When Eisenhower was called to Washington in early 1949 to oversee the military budgeting process, he decided that the military needed a coordinated plan for war. The first step was to agree upon a minimal "disaster averting" military budget, "Alarmist Ike" told both Forrestal and his diary. He had tried to slow postwar demobilization to "a rate that would avoid destruction" of the nation's military capability. But the Congress had not listened to his warnings. Now it was necessary to catch up, quickly.[12]

By late April he had worked out a plan (eventually named Offtackle) that called for stopping a Soviet advance in Western Europe while launching "at the earliest practicable date, a strategic air offensive against the vital elements of the Soviet war-making capacity." Yet just a week later he wrote to Secretary of Defense Louis Johnson that he was "a bit astonished" that the military still had no clear view of what the air offensive could be expected to achieve. "We have made an early bombing offensive such an important feature of all our specific war plans that I had assumed there was a general agreement on the minimum results that would probably be obtained." Of course in the interim he himself had developed no definite answer to this question, even though an early bombing offensive was an essential part of Offtackle. So he now urged an immediate study of the subject, apparently without recognizing the irony.[13]

By the summer of 1949, Eisenhower was willing to venture an initial judgment about the bomb's usefulness: even a "sudden, powerful" atomic bombing would not end a war by itself, he told Louis Johnson, but it would help to retard or cripple the enemy. "An early atomic attack may not yield all the results for which we hope, but it is the only move that promises any deterrent or delaying effect," so a "D-day force" of atomic bombers was needed to execute it. He urged Johnson to build that force, even if it meant cutting funds for other military services. Bernard Brodie's dictum that from now on the purpose of weapons would be not to win wars but to deter them understandably made little impression on him, because he still saw no essential difference between using a weapon to deter war and using it to win a war. For him, the ability to win a war was itself the only meaningful deterrent.[14]

Not until July 1949 did he address atomic deterrence explicitly, telling Secretary of Defense Johnson that "many authorities" stressed the value of deliverable atomic bombs as a deterrent to war. This was a strong argument for building up U.S. air power, he said, "assuming any validity to this general line of reasoning." The caveat indicates that Eisenhower was not fully persuaded of the argument. He also made it clear that the bomb would deter war only as part of an overall war plan that was sufficiently frightening to a potential aggressor. He was "in absolute agreement" with Bernard Baruch that a careful plan for war, including an atomic strike as only one component, was the best deterrent to war; therefore the United States should maintain its nuclear advantage He told Swede Hazlett a "fine, properly balanced" atomic strike force "would not only have a deterrent effect upon potential enemies but would give us a splendid 'fire department' in the event of aggression." [15]

As early as 1948, Eisenhower indicated that he expected nuclear weapons to deter more than World War III. When he set down in his diary "the main facts of our present existence," he called for the United States to develop "a position of strength from which it can speak serenely and confidently." Speaking "serenely and confidently" meant being able to shape world conditions with words alone. As he put it to James Forrestal, he wanted the United States to be able to employ "power diplomacy." The United States needed allies and access to raw materials; these were his final "main facts." Power diplomacy would keep allies in line and protect access to raw materials without the active use of force and its attendant risk of war. Military strength would provide the symbolic gestures that would create successful power diplomacy.[16] Chief among these symbolic gestures was continued production of atomic bombs and development of the H-bomb. As during his Pentagon days, the general assigned these weapons a central role without knowing, or caring much about, their precise strategic function. He perceived them more as symbolic than as practical weapons.

In order for these symbolic tokens to be deployed, they would have to be at least tolerated, if not actively embraced, by the public. Although the public's fears of nuclear weaponry were waning in the late 1940s, Eisenhower was apparently still concerned that the public might not fully support nuclear armament. He sought to soothe public fear after the first Soviet atomic explosion, joining the chorus of national leaders who assured the public that this had been foreseen years ago and thus called for no major changes in U.S. policy. When the U. S. response—the decision to make the H-bomb—was announced, he went out of his way to try to calm and transcend fear. He declared that to calm public fears it might be necessary and worthwhile to divulge some previously secret information to the public, whereas previously he had called for full secrecy.[17]

Eisenhower made a conscious effort to put the uniquely apocalyptic implications of the new weapons out of mind, and he urged others to do the same. There was no reason to "hide from the horror of the H-bomb in ignorance," he told one audience. "Every invention of mankind has been capable of two uses, good and evil. It is up to the moral fiber of mankind to decide to which use an invention is put." "Every generation has had its problems," he told a group of students. "Everyone has had to face A-bombs and social unrest. . . . Don't let them make pessimists and defeatists out of you again." He refused to consider the bomb as a new reality in and of itself. Even the H-bomb was only a danger in certain contexts, contexts that resembled familiar forms of "social unrest," where clear thinking and reasonable action, the fruits of self-discipline, no longer prevailed.[18]

For Eisenhower, clarity in the postwar world meant recognizing the apocalyptic magnitude of the danger stemming from insufficient self-discipline, whether embodied in communism or a "hot" war against communism. Although the bomb would be used in that war, he saw the bomb itself posing little threat. Civilization had faced apocalyptic threats before nuclear weapons were invented, he insisted, and the destructiveness of war would be as great (or nearly so) without nuclear weapons since the next war would, in any event, resemble the last one. His reaction to the hydrogen bomb reflected his general tendency to demand a consciously willed optimism from himself as well as from others. In the larger context of his ideology it appears as one more kind of self-restraint—consciously repressing fear and its effects.

Yet this repression could never be complete, for his reassurances were freighted with images of the fear he urged others to avoid. "Everyone seems to enjoy the terror we've generated for ourselves," he told a group of young people, who may have wondered where he got such a strange idea. Urging them to fear no weapons, he assured them that no one was going to drop a bomb and "make the U.S. disappear." Explaining these words in private correspondence, he held that "no one was doing a real service to the public if he went around threatening us all with complete extinction without warning and, as a result, producing among us a tension that would be an obstacle to clear thinking and reasonable action. As a practical matter, if we are all to be destroyed in the twinkling of an eye, what is there to do about it?" Such words did not reflect unalloyed confidence that the United States could "whip the world," but an ongoing struggle between confidence and fear.[19]

Eisenhower's words about war from 1948 to 1950, while both confident and fearful, remained surprisingly distinct from the rest of his discourse, as if military affairs were a more or less separate compartment of his life. Freed from the responsibilities of an official military post, he no longer had to direct his public rhetoric solely to such matters. In his private discourse he attended to them as rather technical matters, not significantly related to his other concerns. The only major link between military issues and the rest of his discourse lay in his fear of excessive federal spending, for military as well as other purposes. This was an increasingly frequent topic, but it did not in any sense dominate his discourse. Of course the question of the military budget was rapidly becoming a political mine-field. Anything Eisenhower said about it was likely to create more problems for him, so he was well advised to avoid saying anything, whenever that was possible. But he was also using his newfound freedom to speak privately as well as publicly on other matters, rarely addressed in his previous discourse.

## "MY FAVORITE SUBJECT"

Eisenhower began civilian life as he had ended his active military duty, declaring that the crucial factor in saving civilization was the mental and spiritual state of his fellow citizens and their leaders. Soviet communism was still cast as a mortal threat to civilization. He told Douglas Fairbanks, for example, that the United States would defeat communism only if "each of us gets out his spiritual armor, shines it up, and goes out to fight until victory is attained." (In more prosaic terms, he explained, this meant that each person must "voluntarily do his part.") He stressed spiritual values most often when responding to correspondents who had stressed that factor themselves. "I agree with you that the times call for leaders who are 'enlightened Christians,'" he told one, though he was more likely to support a generalized sense of spiritual values and "an offensive against corroding materialism."[20]

His agreement with one such correspondent was particularly revealing: "I think you are correct in asserting that, at present, moral and religious grounds provide the central appeal for efforts to sustain freedom abroad. Ultimately, of course, it must be seen by all our people that any further gains by totalitarianism [read: the Soviet Union] would shift the world balance of power irretrievably to the hands of despots . . . [and] degrade our civilization to their own unfathomable level." Religious arguments were useful for the present, he seemed to say, but the real issue was self-preservation. The problem, as always, was that only a few insightful leaders understood this. Americans "just don't believe we ever will get into a real jam" and don't see the consequences of their complacency "until we get into serious trouble." This was much the same line he had taken as C/S.[21]

Having left active service, though, Eisenhower felt free to take a broader view of "the danger into which we are drifting." The danger now went far beyond complacency about military matters. At the very outset of his tenure at Columbia, he wrote: "I believe that all of us should be taught the inevitable results of adopting statism either through unthinkingly drifting into it or through conquest from without. . . . At first hand I know something of the human stultification that comes about through paternalism that finally results in complete loss of freedom and in the surrender of all personal initiative to absolute governmental regimentation."[22]

After Truman's 1948 re-election, the unthinking drift from within rather than conquest from without became the dominant theme in Eisenhower's private discourse. When Thomas Dewey came to visit him that November, they did not discuss military preparedness, the Soviets, or the threat of war. Eisenhower told his diary that Dewey had come to persuade him that only he, the great war hero, could now "save this country from going to Hades in the hand basket of paternalism—socialism—dictatorship. He knows that I consider our greatest danger the unawareness of our majorities while aggregated minorities work their hands into our pockets and their seats to the places of the mighty: So he dwelt at length on the preservation of freedom—my favorite subject!!!! . . . He is most fearful (as are thousand of others, including, myself, in varying degrees) that we, as a nation, will fail to see the danger into which we are drifting."[23] Eisenhower insisted that he had serious doubts whether he should run for president. But he had no doubt that the U.S. was in grave danger of sliding into socialism, which would inevitably mean totalitarianism. Judging from his private correspondence, it was indeed a favorite subject. He addressed the subject several times in 1948. During 1949, it became a standard refrain and central theme in his private discourse.

At times he explored the issue in temperate and reasoned language. For example, at the beginning of 1949 he told labor leader Phillip Murray, "I most earnestly believe that whenever these matters can be solved locally or by private institutions we are badly advised to permit federal participation." But it was often difficult for him to control himself. The most important point about his new discursive turn was not its content, but the intensity of the exaggerated fears that fueled it. The very next day he expressed positive interest in a correspondent's claim that the Truman administration's policies would lead to a welfare state and then a police state. Two days later he congratulated conservative columnist George Sokolsky for writing that the income tax "turns free men into the things of the Government."[24]

That same week he participated in a conference with business executives on the purpose of education. Moved to get his thoughts on the subject in order, he penned a lengthy diary entry that began: "The trend toward government centralization continues—alarmingly. In the name of 'social security' we are placing more and more responsibility upon the central government—and this means that an ever growing bureaucracy is taking an ever greater power over our daily lives. Already the agents of this bureaucracy cover the land . . . they nag, irritate and hound every businessman in the U.S."

The diary reflection admitted, in passing, that the solutions to modern problems often required coordinated efforts rather than rugged individualism, and "in certain limited fields the Federal Govt. could properly take action that would have some indirect, beneficial, results." But it stressed at length the dangers of excessive reliance on government:

> The real hope of the short sighted is to get Federal money to support institutions . . . The proposition is immoral—and its adoption, in this general sense, will lead to statism and, therefore, to slavery. And the best way to establish dictatorship is to get control of the educational processes in this country. This trend must be halted in its tracks. To help stop it is one of the reasons I've taken on this strange, difficult and often frustrating task. Except for a few young and able men here—there seems to be little awareness of what is happening to us—or threatening us.[25]

Here was another opportunity for Eisenhower to denounce self-seeking, to cry out a warning against it, and to pride himself on discerning a danger that most others were too short-sighted to see. The approach he took to education would soon be applied to every facet of domestic life. As 1949 went on, his fears of creeping socialism and incipient dictatorship became more pronounced: "Let me remind you," he told a proponent of federal aid, "that governments have more than once slipped into dictatorship under heads who were originally elected to their offices. One thing certainly must be clear—complete dictatorship is a necessary result of complete socialization, and such a result means the end of liberty."[26]

Eisenhower most often expressed such ideas to his powerful, influential friends and correspondents. He urged Eddie Rickenbacker to keep on spreading his message that too many in the United States wanted something for nothing, and they would soon lead the nation "down the road to ruin." There was little to fear from communists who openly attacked the American system, he wrote to Texas millionaire Amon Carter: "Their attack can be easily detected and countered unless we go completely asleep." The real danger came from "individuals who are essentially humanitarian and altruistic in purpose even though they are fuzz-minded in their thinking." Such "liberals" were well-meaning, but they offered only material comfort, not "what the human soul craves"; i.e., the ensemble of individual freedoms "that are the very core of all our deepest desires and aspirations." So the liberals promoted ideas that "would merely advance us one more step toward total socialism, just beyond which lies total dictatorship." Eisenhower called upon his friends to help him "combat remorselessly all those paternalistic and collectivistic ideas," which would eventually cause "the collapse of self-government." He portrayed this battle, like all his battles, as a contest of spiritual values against their materialist foes. So it would have to be an apocalyptic crusade waged to the bitter end.[27]

He voiced similar fears to old friends and acquaintances. He signaled his "complete agreement" with Gen. Percy Bishop that Americans had converted to the "something-for-nothing philosophy," and he assured Bishop that he was working to reverse that trend. To his in-laws' physician he wrote, "the times are serious and everyone must be ready to do his duty if we are not to fall prey to false ideas and to political trends that seem to have rather terrifying potentialities."[28]

Occasionally he deigned to share his thoughts with humble strangers, as in a letter to an engineer from Alabama: "If we go completely to the socialized state, I firmly believe that we will become nothing less than a regimented state. . . . If we are to become fully socialized, we will become also fully regimented." The engineer might well have rejoined that the great general did protest too much. The engineer had merely suggested that it would take some effort on the part of the federal government to improve the lot of the average person rapidly. Like so many others of his day, he viewed moderate governmental authority as a reasonable and beneficial compromise, nothing more. Eisenhower himself admitted that the complexity of modernity made some governmental authority necessary. But given his discursive framework, Eisenhower could not avoid exaggerating the prospect of federal aid into the threat of full-blown socialist dictatorship.[29]

## A CLASSICAL REPUBLICAN

The exaggeration stemmed in part from the roots of his ideas. He had a coherent theory to explain his concerns, though in no single place did he articulate it completely. It began, as did his approach to every issue, with his view of human nature. "The facts of human nature" dictate that people are best motivated by individual differential rewards, he assumed. "None of us likes to face up to the fact that he himself must sweat and slave if he is to realize an ambition. It is a comfortable human failing to pass disagreeable responsibility to an indefinite, indefinable whole. This is the kind of thing I believe we must combat." Only a system of differential incentives, with no limit on the potential rewards, could coax hard work out of the self-indulgent, lazy side of human nature; only a capitalist system could achieve maximum productivity. Individual freedom was humanity's "deepest desire" because everyone wanted to be free to pursue private gain without public responsibility.[30]

Here was a fundamental paradox in Eisenhower's emerging ideology. Capitalism was a product of selfish impulses, yet it was simultaneously the strongest barrier to the ultimate, chaotic triumph of those impulses. Unless capitalism were universally and rigorously enforced, people would happily let the government take care of their material needs and take responsibility for all the problems of life. Government, run by even more selfish people, would eagerly take the powers granted to it and usurp much more. This was a vicious circle: lazy people would ask more and more from government; government would give more and more, because the more it gave the more control it gained over people's lives. Once the habits of self-reliance and individual differential reward were interrupted, even the slightest bit, this spiral would set in and there would be no stopping it. With little difficulty it could lead to the full-blown regimentation of "statism."

There was nothing original in this theory. It could be traced back to the classical republicanism of Cato's Letters and the Revolutionary War era. It had strong affinities, too, with the populist tradition that grew out of republicanism, pitting the ordinary citizen against the invasive overweening powers of government.[31] Republicanism assumed that the selfish side of human nature, like the devil of traditional Christianity, was seductive, implacable, and hence immensely powerful. The Godly and civic virtues of self-control were, conversely, quite fragile. They represented what people really wanted, but most people were too weak and undisciplined to attain them. So the system of economic and political freedom that depended on voluntary self-control was always on the verge of being overcome by "statism." For Eisenhower, as for the Founding Fathers, these were not theories to be tested against empirical evidence. They were a set of interlocking foundational assumptions, a lens through which all empirical evidence would be perceived and interpreted. Their truth could not be open to question.

Therefore, the reality of the dangers did not have to be demonstrated, nor even spelled out, in any detail. Terms such as paternalism and statism had to be left vaguely defined, because they were symbolic markers that represented the entire ideological system. Indeed, their vagueness was the foundation on which the system was built. They were not empirical realities, but terms by which disturbing empirical realities (labor strikes, taxes, aid to education, etc.) were given meaning. They were societal projections of the vaguely defined diabolical side of human nature. It was dangerous to get too close to them, even for purposes of understanding. One needed to know only that they were wily and terribly compelling if given any chance at all to guide behavior. Only the eternally vigilant would foresee the snares that the evil powers set; only the spiritually strong would resist them.

Although Eisenhower may have entertained such ideas for a long time, he had not expressed them as C/S. Perhaps he felt constrained by his position, even in private discourse. He had warned loudly against the dangers of regimentation. But then it had been social and political chaos abroad that might trigger statism. Now it was primarily laziness and self-indulgence at home. Though regimentation was his main fear, he sometimes worried about a descent into domestic chaos too. In his discourse, these were all manifestations of the same root problem of selfishness. Classical republicanism was not the constant element in his discourse. It was merely one way of expressing the underlying constant: the age-old struggle between the freedom of self-control and the selfishness that led to statism.

Like many others before him, Eisenhower set his republican views in an apocalyptic context, which led him to exaggerate the dangers even more. The self was its own most dangerous enemy and had to be combated without quarter. There could be no middle ground between good and evil. Every step toward self-indulgence, no matter how slight, would pose a mortal threat to virtue; any federal government power was not only unfortunate but dangerous. The dualism that formed the deeper structure of his discourse required him to frame the problem in absolutes. The danger of statism, absolutized, had to be portrayed as unlimited, whether it came from foreign or domestic enemies.

In the face of a discourse that generated such immense fears, "Alarmist Ike" naturally tried to muster a consciously willed optimism: "If those who believe in constitutional America are to go down, I am certain of one thing, they will go down fighting and with their flags flying. By the very nature of their task, they cannot give up—they cannot bow to pessimism and discouragement. I number myself among members of this band."[32] But such expressions of optimism in his private discourse were very few and far between.

On the other hand, he confessed his outright discouragement only occasionally, as in October 1949 when he wrote to wartime friends: "Rarely can I find in my morning newspaper any single item that implies bright prospects for the future. The contrary seems always to be true, and it takes an overwhelming faith and stout heart to remain optimistic in considering the world that our children and grandchildren will have." A few days later he wrote, "There is no easy road to that repose and contentment everyone has come to long for to intensely." It would be comforting to believe that hard work would bring "a feasible and satisfactory solution. . . . That was, of course what sustained us during the war; we always knew we could win if we kept trying."[33]

Although Eisenhower might have been depressed by the recent news of the Soviet atomic explosion and the triumph of the communists in China, he particularly emphasized domestic labor strife: "We are having great strikes . . . reducing our productivity. . . . With great portions of the world looking for and needing the products of our industry, it seems to me that we are getting into a very serious situation."[34] Concerns over productivity had been central in Eisenhower's life since his early service in Washington before the Depression. Now he worried that selfishness, in the form of excessive labor demands and a drift toward socialism, would undermine productivity. This could lead to further demands for a regulated economy, reduce resources for the support of foreign nations threatened by communism and, perhaps most important to the general, reduce the resources available to the military both in peacetime and in "an emergency."

As head of the occupation and chief of staff, he had worried constantly about the lack of economic productivity in Europe. The chaos he lamented was, above all, the absence of a smoothly functioning production system; if capitalism appeared ineffective, it would open the door to communism. He continued to harbor that fear during the Columbia years, but his story now focused much more on a growing fear that the same kind of chaos might engulf the United States, robbing the military of resources and leaving regimentation by the federal government as the only alternative.

## EXPLANATIONS

Why this shift in the private discourse? Some biographers trace it to what Piers Brendon calls his "clandestine campaign" for the presidency.[35] They argue that he was surrounding himself with new friends from the wealthy Republican corporate elite. These friends were supposedly teaching him the language they wanted him to use as their political figurehead, and he was showing how well he was learning his lessons. He was telling them what they wanted to hear because only they could make him president. There is evidence to support this interpretation. But in the end it is not convincing.

No one will ever know for certain whether Eisenhower really wanted to become president. He himself probably did not know, at least at this time. But a few facts are certain. At times he was preoccupied with the controversy surrounding his political future. His diary and private letters during the Columbia years indicate frequent reflection on it, whenever the "Eisenhower surge" resurfaced. He consistently arrived at the same conclusion: he did not want to be president and hoped to avoid that fate. He was also consistent in explaining why: politicians were ambitious, hence selfish, people, and he would not join their ranks by seeking office. He insisted he could not close the door completely, however, because he might some day be persuaded that it was his duty—the very opposite of his desire—to run.

One other point is certain. During his years at Columbia, when Eisenhower was preoccupied with the military, the presidency, and fears of creeping socialism, the discursive opposition between selfishness and duty was at the center of his reflections on all three subjects. This was especially evident in a diary entry written in the first week of 1950, his one attempt to combine all his reflections into a something like a theoretical whole.[36] Many people were pressing him to declare as a Republican and begin his overt political career. He wanted "to clarify my mind" on the issue, to be sure that he knew his principles and was sticking to them. So he set down his reasons for remaining publicly nonpartisan. He complained in generic terms about all those who were betraying "the basic tenets of Americanism," the most important of which was the value of allowing individuals to earn their security and comfort by hard work. He discussed his commitment to the army and several ways in which a partisan declaration might harm the army, "this country's most devoted, most efficient and best informed body . . . the finest organization in government—any government." After pausing to remark, "As between the so-called concept of the welfare state and the operation of a system of competitive enterprise there is no doubt where I stand,"[37] he continued with an attack on selfish politicians.

He concluded the entry with a seemingly irrelevant reflection on the *New York Sun* going out of business. The paper's final editorial, amidst "a series of catchwords of conservative orthodoxy," complained that it could no longer afford rising labor costs. Eisenhower signaled his accord with the catchwords and commented: "Labor leaders have become so unreasonable in their demands that they are defeating their own ends." Then he pasted in his diary a Rube Goldberg cartoon, from the paper's last edition. It depicted the United States sinking into a sea of debt, while a piano-playing "Harry" sang about "the welfare state" and "the gravy train." Above this, Eisenhower noted that the *Sun* stood for "the things in which I believe." The death of the *Sun* symbolized, for him, one more step toward the death of traditional American principles. The question was whether those principles were "now to go into the discard." If so, he vowed to himself, "I'll go down fighting."

This reflection on the *Sun,* including the cartoon, was actually quite relevant to his consideration of party politics. They made it clear that he was a partisan, for he saw Truman's Democratic Party as a danger to the nation. The Democrats and their labor supporters were, in his mind, the party of selfishness. As a general and a consultant to the Truman administration, he felt constrained to avoid political polemics. "I've seriously considered resigning my commission," he wrote in his diary, "so that I could say what I pleased—publicly." But throughout his tenure at Columbia he was scrupulously careful to decry the dangers of socialism and paternalism only in the abstract, never attacking the Democrats directly. In public as well as in private, though, one could hear his indictment of Truman and the Democrats clearly enough between the lines.[38]

This diary entry does not prove that Eisenhower either wanted or did not want to become president. Nor does it prove that his fears for democracy and capitalism were genuine. It proves only that he was ably to descry, even if somewhat dimly, the consistent dualistic principle underlying his discourse. It was democracy, capitalism, individualism, the army, and all the institutions built on a sense of duty, battling against political ambition, Truman, the Democrats, federal aid programs, organized labor, and all the institutions built on selfishness.

This was the same moral and spiritual civil war that Eisenhower had first described in the early years of World War II. There was nothing essentially new in his principles, nor in the exaggerated fears they produced. The specific fears he articulated, while more focused than before on internal threats to U.S. capitalism, were all logical extensions of the fears he had already been expounding. Moreover, the new emphases were fully evident in his public discourse during 1948 (see chapter 9 below), while they did not enter his private correspondence with his friends in substantial ways until 1949. In light of his previous complaints about not being able to speak freely, there is no need to assume that he learned this new language of fear from his new friends. It seems more likely that, as he claimed, he was now saying things he had long wanted to say. There is no convincing evidence that his warnings were uttered just to impress his friends and/or advance his presidential candidacy.

Moreover, even if he were subtly maneuvering toward the presidency, he had no need to impress these friends. They sought him, as he acknowledged, because he was so eminently electable.[39] Moreover, he was equally electable on either party ticket (as some Democrats acknowledged in 1948 by offering him the head spot on their ticket). It hardly mattered what he said, because he did not need to prove himself to his friends by saying the right things. They needed him more than he needed them.

Eisenhower could fall in quite easily with his new friends because they offered such a willing audience for his warnings of impending doom. He bonded with them so readily because all shared the same language; both the content of their views and their style of expression were congenial to his own. As Robert Griffith says, these friends wanted Eisenhower to run because "he was pre-eminently electable. More importantly, as they were soon to discover, his political and economic views in many ways closely approximated their own."[40] Eisenhower joined a community in which all mutually confirmed and reinforced for each other the validity of their common views and fears. This made him neither a leader nor a follower, but rather what he always said he wanted to be: a useful member of the team.

Griffith has explained the mission of this team quite clearly. They wanted to use governmental powers for "moderating economic conflict, regulating domestic markets, promoting international trade, and sustaining economic growth." But they wanted to avoid continued and expanded New Deal policies that might "ultimately destroy private enterprise. . . . The strategic problem faced by corporate liberals in the postwar era was, thus, how to obtain the benefits of state intervention while avoiding its dangers. Their immediate, tactical problem was how to win political power."[41] Eisenhower himself rarely mentioned the benefits of government-business partnership. His focus was almost entirely on the team's fears.

Therefore, he was more than willing to join the team's effort to win political power by adopting its favorite tactic: spreading the gospel of fear of the Democrats.

There is no reason to believe that this tactic was disingenuous. The more the members talked to each other, the more they convinced each other that their fears of "paternalism—socialism—dictatorship" were realistic. As in any community, conversation served to legitimate the dominant view and insulate it from reality testing.[42] They created a spiral of mutually reinforcing and enhancing fears, convincing each other that these were perfectly reasonable, particularly after Truman's victory in 1948. Once in the group, Eisenhower or any member would be more likely to intensify his expressions of fear, simply because that was the language they shared.

These new friendships were a sign, though not a cause, of the one respect in which Columbia's president had changed. At the decade's outset he had warned of a coming war with Germany. Even if at the time he had seemed excessively alarmist, in retrospect his warnings appear reasonable enough. In mid-decade he had warned of the threat of communist expansionism, not through war but through political subversion in war-torn countries. The reality behind this fear remains hotly debated by historians; some, at least, find the fear quite realistic and appropriate. By decade's end, Eisenhower's most vivid fears had taken a decidedly unrealistic turn. He spoke seriously and consistently of Harry Truman leading the nation, by 1956, to an irreversible descent into full-blown totalitarian state socialism. He was not alone.

In hindsight, one can only wonder how so many seemingly intelligent and perceptive people could have shared such a bizarre belief. As Republicans, of course, they could very easily see themselves as moderates, since so many Republicans to their right were hawking fears that the internal drift into socialism was being orchestrated in Moscow. The "war scare" fear heightened the right's growing fears of communist subversion. Eisenhower and his friends did not totally discount this fervent right-wing anticommunist view, but they gave it relatively little attention. In this sense they could assign themselves the "middle of the road." But this does not mitigate the unrealistic nature of their own deepest political fears. The anticommunist hysteria of the far right and the anti-federal-government hysteria of the "moderate" right were simply two different ways of creating a politics immune to reality testing.

The growing anticommunist hysteria does help to explain Eisenhower's shift from foreign to domestic fears. He had always prided himself on warning others of a danger that he was convinced most were ignoring. By 1948, as he would tell an audience soon after arriving at Columbia, it was "profitless . . . to talk too much about any threat that may come from without. Such threat as there is in the world today is plain to all to see."[43] If anything, the threat was felt too plainly, as the general's efforts to dampen war talk indicated. Yet he could hardly debunk the war scare completely, any more than he could continue to talk of reconciling differences with the Soviets. To do so would endanger not only the military budget, but also the revived hopes for his once-cherished project of Universal Military Training.

He resolved this dilemma by saying little at all about relations with the Soviet Union. He simply changed the subject. This allowed him to align more easily with the "moderate" Republican elite. They saw little profit in a war, but great political profit in a crusade to gain control of the federal government. They also saw profit in minimizing the most potent issue of their intra-party rivals, which was anti-communism. No longer a full-time official of the Truman administration, Eisenhower felt somewhat more free to join the ranks of the moderate Republicans, as long as he scrupulously maintained the appearance of being apolitical.

## THE COLUMBIA CONNECTION

If Eisenhower's political ambitions remain in doubt, there is no doubt that most of his new friends were actively promoting his candidacy. There is some reason to believe that he had been recruited to Columbia in part to keep him in the public limelight. But he had also been recruited because Columbia needed a popular leader to replace the aged Nicholas Murray Butler and revive its flagging fortunes. He knew this very well. As Robert Griffith says, "His job as president of Columbia was also, he believed, in large measure one of public relations. He was himself, by virtually every account, a master of the art." Most of all, Eisenhower believed, Columbia needed money. Here, too, he was "Alarmist Ike." "Unless we get this money business straightened out," he wrote to the dean of Barnard College, "disaster looms." Faced with disaster, he dreamed of perfection. He had a "dream for this institution's enlarging usefulness in this time of trouble and confusion," he told a public relations consultant. "If I could solve the money problems of the University," he wrote in his diary, "I would not only regard this as almost an ideal place, but I'd have great opportunity & time for personal study. But it's the nagging money problem that keeps me going always—including nights."[44]

There are different estimates of how much time and energy Eisenhower actually put into solving Columbia's problems. But it is clear that he saw Columbia through his typically apocalyptic lens; it was either utopia or disaster.

In a revealing letter to Swede Hazlett, he applied the same dualism to himself. He would have liked to give his sole attention to Columbia matters, he claimed, but there were so many other claims upon his attention. Sometimes he got so confused that he vented his frustration in irritated outbursts "directed at myself for allowing confusion and uncertainty to arise where system and serenity should prevail." These outbursts were sometimes mistaken for dissatisfaction with his job.[45]

Many of Eisenhower's personal relationships, particularly with his newer friends, were entwined with his fundraising activities. When the head of the alumni association cautioned him against this, he responded, "because of my constant preoccupation with the serious financial problems of the University, these problems seem to provide a never-changing backdrop for everything that I say and every action that I take." Consequently, he continued, his social life was always influenced by "the realization that the financial problem is still there."[46] As a university president, he would have to develop his relationships with the rich and offer them not only his personal fame and charisma, but some good reason for giving large sums to Columbia. Once again, he had to tell a story to serve a practical purpose.

One possibility was to continue the story he had been telling as chief of staff, to put Columbia forward as a primary bulwark against international communism. But that path was no longer appealing to Eisenhower; he had little new to say about it and perhaps wanted to say as little as possible. So he turned to another side of his ideological story, the domestic side, which had been only slightly developed. The letter to Amon Carter cited above, for example, decrying the "fuzz-minded liberals" and the drift toward socialism, was a fundraising letter meant to be circulated among potential donors. It stressed Columbia's commitment to "perpetuate our basic ideals for practice by our grandchildren" and warned that universities must "be alert in warning us against all the insidious ways in which freedom can be lost." But it closed with the bottom line: "We need material things—money."[47]

Carter passed the letter to Richard Simon, of Simon & Schuster. Thanking Simon for praising the letter (and sending a check), Eisenhower averred that his only ambition was to revive respect for basic truths that were "absolutely essential to the preservation of freedom in this country and, therefore, in the world. Without trying to scarehead the subject, I still think that there is discernible a trend toward the neglect of basic values and concepts in favor of immediate advantage and fancied safety."[48] Eisenhower wrote many such letters to wealthy potential donors around the country. He (and his aides) displayed a marked talent for telling them what they wanted to hear and "scareheading the subject" just enough to raise millions.

The main themes of these letters, and of Eisenhower's discourse as a whole, were summarized in a series of public letters to "alumni and friends" (read: potential donors) of Columbia. "There are two ways for a government to become a dictatorship; one is to slide into it, and the other is to be enslaved by a stronger military power. The United States must be vigilant against both dangers. It can remain free and can maintain the freedoms of the individual American, only if it trains succeeding generations of youth in more effective citizenship. That is a Columbia objective."[49] Indeed, he often proclaimed this to be Columbia's principal objective; and effective citizenship meant supporting and defending capitalism.

Columbia's president had not forgotten the rhetorical power of the themes he had developed in his previous job. Invoking his personal fame (and the popularity of his recently published war memoir), he alluded to World War II as "a crusade to preserve human rights. As we now realize, this crusade against oppression is not over. . . . At Columbia we are engaged in a crusade in the best sense of the word. . . . While democratic values are threatened by forces abroad and at home, Columbia is optimistic. We intend . . . to enable our children to have all the individual rights that we have enjoyed, necessarily including economic rights." Every school, he told the Columbia University Club, should teach the virtues of free enterprise and hold as its aim to "avoid the destruction of the free enterprise system." The implication was plain, if somewhat surprising: World War II, though ostensibly a crusade against fascism, had been primarily a crusade against the Marxist economic system.[50]

It would be unfair to suggest that Eisenhower developed this discursive line only as a fundraising ploy. If fundraising were the only concern, he might have chosen other lines that could have worked just as well, or better. But this particular line had the virtue of being consistent with all of his previous words as well as being appealing to potential donors. It certainly may have grown out of genuine conviction. (On one occasion, biographer Steve Neal reports, "Ike burst into a rage, a large vein on his forehead throbbing, as he said [speaking of Columbia's graduate students], 'Dammit, what good are exceptional physicists . . . exceptional anything, unless they are exceptional Americans.' He went on to say that every student who came to Columbia must leave it first a better citizen and secondarily a better scholar."[51]) In any event, Eisenhower had a strong sense of duty. Whatever job he took on, he wanted to do it well, whether it was invading Europe or raising money for Columbia. The success of this story in raising Columbia's fortunes must certainly have encouraged him to repeat it on every possible occasion. As president of Columbia, Eisenhower found—and made—many occasions to tell his story. This was perhaps the most fundamental continuity between his service as chief of staff and as university president.

## A CONVENIENT PLATFORM

Eisenhower went to Columbia with much more on his mind than fundraising. When he told Hazlett that he was merely changing his headquarters, he went on to explain the point in a brief sermon that began, "I believe fanatically in the American form of democracy." After outlining that form and declaring it the only basis for "world order," he concluded: "It is these simple conceptions that I will take to Columbia. If by living them and preaching them I can do some good I will hope to stay on indefinitely. I did not mean suddenly to become pontifical." But of course he did mean to become pontifical, or at least homiletical. By his own admission, preaching was one of his major goals at Columbia. As Peter Lyon says, "he fancied that Columbia would afford him a convenient platform from which he could exhort the nation." Lyon notes that when the trustees set out to lure him to Columbia, "the magic word to bring Eisenhower round was duty." Chief among those duties, as he saw it, was inspiration and motivation through the spoken word.[52]

At the outset of his Columbia tenure he assumed that his speeches would continue to follow the War Department (now Department of Defense) line. He would continue speaking largely about issues of national security and extend his range to broader foreign policy concerns. He told the new secretary of defense, James Forrestal, that his speech of 7 May 1948 was a good example of the general line he took in all public talks; he would promote the European Recovery Plan as part of a broader plan to enhance the national security. Then he asked Forrestal if the defense establishment would want him to emphasize any other topics. A few days later he told Forrestal that he would stop speaking altogether if Forrestal thought it best. Soon after, he told journalist Drew Middleton that he was now more free to speak his mind on foreign policy issues (though he was technically still a soldier and thus under some constraints).[53]

As it turned out, though, he used his new freedom more often to speak out on issues of domestic policy. He had entered the educational field "to be helpful in the perpetuation and enrichment of the American system," he told one correspondent. "Every University and the people in it have a continuing responsibility to assist in cultivating unswerving devotion to that system." This letter was typical of many. To an old friend from Abilene he wrote that he wanted to give students "the certainty that they are standing on a firm foundation and not merely whirling around in a state of complete mental confusion." This image may well have exaggerated the mental distress felt by young people in 1948. It did, however, sum up "Alarmist Ike's" view of the nation's—and perhaps his own—most basic problem: if civilization was battling the forces of chaos, the most dangerous form of chaos was confusion about values.[54]

As a university president he aimed to speak not just to students but to the entire nation. He told an old army friend, Gen. George Van Horn Moseley, that there were plenty of politicians promoting their own ambitions, but too few people "preaching such simple things as the love and preservation of freedom, both political and economic freedom. . . . It is because of my almost fanatical belief in the American system—that is in a capitalistic economy and a political republic— that I am occupying the job I now do and so frequently undertake tasks that would be otherwise distasteful. It is my ambition to see every American become consciously aware of these basic truths." He was "astonished" to learn that only fifty-seven percent of Americans thought capitalism essential to democracy. He took the connection as "axiomatic," and he aimed to convince all Americans likewise.[55]

The clamor for his presidential candidacy heightened his sense of the potential influence of his words. He knew that Republican leaders wanted him because he was electable; he knew that they used the word *duty* because it was the only appeal that might succeed, and he never denied that it might succeed. At least once he allowed himself to fantasize about "an American miracle . . . someone being named by common consent," rather than through the ordinary machinations of politics. Under this circumstance, he told Beetle Smith, he would deem it his duty to become president. It seems likely that he really did want this miracle to come to pass. "I must say," he confided in a diary entry on the presidency issue, "that, as of this moment, my imagination cannot conjure up any picture of emergency, disaster, or danger that would point irrevocably to me as the sole savior of the United States. Put that way, the thing sounds silly."[56]

Despite the tacked-on disclaimer, Eisenhower's imagination clearly was conjuring up just this picture. He had no trouble imagining the nation in a desperate emergency that might spell damnation. ("As of this moment" was written by a man extremely careful with the written word.) He also had plenty of encouragement to imagine himself the savior.[57] On occasion, it seems, he could not resist imagining himself as the first president since Washington to ascend the "bully pulpit" leading a unified nation on a crusade, not leading one political faction against another. His fantasy of becoming president by common consent would mean the fulfillment of his dream: unifying the nation under the umbrella of a universally shared value system, through the power of his own person and discourse. It would be the ultimate proof that his simple, clear message had ended the mental chaos threatening the United States and all of civilization.

All of Eisenhower's private reflections about his role point to the same basic premise: his unique public stature gave him a unique opportunity to lead the nation toward a unity based on common commitment to shared values. In his long diary rumination on politics and the presidency, he argued to himself that all Americans shared the same "basic tenets of Americanism," but many held them only unconsciously. His special field of work was "the bringing of these basic tenets to our CONSCIOUS attention." Since he was to be the great unifier, he could not identify publicly with either party. He would await the call of a unified people. As he told his predecessor at Columbia, Nicholas Murray Butler, he intended to work "to preserve our national life, if not civilization itself." He could imagine his preaching saving civilization not only by its content but by its simplicity and clarity, which would dispel the public's mental and axiological chaos.[58]

By June 1949, he was frustrated that his efforts were not bearing enough fruit, and he sought a way to be even more influential. He told Bernard Baruch that all of his speeches "emphasize one theme," which was the danger of "looking to the government for the cure of all social and economic ills." He was concerned, however, that his lone voice might be "shouting futilely and uselessly," so he asked Baruch's help in finding a way to be "more emphatic and effective."[59] Two days later he made a similar point at greater length to Arthur Page, head of the National Committee for Free Europe. This letter gives a particularly full picture of Eisenhower's understanding of his role as a public speaker, as well as his efforts to work out a rudimentary political-economic theory.

"There seems to be little question," he began, "that some 80% or 90% of what might be called the 'studious' public are aware of both the open and insidious attacks upon the average American's freedom of opportunity." But millions of workers were not very studious. In a free enterprise system "where people are rewarded unequally (if for no other reason than their differing contributions to society)," these workers compared themselves with their richer bosses (rather than workers in other countries) and felt dissatisfied. "Because there are always more workers than owners, it is easy to create a situation in which communistic seeds can grow. Always in our past we used this characteristic of our economic system [i.e., differential rewards] to spur the ambition of every human." The schools taught "that talent, energy, devotion to duty, and persistence would surely bring success." Now "many places decry or sneer at opportunity and merely scream 'injustice.'" Eisenhower wanted all schools to return to their former indoctrination. But a problem remained: "How to get the necessary lessons home to people who, for one reason or another, are not swayed by long and laborious argument based on logic. I rather think the issues will have to be sloganized" so that the arguments for capitalism would be "instantly and universally understood."[60]

Eisenhower was surely aware that he was sloganeering. While preparing a speech to launch the "Crusade for Freedom," he wrote to advertising executive Bruce Barton that speaking in praise of freedom was "something on the order of being against sin!" But he was also acutely aware of the power of slogans and platitudes, for he had been deploying them masterfully since the war's end. After a brief time of relative absence from the rostrum in the first months of 1948, he resumed his normal schedule of frequent speaking and continued it throughout his term at Columbia.[61]

He continued to complain about having to make so many speeches. He was "the victim of every organization that needs a top-flight drawing card," he lamented to Beetle Smith in the spring of 1949. "I am proof, fortunately still living, of the dangers of the so-called ptomaine circuit." A year later he was still complaining in his diary, "Public speaking gets to be more & more of a burden. . . . How I hate it!" But such complaints were another way to assure himself that he spoke not for selfish reasons, but solely out of obligation. "Life in New York seems to inflict upon me a series of defeats," he lamented to his brother Milton. "These consist in yielding always to the demands of things that I 'must' do rather than to personal desire." He complained especially bitterly when anyone accused him of speaking as a politician. In his own self-interpretation, it was absolutely crucial that he not be confused with politicians, who spoke for selfish reasons, not out of duty.[62]

The desire for a public pulpit was hardly his only, nor perhaps his principal, motivation for becoming president of Columbia. As he told Swede Hazlett: "There are dozens of different considerations that finally influenced me to say 'yes' to the Columbia Trustees."[63] But this particular consideration adds an important perspective to the study of his discourse. It reveals at least part of his frustration as chief of staff: he had felt unable to speak candidly about domestic issues and the economic values Americans should practice if they wanted to save civilization. In this sense, Eisenhower had indeed only moved his headquarters. He planned to continue telling a symbolic story that would offer a stable sense of meaning to the nation. He never separated his consciousness-raising as a national icon from his fundraising as a university president; since the story he wanted to use for both purposes was essentially the same, he saw no need to separate them. Implicitly, at least, he was saying that in his new pulpit he would continue, on behalf of

Columbia and the nation, the same battle that he had waged during World War II and as chief of staff. For those still unsure of the nature of that battle, he was inviting them to seek understanding from his public words and activities while president of Columbia.

## CHAPTER 9

# The Public Discourse

D uring his years at Columbia, Eisenhower told one story that reached far more Americans than any other. It was a story in the strict sense, the story of his experiences in World War II, published under the telling title, *Crusade in Europe*. He had written the memoir during his three-month hiatus between the Pentagon and Columbia; it was published in November 1948. For the next two years or more, when the book was a great bestseller, serialized in newspaper and television, it would constitute his primary impact on the public. It allowed him to tell his story of the war in much more detail and to a much wider audience than ever before. But the author left no doubt that he meant his recounting to shed light on the present and future as well as the past. So *Crusade* served as the capstone to his storytelling career as C/S. At the same time, it initiated his new career as a university president and civilian spokesman for liberal international-ism and what he termed the political "middle way." It was the most successful of his efforts to speak to the entire U.S. public. During his Columbia years, what-ever he said and did would be received within the context created by the book. A close analysis will show that the book was very much in line with the program of public consciousness-raising that his private discourse announced.

## CRUSADE IN EUROPE

*Crusade* stated its theme in its very first pages. "Two miracles" had enabled the Allies to gain unconditional victory. First, the United States had undergone a "rev-olutionary transformation" from weakness to preeminence. It had started out in "appalling danger" from its "almost complete military weakness," due to public complacency and competing views of "what was demanded of us." But once Pearl Harbor "converted the issue into a struggle for survival . . . each began, step by step, to learn and to perform his allotted task." By war's end, the United States had achieved "astounding strength and effectiveness." The second miracle was the development of "near perfection in allied conduct of war operations," made possible only by "voluntary co-operation . . . concessions voluntarily made." As Martin Medhurst notes, the theme of cooperation "would run throughout the 478 pages of *Crusade in Europe* and be linked with such related terms as unity, teamwork, allies, and partnership." Eisenhower clearly wanted average Americans to feel that each had made a significant contribution to the victory by performing his "allotted task." Yet his narrative said little of the specific contributions of the average American (he had no direct experience of civilian life during the war, of course), and his references to the role of the average soldier were relatively cursory.[1]

His theme was embodied principally in a story of outstanding military leaders. These were the people with whom he had spent virtually all his time during the war. In his book, as in his ideological framework, they become symbols of all that was best about the United States and Western civilization. Above all, he told a tale of clear-sighted, highly rational, selfless officers who used these virtues to create an amazingly efficient military machine. When conflicts arose among them, they set aside selfish concerns in favor of the common good. Thus every conflict was resolved, and the team, working smoothly together, moved inexorably toward total victory. These leaders did what storybook heroes do—solved seemingly impossible problems and overcame seemingly insurmountable obstacles—because of their exemplary virtue. They were the ones who rescued America from appalling danger by their nearly perfect voluntary cooperation. They were models that every American would be well advised to emulate in an era of cold war.[2]

The structure of the book left no doubt that it was meant to be a lesson for the emerging cold war. The chronological narrative, ending with "Victory's Aftermath," was followed by a chapter titled "Operation Study." Here the reader learned the lessons of the war, which turned out to be the stock themes of the author's postwar discourse: the global scope of war and peace, the need for industrial mobilization and military preparedness in peacetime, the need for teamwork among both the military services and the allied nations (especially the United States and Britain), the crucial role of morale and optimism, and the need for universal sacrifice. The atomic bomb had created a new era of warfare, in which air power was the key to military success. But public morale was still the winning weapon. A democracy could be as brave and productive as a dictatorship if its citizens had inspiring leaders to encourage them by giving them a clear idea of their nation's values and the justice of its demands upon them.[3]

The author himself expanded on these lessons at a publisher's event to celebrate the publication. It would be "useless and a mistake" to write the book, he told the audience, if it did not contain "a few lessons to apply to the future." The most basic lesson was the need for teamwork and "one common purpose" in order to achieve victory. That purpose, he continued, was the protection of democracy, the "political expression of a deep and abiding religion," against the state. "We believe [man] has a soul. It is that simple." An America unified by belief in "a Great God" could solve all domestic and international problems. No global war was "on the immediate horizon," he said. But if another war broke out, the United States would win and come out "with democratic concepts clear and unsullied."[4] Neither the religious framework nor the confidence in post–World-War-III democracy was reflected in the book itself.

## RUSSIA

It was clear that the book was designed to inspire the nation to wage cold war, as contemporaries recognized.[5] Lest anyone be left in doubt, Eisenhower concluded his work with a chapter simply entitled "Russia." Here he faced the delicate task of raising enough, but not too much, alarm. He had to cry out the continuing danger and call the nation to continuing struggle in defense of freedom. This had been the moral of his story since May 1945. His story still had to have a moral—the war still had to be made meaningful—and he could hardly adopt a new ending now. He knew, too, that the military was still struggling to get the resources it thought necessary to prevent Soviet gains. Like all his colleagues, he insisted that the United States was woefully unprepared for deterrence or another war. He wanted military unification, reinstatement of the draft and, most important, a bigger military budget. To many, it seemed that the only way to achieve those things was to promote a fear of imminent war.

That fear arrived, full force, just as Eisenhower was in the midst of writing his memoir. The war scare, triggered by the fall of the Czechoslovak government, was the dominant public context in which he worked. Now he had to fear not only complacency on military matters but also its opposite. To maintain his "middle way," he had to conclude his story of World War II with words that would keep up the popular enthusiasm for a cold war and increased military strength yet restrain the impulse to use that strength.

The result was an ambiguous picture of the Soviet Union, its leaders, and its intentions. The chances for cooperation at the war's end were very high, he recalled, as well they should have been, since the ordinary Russian "seems to me to bear a marked similarity to what we call an 'average American.'"[6] He wrote at length about his warm relations in the early postwar months with Soviet leaders, including Stalin and especially Zhukov. These were not people whom anyone would want to annihilate in an atomic slaughter. Rather, the author said, it was perfectly possible for the Soviet and American systems to coexist, as long as each did not trespass against the other.

There remained a fundamental gulf between the two sides, however. Cooperation with the Soviets had never been too good, even during the war, he claimed; had the Soviets been more a part of the team, the peace would now be more secure. After the war's end, Zhukov was stifled by excessive state control, and his personal friendliness was not matched by other Soviet officials. As time went on, relations worsened for some reason that was unexplained and "may possibly never be clearly understood by any of us." Eisenhower carefully refrained from placing all the blame on the Soviet side. The Soviets were wholly misguided at present, he implied, but not wholly irredeemable.[7]

Yet the very title of the book left no doubt that it was too late for compromise. Eisenhower explained the title in describing his refusal to shake hands with a captured German general. Now, as then, he implied, the time for diplomacy and mutual reconciliation had passed. Now, as then, absolute good was pitted against absolute evil; as always in such situations, the good had to launch a crusade to vanquish the evil.[8] He explicitly equated the situation of 1948 with 1938. The great danger was still diplomacy, which could easily become appeasement. Only moral rectitude, economic power, and military strength could save the day, he insisted.

Most important, though, the United States would have to "annul Communist appeals to the hungry, the poor, the oppressed, with practical measure untiringly prosecuted for the elimination of social and economic evils that set men against men." Here was a scarcely veiled appeal to follow the path named for the author's revered mentor, George Marshall. Eisenhower shared Marshall's fear that an excessively belligerent U.S. stance might trigger war.[9] The Marshall Plan, he argued, was the route to solidifying the U.S.-led Western alliance, which was in turn the only route to winning the cold war while avoiding hot war. In addition, the Marshall Plan suggested that, just as the once-heinous Germany was being incorporated into the U.S.-led world order, so might the now-heinous Soviet Union some day be forced to follow suit. In a broader sense, Eisenhower was urging the public to make the capitalist system work well enough to meet the basic needs of all people, thus demonstrating its superiority to its ideological rival.

Eisenhower closed his memoir on an eschatological note, with a plea for the kind of internationalism that won the war. There was plenty of reason to be alarmed, he suggested, but ultimately no reason to fear. If all Americans performed their allotted tasks with "the moral integrity, the clarity of comprehension, and the readiness to sacrifice that finally crushed the Axis, then the free world will live and prosper, and all peoples, eventually, will reach a level of culture, contentment, and security that has never before been achieved."[10] Rapprochement was no longer possible. But some day the cold war would be won, the Soviet people would become part of the "free world," and capitalism would be forever free from any threatening alternative.

Whatever Eisenhower said and did as a civilian, he would be associated with his story of World War II. But the story had now changed in a subtle yet profound way. The closing sentence contained the only implicit reference to world peace in the entire book; even there, he spoke of "security," avoiding the word *peace.* He was telling a story of a bitter and unfinished ideological struggle whose goal was not so much world peace as simply victory. He was applying the paradigm of World War II to the cold war: a seemingly irrational enemy was threatening civilization, for no comprehensible reason, and the conflict would have to be fought through to unconditional surrender. (The image of World War II as an anticommunist crusade would come later.) He acknowledged that he no longer needed to persuade the nation to wage the struggle and pursue victory, but he did need to persuade the nation to pursue it with a minimal risk of massive bloodshed. Since the battle was over values, he argued, it would be won by the side that exemplified superior values in its method of fighting.

When he had an opportunity to write for the *Reader's Digest,* and reach even more readers than he could with his book, he took for his theme not the struggle against the Soviet Union but the value of education. In "An Open Letter to America's Students," he told young people that the war had been won not by a few leaders (as readers of *Crusade in Europe* might assume), but by millions of Americans of all ranks acting, "if for only a few minutes in some desperate crisis," as leaders. He called on all students to prepare for their moments of crisis by learning the virtues of leadership: "audacity, initiative, the will to try greatly." These virtues would keep free enterprise alive and avert the "needless concentration of power [that] is a menace to freedom." His "Open Letter to Parents" began by reprising the theme of the unfinished war, inviting all readers to see themselves as "veterans of a war in which freedom and free government were at stake. Our victory, won at staggering cost, will not be thoroughly consolidated until we, and our children and grandchildren, know the manifold ways in which freedom is still subject to attack and are equipped mentally, spiritually and physically to defeat every threat. Such fullness of knowledge and of able readiness is a direct function of education."[11]

The message from this pair of articles was clear. The primary purpose of war, and of education, was to defend the value system undergirding capitalism. The great threat to capitalism, unheeded by the public, was no longer centered in central Europe or anywhere abroad, but in every city, town, and school of the United States. This, the message delivered between the lines of his memoir, would be the clearly spoken message of his public discourse as president of Columbia.[12]

## THE PUBLIC STORY

In 1955, when asked about the finest speeches of his career, Eisenhower named only one from his tenure at Columbia. It was a Labor Day address to the American Bar Association on 5 September 1949.[13] At the speaker's own suggestion, this speech can be taken as a useful precis of the public story he chose to tell during the Columbia years. It began by delineating *"three fundamental principles* of American life":

> *First,* that individual freedom is our most precious possession . . . and the central target of all enemies—internal and external—who seek to weaken or destroy the American Republic.

> *Second,* that all our freedoms . . . to buy, to work, to hire, to bargain, to save, to vote, to worship, to gather . . . are a single bundle. . . . Destruction of any inevitably leads to the destruction of all.

> *Third,* that freedom to compete vigorously among ourselves, accompanied by a readiness to cooperate wholeheartedly for the performance of community and national functions, together make our system the most productive on earth.

> These three principles express the common faith of loyal Americans. . . . The middle of the road between the unfettered power of concentrated wealth on one flank, and the unbridled power of statism or partisan interest on the other. Our agreement in these three great fundamentals provides the setting within which can always be composed any acute difference.[14]

Here were most of the themes that dominated Eisenhower's public story from 1948 through 1950. They were the same themes that dominated the private discourse. Indeed, the public language often developed his theoretical framework in more detail than the private. In this time period there would be no significant difference between public and private discourse, as there had been when he was chief of staff.

Although there would be no major departure in these years from the theoretical foundations he had developed as C/S, new elements and new emphases gave a different tone to the whole. Now he put more stress on the internal rather than the external threats to individual freedom. All freedoms were still tied together, but the paramount freedom was economic in nature (the first five of his eight enumerated freedoms were economic).[15] A competitive free enterprise system was the essential value to be saved, for it was the crucial link between maximum freedom of every kind and maximum national productivity. It could be saved only if individual acquisitiveness were mitigated by cooperation for the common good; with good will, cooperation could solve every problem. This was Eisenhower's famous "middle way."

On either side lay the fearful "isms." On the right, the danger was domination by the rich few; on the left, domination by the state. But the rest of the lengthy text of the Bar Association speech gave the two dangers rather unequal treatment. The "ism" of the right remained curiously unnamed, although only four years had passed since the end of the great crusade against fascism. And it remained curiously unexamined.[16] Virtually the whole speech was given to an attack on the left and its "shibboleth of an unbridgeable gap between those who hire and those who are employed." Eisenhower insisted at length that every "intelligent, educated and energetic working man in America" could go virtually as far as his talents and energy would take him. Nearly all American workers knew this and enthusiastically supported capitalism, he averred. Workers and bosses cooperated, each wanting the best for the other, because they recognized that "the interests of labor and management in most situations are identical"; all had "common social purpose, common economic attitude, and, above all, identical aspirations." Thus they gave the lie to the Marxist premise of inevitable class conflict.[17]

Lest he sound too optimistic, Eisenhower reminded his audience that "selfishness and cupidity—the source of those errors—will never be wholly eradicated from within us." He did not fear the selfishness of those who took "the middle way," for that was the way of self-control. But the burden of his speech was to bolster the will of the audience to fight off attacks from the right and, more particularly, from the left. "Alarmist Ike" was ever ready to portray the dire consequences of failure. "Soon only the specious promises of the extreme Right and the extreme Left may make themselves heard," he warned. "When the center weakens piecemeal, disintegration and annihilation are only steps away. . . . Bureaucratic plans, enforced on both [labor and management] by government, pave the way to despotism." If the nation followed politicians who "falsely declare that only government can bring us happiness, security and opportunity" and offer "crackpot fantasies of reward without effort, harvests without planting," it would soon find both its productivity and its freedom destroyed by stifling government controls.

In his conclusion, Eisenhower advised the lawyers to "clean out the ambush of catchwords, tags and labels in which the plain citizen, including the old soldier, is trapped every time he considers today's problems. How can we appraise a proposal if the terms hurled at our ears can mean anything or nothing? . . . If our attitudes are muddled, our language is often to blame." This was a rare and startling public admission that he himself, an old soldier, was caught in a confusion of catchwords and labels that could mean anything or nothing. As he did so often, though, he depicted himself as a victim of nefarious forces. He did not take the obvious next step and admit his complicity in the problem.

A careful analytical listener would have grasped the point quickly enough. Eisenhower's seemingly logical arguments were built out of appealing catchwords such as *individual, freedom, opportunity, cooperation,* and scare words such as *extremism, statism, bureaucrat.* These terms functioned as virtual synonyms. Any of the "good" words could be substituted for any other, for each was a synechdochical representation of the "American system" and all its virtues. The "bad" words were virtually synonyms, too, for each served to denote all that opposed the "American system." The specific meaning of each term, as well as the logical relations among them, was only loosely examined. But Eisenhower's speeches were never meant to clarify issues for analytical listeners. They made their impact by the force of their rhetorical emotion (and the speaker's fame), not the force of their logic. "Eisenhower became an embodiment of the force of personal persuasion," as Richard Crable puts it. "As astute observers of the period concluded, his messages did not need to stress content and details because Ike was the message."[18]

Historian Travis Beal Jacobs says, "In mid-twentieth-century America no other public figure expressed such a fervent interest in citizenship in a liberal democratic society."[19] His fervor was intended to confirm and deepen cold war emotions by pitting absolute right against absolute wrong, with no middle ground allowed. To this end, he constructed a rhetorical world of irreconcilable polar opposites, a world in which the urgent task was not to think carefully but to choose sides, to fight, and to win. Here was no subtle nuance, but the simplicity of a preacher identifying a devil and declaring a crusade against it. The result could only be that his own attitudes, and those of audiences he influenced, would be even further muddled.

Commemorating Columbia's John Dewey, Eisenhower underscored his own dualism (while co-opting the famous progressive educator as a symbol of conservative politics): "We are rapidly approaching a split in the road. Are we going to bow our heads to centralized government or be free to follow John Dewey's 'freedom to learn'?" In another of his most important addresses, on the occasion of his installation as president of Columbia, he announced at the outset: "In today's struggle, no free man, no free institution can be neutral."[20]

## "YOUR HUNS AND VANDALS"

As he described "today's struggle" in his many speeches, Eisenhower called for continuing war against the Soviet threat. But he entwined that call with his new focus on the less obvious danger at home. The threat of communism abroad was now "easy to recognize," he said at his Columbia installation, as was the threat of Moscow-directed subversion at home. "Less easy is it to see the dangers that arise from our own failure to analyze and understand the implications of various economic, social and political movements among ourselves."[21] In a public letter to a congressman, which stirred some controversy, he went even further: "I firmly believe that the army of persons who urge greater and greater centralization of authority and greater and greater dependence upon the Federal Treasury are really more dangerous to our form of government than any external threat."[22] This less visible but more potent danger was now "Alarmist Ike's" great theme. He had ascended the national pulpit to offer a description of the domestic political-economic scene that would lay bare the unseen danger.

The Columbia inaugural address, given in a national media spotlight, offered a prime opportunity to explain those dangers. It built upon the new president's rudimentary social theory: "The society must be stable, assured against violent upheaval and revolution; otherwise it is nothing but a temporary truce with chaos." These were the two choices: either a merely transient protection from chaos or the permanent protection known as "stability." He continued, "But freedom for the individual must never degenerate into [the] brutish struggle for survival that we call barbarism. Neither must the stability of society ever degenerate into the enchained servitude of the masses that we call statism." These were the familiar twin forms of chaos, one the raw form of chaotic barbarism and the other its excessive countermeasure. Only the "middle way" of individualism tempered by cooperation could steer the narrow path between them and lead onto the broad plain of "stability . . . the fullness of orderly, civilized life."[23]

The barbarism of the wholly unregulated marketplace was only briefly addressed in the inaugural address. And it turned out that the real danger came not from the predatory rich but from the victimized poor: "Extremes of wealth for a few and enduring poverty for many [would] create social explosiveness and a demand for revolutionary change." Perhaps the speaker wanted to suggest this as a genuine threat; perhaps he was simply signaling that he did not want to see the New Deal safety net entirely dismantled. It was hard to tell, because he spoke principally in catchwords, carefully avoiding specific policy issues.

His catchwords were clearly aimed primarily at President Truman and other Democrats who would expand the New Deal's buffers against poverty. As chief of staff, with Truman as his commander in chief, he had never directly warned of the dangers of "statism." Now he felt free to do so (though he still never attacked Truman or the Democrats explicitly by name).[24] The main problem with government programs was not, as so many claimed, their "historic inefficiency." It was their threat to individual initiative: "A paternalistic government can gradually destroy by suffocation in the immediate advantage of subsidy, the will of a people to maintain a high degree of individual responsibility." Without the profit motive, "all rights would soon disappear." When critics of capitalism issued "demagogic appeals to class hate . . . [they] would lead to the extinction of our democratic form of government . . . either civilization or liberty must perish." The United States might be "as fearfully plundered and laid waste by barbarians in the twentieth century as the Roman Empire was in the fifth. . . . Your Huns and Vandals will have been engendered within your own country by your own institutions."[25] The peril from both forms of excess, barbarism and regimentation, was clearly assigned to the Democrats and the liberals. They now represented the primary agents of the chaos against which Eisenhower still called the nation to battle. This left the Republicans as the only champions of the order and stability of "the middle way."

In a speech at IBM he fleshed out his dystopian vision. If the government, or "a particularly small group of individuals," owned all the property, all economic functions would become one "tremendous, staggering business." In order to make it a success, the rulers would have to bar strikes and freedom of the press, and eventually all individual freedoms would disappear.[26] Thus individuals would lose the inherent rights that all possessed simply because they had divinely created souls. "To prove that, ladies and gentlemen, we must go back and depend upon faith and faith alone, and I say it is a faith akin to religion, to most of us, Christianity." Such an explicit linking of Christianity and capitalism was rare in Eisenhower's discourse, but it was understandable given that the logic and problematic of his public and private discourse still rested on assumptions about human nature that were deeply rooted in Christian traditions.[27]

All of his conclusions could have been argued from strictly secular premises. But he never took this route. He assumed selfishness as both the prime motivator and the primary danger of human life, causing an inevitable conflict between self-indulgence and self-restraint. He consistently relied on his apocalyptic worldview to explain why capitalism was the most productive system; why workers should embrace capitalism; why socialism would lead to totalitarianism; why self-indulgence would lead to anarchy; why revolution posed a grave threat; why emotion was dangerous; and why the only alternative to voluntary self-discipline was barbarism or dictatorship. He assumed that human beings were superior to other animals only because they had divine souls. Otherwise, he asked one audience, why not treat humans and mules on the same footing, as the Marxists did, all "harnessed to the plough, whipped and goaded to work"?[28]

## "CAVIAR AND CHAMPAGNE"

The great danger now was that Americans would forsake their spiritual values and choose to be treated like mules: "Too often, today, we incline to describe the ultimate in human welfare as a mule's sort of heaven—a tight roof overhead, plenty of food, a minimum of work and no worries or responsibilities. So far have we strayed from our sense of values."[29] The only way to reclaim spiritual values was to reject every hint of socialism within the United States. The life of hard work, responsibilities, and worries was the true life of the spirit.

Eisenhower sometimes called the nation to this spiritual life by conjuring up a clear, satisfying image of eternal verities learned in his childhood. This was a powerful rhetorical technique. He would draw a vivid contrast between a spiritual past and the materialist present, then project the discouraging picture into a dystopian future of totalitarianism. Addressing a group of high school students he could not resist "the temptation to reminisce":

> In those days we didn't hear so much about the word security, personal security through life from cradle to the grave, some kind of assurance that we were not going to have to go out with a tin cup or sell apples on the streets. But there was constantly around us the right and the opportunity to go out and do better for ourselves. . . . If we allow this constant drift toward centralized bureaucratic government to continue . . . there'll be a swarming of bureaucrats over the land. Ownership of property will gradually drift into that central government and

finally you have to have dictatorship as the only means of operating such a huge and great organization."[30]

Toward the end of 1949 he revived this theme in a pointed attack on what he saw as a growing trend toward self-indulgence. Americans had "lost some respect for mere thrift and independence," he proclaimed. "Maybe we like caviar and champagne when we ought to be out working on beer and hot dogs."[31] A few days later he reminded an audience of the three principles of freedom from his ABA speech, and then added: "Maintain that sort of freedom and we will have security, true security—not the slothful indolence and ease and stagnation that is the lot of those who abandon freedom to become the slaves of others." The next day he again warned against the false kind of security: "If all you got out of life is security, if that is all you want, why not commit some kind of offense that will put you in prison? You will never have to worry." He urged people to eschew safety, to take risks, to make sacrifices, not only for their personal advantage but also for the good of the nation. "True security" meant the ensured survival of the American way of life, a way inherently full of risk. "Life is certainly worthwhile only as it represents struggle for worthy causes, and there is no struggle in perfect security," he had told Columbia students a few months earlier (adding here, too, that "perfect security" would be "a lifetime in a federal prison"). Risks (and, presumably, the failures that they sometimes engendered) were essential to maintain the American system as he understood it.[32]

This set of speeches evoked some outcry. They obviously caricatured the New Deal in a pejorative way. Commentators such as labor journalist James G. Crowley found it ironic and "indecent" that General Eisenhower, of all people, would urge others to eschew the safety of government funding for the risks of the marketplace. Crowley pointed out that the general had gone to West Point to obtain a government-paid education, had lived his whole adult life on a government paycheck, and was still receiving a very handsome government salary and expense account in addition to his salary from Columbia.[33] As many biographers have noted, this money did not make Eisenhower really rich (though it made him quite comfortable). His rapidly growing coterie of immensely rich friends, however, offered him a lavish lifestyle far beyond his own means. He knew that he would never want for anything.

There is no evidence that Eisenhower was aware of this irony, nor that he chose his friends in order to gain the comforts they could provide. He saw both himself and his friends as risk-takers, and he offered them as outstanding examples of the benefits the American system offered to risk-takers. To most American workers, though, they seemed to have a security unimaginable for the average person, as they took their ease amidst caviar and champagne. Always sensitive to criticism, Eisenhower soon complained to his brother Milton, "I grow very, very weary of the whole business. I am about to blow up."[34] He was apparently most anguished not by the charges of hypocrisy or insensitivity, but by the charge that he chose these words for political effect and thus revealed himself as an undeclared candidate for president. For whatever reason, he ceased public speaking for a time, and he stopped charging that ordinary workers were living in luxury. But the sentiment remained central to the public rhetoric.

As Blanche Wiesen Cook writes, "Eisenhower tended to regard workers much the same way as he regarded troops in wartime: They had a job to do for the good of the nation." Their job now was to risk not their lives but their guarantees of minimal material comfort. The willingness to hazard poverty would protect the system against internal collapse simply by embodying, and thus perpetuating, the system. It would be the most important evidence in peacetime of the self-discipline and self-sacrifice needed to defend the system against its enemies, foreign and domestic. He encouraged the students at Columbia to think of themselves as troops too. The military existed to protect a way of life through sacrifice and death, he told one student gathering. Now all citizens had the same responsibility. If the young people wanted a better standard of living or "a better anything, then each of us has the responsibility to defend with his life the liberty and the rights that have brought all this about." He proposed to the editor of *Reader's Digest* a series of articles by Columbia faculty on a single theme: "courage of a high order and unique character is required of the average American today if he is to resist and eventually to defeat those who would lead him to surrender his freedom as an individual in exchange for a servile security." As *Crusade in Europe* implied, the values of the successful warrior now had to be practiced on the home front; the crusade had to be brought home.[35]

For Eisenhower this crusade, like every crusade, was about defending the fragile forces of good against implacable evil. Although he generally avoided the explicit language of a continuing war, his discourse at Columbia was built on the link between fighting wars and feeling beset by danger on every side. War and danger implied each other, and he was always ready to enlist audiences in his crusade by preaching impending danger. "The impact on us of every international fact and crisis is immediate. We are seldom free from anxiety as each day's events crowd instantly upon our attention," he told the Columbia graduating class of 1949. "False teachers, who magnify acknowledged errors in the practice of democracy, attempt to destroy our faith in man's right to self-government. . . .

Millions of us, today, seem to fear that individual freedom is leading us toward social chaos; that individual opportunity has forever disappeared; that no person can have rightful title to property. . . . To these fearful men, the free human individual is a social anachronism."[36]

The university's president immediately protested, "On every count the fearful men are wrong." But he had offered a catalogue of the very fears he himself was disseminating throughout the land at every opportunity. He could represent these fears so convincingly to his audience because, despite his protestations of optimism, they were the foundation and central axis of his discourse. "The American Dream may become the American Nightmare," he warned the *New York Herald Tribune* Forum. "Today, internally and externally, our affairs seem framed in an unending series of crises. . . . More and more bureaus, more and more taxes, fewer and fewer producers; the final result is financial collapse and the end of freedom."[37]

Even when he urged optimism, he sometimes fell back into an absolute dualism that ended up reinforcing the fears he ostensibly discounted. For example, he told an IBM audience: "There is a growing doubt among our people that democracy is able to cope with the social and economic trials that lie ahead. . . . Unless such fear is banished from our thinking, the sequel will be either the heavy curse of tyrannical regimentation or the collapse of our democracy civilization in social anarchy." Despite his clear understanding of the dangers of excessive fear, the structure of his discourse drove him again and again to speak as "Alarmist Ike." Yet he never acknowledged that his own fear-laden language might be part of the nation's problem. He spoke as one convinced that his own analyses were the product of calm, objective perception. He assumed that he was offering not too much, but just the right amount, of fear and alarm. This was one more application of his philosophy of "the middle way."

## THE MIDDLE WAY

Eisenhower assumed that selfishness was the source of anarchy, regimentation, and extremism of every kind. Its opposite was always sober, reasoned, self-restrained moderation. One had only to find the rational mean between the extremes, and there lay "the middle way," the key to stability. By pitting the middle against the extremes, Eisenhower's discourse could maintain its fundamental bipolar structure, yet at the same time mask that structure behind a facade of moderation and compromise. So he called for a middle way to balance individual freedom against government control, military strength against fiscal economy, pessimism against optimism, fear against hope, etc.

"The middle way" was a fantasy of perfect rationality, perfect balance, and therefore of perfect control. Eisenhower had to argue that there was value in both elements of every pair of opposites, as long as each was taken in moderation, while there was danger in each element if taken to excess. Thus no one of these elements should be abolished. Rather all should be controlled rationally. This meant finding and implementing precisely the most rational amount of each. The same procedure held for both tangible behavior (taxation, building aircraft carriers, etc.) and intangible feelings such as hope and fear. The wise society would control all, under the guidance of well-informed, rational leaders. Even on the most fundamental polarity, selfishness against self-restraint, he had to advocate controlled exercise of both (since capitalism depended on a sizeable dose of selfishness). So the optimal levels of selfishness and self-restraint would have to be determined. His discourse could allow no room for ambiguity on this most crucial question.

More than once, however, he acknowledged that he did not know exactly how to define the delicate balance. In a major speech, he told the *New York Herald Tribune* Forum that "it may be impossible for any individual to define accurately the line dividing governmental and individual responsibility." The dividing line between government authority and individual freedom "never is completely fixed; never is static. It oscillates constantly, in a middle area."[38]

There was an interesting example of this conceptual confusion in October 1948, when Eisenhower was briefly fascinated by the idea that "each man and each woman is the center of the universe . . . because all the world is known to him only by its reactions upon him." He made this point in a speech at the Riverdale School, to explain why every person is inevitably selfish. But in his "Open Letter to America's Students," published that same month, he turned the same idea into an essential virtue: "If your generation fails to understand that the human individual is still the center of the universe and is still the sole reason for the existence of all man-made institutions, then complexity will become chaos." This was the prelude to a typical Eisenhower sermon on the virtues of free enterprise and the dangers of governmental control. Only a dictatorship, the political fruit of excessive selfishness, would deny that the individual is the center of the universe. To compound the confusion, the article concluded that being a good American meant "placing the common good before personal profit," which might sound to some like a socialist principle.[39]

Eisenhower argued along the way that there was really no contradiction to be resolved: "Never forget that self-interest and patriotism go together. You have to look out for yourself, and you have to look out for your country. . . . They are partners." He illustrated the point by mentioning the millions of poor in U.S. cities who demand more security. "If they feel too insecure, their discontent might some day undermine your security, no matter how personally successful you might be."[40] This was a plausible (if somewhat crass) way to dispose of the conflict between self and society, and he might have been expected to focus on this theme in the coming years. In fact, though, he mentioned it only occasionally. He was far more likely to place an unavoidable need for government and a demand for maximum individual freedom side by side, without trying to resolve the contradiction.

The one tangible product of this confusion was Eisenhower's proudest achievement at Columbia—the founding of the American Assembly. The idea, he told potential donors, was an ongoing series of conferences bringing together leading figures from academia and every other walk of life to explore issues of vital public concern. The ultimate goal was to answer "one of the most vital questions" of the day: 'What is the proper dividing line between the responsibilities and rights of the individual on the one hand, and the necessary controls of the central government on the other hand?' This must be answered. Soon!" Here was another opportunity for Eisenhower to warn the world of a danger he had foreseen long ago: "When I came out of World War II, I had a profound conviction that America was in danger for two reasons: (1) The Communist threat from without. (2) The failure of most of us to remember that the basic values of democracy were won only through sacrifice and to recognize the dangers of indifference and ignorance." Now "millions of our citizens" feared that "we shall destroy our competitive economy and therefore lose individual freedom." The public needed to understand "the political experiments constantly urged upon us, if American democracy is to survive." The American Assembly would be a step in this direction, he implied, because it would define the "middle way" in objectively logical terms, free from bias, and thus provide a program that could unite the United States and, eventually, the whole "free world."[41]

The American Assembly grew out of Eisenhower's refusal to accept the ambiguity that he told the *Herald Tribune* Forum was unavoidable. It grew, too, out of his vision of education as a servant of larger national interests, especially the interest of saving capitalism from its purported enemies. Of course there was also obvious benefit to Columbia in having so many wealthy and powerful elites enter through its gates, even if only for a few days. The assembly also allowed Eisenhower to steer Columbia's resources in the direction he wanted the university to take, despite serious resistance from much of the faculty.[42] Yet as he explained the need for the American Assembly he suggested that the problem it aimed to solve might be insoluble, which meant that the goal he set for himself, Columbia, and the nation—a clearly defined value structure shared by all—might be unattainable. For a leader who needed to provide (and desperately wanted) clear, simple definitions of right and wrong, this might be the most alarming danger of all.

## CHAPTER 10

# The Meaning of Peace

I n his years at Columbia, as during his years as chief of staff, Eisenhower virtually never raised the topic of peace voluntarily in his private discourse.
When he discussed peace, it was always in response to someone else who had
raised the issue, or in connection with Columbia fundraising.

## PEACE IN THE PRIVATE DISCOURSE

"The world can never be assured of peaceful settlement of its problems until
there is sufficient power and authority centered into some single world federation to enforce conciliation and peaceful adjustment of difficulties." Eisenhower
wrote these words to his friend Aksel Nielsen, in response to press reports that
he had joined the World Federalists. He had not joined that group, he assured
Nielsen. In a letter to another correspondent he explained why: "Eventually there
must be some type of federated control if there is to be world-wide confidence in
peace . . . [but] the world is not *now* ready for such a development. . . . This will
continue so long as the two-world pattern exists." Two important assumptions
were revealed in these letters. First, a world federation would have to be based on
a single political-economic system, as he had always maintained. Second, even if
such a system were established, it would inevitably face resistance and need to
enforce its dictates. Civilization would always be challenged by chaotic forces, and
it would have to be prepared to use force to keep chaos at bay.[1]

Eisenhower was also drawn to talk about peace, at least tangentially, by his
work with the Council of Foreign Relations study group he chaired. In the spring
of 1949 he initiated a statement by the group recommending that the new NATO
organization become the prototype for a series of such alliances spanning the globe.
He urged the Truman administration to issue "a flat warning that aggression in any
form, in any part of the world, will always be considered as 'dangerous to our [U.S.]

peace and safety.' This is the language of James Monroe, and we believe that it now applies to the whole world."[2] This made explicit what had long been implicit in his discourse: if a peaceful nation meant a nation permanently stabilized and secure against chaos, then chaos anywhere would be a threat to the nation's peace. Peace required vigilance that was spatially as well as temporally without end.

Other references to peace were embedded in fundraising letters. Touting the university's new nutrition center, he wrote that he had become president of Columbia because he believed education was the surest path to world peace. The nutrition center would explore ways of "lessening those economic tensions that gradually build into wars and make it more and more difficult for individual freedom to survive in the world."[3] In other words, if capitalism could find ways to feed more people more cheaply, it could better withstand the challenge of Marxist alternatives. Those alternatives, as the current embodiment of chaos, might never be wholly eliminated. But only when they were permanently contained would world federation and peace be possible.

Another project at Columbia gave a major boost to Eisenhower's reputation as a seeker of peace: the Institute of War and Peace Studies. "I think it almost incomprehensible," he told a potential fundraiser, "that no American university has undertaken the continuous study of the causes, conduct and consequences of war—the greatest ill to which our civilization is heir."[4] Here seemed to be clear evidence of the general's continuing desire to promote peace.

In fact, though, the institute as Eisenhower conceived it was much more about war than peace. It began as a way to save the American Military Institute (AMI), publisher of the journal *Military Affairs*. AMI was a private organization that had received funds from the army, until the funds were cut off in October 1949. Its chief fundraiser, Edwin Clark, interested Eisenhower in linking the institute with Columbia. By early 1950, negotiations were under way to alleviate the institute's financial difficulties by bringing it under the auspices of Columbia. Eisenhower met with the history department to encourage its interest in the then-novel field of military history. By early March Eisenhower met with Ed Bermingham and Douglas Dillon to plan serious fundraising efforts. Inviting Bermingham to the meeting, Eisenhower added a typically alarmist note: "There are many, many ways to go wrong in the business of mobilizing support . . . But I do know that if we attempt nothing, we face certain ruin." At the meeting Eisenhower remarked that millions were spent to eradicate diseases, "but no money has been provided for study or research of the greatest killer of them all—war." The next day he sent Bermingham a memo on a "Professorship for Causes, Conduct and Impact of War"; i.e., a plan for the study of military history.[5]

By late spring, Eisenhower told Bermingham that he had "been encouraged by numbers of people" to widen the plan beyond a merely academic study of military history. Now it would involve "frequent convocations of business and professional men" who would give the findings of the academics "instant application in their daily lives." Edwin Clark was still busy cultivating foundation support, he added, and the institute would ensure "continuation of the quarterly magazine known as 'Military Affairs.' (Maybe I am wrong in that name, but, anyway, it has a subscription list of 1200 that we do not want to lose.)"[6] This was the kind of project that would benefit Columbia (as well as AMI) financially.

In the fall of 1950, when Eisenhower asked George Kennan to head the new program, he said it would have two purposes: "to help in the development of peace and serve the interests of America." In deference to the "realism" both shared, he allowed that "war and conflict are so deeply imbedded in human nature" that no study would ever teach the world how to end war. But one could well study "the *conduct* of war. Obviously, if the military and economic strength of a nation are important in preserving peace—or at least in winning a war," then it would be valuable to learn how to "achieve victory expeditiously, surely and economically." The United States had always depended on plans "produced almost on the spur of the moment" to win its wars. Now, "that is simply not good enough." The institute would help the nation develop more effective advance planning to win the next war and ensure that, "at the end of the war, our individual liberties will emerge unimpaired."[7]

In this description of the institute, the prevention of war seemed to take a distinctly second place to the winning of the next war. Perhaps this was only telling Kennan what Eisenhower thought he wanted to hear. As a fundraiser, Eisenhower used all his skills of rhetorical flattery and was quick to tell each potential contributor whatever would sound most appealing at the moment. On the same day, for example, he wrote to a wealthy executive that the institute would study how to organize the United States for war "efficiently, effectively, and *economically*," and how to emerge from a war with individual freedoms intact. His proposal to study war as "the great killer" may have made a lucrative appeal to some potential donors.[8]

There is no way to know how much, if any, of this language was more than simply fundraising rhetoric. On balance, it would seem that the institute was designed to study the conduct and winning of wars much more than their prevention. It is difficult to see it as evidence of any sincere desire for peace; it is easy to see it as evidence of a sincere desire to promote Columbia's fortunes. Eisenhower was ready to develop links with any segment of society that might bring more support to Columbia. Here he saw a way to connect with the military and its supporters, which no other university had yet done, and to use that connection to bring more business leaders into the Columbia orbit as well. It was a major step toward making academia a pivotal link in the emerging military-industrial complex that Eisenhower would one day famously warn against.[9]

## PEACE IN THE PUBLIC DISCOURSE

To promote the proposed institute, the president had to pay the price of preparing a long formal address. Leo Silver had offered to endow an annual lecture on peace, named for his father, Gabriel Silver, on condition that Eisenhower give the inaugural lecture. On the day he gave the speech, Eisenhower wrote to a wartime friend: "I am trapped into making another long speech this evening, this time on 'peace.' . . . Peace happens to be one of those subjects that is easy enough to talk about—for hours—but it is certainly difficult *to do* anything about. Consequently, a talk becomes more of a sermon and exhortation to spiritual greatness than a blueprint for practical action. This characteristic in the speech is, for the soldier, nothing less than a tragedy—however I think I shall get through the ordeal." He had no illusions that his speech would materially advance the cause of peace. Indeed, at this time he seems to have had little enthusiasm for any efforts to advance peace. He did, however, hope the speech would materially advance the cause of Columbia; years later, in a memoir, he explained that he agreed to give the speech because "I could not allow an opportunity for a [financial] contribution of that sort to go by the board. . . . Fortunately, the good benefactor provided the promised endowment." He also saw it as one more occasion to mount the pulpit and exhort the nation to avert the dangers of which he constantly warned. This meant an opportunity to broaden his discursive framework by linking his former guiding ideal of world peace to his new guiding ideal of domestic spirituality and capitalism.[10]

Listing his university's various contributions to peace, the president announced: "We hope to establish here a Chair for Peace, possibly an Institute."[11] The goal was a scholarly study, "free from emotional bias . . . [of] the most malignant cancer of the world body—war." This was the first mention, in public or private, of a new institute, or even a chair, devoted to peace rather than war and military history. At the outset of the speech, though, he linked peace with spiritual greatness paradoxically, by praising "those things of the soul and spirit which great men of history have valued far above peace. Without those values, peace is an inhuman existence. Far better risk a war of possible annihilation than grasp a peace which would be the certain extinction of free man's ideas and ideals." Freedom was the code word that signified all these spiritual ideals. "The pact of Munich was a greater blow to humanity than the atomic bomb at Hiroshima," he argued, for the bomb destroyed only material things (here he ignored the lives lost), while appeasement brought "suffocation of human freedom among a once free people," a "more far-reaching" and more dreadful fate. Now the great goal of the ongoing struggle was not peace but the Anglo-Saxon ideal of freedom. Peace was a nice ideal, he seemed to say, but it was better to be dead than Red.[12]

The ultimate ideal was the millennial vision of peace with freedom. To make this point clear, Eisenhower articulated a semantic distinction that had always been implicit in his public discourse: "We constantly use the word 'peace' in two senses which differ sharply. One is the peace of our dreams—a peace founded in noble impulses, universally shared. It is always the ideal, the pole star that guides us on the proper path. The other peace is *something* of an armed truce; but today a half-loaf is better than none." Armed truce had to be maintained by force, and it required the United States to build up its military strength. But "we hope to reach the point where this peace becomes the starting point of the *real* peace we seek." Here the general was building on his frequent distinction between relative and absolute security. He used the word *peace* to legitimate military force as a tool for the "slow evolutionary processes" that would lead to the great apocalyptic transformation. (In a private letter two weeks later, he referred to "what we now call peace—specifically the cold war.")[13]

The bulk of the Silver speech told the people of the United States what they had to do to move the world closer to the millennial ideal, "an enduring world-wide and secure peace." Americans had to understand that "their own self-interest requires them to teach others the techniques of raising human standards of exis-tence." The crucial point here was not the harmonizing of altruism and self-inter-est, but the need for the United States to be a model. If the poor and immiserated around the world did not see capitalism working to their benefit, they might well turn to Marxism, which would only continue world conflict and chaos. To create an attractive example, Americans first had to protect their domestic economy, keep-ing the U.S. free enterprise system working smoothly and productively, avoiding "any risk of submission to the all-powerful state. Moreover, only thus can the world have any hope of reaching the millennium of world peace. For without the exam-ple of strength, prosperity, and progress in a free America, there is nothing to inspire men to victory in today's struggle between freedom and totalitarianism." Real peace meant no accommodation with the Soviet system, but a full victory over it, leaving the world no option but to emulate the American system.[14]

Intertwined with this argument was another point (though the speaker did not make the connection explicit). Soviet armaments were wielded by a society that was not spiritual and hence had no self-restraint. If the Soviets were not externally restrained, through disarmament enforced by a U.N. "world police force," the armaments would inevitably be used to threaten the West. The West, being spiritual and capitalist, was self-restrained. Therefore, the world had nothing to fear from the West's armaments, which would be used only defensively. Arguing this point at some length, Eisenhower mentioned that the United States had proven its benign intent by disarming "to the extent—in some directions even beyond the extent" that he would judge advisable. This line, though parenthetical in the speech as a whole, captured the next day's headlines and the attention of Congress, which immediately summoned the general to Washington to explain what he meant by "beyond."[15]

In his testimony, he detailed the additional expenditures he wanted to see, but stressed that they were quite minor. "Interwoven throughout his presentation were eloquent appeals for domestic unity," the *New York Times* told its readers the next day. "He described moral and spiritual strength, as well as a healthy economy, as essential, since 'arms are merely the cutting edge.' He characterized 'unity of thought and effort' on basic principles as the 'greatest weapon the United States has, and it doesn't cost a nickel.' . . . Meanwhile, he said, there must be a 'never-ending crusade' to enlighten the people of the world and convince them of this country's 'good will and decent purposes.'" This journalistic report missed the key point, however. For Eisenhower, domestic unity and spiritual strength would not develop concurrently with an international crusade; rather, unity and spiritual strength now were defined as the essence of the international crusade. The general was probably pleased to have both Columbia and Congress give him a national platform to expound his new vision of peace through a combination of internationalism and domestic commitment to capitalism, the inseparable twin keys to cold war victory. And victory was now the only way to peace.[16]

He had begun to develop this new line in his rare public references to peace in 1948. When his appointment to Columbia was announced, he explained his decision to a press conference: "Wherever I am, the interest of the Army and of the National Security will always be Number One with me. . . . The future of civilization is absolutely dependent upon finding some way of resolving international differences without resort to war. . . . I told them [at Columbia] that I had a conviction of what the American way of life is, and if it could be practiced throughout the world that only a secure America can lead in that direction." Asked whether "peace is secure for a reasonable length of time," Eisenhower avoided a direct answer. Commenting only that the world was "bewildered and fearful," he advised maintaining "our own path of moral rectitude. . . . I intend to continue work along that line." This press conference foreshadowed his new focus on the domestic rectitude of "the American way," but it gave little indication of how rapidly the peace theme would fade from his public discourse.[17]

In October 1948 he devoted a speech at the Riverdale Country School to the subject of peace (apparently because of a special request). The military's job was to defend a way of life and a system of government, he said, which "needs a certain fundamental foundation stone on which to rest. Among them [sic], and I'm not going to try to enumerate all of them, but among them is a system of free enterprise." After stressing the central importance of internationalism, he continued, "We are apt to fall into the great error of thinking of people either as black or white, and I am speaking in a spiritual or moral sense." In fact, every person has "the nobler virtues that we refer to as courage, the spirit of self-sacrifice" but "inescapably, each man and each woman is the center of the universe, he must be and is compelled to be that center because all the world is known to him only by its reactions upon him and, therefore he is also a selfish human being. . . . So the problem then in peace is to get these nobler virtues in control . . . In the drive for peace, just like winning a war, the attack must be on a very broad front." Ordinary people were the essential infantry in this attack because "they bring home to each of us that wars are started inside each one of us, not merely by some wicked person or some wicked nation elsewhere. . . . We have got to find a way to bring home to each of us the individual responsibilities we bear." The elusive problem of peace was the elusive problem of capitalism: finding a way to ensure that noble self-restraint would prevail over selfishness. "The problem is to defeat it before they [the selfish] can bring again a catastrophe upon the world."[18]

Among more than thirty official messages he issued in 1948, only one referred to peace as a major goal. Permanent peace was an ideal that "hangs over the horizon as a beacon by which to steer," he said, again making explicit a notion that was always implicit in his discourse. The way to approach the ideal was to keep the United States strong in every way, to defend against the twin dangers of assault from without and "creeping paralysis from within." In a 1948 Fourth of July oration to a veterans group, Eisenhower called on the military to "maintain the integrated national strength that will discourage any from attacking us, while you work unceasingly for the growth of international understanding that will eliminate war." But these were rare references to peace. In 1949, as in 1948, the subject of peace remained generally absent from the public discourse.[19]

During the spring of 1950, as Eisenhower began raising funds for the Institute of War and Peace, he also began to make war and peace a more prominent focus in his public speaking. Shortly before the Silver lecture he told another college audience that the way to peace was "to encompass within our camp all people everywhere" in the American way of life. He warned against pursuing this goal through "a police state or garrison state" of excessive militarization, but he also cautioned against negotiations with the Soviets, who would never "respect a treaty which mainly states that everything is going to be sweetness and light." Though many U.S. leaders were openly concerned about creating a "garrison state," few if any were talking about a treaty with the Soviets. Eisenhower himself rarely mentioned the idea, so it is difficult to know how to interpret his implication that a treaty would be "sweetness and light." Apparently this was yet another example of simply creating an image of two extremes so that he could propose a "middle way." This was, in fact, his conclusion. The only way to peace was to offer the world an appealing example of "the middle way": "140,000,000 united Americans working for our economy and facing the world is the strongest power there is under the Almighty."[20]

## THE NEW MEANING OF PEACE

It would be misleading to attach much importance to these speeches, for they were so few in number. During Eisenhower's years at Columbia, the theme of peace almost vanished from his public discourse, relative to its constant emphasis in the preceding two and a half years. This striking fact calls into question a standard view among scholars—that his supposed desire for peace was the most constant theme in his discourse from World War II through his presidency. This view typically argues that only in 1948, under the influence of his new Republican friends, did he develop an interest in domestic economic issues, which led to his virulent antisocialist sentiments.

In fact, the evidence seems to point in the opposite direction. In his semi-retirement, Eisenhower still had access to the highest levels of the U.S. government. Yet he did nothing to promote any kind of reconciliation of differences between the United States and the Soviet Union, and he no longer even paid lip service to that ideal. On the contrary, he now declared that all such efforts were useless. The explicit goal was now to protect the U.S. system, which meant victory in both the cold war and the domestic political fray. When he did occasionally speak of peace, he still defined it as a sort of global corporate commonwealth, a guarantee that the whole world would model itself on the capitalism of the "American system." He hoped that the world would "finally reach that point where there are no ideological differences," he told an audience in the summer of

1948. Then, "armaments may disappear, and all men may live at peace with each other."[21]

At Columbia, Eisenhower also spoke less about the cold war dangers from abroad. As the immediate concerns of World War II faded from public memory, he referred to the war less and less often, and he used the image of a continuing war less and less frequently. It is no coincidence that he also spoke less about peace. Although he still insisted that the Soviets should not be allowed to expand their sphere of influence, he would not endorse concrete measures to reduce that sphere. Despite his apparent demand for cold war victory, he implicitly accepted the current division of geopolitical power and urged that the United States and its allies simply hold the line. He expressed a relatively high sense of confidence that this could be done—relatively high, that is, compared to his paucity of confidence about the domestic scene. In Eisenhower's discourse, if not in the public view, the cold war was gradually settling into a fixed pattern. Therefore, there was less urgency to talk about the cold war, and there was less to say on the subject of peace.

This rhetorical shift made it clearer than ever that his previous eloquent expressions of hope for peace had been rhetorical weapons of cold war, not expressions of any deep genuine belief. The high-profile peace talk had marked the main difference between his public and private discourse as C/S. With that difference largely removed, there was noticeably more similarity between his public and private discourse as the president of Columbia. When he did speak of peace, he argued against preventive war and excessive military expenditures because of the risks they posed to democracy and capitalism. He argued for the Institute of War and Peace because it would teach the nation how to prepare for and, if need be, how to fight a war, without endangering the fundamentals of the domestic system. He used the language of peace primarily to reinforce his exhortations about the domestic scene.

The constant thread in Eisenhower's postwar discourse was not the need for peace but the dangers besetting "the American way," dangers coming primarily from the left. He now treated the Soviet threat and the threat of "creeping socialism" as inseparable twin manifestations of the same peril. This broadened imagery of threat made "the American way" seem more fragile than ever. Now the cold war and the hope for peace were both constructed as expressions of that fragility; his antidote to that fragility was an exemplary practice of "the American way" that would secure it against the "red menace." He called for a single crusade that would preserve domestic capitalism, win the cold war, and secure world peace. The goals, like the dangers, were inseparable, and the goals were inseparable from the dangers. He could not talk about either peace or victory without evoking, and thus reinforcing, the domestic as well as the foreign fears that pervaded his discourse.

The intimate link between peace and domestic capitalism intensified fear in another way, too. Not long after the Silver lecture, Eisenhower returned to the peace theme but gave it a surprising twist. World War II had given the nation a great hope for peace, he reminded an audience of journalists, but "the shattering of that dream of actual and permanent peace . . . [brought] a confusion that is almost a bewilderment. . . . If the world makes a mistake about our essential confidence and courage . . . we incur very, very great dangers." The United States had to have a commonly understood goal and pursue it "strongly, persistently and invariably until victory is achieved, and that means to pursue it forever." Unlike war, he explained, "peace is never completely won because each new day brings a new problem, and what was right a few days ago is not necessarily correct today."[22]

The journalists may have been surprised to hear that lasting peace, the goal he had held out so often as chief of staff and so recently in the Silver lecture, was in principle unattainable, a chimera. But this public admission had already been echoed in other, seemingly stray, public references to peace as a "pole star," an ideal always "over the horizon," the object of a "never-ending crusade." The new turn in Eisenhower's discourse made this view more necessary than ever. He had always depicted peace as the product of an internal spiritual struggle, a civil war running through rather than between nations. Since the enemy was an eternal fact of human nature, permanent victory was doubtful at best. Now he intensified the dilemma by pinning hopes for victory upon universal support for the capitalism of the "middle way," with its elusive perfect balance between selfishness and self-restraint. Eisenhower himself had admitted that this perfect balance might never be found. If real peace depended on first defining and then achieving the "middle way," it seemed that peace would indeed be, as he admitted here, an unattainable ideal hanging always over the horizon. There would always be an enemy to fear.

## KOREA IN PRIVATE DISCOURSE

On 26 June 1950, Eisenhower wrote to Averell Harriman: "I am convinced the solutions of our internal problems will go a very long way toward achieving our international aims, particularly that of preserving the peace."[23] This sentence summed up the marked shift in his discourse since leaving the Pentagon. It also showed that he could, on occasion, refer to the cold war as an era without adding any qualifier to the word. He did not know that, as he was writing, the Truman administration was committing itself to a war in Korea that would make this usage of the term *peace* impossible for at least the next three years. The first full-scale fighting since the end of World War II would have a significant impact on the American Assembly and all of Eisenhower's other plans, as well as his discourse. He would use the opportunity to articulate more fully the ideological lines connecting his lifelong military concerns with his new career as defender of free enterprise.

From the outset, he unequivocally supported the administration's forceful response in Korea. On 27 June he called President Truman "to congratulate him on his stand." The next day he conferred with "a number of friends at the Pentagon." As he summarized the visits in his diary: "My whole contention was that an appeal to force cannot by its nature be a partial one. This appeal having been made, for God's sake, get ready! Do everything *possible* under the law to get going." He added, "Our side can never be too strong!" The United States must be prepared to use every kind of force available to it, "even if it finally comes to the use of the A-bomb." At this point he added parenthetically "(which God forbid)," an expression of concern about using the bomb that was rare in Eisenhower's discourse. The general's penchant for an all-out apocalyptic assault had not abated since World War II; if anything, it had grown stronger, just as the power of U.S. weaponry had grown stronger.[24]

The diary entry also noted another reason for urging force, which he had not mentioned to his friends: "We'll have a dozen Koreas . . . if we don't take firm stand." He explained to a British friend that a global war could break out, not through intentional planning but because of miscalculation. If the U.N. forces did not use massive force, it "would be interpreted as nothing less than another kind of Munich," which would only lead to further "powder keg" wars. Eisenhower could endorse his friend's optimism about the world situation, he said, only if the United Nations "will stand absolutely firm in the present crisis." For Eisenhower, the purpose of the Korean War was to keep the boundary between the United States and Soviet spheres demarcated with absolute clarity, and thus made inviolable. This was the best way to prevent war, he argued. In the context of his discourse, this was merely a geopolitical expression of the more urgent need for clarity in the endless battle against innate evil impulses. Unless the wall erected against them was absolutely inviolable, those nefarious impulses would inevitably find a way to undermine the forces of virtue. Thus his apocalypticism and his dualism combined to demand total victory in Korea. As he told Alfred Gruenther: "I just want the thing over quickly and decisively."[25]

Predictably, though, "Alarmist Ike" saw signs that others did not recognize the dire peril. The day after his visit to the Pentagon he told Clare Booth Luce, "One gets the feeling that Washington considers it is swimming in strange and swift currents—and there are rocks, rapids and terrors on every hand." A week later he was back in Washington, telling Truman that his decisions "must be *earnestly* supported." Secretary of Defense Johnson spoke "complacently," however: "As [to] inquiries as to the time element—he said 'Pretty good.' God, how I *hope*. But there seems no disposition to begin serious mobilizing! I *think* that it is possible that military advisers are too complacent when talking to H.S.T." On both trips to Washington, he told Bernard Baruch, he had "urged that this is no time for dawdling. . . . We should not treat the present crisis as just a mere inconvenience." When China entered the war he returned to this theme, telling Gruenther, "the one thing that does puzzle me is a seeming lack of urgency in our preparations, starting last June 25." In his diary he continued the lament: "The Korean situation is tragic . . . What have we been doing here [in the U.S.] for 5 mos.?? Something is terribly wrong," because no one had heeded "the fine advice I gave on preparation."[26]

He made the same complaint to Swede Hazlett. Civilian leaders had ignored him: they had not built up a permanent "striking force," the kind of "splendid 'fire department'" that could have quickly subdued the enemy in Korea; and they had wrongly believed the United States would always have a "cushion of time" to respond to any crisis. He hesitated to speak out on such issues, he told another officer, because he was still a soldier and did not want to contradict his superiors publicly. But "we are up against something entirely new, more full of risk and danger than anything we have yet encountered."[27]

Eisenhower's alarm about Korea was soon interlaced with his new focus on the alarming domestic drift toward socialism. He often used the Korean situation to bolster his crusade to preserve the American system. He feared that politicians and bureaucrats were using the crisis "for furthering selfish ambitions," the very problem he hoped to attack with projects such as the American Assembly. This war was not an isolated incident, he told Donald Kennedy, a Columbia fundraiser who wanted to suspend solicitations until the Korean situation stabilized: "I doubt that we can permit such affairs as the 'Korean Crisis' to affect materially a long range plan for improving understanding and exercise of citizenship. . . . These crises are going to become a nagging part of our lives." In other words, Kennedy should keep raising funds for the American Assembly. Indeed, "now that we are at war" the American Assembly was more important than ever, he told its supporters. Since every war takes away some liberties, "we must be assured that at the end of the conflict we have the same individual benefits which we possessed at the beginning. For if we were to sacrifice lives and our National resources and end up as members of even a semi-dictatorial or regimented state," the sacrifices would be in vain. His fear of World War III was increasingly focused on this point: even a U.S. victory would "leave the world so prostrated" that free institutions "could not possibly exist."[28]

He was most disturbed, though, by the skyrocketing military budget. Typically, he claimed to have foreseen the danger long before others. He had already decided during World War II, he told Secretary of Defense Johnson, that the postwar era would see "a long period of unsettled international relations," requiring the United States to maintain unprecedented military forces in peacetime, "and this had to be done without breaking our economy." But he had not expected the shocking rise in military spending now proposed by the Truman administration. Now he claimed to foresee, better than others, the possibility of disaster ahead: "Some of these officials think we can *buy* security; solvency and security can scarcely be separated—yet I hear talk of 55 billion a year for *several* years. Tragic." "We have lived too long with our heads in the sands," he wrote to a salesman from Kansas. The United States had to understand the true magnitude of the communist threat and meet it with military force that was both sufficient and affordable. Otherwise the nation would soon "come squarely to the crossroads of choosing either the path of war or of being bled white economically."[29]

To a mother who hoped to keep her son out of the war he wrote, "The question is what must we do to preserve a way of life . . . without becoming nothing but an armed camp. . . . It is more than ever necessary that we be certain of our own moral integrity and purpose. . . . Each of us must do his own duty."[30] This letter reflected the emerging synthesis in Eisenhower's discourse. Moral purpose and duty meant rational self-disciplined behavior. It would err neither toward complacency nor undisciplined military spending; either one would lead to state controls and eventually a regimented society. In military spending, as in everything else, the nation would be saved by rational leaders, who could precisely calculate the optimal "middle way," and by masses who would make the sacrifices necessary to adhere to it.

Eisenhower worried about the masses. To Swede Hazlett he wrote of his "shock and dismay" in World War II at young Americans' "lack of knowledge of the age-old struggle between individual freedom and dictatorship." (Universal Military Training would solve both this problem and the military readiness problem simultaneously, he argued.) "So often the individual citizen feels helpless and lost in the overwhelming mass of 150 million people." Yet a clear message, delivered clearly to the world, was essential to winning the cold war. The United States had to appear to the world "as champion of the great human values." If all people did not see in the U.S. system a way to fulfill their own aspirations, "then we are doomed as surely as if we today were completely defenseless before the Communistic and Russian purposes." Korea demonstrated that the United States would have to support "our weaker friends all over the world in order that the system of free government does not crumble inch by inch and finally leave us an isolated island in a whole sea of enemies."[31]

The way to avert catastrophe was through better public relations. "If Communistic propaganda goes unchallenged," the United States would lose the global ideological struggle, and "if this happens, we have no escape from dictatorship." To solve this problem he wanted the truth of the U.S. commitment to peace "nailed, banner-like, to a staff." One way to disseminate the truth, he suggested, was via the popular radio personality Arthur Godfrey. Godfrey could reach many millions, he told several senior military and civilian officials: "He could be of great help to our country whenever a piece of important information could be appropriately fitted by him and his experts into his particular type of program."[32]

Eisenhower, however, was still not quite certain exactly what the truth was, nor how it should be expressed. He proposed that Ferdinand Eberstadt (author of the military service unification plan) head a study to define the fundamentals of U.S. belief, starting from an "obviously moral platform." He wanted "simple, easily understood conclusions" that could be "put down in simple, almost diagrammatic form," to relate the core ideas of foreign policy to "the many great internal problems." The findings of this study would be used to guide and unify the American public. Writing to Eberstadt about "the sorry state in which we find ourselves," he claimed that fear was "the greatest obstacle to reasonable arrangement of men's affairs." But the most troubling problem was ascertaining who should be feared, and how much: "We have great difficulty in assigning priorities. . . . It keeps the world upset a great portion of the time." In his diary he allowed himself a moment of uncertainty about his own habitual fear, but he quickly retreated to his reassuringly familiar stance: "While sometimes I wonder whether I do not exaggerate in my own mind the seriousness of the world situation, I likewise am not certain that some of our office holders are not either complacent or too slow to treat the American people with the *bald* facts of the world situation. . . . And poor H.S.T.—a fine man who, in the middle of a stormy lake, knows nothing of swimming. Yet a lot of drowning people are forced to look at him as a life guard."[33]

## KOREA IN PUBLIC DISCOURSE

In public, even more than in private, Eisenhower used the war as a rhetorical device to continue his domestic crusade. The "dark clouds of the threat of war" had been spawned by a lack of knowledge, he told Columbia students. But what the world needed to understand most was American principles and how the American system works. This was, apparently, the best way to avoid war. He used similar words of alarm and reassurance addressing the Boy Scouts: "Few of you can remember a day free from war, rumor of war, fear of war! That you may not, in your young manhood, be sacrificed *to* war is indeed the primary purpose of our foreign policy today. And you *shall* not be, if the pledge of allegiance stands always before the world as the guiding light of our national life." These words were sandwiched between exhortations to a more virtuous domestic life. "Every society, every crowd has its weaklings, its cowards, its self-centered individuals," the general affirmed. He urged the Boy Scouts to "escape the shame" by unselfish sacrifice, and implied that this was the true meaning of the pledge of allegiance. Foreign policy and peace were functions of exemplary virtue within the United States.[34]

A speech in Pittsburgh, in the fall of 1950, began with a rudimentary theory of the evils of communist totalitarianism. Since such a system offered no stimulus through differential economic rewards, it could motivate only through punishment, and it had to "ever increase the punishments visited on the laggard" until he had nothing to lose by revolt. To mask this internal weakness and postpone its inevitable downfall, "its policy must be to destroy freedom everywhere." The problem was to defend freedom against "pillaging hordes" of "Communistic fanatics" without "suffocating" freedom at home. The United States should maintain enough military strength to deter the enemy "in the final showdown." (Eisenhower added an unusual public rejection of "preventative war": "None has yet explained how war prevents war. Worse than this, no one has been able to explain away the fact that war creates the conditions that beget war.")

In order to build a large enough military force, everyone needed "to subordinate our ease, our plans, our pleasure to the hard necessities of the country's safety and the world's freedom." Too many Americans worshipped the dollar and saw, "even in crisis, a chance to profit, to further selfish aims." "Selfish grabbing, heedless spending of dollars" was more dangerous than ever, given the spiraling military costs: "If solvency and security are not synonymous, they are so closely related that the difference is scarcely discernible." So the Korean War, like World War II and every war, offered an opportunity to defend the freedom to be voluntarily self-restrained by embodying self-restraint in the course of the battle. Exemplary behavior was the winning weapon.[35]

Despite the pervasive awareness of the ongoing war, on some occasions Eisenhower seemed to forget that peace was the primary U.S. goal. His most important speech of the latter half of 1950, initiating the "Crusade for Freedom," mentioned only in passing "our aspirations for peace, our hatred of war." As Martin Medhurst has noted, this was "an archetypal example of Cold War discourse." It was "constructed as an agon—a contest or battle between two opposing forces," warning of the "probably prolonged struggle" between freedom and totalitarianism. The speech was ostensibly an appeal to answer communist propaganda with the words broadcast by Radio Free Europe, funded by the "Crusade." But it covered much more ground. Medhurst finds that it included every typical feature of cold war discourse: stark polarizations, fear appeals, biblical allusions, images of death, use of ultimate terms, savagery of the enemy, righteousness of America, and the fragility of liberty.[36] Although he calls it "the first major address in which Eisenhower dons the mantle of rhetorical cold war," all of these features had long been typical of Eisenhower's discourse.

In this speech, though, the characteristic new emphases of Eisenhower's discourse were brought to bear on cold war issues. Public imagery was the central concern. Communist propaganda told the world that "we Americans are physically soft and morally corrupt; that we are disunited and confused; that we are selfish and cowardly," he said. Of course this "propaganda" only echoed his own oft-repeated description of the direction the nation was taking. A few moments later he warned, "It would do no good to defend our liberties against Communistic aggression and lose them to our own greed, blindness, or shiftless reliance on bureaucracy and Federal Treasury." The way to win the cold war was to show the world a different image.

The bulk of the speech was a call to "tighten our belts, both nationally and individually," and defend American freedom. High productivity and financial stability were as essential as a prudent military buildup. Excessive personal spending at such a time would only give the Soviets pleasure "in bringing us further inflation and closer to economic ruin." Without "Spartan frugality" and a unified national commitment to the values the general espoused, "the system of government established by our forefathers will disappear. The American record, from Washington to the day of that disaster, will be only a blank page in history."[37]

The Korean War allowed Eisenhower to fuse foreign and domestic sources of impending catastrophe and to speak of the two as twin facets of a single omnipresent threat. The crucial link between the two was his emphasis on exemplary domestic behavior. The virtues he had been promoting as a necessary bulwark against domestic socialism now became the bulwark against foreign communism, the winning weapon in the cold war and thus the path to peace.

CHAPTER 11

# President of Columbia: Conclusions

When Eisenhower told Swede Hazlett, "Going to Columbia is merely to change the location of my headquarters,"[1] he suggested not only a way to understand his move to Columbia, but also a criterion by which to interpret his work there. To what extent was he merely using his office at Columbia as a place to continue his previous work? How much continuity was there between his military career and his university presidency? What stayed the same and what changed? At first sight, it would appear that the move to Columbia marked a radical break in the general's work. In public as well as in private he talked less about foreign dangers, not at all about peace, and dramatically more about domestic dangers. But at a deeper level there was striking continuity.

### THE ENDURING PRINCIPLES

Three main themes dominated both the public and private discourse of the Columbia years. The first theme was the ongoing battle between the forces of selfishness and the forces of self-restraint. The second theme was the grave danger this battle posed to the U.S. political and economic system. The third theme was the need for national unity, based on clearly defined and universally supported value principles, in fighting the battle. These were also dominant themes in Eisenhower's discourse as chief of staff. There was nothing essentially new here. He did not shift his discursive stance so much as broaden it, applying the same principles to new areas, spelling out themes that had always been there implicitly.

Because the principles remained the same, he was able to incorporate these new areas easily, logically interweaving new discursive elements with the old. The public and private discourses, now so similar, formed a strikingly unified, internally consistent whole. Eisenhower attested to this inner coherence by frequently reiterating, as a basic principle, that all individual rights and freedoms are linked together, so that a danger to one is a danger to all. Most prominently, of course, he argued repeatedly that capitalism was an essential prerequisite for democracy and that a growing threat to economic freedom imperiled political freedom. (Rarely did he argue that democracy was a prerequisite for capitalism).[2]

The consistency of Eisenhower's ideology lends credence to his claim that going to Columbia was merely changing his headquarters. He saw himself fighting the same battle he had waged on active duty, a battle defined by his ideological framework. Once free to express himself more fully, he did not abandon his previous concerns but only expanded their meaning by revealing their full ideological context.

He had made it clear to the Columbia trustees, when he accepted their offer, that he would continue to be a general and that the government would always have first claim upon his time. Military affairs continued to consume much of his attention. Military leadership continued to be a paradigm by which he constructed his values in every aspect of life. The military paradigm encompassed the basic themes of his discourse: a good officer identified dangers well in advance, united his troops to defend against them, motivated his troops by effectively communicating shared principles, and exemplified self-discipline. These were the virtues he praised consistently throughout World War II and the postwar years and hoped to extend to the whole nation.[3]

The struggle over the military budget, which took up so much time and attention, also had an impact on the broader discourse. Now he worried not only whether the nation would provide enough resources but whether it might allocate too much of its resources for military preparedness and thus dislocate the economy, increase central government control, and reduce individual freedoms. This concern is hardly surprising, in light of his lifelong immersion in military affairs and the central role this issue played in his presidency. In fact, the surprise is how relatively secondary this concern was in both his public and private discourse at Columbia. He made the point any number of times. It was one important way to connect his ongoing military concerns with his newfound passion for saving the domestic capitalist system. It was not in any way the dominant theme, though; it was only one among many expressions of his newfound passion.

Nuclear weapons were even less prominent in his discourse. Eisenhower continued to treat them as simply one part of a much broader picture of weaponry issues. He still focused principally on their symbolic value. He went out of his way to try to calm public fears about the new weapons. In this respect he agreed with most other elite leaders (at least outside the navy) that the weapons some people saw as a world problem were actually an essential part of the solution to world problems. The military budget presented a similar paradox: it could be seen both as problem and solution, a source of danger as well as safety. In both cases, Eisenhower was seeking an ideal balance between danger and safety. But his tendency in this period was to repress nuclear fears while gradually fostering growing fears about the cost of excessive rearmament.

This was both a sign and a consequence of the shift from foreign to domestic dangers as the primary source of threat. He certainly still worried about winning the cold war, but with his alarmism now focused preponderantly on socialism and statism at home, he subsumed all cold war and military issues to this domestic fear. This might suggest that he was more concerned about defending the U.S. system at home than defending U.S. interests abroad. But it seems more accurate to say that he blurred the distinction between the struggle abroad and the struggle at home to such a degree that virtually no difference remained. Was domestic capitalism to be defended as a means to winning the cold war, or was it vice versa? The question no longer had any meaning, for the two goals had essentially become dual means to the same overriding goal: preserving the American system.

For Eisenhower "the American system" and "the American way" meant more than simply the reality of life as lived in the United States. These were catchwords, not unlike *freedom, statism,* and the others. They denoted a symbolic, not an empirical, state of affairs—an ideal, a fantasy of perfection. Although Eisenhower located this ideal in the rural United States of his childhood, it really could not be identified with any empirical place or time. It functioned more as a universal ideal. Since it was the manifestation of spiritual good, it would have to be defended everywhere and always against the evil that threatened it. National boundaries were ultimately irrelevant. The battlefronts, whether foreign or domestic, were all parts of the same apocalyptic war.

He made this clear when he urged the nation to win the cold war not so much by superior weaponry (though he insisted that the United States should maintain superior weaponry) as by superior words and images. His principal point in this regard was the need for better propaganda. It was crucial to persuade other nations to believe that the United States wanted only what was best for others and that the U.S. system was demonstrably best for others. So Eisenhower promoted fidelity to and confidence in the American system as a way to win the cold war, which was in turn a way to save the American system. In a September 1949 press conference, asked how far the United States was from "winning the peace," he replied that he was more optimistic than he had been in two years. The United States would win "by remaining true to the principles of freedom—economic, political, and all the others."[4] More clearly than ever, he was merging the two fundamental processes of social restraint within his discourse: the United States would restrain the threatening other by restraining itself, and vice versa. But his body of discourse, taken as a whole, showed more doubt than optimism that the United States would develop this weapon and wield it effectively against the enemy. He no longer spoke of peace as his goal, but merely of protecting the American system from total collapse.

## THE MIDDLE WAY

Eisenhower's prescription for saving the U.S. system was to find and follow "the middle way." By giving his ideological structure this title, he could claim that he followed no ideology, but only the dictates of thoughtful, moderate rationality. Of course "the middle way" was itself an ideological and discursive construct. It was the essential feature of that timeless ideal, "the American way." Once the optimal "middle way" was determined for the United States, it would become the exemplary "city on a hill," and "the middle way" would be extended to the whole world. With the rest of the world still plagued by postwar chaos, the United States was the only country with the opportunity to make a correct determination on this most vital matter. So it was not at all objectionable, in fact it was perfectly reasonable, that the United States should set itself toward a benign form of global preponderance. It was equally reasonable that ideological words should be its primary weapons, since ideological control was the primary goal of the battle. "The middle way" functioned as a sign of perfect clarity and order, representing a universal good, a goal beyond ambiguity and thus beyond history.

When Eisenhower was chief of staff, peace had been the crucial term representing millennial fantasy in his discourse. Now that term was largely dropped in favor of "the middle way." But this revealed deeper structural continuities between the C/S and Columbia eras. In both discourses, the millennial term was employed to create an image of optimism and hope, but there was little in the substance of the language of either discourse to support that optimism. The language spoke primarily of threats and dangers, with only vague catchwords to spell out the ways to defend against those dangers.

The use of the term "the middle way," like the earlier use of peace, was much more prominent in the public than in the private discourse. Eisenhower's private discourse as president of Columbia was marked by a powerful tone of fear for the future of the nation and the world. There was little optimism about finding a saving "middle way." For the most part, there was only dread of the demise of capitalism and individual freedom. "The middle way" was thus an artificially constructed language to buoy the public's optimism that its problems could be solved. It was the central catchword, representing a promise that solutions would be found, without giving any specific idea of what those solutions might be. Eisenhower could do no more, for he was unable to define "the middle way" with any specificity, as the private discourse showed.

In this respect his fundraising for Columbia played a particularly interesting role. It was in some respects public and in some respects private. It promised solutions to the nation's problems, yet it admitted (particularly in letters for the American Assembly) that no one could define "the middle way" in any operational terms. Such definitions were the goal of the assembly and, by extension, of all Columbia's educational activities. Yet Eisenhower asked for immense sums of money precisely because this term held out a promise of millennial perfection, if only it could be given precise content and disseminated to national leaders. They, in turn, would use that content to affect the precise rational control that the term promised. The fundraising literature for Columbia marked a sort of discursive middle way between hope for a middle way and fear that it might never be found; i.e., that the nation's problems might never be solved. Discovering a new millennial symbol gave the university's president another arena in which to worry that the nation would fall short of its goal.

### IRONY AND ANXIETY

Eisenhower showed the continuity between his active duty and civilian careers by his ideological commitment, his use of millennial fantasy, and his alarmism,. He had truly never left the army. The discourse of the Columbia years also resembled the discourse of the Pentagon years in its sizeable component of irony. He was still trying to use language to create a sense of stable order, and the language that he used was still undermining his effort, for he was still drawing on a variety of conflicting discursive traditions. The discourse of peace he had used as chief of staff had carried its contradictions along unresolved. Now the same traditions that had created those contradictions were sustained and broadened to encompass new issues, which only amplified the contradictions.

In Eisenhower's attacks on the purported drift toward socialism, his debts to these traditions became clearer than ever. When he asserted that all humans feel themselves to be the center of the world, and assigned this a positive meaning, he was pushing the classical liberalism of John Locke and Adam Smith to its limit. But his sustained attack on the self-seeking officeholders and bureaucrats exemplified the powerful Augustinian impulse in classical republicanism and populism, with their vision of history as a struggle of the many to restrain the powerful few. The private discourse, in particular, was also marked by the tragic Augustinian sense: as long as history endures, governments will be unfortunate necessities, the dilemma of power will remain insoluble, and the many will have to struggle endlessly against the abuses of power. Of course the whole was still expressed in apocalyptically dualistic terms.

Eisenhower upheld each of these views as ways to promote his ideal of voluntary self-control. Since all met at this hub of the ideological wheel, he may have assumed that all would contribute to his goal of certainty and unity. Here, too, he was building (though unwittingly) on a rich historical precedent. These traditions had already been intertwined in the Revolutionary War era, and they had forged a synthesis that survived almost unchanged in Eisenhower's ideology. Historian James Kloppenberg has shown that this synthesis linked political and moral concerns through its pivotal term, *autonomy* (literally self-rule; i.e., ruling and restraining one's own passions). "Americans sought independence as a nation," he argues, "to secure autonomy as individuals." Ernest Tuveson, studying the same era, has found abundant evidence of Christian apocalypticism in the writings of political elites.[5] Eisenhower's ideological discourse offers a fine example of how all these traditions could be synthesized. The powerful few, imposing external restraint on others, could be cast as the forces spawned by chaotic excess and leading to apocalyptic collapse. The masses could be rallied to an apocalyptic war against them in the name of individual autonomy.

But confusion remained. At times Eisenhower said clearly that there was a preexisting harmony in human society, which rationality and education could surely discover. This premise, which fueled his Wilsonian hope for world peace, also provided a promise of finding a secure domestic "middle way." At other times he pinned his hopes for domestic harmony on a spiritual victory over conflicting human impulses. At still other times, he assumed an ineradicable selfishness that would produce inevitable conflict in society. This Augustinian premise, which left containment the only hope in foreign affairs, also entailed a permanent threat of conflict and chaos on the domestic scene. Merging these traditions left basic questions unanswered: If people are rational enough to control their selfish impulses to precisely the right degree, why is conflict so pervasive in U.S. society? Why should New Deal policies inevitably lead to socialism? And why should socialism inevitably lead to political totalitarianism, not the democracy that European democratic socialism foresaw?

Eisenhower found it convenient to leave such questions unexplored. Weaving so many traditions together, he could be all things to all people, which certainly broadened his political appeal. To do this, though, he had to avoid precise language that might reveal the contradictions among the various traditions. He had to rest content with the evocative catchwords that he had deplored in his ABA speech. His own discourse provided a good example of his warning in that speech: "If our attitudes are muddled, our language is often to blame."

The muddle was compounded not only by the broadened parameters of the discourse, but also by its new millennial term. Peace was a word that bespoke a promise of unity, harmony, and consistency, but "the middle way" was at best a compromise. It was never presented as a way to transcend the tensions between polar opposites, nor to sublate them, but only to keep them under control by mitigating excesses at both ends of every polarity. Within Eisenhower's own discursive framework, this fantasy of perfect rational control was bound to be only a fantasy. Reality, rooted always in the conflict between selfishness and self-restraint, was bound to be constantly unstable, always less than perfect.

It is hard to see the discourse about "the middle way" as a meaningful effort to find any concrete resolution to the anxieties it claimed to address. The discourse can better be understood as a continuing effort to negotiate a chaotic semantic field, playing creatively among the many sets of opposites it generated. The discursive process did often create an impression of mastery, simply because the speaker appeared to have the language, and therefore the reality, largely under his rational control. He was able to connect all the goals he posited and all the fears he evoked within a single rhetorical web, which reinforced the impression of substantial control. But "the middle way" could replace peace as an eschatological term only because it promised perfect rational control and hence perfect balance. So the discourse had to promise perfect mastery, while its own process demonstrated how illusory this impression was.

The promise of perfect balance was necessarily a promise of an endless, and endlessly frustrating, quest for perfect balance. The destabilizing discursive struggle between opposing terms was bound to go on forever. This was always the implicit foundation of Eisenhower's discourse. Sometimes it was openly admitted, as when he said that the dividing line between government authority and individual freedom "never is completely fixed; never is static. It oscillates constantly, in a middle area."[6] More often, though, it was denied (especially in the public discourse), which made the discourse even less stable.

By raising expectations that it could not fulfill, talk of "the middle way" increased the uncertainties and anxieties that it aimed to relieve. In the process, it made every excess or imbalance in any direction seem irrational and dangerous, a force of chaos powerful enough to drown civilization. If the language of peace generated and reinforced the very fears it was intended to assuage, the language of "the middle way" did so even more intensely. With those threats so consistently expressed in apocalyptic terms, the result was frightening indeed. The audience would ultimately have felt less anxiety had the speaker recommended simply accepting an inevitable modicum of imbalance and tension, interpreting it as an acceptable mode of order rather than a perilous chaos. In Eisenhower's ideological discourse, however, this was not a viable option.

## HOPES AND FEARS

Herein lies the ultimate irony of that discourse. He was seeking rational order to stave off the stresses of uncertainty in a postwar "country unfamiliar emotionally," as Geertz puts it.[7] To fulfill this purpose, his ideology had to be held so rigidly that every conflict or problem became an apocalyptic harbinger of social disunity, political and economic disintegration, and cultural chaos. Without this premise, his entire body of discourse would have lost its underlying structure. Logically prior to this was the premise that there would always be conflicts and problems, stemming from human nature itself. So his discourse would first assume an inevitable threat to unity and order, then search for specific examples to validate the assumption, and finally express those threats in apocalyptic terms.

In other words, he had to be "Alarmist Ike." He had to respond to his fears by painting frightening pictures of apocalyptic threat. He knew no other way to speak about the world. Changing the name of the foe from "Soviet communism" to "creeping socialism" did not change this dynamic. The language continued to exacerbate the fears it sought to overcome, raising uncertainty to new heights. Seemingly innocuous platitudes such as, "We Americans need fear nothing of the future if we live in the unity of common purpose,"[8] were freighted with this whole ideological edifice. Apart from the empirical unlikelihood of unity of purpose, which undermined the statement's assurance, the discursive structure itself was bound to take away the hope the statement offered. A call for unity assumed that the only alternative was total disintegration. In this context, the words "we need fear nothing" were actually a way of saying that we should fear everything. The apparent assurance was meaningless unless it first evoked the fear it could then claim to overcome.

Eisenhower used this linguistic process to construct an ideal image of "the American way of life," filled with consensus, cooperation, and confidence. He gave that image a semblance of reality by placing it in an imagined past. He intended it to ease cultural strains and fears. But he constructed both "the American way of life" and the idealized past, as he had constructed his image of world peace, by constructing a broad array of threats to them. All these constructions were essential parts of a single discursive process, so there was no way to separate "the American way" from the threats to it. Since he pursued the image by creating more fears, he only put more strain on the whole system. Therefore it had to become ever more rigid and express its fears in ever more absolute terms.

Caught in this self-perpetuating dynamic, Eisenhower invoked fear of a dreadful future, not hope for a better one, as the motive for societal change. The change he urged was primarily a return to the past, not movement toward a different, better future. At times, "the middle way" did seem to represent something new for the future, but it was very vague and sunk in its ambiguities. Eisenhower was much more concrete and emotionally convincing when he created nostalgic images of the past and offered them as the most dependable guide to finding "the middle way." He could speak of this hope for reviving the past, however, only by contrasting it with a frightening future; he left it unclear whether "the middle way" was in fact an innovation or a return to the past. This unresolved tension between past and future only added further ambiguity to the meaning of "the middle way."

The defensive mode of his discourse was reinforced by its new turn toward domestic issues. In his Columbia years, Eisenhower paid less attention to extending U.S.-style freedom around the world. He continued to stand for internationalism, praising the benefits that would accrue to the world from a preponderance of U.S. power and influence. He praised the extension of the U.S. system not as an end in itself, but as a means of defending "the American way." The crucial issue was not whether the U.S. system would expand internationally, but whether it would survive at all. When Eisenhower invoked Jeffersonian rhetorical flourishes, he drew on an ideological system that had legitimized, and indeed required, U.S. expansion. But he did not use those flourishes to urge confident expansion of the U.S. system, but rather fearful protection of it. This was particularly evident during the Columbia years, when the discourse turned so sharply toward domestic fears. More than ever, expansion of the U.S. system was only a means to its protection. He always brought the argument back to the domestic preservation of the U.S. system.

This broadened the apocalyptic dimension of his discourse. The only admissible alternatives were the most extreme: either a U.S.-led system (some would call it hegemony) throughout the "free world," or a total loss of "the American way" at home as well as abroad. As Eisenhower acknowledged, though, the problems abroad were plain for everyone to see; there was little reason to feel confident about preponderance. When he turned to focus on domestic issues, he simply expanded the range of perceived threats. By treating "the American way" at home and abroad as a single fragile ideal, he honed his ideological system further toward a single all-encompassing polarity. Because he constructed that ideal by constructing its foes, hopes for its success anywhere had to evoke fears for its survival everywhere. So the intertwining of the world's fate with that of the United States only increased the sense of apocalyptic peril at home. Hopes for the "free world," like hopes for "the middle way," were bound to heighten fears.

The true measure of those fears was most evident in the new central vision of Eisenhower's discourse, the vision of Harry Truman leading the nation into socialist dictatorship. When such an unrealistic fear becomes the leitmotif of a person's discourse, the word *paranoia* may come to mind. Eisenhower was obviously not clinically paranoid. But did he employ what Richard Hofstadter has called "the paranoid style in American politics"?[9] Hofstadter traced a long historical tradition of political expression, whose central image is fear of "a 'vast' or 'gigantic' conspiracy as *the motive force* in historical events." It was propagated by "uncommonly angry minds" full of "heated exaggeration, suspiciousness, and conspiratorial fantasy. . . . The feeling of persecution is central." Based on this definition, Eisenhower should not be classed as a practitioner of the "paranoid style."

Yet he came surprisingly close. He did view the implacable threat of totalitarianism as the motive force in history, and he sometimes spoke of it as a conspiratorial force. He was certainly given to heated exaggeration and, at least occasionally, he expressed a feeling of being persecuted by various kinds of evil.

Eisenhower's discourse displayed nearly all of the other features of the "paranoid style," as delineated by Hofstadter: "Social issues could be reduced rather simply to a battle between a Good and an Evil influence. . . . The Evil influence, if not soon curbed, would bring about a terrible social apocalypse." "All our ills can be traced to a single center and hence can be eliminated by some kind of final act of victory over the evil source. If the warnings of those who diagnose the central treachery are not heeded soon enough, it is argued, we are finished: the world confronts an apocalypse." In Hofstadter's analysis, the paranoid style is "always manning the barricades of civilization. . . . Time is forever just running out." This style "runs dangerously near to hopeless pessimism, but usually stops short of it. . . . As a member of the avant-garde who is capable of perceiving the conspiracy before it is fully obvious to an as yet unaroused public, the paranoid is a militant leader. . . . The quality needed is not a willingness to compromise but the will to fight things out to a finish. Nothing but complete victory will do." Thus the leader calls for an "all-out crusade."

A leader who practices this style typically defends it on moral grounds. The enemy is "amoral, ubiquitous, luxury-loving." The leader often expresses a "fear that the decline of entrepreneurial competition will destroy our national character, or that the same effect will be brought about by our hedonistic mass culture and by moral laxity." He continues, "His sense that his political passions are unselfish and patriotic, in fact, goes far to intensify his feeling of righteousness and his moral indignation."

It is striking that Hofstadter, who probably never meant to class Eisenhower with McCarthy and Goldwater as "paranoids," could describe Eisenhower's discursive style so precisely. It was difficult to see his affinity with these more extreme Republicans, in part, because most of his language seemed so sober and reasonable by comparison. But Hofstadter has noted that this, too, can be a mark of the "paranoid style." Its discourse can be very convincing by its powerful appearance of logical persuasion. It sets out from defensible assumptions and accumulated facts, though it uses them to arrive at unrealistic conclusions. "It is nothing if not coherent—in fact, the paranoid mentality is far more coherent than the real world, since it leaves no room for mistakes, failures, or ambiguities. It is, if not wholly rational, at least intensely rationalistic." The political paranoid uses rich factual information and complex logical arguments as "a defensive act, which shuts off his receptive apparatus and protects him from having to attend to disturbing considerations that do not fortify his ideas." Distanced from reality, he is likely to strive for unrealistic goals, which only increases the level of frustration. "Even partial success leaves him with the same sense of powerlessness with which he began." So the conviction of an implacably evil enemy, to be faced in an apocalyptic showdown, grows even more persuasive and inescapable.[10]

Of course every ideologue blocks out reality in this way, and not every ideologue employs the "paranoid style." Yet Hofstadter's classic essay is one more reminder that the line between Eisenhower's "middle way" and McCarthyite radical Republicanism was never a very clear one. The differences are certainly very important, as the copious literature on the period makes clear. But that literature has been less attendant to the similarities, which may be equally important. By placing Truman Democrats, Wallace progressives, and Stalinist communists on a single continuum of evil, Eisenhower was making it more difficult for the public to distinguish among those groups. He was expanding the range of those to be feared.

When McCarthy and his followers turned that fear to hysteria, Eisenhower was complicit in heightening the hysteria he claimed to reject. He may have increased the level of hysteria even more by labeling so many kinds of anxiety as hysteria, rather than addressing the causes and nature of the anxieties in realistic empirical fashion. He used the charge of "hysteria" to denigrate policies that he opposed. But it is hard to resist the psychologizing conclusion that he saw so much "hysteria" in the land, and feared it so much, because he was striving so hard to repress his own tendencies toward hysteria. Certainly, he consciously intended to repress widespread public doubts about the viability of the U.S. system. There is no need to resort to psychological theory to see why the repressed doubts were bound to return; the "paranoid style," regardless of its psychological causes, always relies on language that evokes the very fears it seeks to overcome.

This explains why the "paranoid style" so often serves a conservative ideology, as it did in Eisenhower's time. It discursively constructs a world filled with peril on every side. When it offers a vision of genuine innovation and a better future, it does so only by constructing new threats that bar the way to that future.

So its words of hopeful encouragement for change end up increasing, rather than assuaging, doubts about both present and future. Paranoid language makes every movement into the future seem as dangerous as the present, which inevitably reinforces resistance to change of any kind. So it turns to an idealized past. When that is not available, it makes the status quo seem the lesser of two evils, safer than the risk of an unpredictable, hence uncontrollable, future.

Hofstadter's "paranoids," like Geertz's ideologues, see the world as out of control and feel frustrated by their powerlessness and lack of control. Eisenhower's language displayed the same dynamic. His appeals for "the middle way" and the American Assembly made it clear that the essential issue was control. Whatever could not be brought under the control of elite leaders was defined as chaotic and threatening. Since the future is always beyond control, insistence on controlling it is bound to breed frustration and anxiety. So "the middle way," presented as a path to a better future, could only heighten apocalyptic fears and make any genuine change seem a path to catastrophe. With both the present and the future hemmed in by such immense dangers, and with no way back to the idealized past (as Eisenhower himself admitted), the world became a trap or, at best, a fortress. There was no way to remove the danger. The best to hope for was to keep it forever at bay and prevent it from destroying civilization.

This conclusion was, of course, predetermined in the fundamental premise, the hub of Eisenhower's ideological wheel, the "single center of evil" (in Hofstadter's words): the ineradicable selfishness innate in human nature. Yet the final ironic twist in the ideological wheel was Eisenhower's insistence that the only salvation lay in the free moral decisions of 140,000,000 individual Americans. If the problem began not in class conflict, not in economic or political systems of any kind, not in historical roots and trends, but in the human soul, then the weight of the world lay on every pair of human shoulders. This was the only hope that Eisenhower could ever offer. But it had to be, at the same time, the ultimate reason for dread, and the responsibility that it entailed could only increase the anxiety it was meant to relieve. At every turn, Eisenhower was caught in the discursive trap he had created. The more his words entered the mainstream of public discourse, the more firmly the public, too, was ensnared in a web of words that allowed hope for nothing more than staving off the ultimate disaster.

# Part IV

## Toward the White House

CHAPTER 12

# Supreme Allied Commander, Europe

In September 1950, the government of the United States embarked on a major effort to make NATO a genuine fighting force by rearming its Western European allies, including West Germany.[1] President Truman and his advisors knew that it would be no easy task. As Blanche Wiesen Cook has noted, they were promoting

> some of the most unpopular postwar ideas imaginable: the military unification of Europe under U.S. domination, the revitalization of widely hated German industrial power, the rearmament of the German behemoth, the notion that world peace could be ensured only by intensive and expensive preparation for world war, and the notion that communism meant slavery while capitalism meant freedom. . . . Practically all Europe seemed to be moving toward socialism. . . . Not one European country had yet committed itself to a single issue relating to this entirely hypothetical force. NATO was, in sum, an American dream.[2]

Realizing how unpopular this plan would be, the Truman administration offered three inducements to its NATO allies: more American aid (particularly military aid), four divisions of U.S. troops to protect against the possibility of either Soviet or German aggression and, to head the unified allied military force, an American commander—not just any commander, but the most popular of all in European eyes, the wartime hero, Dwight D. Eisenhower. Eisenhower was picked for the job of Supreme Allied Commander in Europe (SACEUR) in October 1950.[3] He made a brief tour of European capitals in January 1951, returned home to report his findings, and by late February was permanently established at the Supreme Headquarters Allied Powers in Europe (SHAPE) in Paris.

## DEFINING THE MISSION

Historians debate the exact nature of Eisenhower's ultimate mission. Some see the Truman administration as wanting primarily to shore up its buffer against potential Soviet military moves westward. Some see it as more concerned with shoring up its geopolitical ties with Western Europe. Still others see the administration as motivated more by economic concerns. The Marshall Plan had accomplished all it could, but Western Europe was still suffering a dollar drain; huge infusions of military aid and U.S. troops would allow the United States to continue pouring dollars into Europe. Secretary of State Dean Acheson seems to have had all these in mind when he wrote that NATO was more than just a military alliance; it was "a means and a vehicle for closer political, economic, and security cooperation with western Europe." Eisenhower was sent to Europe as "the embodiment of NATO" (in Acheson's words), the symbolic vehicle for intertwining and achieving all of these aims.[4]

There was also a domestic political side to the appointment of Eisenhower. Truman knew that the decision to station troops more or less permanently in Europe would be widely criticized. Putting Eisenhower at their head might soften those criticisms a bit. Perhaps Truman also wanted Eisenhower out of the public limelight, since the "Ike for President" bandwagon was still rolling along. If so, he may have made a mistake. As Piers Brendon has noted, Ike's new post

> enhanced his stature as a statesman, while conveniently making it impossible for him to get his hands dirty as a politician . . . [It] reminded voters of Ike's unique achievements in the field of coalition conflict. It restored him to a military position at a time when the country was once again at war, in Korea. . . . It also enabled him to distance himself from the Democratic administration while presenting a sober alternative to the isolationist wing of the Republican party. . . . Ike could avoid making public pronouncements on partisan matters. . . . He was above the grubby political [and McCarthyite] fray at home but in the front line of the cold war against Communism abroad.[5]

Eisenhower was surely aware of all these factors. In fact, by the time he moved permanently to France he had probably decided to run, or at least to consider quite seriously a run, for the presidency.[6] In his most private as well as his most public words, though, he refused to admit that political considerations had any effect upon him. He continued to insist that it was all a matter of duty.[7] In the terms of Eisenhower's own discourse, then, he had probably decided that it was his duty to run for (and presumably become) president. Though he was still ambivalent, he began taking more overt steps in that direction. Many of his ostensibly private letters were written to influential Americans who could help his political fortunes. These letters were quasi-public, for he could assume (and he probably hoped) that their contents would be circulated in elite circles.

As he began his SACEUR duties, he sent such a letter to a key political operative among conservative Republicans, Edward Bermingham. He wrote, he said, because he knew that Bermingham would "from time to time be asked by others" about the potential candidate's views; he knew that this message would be spread throughout the Republican land. "I assure you," he began, "that I approach this whole matter from no other standpoint than that of the enlightened self-interest of our country." If "all the other countries that are important to us have fallen, one by one, under Soviet domination," the United States could not "sustain our economy, our prosperity, and, indeed, our very existence." To prevent this disaster, he was advocating "the middle ground." Isolationism would eventually leave the United States "waiting for our starvation or destruction." On the other hand (in a nod to the Republican right), neither could the United States "carry the world on its own shoulders." He wanted only to help other nations become able to defend themselves. This did not make him a member of the Truman administration, he insisted, nor "a partisan or a member of any political or any other group." He was obviously trying to protect his right political flank while keeping his options open.[8]

Eisenhower had barely arrived in Paris when he sent another letter to Bermingham, covering the same ground in more detail.[9] (To make sure his words were widely heard, he sent copies to two other trusted and influential Republican friends.) He eschewed the complexities of policy that engrossed Truman's advisors and still engross historians. Instead, "Alarmist Ike" opted for the familiar simplicities of his ideology: ruthless communism was intent on "*world revolution and subsequent domination of all the earth.*" The "free system" of individual dignity and "a capitalistic economy" had never been so threatened. "Definite, prompt, and comprehensive measures are necessary if we are to survive." The first need was for the United States to "remain solvent; bankruptcy for us would be a tremendous, if not a decisive, victory for the Kremlin." Both preventing and winning a war required a sound economy. Both the military and economic threats required strong Western European allies. Losing Western Europe to the communists would mean losing all of Eurasia and most of Africa too: "Among other areas, the Belgian Congo, the Mid-East, and the Suez Canal would be gone! . . . The existence of such a vast organism, hostile to us, would pose a military problem that would defy solution."

The economic problem would be equally grave: "Where would we get the materials needed for our existence? For making steel, for making atomic bombs? It is
this kind of problem that keeps me awake nights."

The way to fend off these catastrophes was not to keep U.S. troops in Europe
forever, Eisenhower continued: "We can not be a modern Rome guarding the far
frontiers with our legions." If all U.S. troops were not withdrawn within ten years,
his mission would have failed. The mission was, above all, "to rejuvenate in
Europe a feeling of self-respect, of self-confidence, and of self-dependence—
including the burning purpose and desire of self-defense. . . . The present question is how to inspire Europe."

These words, written to political allies, may have been intended for political
purposes. Certainly they reflect a military officer whose conception of his role goes
far beyond purely military matters, an officer taking the broad view that would be
appropriate for a president. But they should not be discounted as mere political
manipulation. Both their content and their alarmist tone were perfectly consistent
with everything Eisenhower had said in private before becoming SACEUR, and
they summed up the gist of everything he would say about his mission throughout his fifteen months as SACEUR. If Eisenhower had another "true" set of private
beliefs, he never wrote them down, and they must remain irrelevant for history.
All of his private words revolved around the key ideas outlined in these letters.

He first began to develop this pattern of language when he headed the
Council on Foreign Relations study group, two years before his appointment to
NATO.[10] It was already fully evident when he returned home briefly in late
January, after his initial tour. Eisenhower and Truman lunched together, and then
the president convened his top advisers and asked the SACEUR to repeat the
report he had given over lunch.[11] "I believe that our civilization is in one hell of a
hole," Eisenhower lamented. "Western Europe is the seat of our culture and our
civilization," he explained. Despite its great economic power, it was "afraid of 190
million backward people"—the Russians—only because Russia was united and
Western Europe was not. His job, he said, was "to bring about a unity in the
defense of Western Europe," and thus end the danger.

But what was the real source of danger? Eisenhower asserted that "he
doubt[ed] very much that the Russians want[ed] to fight now. 'I personally think
those guys in the Kremlin like their jobs.' . . . There was always a possibility that
something could happen, but he doubted it." In all the capitals he had found
"confidence that the [indigenous] communists in Western Europe presented no
grave menace." "The real communist danger at the moment," Eisenhower
explained, "is in its latest manifestation, that of 'neutralism.' . . . Neutralism is only

a wishful hope, but we have to recognize that it has a fairly wide appeal." The "unity" Eisenhower wanted was a solid wall of well-armed European nations, siding with the United States against the Soviet Union. In all the European capitals he had visited, "he got everybody to agree that the Western nations could tell Russia to go to hell if they only would get together, raise enough men, and produce enough equipment."

The Europeans would choose that "unity," he argued, only if they found it in their own interests and trusted the United States to support those same interests. Eisenhower's code words for this pro-U.S. stand were "confidence" and "morale": "The way we can give them that confidence is by sending equipment and by sending some American units over there to help morale. . . . We've got to get them the equipment to end this idea of neutralism." He wanted U.S. troops in Europe to "boost their morale. Nothing would convince the Europeans more than the sight of 10 or 12 United States divisions that we mean business. Of course, we should not plan on keeping our divisions there forever." Once the Europeans built up their own force, "the Americans can come home." Even for the present, he estimated, the U.S. forces would supply only about one-fifth of the troops needed to defend against a Soviet ground attack. So the U.S. military presence in Europe would be valuable principally for its symbolic, not its practical, significance. Yet that symbolic meaning held the key to the future of civilization, he concluded: "The difference is whether our civilization goes up or goes down, and so I am ready for a tremendous sacrifice."

There was nothing new for Eisenhower in this lengthy report to the president and his top advisors, nor did he develop any significant new ideas during the next sixteen months in Europe. Rather, he elaborated his old ideas in a new context. He was back in daily contact with the issues that had been most central in World War II: holding together a Western alliance to face a totalitarian enemy. The enemy was a new one, with a new kind of ideology and new weapons to advance it, but Eisenhower's own ideology was essentially the same. He was dealing with the same issues and the same ideology that would dominate his presidency. So his long stay in Europe gave him a valuable opportunity to hone his central ideological tenets as he continued his ambivalent advance toward the White House.

## DEFINING THE THREAT

His most basic tenet was that the Soviet Union was irrevocably bent on dominating the whole world. Reading a long essay on cold war strategy by Leslie S. Stevens, Eisenhower came across a quotation from Lenin, declaring "the most frightful collisions" with capitalist states to be "inevitable." "This belief has never changed," he jotted in the margin. When Stevens argued that it was ideology, not nationalism, driving Soviet policy, Eisenhower noted: "This is 180 degrees different from what I've believed. If he is right I think the USSR is even more dangerous than we have assumed." Apparently he found Stevens's argument sufficiently persuasive to modify, though not change, his own belief. Soviet leaders were compelled by an "unholy wedding" between Marxist ideology and traditional Russian imperialism, he wrote to Stevens. Neither factor was dominant, but each reinforced the other.[12]

Eisenhower's marginalia endorsed Stevens's claim that the Soviet Union, still depleted from World War II, was unlikely to start a war soon. It would be a foolish move, unless the Soviets were directly attacked. (Here Eisenhower's notes referred to "the Mother Russia complex.") Stevens warned, though, that "the logic of the situation as regards war and peace may not be controlling." Eisenhower agreed that this was "sad but true." It was "a most important point," he noted, that the Soviets might not think in the same way as Americans. As he explained to a friend, the Soviet Union was a juvenile and irrational nation, which might really start a war.[13]

In the event of war, "we will have to use everything we have," he told his chief of staff, Gen. Alfred Gruenther. Of course this meant using nuclear weapons. A letter to President Truman, drafted by Eisenhower on behalf of his Council on Foreign Relations study group, called for enough strategic air strength to mount an "effective" bombing attack against Russia. But Eisenhower still saw no great revolution in warfare. "Most of my associates have not so simplified the problem as to make the atom bomb situation the single decisive factor," he noted in the margin of Stevens's essay, and then wrote: "Air-men might believe this. I do not." He did not think a preemptive attack (which he always rejected) would bring the Soviet Union to its knees or prevent a Soviet attack on Europe. It would be wrong to rely too much on air power, he told Army Chief of Staff Joseph Collins. The next war would still be a traditional war, won on the ground. Such a statement from the SACEUR would certainly help Collins keep up funding for the army. At the same time, he could please air force and navy constituencies by declaring that they would carry the bulk of the U.S. involvement in the next war because most of the ground troops would be European. This was, in fact, part of NATO doctrine.[14]

Eisenhower's statement to Collins also reflected the SACEUR's basic approach to war planning. He expected a long war in which industrial production would be decisive, as it had been in the last war. The main value of strategic bombing, he told Collins, was to destroy the enemy's military industries and thereby its will to resist. In case deterrence failed, though, the United States needed to keep up its industrial production and stockpiling. Civilian leaders such as Truman were ignoring his pleas for readiness, he complained in his diary; he resolved to go on "preaching" to them until they listened and to "go to town" on stocking military materials. These were the same kinds of complaints he been making since the early months of World War II (as he noted in another diary entry). He was still preparing to refight the war that he told the public had never really ended.[15]

If the Soviets did attack, the United States would have to fight, Eisenhower insisted, because Europe was only the first domino. A communist victory there would lead to communist domination throughout Asia, Africa, and "possibly even parts of South America," he told one correspondent. Eisenhower did not fear direct military conquest of the United States. Rather, he feared the economic consequences of these falling dominos. After reading a major article by John Foster Dulles in *Life,* outlining a theory of massive retaliation against Soviet aggression, Eisenhower wrote to Lucius Clay that he agreed with Dulles in cases of military aggression. But he questioned whether this would work against political aggression, which could be just as damaging to "our resulting economic situation." The United States would be cut off from trading partners, and the basic rule of foreign policy, he wrote, was to know what countries must be friendly trading partners to allow the U.S. economy to flourish. To his brother Edgar he explained that the United States needed raw materials as well as trading partners, and communist world domination would make both impossible. The threat to raw materials was becoming his favorite theme. When a mining executive pointed out that the United States was rather self-sufficient in many minerals, Eisenhower admitted, "occasionally I overstate or oversimplify my raw material argument." It was only one part of the overall picture, he implied, but it was a crucial part.[16]

Without a successful NATO, he argued to *Reader's Digest* publisher DeWitt Wallace, the United States would have to stave off the communists alone. But this would push military costs so high "that we could scarcely manage and expect to retain, over the years, a free economy." Eisenhower no longer distinguished between security and solvency; the United States had to win the cold war to protect its economy, and vice versa. The question was how to protect the nation militarily and economically at the same time. The answer, he told his diary, was to find "the most economical & efficient methods" of combating communism. But how did you impose efficiency in a free enterprise economy? He knew that government controls were bad; the law of supply and demand should always be obeyed. But what if the government had to make extraordinary demands for military procurement? He confessed to financier George Whitney that the problem

baffled him. (Indeed, he admitted to another wealthy friend that the overall economic situation in the United States was too complicated for him to understand.)[17]

By early 1952, after extensive correspondence on economic issues with stal-
warts of the Republican corporate elite, he had formulated some basic principles.
These were sketched out in a lengthy diary entry. The immediate problem was an
overly rapid military buildup aiming at a particular "D-day." This buildup was
uncalled for, since no "emergency" (i.e., war with the Soviets) was likely in the
near future. Eisenhower argued that the resulting boom-and-bust budgeting was
costly and inefficient. He had been well tutored by his corporate executive friends
to understand that "reasonable men have no recourse except to plan on the basis
of stable, relatively assured income and outgo." The nation, like a business,
needed long-range planning and a steady level of military spending that could be
sustained "as long as there appears to be a threat in the world capable of endangering our national safety." Of course in Eisenhower's private discourse this meant,
in effect, a spending level sustained in perpetuity, for he would always see a threat
to the nation. But he saw no threat in substantial military budgets, as long as they
could be maintained without inflationary pressures. Inflation was now the main
danger facing the nation.[18]

Eisenhower added that, as SACEUR, he could not publicly criticize the
Truman administration's excessive military budgets. The slightest political word
"would be disastrous to the vital work I am trying to do," he cautioned his brother
Milton. He also worried that public criticism from others, with whom he agreed,
might do more harm than good. When Phillip Reed, president of the National
Association of Manufacturers, publicly stated that the Soviet threat was overstated
and urged less military spending, "Eisenhower was furious," writes Blanche
Wiesen Cook. Eisenhower "agreed that it was possible 'to go broke in the process
of rearming and destroying the very economic and social fabric we are trying to
defend.' But Eisenhower feared that Reed's talk gave too much comfort to those
who opposed all rearmament and preferred simply 'to put off unpleasant chores'
and do nothing." If one had to err, it was better to err on the side of too much
rather than too little military spending, because the risk was infinite; this was
Eisenhower's implicit argument.[19]

### "DANGLING BY A THREAD"

The SACEUR was as alarmist as ever. To judge from his choice of words, apocalyptic perils on every side threatened "our very existence." Any one of them might

lead to U.S. bankruptcy, thence to dictatorship. He was fighting to save the U.S. free enterprise system, which meant the "American way of life," which meant civilization itself, he told several correspondents: "This whole political and economic order is being challenged from every angle." The cold war was one of "those occasions in civilization's history in which complete priority must be given to problems of national survival." He told his NATO staff members that success in their mission was "vital to the civilization we know. . . . The free world must work together and well or there is going to be no free world." "Are you ready to accept complete defeat for the American form of government?" he asked his brother Edgar. If not, now was the time to fight for it.[20]

Every topic Eisenhower discussed in his private discourse was framed in the language of impending disaster. Before leaving for Europe, he met with his Council on Foreign Relations study group to send a letter to the president. He was preparing to deal with "a world crisis," he told the group: "We are dangling by a thread over the edge of the cliff." His draft of the letter warned that "a disunited free world is certain to fall, piecemeal," to the Soviet Union, leading to "the extinction of our treasured ideals." "Without an effective allied force in Europe," he explained to Henry Wriston, head of the council, "all the Russians needed to march to the Channel was shoe-leather." The crumbling effect set in motion by the fall of Europe would be difficult to stop short of the point where America's danger would be acute. Indeed, without allies in Western Europe, the United States would find itself in the most desperate situation of any major government in modern times.[21]

The true catastrophe would be economic: "Our economy must suffer severely, if not fatally, if we allow vital areas of the world to fall successively under the domination of the communists." If the economy were crippled, the U.S. system of free enterprise would be destroyed, he warned his brother Earl: "If the other countries of the free world fall, one by one, under the domination of Russia, we will finally get to the point where we have no friends with whom to trade; and, after that, it would be only a short distance to economic disaster for us and consequent regimentation of some kind." If all the world except the United States became "Communistic," it would "force us into a system of complete controls. In other words, we'd have a dictatorship of our own—and would have lost that for which we are struggling, freedom." So a strong NATO was necessary "if we are to survive as a nation featuring political freedom for the individual and a competitive, free enterprise system." "National security and national solvency are mutually dependent," he told his future secretary of defense, Charles E. Wilson. "The permanent maintenance of a crushing weight of military power would eventually produce dictatorship."[22]

Great military power would prevent the "crushing weight" of greater power in the future. "Industrial mobilization could save our nation—our country is at stake," he wrote in his diary. To President Truman he confessed: "Our biggest problem is production. . . . The element of time may well be critical. How to solve this one without going hysterical I don't know." Present policies only seemed efficient; in reality they were driving the United States "straight toward inflation of an uncontrollable character. Wouldn't the monster Kremlin rejoice to see us admit insolvency!!!" He agreed with railroad executive Martin Clement that inflation was the nation's number one problem, and could be prevented only by higher taxes and lower government spending.[23]

He lamented, typically, that he was among the few who understood the danger and were willing to take the "highly unpopular" steps needed: "We [i.e., the public] want nostrums and sugar-coated pills; but they will be no good against more and more planned economy and Socialistic trends." The danger of socialism remained a central and cherished tenet in Eisenhower's discourse. As he prepared to announce his candidacy for president, a principal political advisor, Henry Cabot Lodge, warned him to stop calling the Democrats socialistic, since few voters would believe that. But Eisenhower resisted; he "felt compelled to remark that I believe what I believe"—any government could claim to be the people's servant but end up as their master.[24]

This left the problem of how to increase military production while avoiding inflation and government control. Such a problem, too, might spell catastrophe: "I begin to experience bewilderment in attempting to understand how the law of supply and demand can control the whole matter in time to avoid disaster." He was sure that the philosophy of work was "the only thing that is going to save the world." He told the audience: "Every American must do utmost in these days of tension and bewilderment to preserve and sustain our nation and our system." But he did not know how to relieve the bewilderment. "The average U.S. citizen is confused—if not fearful and afraid," he noted in his diary. He complained to George Whitney about the "feeling at home that the country is deteriorating; people are just plain scared." He admitted sharing the confusion and fear. In fact, though he did not acknowledge it, he was even more frightened than most people, for he feared that Americans might actually want "to go on an unthinking course to ultimate disaster."[25]

Eisenhower claimed that only dire peril and pervasive fear persuaded him to run for president. He recalled telling Douglas Southall Freeman, in 1946, that anyone should accept the presidency if the nation's leaders deemed him the "only man who could save the country from ruin." Now, apparently, he believed that time had come. His political friends believed that a Democratic victory in 1952 would increase "the risk of the two-party system disappearing . . . a disastrous possibility." For his brother Milton he summed up, in his own words, the advice he had received from those friends: unless Eisenhower becomes president "the country is down the drain." If this was all, to some degree, a rationalizing self-deception, it still demonstrates how central (and how serviceable) alarmist language was in Eisenhower's private discourse.

## SOLUTIONS

The trick was to prevent all these interwoven catastrophes—foreign and domestic, military, political, and economic—without fighting another world war. Eisenhower continued to argue that World War III would be catastrophic even if the United States won. "If I did not believe that our efforts today were directed toward the prevention of war," he wrote to Army Chief of Staff Gen. Joseph Collins, "I most certainly would not be here." He told George Whitney that "the advancing of the Iron Curtain would put us in an intolerable position." But "there is no such thing as a preventive war, at least against a great and monolithic power such as exists in Eurasia today." A victorious war over the communists would "still leave us a chaotic world" where democracy could not grow. "So there is no recourse for the free world as I see it but develop a security situation which Russia *must* respect, which it will not attack."[26]

As long as the Russians were deterred from attacking, and war was avoided, NATO would be preserving the peace. For the first time, peace became a significant (though still not frequent) theme in Eisenhower's private discourse. He stressed his desire for peace to ordinary citizens such as Elizabeth Rankin, who chastised him for misusing the New Testament to justify his policy of peace through strength. "We both seek a lasting peace. I agree with you that complete disarmament of all nations and complete adherence to Christian principles by all would bring peace." Communist warmongering, however, made this impossible. "Our best hopes for peace lie in the timely provision of military and economic strength sufficient to convince an aggressor that he cannot gain through war. Like you, I hope for the day when people everywhere will be able to live in peace—free from fear of war." He told Private Gabriel Stilian that, because communists only respect force, the free world must have enough force to prevent them "from putting their case to the test of arms. In other words, we are training and preparing now *not to fight a war but to preserve the peace.* . . . Our basic objective [is] organizing to preserve the peace." Peace now meant primarily the absence of war.

Since there was no war at the moment, peace prevailed, and the only task was to preserve it. Preserving peace would be one, though only one, way to prevent catastrophe.[27]

Perhaps it was not just coincidence that ordinary folks heard this message. He wrote to Ford Foundation president Paul Hoffman, "I do think it important to remember that people want *peace.*" Eisenhower was praising a speech by Hoffman as a fine summary of Repblican principles. His only suggestion was to add some reference to peace. This concern about the rhetoric of peace may have been occasioned by an article by *Look* publisher John Cowles entitled, "Let's Launch an American Peace Offensive." Just the day before writing to Hoffman, Eisenhower had written to Cowles: "The theme of your article was perfect. Frankly, if I did not believe I were struggling to preserve the peace, I would have far less concern in this job." More articles like this should be encouraged, he said, to "establish peace as the real warp and woof of all our propaganda and informational activity." Eisenhower was promoting peace, then, not only to avoid war but also to score propaganda and political points. This was also the theme of Cowles's "perfect" article: the United States should propose a disarmament plan so that, when it was rejected, the Soviet Union would stand convicted as "the aggressor and warmonger." Eisenhower could readily support such a plan since it would both assume and validate the premises of his policy: preserving peace by preparing for war.[28]

In the spring of 1952, as he prepared for his presidential bid, he developed a general position on disarmament, sketched out in letters to two key Republican friends. First, the United States had to confront the Soviets "with the certainty that they cannot hope successfully to attack the free world. Once this goal has been achieved from a position of strength we can begin to negotiate on a practical basis for the development of a plan of co-existence in this world." This would include "a progressive program of disarmament—one that is accompanied by full and free inspection because of the impossibility of trusting the Russian dictatorship. If we cannot bring about such an agreement we can at the very least live, thereafter, in a feeling of relative security." "In the long run" the appeal of the U.S. system would undermine communism everywhere and "the Soviet dictatorship will begin to deteriorate." But, he admitted, "this is a long-term project; I believe the world has gone too far to admit of any easy answer to its colossal problem of working out a plan of co-existence between free government and dictatorship. There is no completely clear cut solution." For the foreseeable future, the United States would have to accept the existence of a mortal enemy in the world and find ways to survive. Peace meant a situation in which both enemies survived, neither taking active military steps to destroy the other.[29]

The only way to preserve this kind of peace, and thus preserve the Western capitalist system, Eisenhower said repeatedly, was collective security. "Collective security is a *must* for the future of our type of civilization," he wrote to his brother. Without it, he told Swede Hazlett, all NATO nations including the United States would suffer "an eventual fate that is worse than any kind of expense or effort we can now imagine." Any alternative to collective security promised "little more than tragic failure; this, it seems to me is the basic truth that we at home—and Europe especially—must understand, *now!!*" But he gave the Wilsonian term *collective security* a somewhat new meaning. Now it meant, in effect, solidifying the "free world" as a U.S. "sphere of influence" mobilized to combat the Soviet sphere in a continuing cold war. If the "free world" could be organized "efficiently and rapidly," he told his wartime aide Harry Butcher, "the communist world will not dare attack."[30]

Reflecting explicitly on linguistic usage, Eisenhower contended that "the word 'neutrality' has become almost meaningless." All noncommunist nations "must be specifically a part of the organization of free nations. . . . To attempt to do otherwise is silly and suicidal." He told columnist Drew Pearson that his goal was "to bring the free world into effective cooperation—and by the free world I am now thinking of practically all areas that still lay outside the Iron Curtain and, of course, all those inside it that want to get out."[31]

In June 1951, Eisenhower wrote in his diary: "I am coming to believe that Europe's security problem is never going to be solved satisfactorily until there exists a U.S. of Europe." Most important, a unified Europe would be a way to bring West Germany into the U.S-led military alliance. "The German problem grows acute," said another diary entry a few weeks later. A U.S. of Europe would also keep down military expenditures that were weakening European economies. Eisenhower supported this idea, soon embodied in proposals for a European Defense Community (EDC), throughout 1951. In a review of his first year as SACEUR, he told Truman that only an EDC would allow Europeans to defend themselves affordably over the long run. Without it, he told a Republican ally at the same time, there could be "no permanent and assured peace for the Western world as long as the communist menace exists in its present form." A few months later, he still fretted over the insoluble question of Germany: "We are either going to solve this German problem or the Soviets will solve it in their favor."[32] Nodding to his political right, Eisenhower sometimes expressed regret that he could find no alternative to collective security. It was unfortunate, he said, because it caused so much political debate. But he insisted that it was an absolute necessity.

Perhaps he also regretted it because the job was so difficult. Replicating his World War II attitude quite precisely, he maintained that there were adequate resources for a strong collective security force; what was lacking was the will. "We *can* do this job if we *just want, badly enough, to do so,*" he wrote to a British wartime colleague. But there was just not enough sense of urgency among the NATO allies, he complained to Averell Harriman. Unfortunately, he lamented to the Army Chief of Staff, the people who had the most at stake seemed most confident. Military leaders had to pressure civilian leaders to "educate" their public to support the U.S. militarization plans, or else the dangers would be "so terrifying and tragic as to make decent peace an unattainable goal in our time." Each country had to develop the morale and will to defend itself; "if not, that particular nation is doomed." As always, Eisenhower counted himself among the few who saw and responded to impending danger.[33]

In late 1951 and early 1952, he occasionally wrote of an improving morale situation. By the spring of 1952, however, faced with a poll showing no favorable public opinion toward NATO membership for West Germany, he was still contemplating the possibility of total failure. Security was a product of spiritual, economic, and military strength, he wrote to George Sloan, using a favorite mathematical metaphor. "If any one of the three factors concerned falls to zero, then the product of the equation . . . likewise falls to zero." He feared that some Europeans might let their strength fall to zero; he sometimes wondered, he told a friend, if people would not "prefer to go on an unthinking course to ultimate disaster."[34]

## "INSPIRATIONAL EFFORTS THAT COST NOTHING"

Such pessimism and defeatism was "one of the big obstacles to progress," Eisenhower complained. Of course he denied the pessimistic overtones of his own alarmist fears. He was still "an incurable optimist" with "almost indestructible optimism," he insisted to friends, though he did confess that "occasionally I grow a little bit weary." At one point he admitted to Averell Harriman that he did not want to testify before a congressional committee because "any honest testimony would have to present the discouraging as well as the encouraging features of this project. . . . I could easily be quoted as being exceedingly pessimistic. Yet the last thing that a leader may be is pessimistic if he is to achieve success."[35]

Eisenhower's self-appointed role was, once again, to inspire others by playing the eternal optimist. "What Europe needs now more than anything else is someone to make her understand how much she *can* do if she really wants to do it rather than someone who is constantly preaching futility and defeatism." "Our basic purpose," he explained to Lucius Clay, "is to re-create the morale that will insure the *self*-defense of Europe." As Thomas Sisk has shown, "Eisenhower believed that the best way to exhibit American leadership in Europe was through an early and massive infusion of troops into Europe."[36]

For the SACEUR, U.S. troops were not primarily a powerful military barrier against a Soviet attack, nor a tripwire to deter that attack. These were only their short-term functions. In the long run, and in the most important sense, the troops were, like nuclear weapons, symbolic tokens in a psychological campaign. The very presence of these troops was supposed to inspire the Europeans to build forces of their own strong enough to stave off Soviet aggression for decades to come. According to this theory, the material presence of U.S. troops would embody the U.S. spiritual values of optimism and morale, stimulate those spiritual values in the NATO allies, and thus lead the latter to create greater material forces of their own. The material and the spiritual were bound together through optimism.

In an official report he told his civilian superior, the new secretary of defense, Robert Lovett: "It seems silly if we do not match our great material expenditures by inspirational efforts that cost nothing and which, in many cases, can be more efficacious than mere financial help." Only "inspired leaders," he wrote in his diary, could persuade the Europeans to form a United States of Europe. Eisenhower was talking, above all, about himself. Though he never quite came out and said it, he left little doubt that he saw himself, both in Europe and at home, as the inspired selfless leader needed to avert disaster. "It certainly looks like the poor old world needs a new Moses," he lamented to a friend in the summer of 1951. Two months later he told Lovett that "NATO needs an eloquent and inspired Moses as much as it needs planes, tanks, guns, and ships. He must be civilian and he must be legion—he must speak to each of the countries, every day of every year—he must be the product of American leadership." This left little doubt who the new Moses would be.[37]

His job, as he saw it, was essentially a sales and public relations job. He had to interpret the symbolic meaning of the U.S. troop commitment, to put the right spin on it. To the secretary of defense he explained: "We must appeal . . . to entire populations—we must strive to reach the heart and mind of every single individual." He intended to achieve this by explaining the U.S. military effort "in such terms that the ordinary man can understand," he told Lucius Clay. "Our problem is so much one of selling and inspiring—of making people see this job from the American viewpoint."[38]

To be an effective salesman, Eisenhower would "occasionally overstate or oversimplify," he said. Others might judge it more than occasional. It was unavoidable, though, from his perspective: "We have got to reduce the issues of the day to their simplest terms, to point out the right and wrong in each instance." This would "inspire optimism and insure accomplishment; without these qualifications, the free world will indeed be in a sorry mess." Blanche Wiesen Cook has rightly observed that Eisenhower had to "introduce new concepts, new meanings, new ideas—to change the very words of public life."[39]

His first appeal was to reason: "The self interest of each nation in the success of the whole should be demonstrated." So he argued that every NATO nation could defend itself more cheaply, as well as more effectively, if all pooled their resources. He made the same point about his own nation. It was only "enlightened self-interest" to keep a strong military alliance with valued trading partners. As he moved closer to outright presidential candidacy, this theme became more prominent. "My motivating principle has been American First," he wrote to Arthur Summerfield, an influential Republican. He told another influential Republican, George Sloan, that Americans serving in Europe were "animated by one compelling motive. This motive is to serve the best interests of our country." This was obviously a message that would serve Eisenhower's political interests as he tried to woo right-wing Republicans.[40]

Given his view of human nature, though, Eisenhower could never rely on reason alone to carry the day. People were not self-disciplined enough to follow the dictates of reason. "A union of minds & hearts is the indispensable formula for success," he told his diary. He wrote to Hollywood producer Samuel Goldwyn (praising him for a recent patriotic film): "The more I live, the more I am convinced that it is the simple truths—the seemingly obvious truths—that need constant telling and retelling." Americans had to be persuaded to defend their own freedom, or else it would not survive. This defense required selflessness, a quality "so difficult to instill permanently in human nature that constant effort is required . . . through every medium," including Hollywood films.[41]

The battle between selfishness and self-discipline was still fundamental to Eisenhower's ideology, and he commented upon it many times in many contexts. To one political supporter he wrote: "All people are made up of combinations of characteristics that divide themselves fairly well into two categories between which there is constant war." The "noble" category included selflessness, cooperation, balance, consideration, and cheerfulness. The "ignoble" was "the exact opposites, or at least the lack" of these, including fear, hysteria, and selfishness. People who sought private gain rather than the national good were "responding to one of the recognized factors in human nature," he wrote to his brother Edgar. To be human, he told George Whitney, meant to have a "full share of ignoble and self-centered qualities"—"the villain who, in one degree or another, lurks within each of us"—as well as "at least some of the ennobling virtues." So group relations were bound to generate conflict and require compromise.[42]

But this did not legitimate compromise on issues of morality. On the contrary, precisely because there was a villain in each of us, moral questions allowed only "black and white." Truth in morality was as absolute as in the "exact sciences." The combination of an absolute standard and innate selfishness meant (as Augustinian theology assumes) that moral failure was inevitable. "Men respond far more easily to a selfish impulse than to a noble one," he wrote to Swede Hazlett. So when people got together to solve common problems, the result was usually "exceedingly disappointing." Even the selfless could not expect any results "too brilliant." "We can't go too far wrong. . . . Possibly this is the most for which we should, individually, seek."[43]

The major problem facing groups was that selfish individuals, wanting more power, tended to make themselves leaders. Thus were born the politicians: "Politics excites all that is selfish and ambitious in man." The closer he came to an overt political commitment, the more Eisenhower condemned the selfishness of politicians. More than ever he wanted to convince the world (and perhaps himself) that he would not enter politics motivated by selfishness; he would always be above the dirty political fray. Eisenhower set himself apart because he was a military man, and military leaders were less selfish than others. Most important, Eisenhower was different because he understood that the nation and the world needed leaders who were "inspired" rather than selfish.[44]

## DEVELOPING THEORY

As he moved closer to the presidency, Eisenhower tried to develop a rudimentary political theory based on his view of human nature. In one letter he felt moved to develop an intellectual argument against socialism. Marxism awards all wealth to society because it treats society as prior to, and therefore more valuable than, the individual. This was clearly mistaken, he argued, because "society itself is composed of nothing more than vast numbers of individuals. . . . Unless each member has a real incentive to produce, the result will finally be a society that has nothing with which to reward." The incentive, he assumed, would have to be individual gain, not merely the improvement of society; selfishness was an innate trait of humanity, he wrote to his brother Milton. But he continued that it should be possible to persuade people that "selfish interests require moderation when excess would lead to disaster." He mentioned smoking cigarettes and receiving government farm payments as examples of disaster. No doubt he was also thinking about military budgets and European rearmament.[45]

The essential problem of political life was the danger that individual excess would lead to disaster for the whole community. This was the burden of a long letter to newspaper publisher William Robinson.[46] The letter was intended as a trial run of the ideas on which the candidate would appeal to Republicans. But it was, for the most part, only an explication of ideas he had preached throughout the Columbia years. Eisenhower stated with marvelous precision the most basic premise of his political theory over the previous decade: "All men recognize the need for some control over their own impulsive actions." Unable to trust themselves to pursue their rational self-interest, individuals band together to establish communal agencies that would compel them to control themselves. "The basic purpose of all organization is to produce orderliness, which means restriction upon irresponsible human action." In the context of Eisenhower's discourse, "irresponsible" was a synonym for "excessively selfish."

No group could be successful without such restriction, he wrote. But there was always a danger that the restricting agencies would exercise either too little control, allowing some individuals to amass excessive power, or too much control, giving the agencies themselves excessive power. The eternal "task of the progressive" is to break down all such concentrations of power, for they all restrict the individual's "opportunities for self-development and advancement," the very opportunities that society is established to advance. Eisenhower now numbered himself among these "progressives."

Protecting the individual against unnecessary domination "requires orderly government," he continued; i.e., government that restricts selfish action just enough, but not too much. Finding this "practical balance is difficult, but *it is the ever-continuing problem of free men.*" It was the problem he was encountering in Europe, as he tried to impose central organization on recalcitrant allies. "The age-old problem of inducing the individual to sacrifice in order to promote the common good of the community or nation," he called it, writing to Secretary of Defense Lovett. "Complete attainment of this kind of spontaneous cooperation is not possible," he told Lovett, because "human beings are fallible." But just for that reason he urged a campaign of inspiration, aimed at "hearts and minds."[47]

In the long letter to Robinson, with his own political fortunes in mind, Eisenhower dwelt more on domestic concerns. He discerned a typical historical pattern reflected in U.S. history: young societies err by giving individuals too much license, but mature societies—such as the United States of 1952—err on the other side. Maturity had its virtues, he had written to publisher Henry Luce. Because the United States was more mature than other nations, its people were more willing than other nations to sacrifice for the common good.[48] No doubt he voiced this opinion hoping Luce would pass it along to his millions of readers. But it also followed logically from, and legitimated, his often-repeated claim that only the U.S. model could save Western civilization.

Since maturity, as Eisenhower used the term, meant less concentration of private wealth and more self-sacrifice, a mature society such as the United States had little to fear from wealthy individuals. Thus he had little to say about the dangers of great concentrations of private wealth. (He knew very well, of course, that some of the greatest concentrations would be tapped to fund his campaign.) As in the discourse of his days at Columbia, he focused almost solely on the dangers of governmental power: "The government penetrates more and more into our daily living." "Doctrinaire Socialists" promoted higher taxes and government grants-in-aid as solutions to social problems. It was most distressing the way these policies took power from the state governments, probably aiming "to bankrupt the states." In fact, the future president argued, their policies would lead to "worthless money and bankruptcy" for the whole nation, thence to more "bureaucratic controls, which must finally give way to autocratic controls."[49]

Of course Eisenhower the politician, like Eisenhower the world leader, recognized the need to simplify ideas in order to win campaigns. So he could summarize his lengthy message to Robinson by saying that all the specific political issues of the day were "closely related to the one great overwhelming struggle involving the world . . . personal freedom and initiative vs. regimentation." He told one corporate executive friend that he would make this the only issue of his campaign. Apart from their political value, though, such simplifications always appealed to Eisenhower. They gave the clarity he prized so much.[50]

As he became increasingly concerned about rising military budgets, for example, he framed the issue within his view of history as a great struggle of freedom versus regimentation. In a private letter to Swede Hazlett he wrote that the world's conflicts were "all part and parcel of the same great struggle—the struggle of free men to govern themselves effectively and efficiently; to protect themselves from any threat without and to prevent their system from collapsing under them, due to the strains placed upon it by their defensive effort. It is another phase of a struggle that has been going on for some three thousand years."[51] For Eisenhower, of course, the internal strains were just as much a product of selfishness as the external threats. In his ideology, both were steps on the path to regimentation, the inevitable end product of selfishness. So the 3,000-year-old struggle was the struggle around which he would build his campaign: individual freedom versus state regimentation.

In Eisenhower's discourse this was essentially a spiritual struggle. This had been clear in his previous private discourse, though generally left implicit. Now, as he worked on more precise theoretical formulations, he also gave more precision to his notion of spirituality. Morale, imagination, faith, a common scale of values, and a common determination to meet risks to those values cooperatively were all part of "the spiritual field," he wrote to Averell Harriman. Similarly, he told George Sloan that the spiritual strength of the people includes "patriotism, self-confidence, intellect, integrity and forthrightness, courage and stamina—in short, all those qualities that mark man as a spiritual being."[52]

His fullest theoretical reflection was written to someone he barely knew, an appliance corporation executive named Victor Emanuel: "Too often when we use the word spiritual, people think that we are referring solely to religious devotion, sometimes to a specific religion. Actually it must comprise that great area of human quality that deals with a composite of moral standards, emotion, and comprehension. The spiritual reinforcement we need is not merely evangelical in character; it is a broad need for greater respect of what we like to call the old-fashioned virtues." These included honesty, justice, and consideration for the good of others (which ultimately works to our own advantage, he added). "It is all those impulses and realizations that will make us work solidly together in a spirit of fairness and team play" among individuals and among nations.[53]

Of course Eisenhower continued to insist that the United States was fighting the cold war to preserve all these spiritual values against communists who would destroy them. When he told Elizabeth Rankin that communism is "the enemy of our Christian faith," he was writing to a stranger who was a devout Christian and might well spread the budding candidate's words. But the words were clearly in line with similar sentiments uttered earlier, with little political import. He would offer a similar thought, rather gratuitously, when promoting himself to the Republican corporate leadership: "The greatest weapon that freedom has against the Communist dictatorship is its ultimate appeal to soul and spirit of man. This we must believe."[54]

To frame the cold war in terms of spiritual values while also promoting it as a defense of the U.S. economy, Eisenhower had to link spiritual and economic values. He made the argument two different ways. First, he posited that "unless each individual enjoys a maximum degree of economic freedom, his spiritual aspirations will likewise be ignored"; a government that controlled economic life would not permit freedom of speech or worship.[55] The implicit argument here was that only in a capitalist system were individuals free to practice self-restraint, the essential spiritual virtue, in the marketplace. Conversely, only when individuals practiced self-restraint in the marketplace could a capitalist system survive.

There was also a more pragmatic way to link spiritual and economic values. "Man's basic physical needs must be met before there can be sustained any truly high levels in spiritual force. . . . Unless economic strength is sustained at reasonable level, there will be a lowering of morale." This, in turn, would weaken the nation's industrial and military strength, thus undermining its security. Eisenhower's whole argument for his NATO endeavor rested on this line of thinking. He was led naturally to his newly favorite formula: security = spiritual force X economic force X military force.[56]

For Eisenhower spiritual, economic, and political values were always a single fabric. The United States needed more morality in government, he wrote to his brother Arthur, which would mean "a spiritual rebirth." Unfortunately its leaders were politicians and therefore too selfish to generate this rebirth. Yet precisely because humans are spiritual, he argued, they respond to emotional appeals. Inspirational leadership was necessary to unite any group. There was no simple formula to "bring real relief to the poor old world today and to restore to us that confidence, serenity of mind, and joyousness of living that should be the heritage of any civilized generation," he wrote to Victor Emanuel. "We must, as you have put it, start a crusade. This I have believed and preached for a long time."[57]

In all of this writing, Eisenhower was implicitly nominating himself as the leader of a crusade. First he would crusade once again in Europe, to spark a spiritual revival in NATO. Europe, however, was turning out to be merely a training ground for the great crusade, the one that would end in the White House. In March 1952, when columnist Drew Pearson warned him that a growing isolationist sentiment might hamper his foreign policy as president, he responded at length. The purpose of all U.S. efforts was to protect "the American system or the free system of life," the letter argued. "Fundamentally, this means the entire fabric of man's moral and spiritual aspirations," along with the economic and political institutions to support them. "Solutions must be firmly based in spiritual and moral values. . . . The vast undertakings in which we are involved cannot conceivably be brought to fruition without spiritual propulsion based upon common understanding of the fundamental issues. . . . We must not lose faith."[58]

"Faith" was a synecdochical representation of the entirety of "the American system." It epitomized all the spiritual values Eisenhower was hoping to advance. One word could stand for all those values so easily because all were strands of a seamless web. Unity of purpose was one of these values; it was also, more importantly, the goal of the spiritual rebirth. If all Americans shared the same values and the same way of life—and all Western Europeans adopted those too—all would be equally committed to the anticommunist crusade and to the defense of capitalism.

Their commitment would build a wall strong enough to contain the communist threat. Thus it was of eminently practical value. The task of the inspired leader was to persuade the public that each of its values was indeed merely a strand in a seamless web; that standing for one required standing for all; that the whole ensemble, as practiced in the United States, was indeed the only guidepost to a virtuous, civilized life; and that the alternative to spiritual renewal was unthinkable disaster, the extinction of civilization itself.

## WARNING THE PUBLIC

Eisenhower intended to discharge the duties of leadership by continuing to speak out publicly. Now, though, he had once again to reframe his public words to match his public role. "He was once again General Eisenhower," as Martin Medhurst says, "and his speeches returned to the standard themes of duty, cooperation, and teamwork that characterized his rhetoric from 1945 to 1948."[59] These themes had also figured prominently in his speeches while president of Columbia. But now, as in his chief of staff years, they were projected onto a global scale, and once again they were placed within a frame of global hope and fear: the hope for peace and the fear of a disaster that could destroy civilization. Yet these two themes were now given a somewhat different twist, because Eisenhower had become a publicly acknowledged and fervent cold warrior.

In his initial tour of NATO capitals, he stopped in London to urge Parliament to support European rearmament:

> It is success in this, or it is "or else" for the Free World. . . . There is no single one of these [NATO] nations which can exist by itself; that can protect itself. . . . One by one, due to the many-sided nature of the Communist attack, the weaker countries will fall. . . . Take the case of Indo-China. What would happen there if we should withdraw support of France completely? And then think of Siam, Malaya, Burma, in succession, and what would happen in India? And soon you see yourself in such a shrinking world that finally even great powers like the United States and Great Britain have to struggle for mere existence. So, from our point of view, it is this "or else." Produce collective security that can encompass us all.[60]

This vision of Asian countries toppling like dominos echoed (almost verbatim) Eisenhower's fears in the first weeks of World War II (and foreshadowed his famous "dominos" analogy of 1954).

On his brief return to Washington, he shared the same fear with the U.S. public, with a suitable domestic twist. "The preservation of free America" depended on rearming Western Europe, he insisted; if that region "should be overrun by Communism, many economically dependent areas in Africa and the Middle East would be affected by the debacle. Southeastern Asia would probably soon be lost. Thus, we would be cut off from the raw materials of all these regions. . . . World destiny would then be dictated by imperialistic powers whose avowed purpose is the destruction of freedom."[61]

Addressing Congress a day earlier, he spoke in equally alarmist terms. Western Europe, "the greatest pool of skilled labor in the world," might "go down the drain," he warned. Communist control of Western Europe would shift the military balance of power "so drastically that our safety would be gravely imperiled, grossly imperiled. . . . It is scarcely possible to imagine the fall of Western Europe to communism without the simultaneous fall" of Europe's colonies, "the very areas from which we draw the materials which are absolutely essential to our existence, our way of life. . . . [We must] keep them friendly to us when we need their trade in order to exist. . . . Standing alone and isolated in a world with the rest completely dominated by communism, our system would have to wither away." In testimony to a Senate subcommittee, later published in a popular U.S. news magazine, he argued that the United States needed to be able to get raw materials from "what we call backward or semibackward places of the world. If these underdeveloped areas were to go, one by one, under the hands of the enemy, eventually we would be standing alone as a sort of island of freedom surrounded by a hostile sea of Communism."[62]

Eisenhower also urged Congress to worry about the danger of U.S. bankruptcy: "We are also concerned with the defense of a way of life. . . . Our system must remain solvent, as we attempt a solution of this great problem of security. Else we have lost the battle from within that we are trying to win from without." He took this theme, along with the fear of falling dominos, back to Europe with him. "The effects of economic failure would be disastrous upon spiritual and material strength alike," he told the English Speaking Union. At a press conference in France he explained, "our standard of living must be such that our people passionately desire to preserve it. In other words, there must be something worth defending." Addressing the North Atlantic Council, he used the same language he would later use as president: "We are defending a way of life. . . . We must not destroy from within what we are trying to defend from without. . . . Without economic support, any amount of arms is futile in the emergency of war." NATO should not "so badly coordinate our military progress with economic capacity that we destroy both."[63]

The danger of losing the cold war, either through military or economic disaster, was the foundation of Eisenhower's public rhetoric as SACEUR.[64] Slightly below this danger, though, he ranked the danger of the cold war turning hot. "Global war would be the greatest tragedy that we could possibly experience, except, of course, loss of freedom," he told a press conference. In his address to Congress he described total war as "tragedy . . . probably the suicide of civilization." Eisenhower often described his task as the defense of civilization. "We are steadfast in our determination to safeguard the freedom, the common heritage, and the civilization of our member nations"; "Our countries are joined with the peoples of Western Europe and the North Atlantic to defend the freedoms of western civilization."[65]

Defending Western civilization meant defending the highest form of human civilization, in the general's discourse, and he referred to it often: "The freedom loving peoples of the world have now embarked on a great collective effort to preserve those things which make life worth living"; "We are defending for all mankind those things that allow personal dignity to the least of us—those things that permit each to believe himself important in the eyes of God"; and "The people of Europe and North America represent the highest culture man has been able to achieve upon this earth. They are responsible for every advance of science, the arts, and culture; they possess on the average a higher understanding than any other people in the world; they have the greatest productive capacity."[66]

"Western Europe is the cradle of our civilization," he told the U.S. public; "from her originally we drew our strength, genius, and culture." But the United States was now "the greatest temporal force that has ever existed on God's earth" and "the leading exponent of scientific civilization." It followed logically that any threat to the United States was a threat to civilization itself, and he voiced this idea to a Senate subcommittee (in remarks later published): "It is not a question anymore, as I see it, of civilization's moving along whether or not we decide to do this [rearmament]. . . . The future of civilization as we know it is at stake." He urged legislators to believe that their decisions on NATO "may determine the course of our civilization, whether or not free government is going to continue to exist upon the earth safely."[67]

Doing his duty as a leader, Eisenhower often encouraged the public with optimistic visions of the future. In his broadcast to the U.S. public, after his initial tour of NATO capitals, he reported that "in every capital, there is a growing desire to cooperate in this mutual security effort. . . . America's record and America's strength certainly should prevent hysterical apprehension of the future."[68] At the same time, of course, he was privately lamenting the lack of cooperation, sometimes in nearly hysterical terms. Though he continued public words of praise for the allies throughout his SACEUR tenure, these words were offset by his continuing recitation of the dangers to civilization.

## "A SECURE WALL OF PEACE"

Just as he returned to casting his alarmist language in global terms, Eisenhower also returned to the theme of peace; the two motifs were still linked, because peace still meant the preservation of civilization. In his first address broadcast from Paris, he urged the Europeans to work for "a secure peace and the continuance and the progress of civilization. . . . Our task is to preserve the peace, not to incite to war" (though he quickly added that there would be no "appeasement"). Returning home, he told the nation: "Our hope remains the achievement of peace based on understanding and forbearance, the only sure foundation for peace. We must never lose faith that such a peace can be ultimately established." He made it clear, however, that "understanding and forbearance" did not mean any compromise, nor any reciprocal give-and-take relationship, with the enemy. Rather, the general continued, "we strive to erect a wall of security for the free world behind which free institutions can live. That wall must be maintained until Communistic imperialism dies of its own inherent evils." "We are going to build for ourselves a secure wall of peace, of security," he said on another occasion. On still another occasion, "We have the opportunity to build a bulwark of peace."[69]

The image of a defensive "wall of peace" was central to the general's public rhetoric throughout his tenure as SACEUR. Appearing as a guest on Edward R. Murrow's television program, he told the nation that NATO was "solely an effort to forge a protective weapon to insure a safe peace." NATO would be "a team for defense; one capable of assuring a lasting and secure peace," he told the English Speaking Union, in a speech widely reported in the United States.[70]Occasionally he spoke about a future without a wall: "We have the capability of building such military, economic, and moral strength as the Communist world would never dare to challenge. When that point is reached, the Iron Curtain rulers may finally be willing to participate seriously in disarmament negotiations. . . . We shall have proved our union the world's most potent influence toward peace among men— the final security goal of humanity. . . . What we do now can grant us peace for generations." A strong NATO could force the communist system "to dry up," he assured a Senate subcommittee. But he quickly added, "some of us sitting here will not be here to see the day." His hope for an end to the wall was always a vague eschatological vision, set in a far distant time, not a concrete goal to be pursued in the present. This vision would be realized only through a long period of massive Western military strength.[71]

So for all practical purposes, Eisenhower suggested, the enemy should be treated as a permanent fact of life. At the outset of his tenure, he admitted to the nation that he aimed only for a "relative peace." It would give "the free world a position of security . . . and economic stability." But it would not actively seek to defeat the enemy. He told Congress, "We have to devise a scheme that we can support, if necessary over the next 20 years, 30 years, whatever may be the time necessary." This premise entailed long-term budgeting, eschewing the notion of any "year of maximum crisis": "Let us not delude ourselves with repetitions of dates and years, be it '53, '54, or any other," he told NATO leaders. This premise had far more than economic meaning; it implied a profound limitation upon the meaning of peace. Whatever the general might mean when he spoke of policies for pursuing peace, his goals would be framed within a permanently bipolar geopolitical world.[72]

A year later he explained his views to journalists in some detail: "The free nations have never said, 'We cannot live with Communism in the world.' It has been Communism that has said 'We cannot co-exist with free government.' . . . We should strive to establish systems of collective strength that will bring about equilibrium as cheaply, effectively and economically as we can." An enduring geopolitical equilibrium, cheaply purchased, was now the effective goal of Eisenhower's policies, and thus his effective working notion of peace. Once an equilibrium was attained, he continued "this situation would merely become a simple struggle between the two ideologies and not a struggle on one side backed up by frightening power that particularly upsets the nations close by. We would be content to trust to the decency and justice of our cause, and its appeal in the long run."[73]

This hopeful vision assumed that no nations, in the present or in the future, would be frightened by the immense military power of the United States and its allies. This assumption might well have been mistaken. Moreover, the vision was logically constrained by a catch-22. Eisenhower always assumed that communism was inherently deceitful and subversive; its nonmilitary means of capturing other nations were now the greatest threat, he argued.[74] There was no place in his ideology for any nation or group choosing communism freely, uninfluenced by communist pressure. So any nation or group's movement into the communist camp would be prima facie evidence of communist coercion and further reason to continue waging cold war. What he called the "Pax Atlantica" would always find in communism a treacherous enemy; a geopolitical "equilibrium" would always be unstable, requiring some kind of defensive wall. Since this wall would eventually become an intolerable economic burden, the "free nations" could not, in fact, accept a permanent communist presence in the world except as an immensely regrettable necessity, something to be constantly contained and resisted.

If the NATO-built wall were the means to peace, that wall would have to keep out the scourge of war. Eisenhower did not expect the Soviets to initiate global war, he told a press conference early in 1952. Even though they were building up "terrifying strength," their leaders must know how foolish war would be for them. But his published testimony to the Senate subcommittee a few months earlier warned that "the threat [of Soviet attack] may continue for a long time." Eisenhower's first European broadcast proclaimed his intent to "build a defense behind which [European] children may prosper and live in peace. . . . Should mankind, through our solidarity, our prayers for peace, and through the mercy of God, be spared the catastrophe of another war, then this organization will have served a noble purpose."[75]

Eisenhower clearly revealed his priorities, however, when he said that "global war would be the greatest tragedy that we could possibly experience, except, of course, loss of freedom." The defensive wall was intended in a secondary way to prevent war; its primary purpose was to keep out the communists: "The integrity of all Western Europe must be defended against predatory forces. In this endeavor, we seek only peace." Ultimately, the two functions of the wall were actually one. Since, by definition, only the predators and not NATO could start a war, keeping communists and war out of Western Europe were merely two sides of the same process. In the general's public rhetoric, that was also the process of preserving civilization against the twin dangers of war and communism, the two great forces of chaos.[76]

Only when all threats were safely contained behind the "wall of peace," Eisenhower argued, could the NATO nations have peace of mind. He sounded this theme quite often. "Our real objective," he told a NATO gathering, "is to gain for our people *at the earliest possible moment* the tranquility of mind, the peaceful and confident security to which they are entitled." "Only through positive action by all our nations," his report to SHAPE concluded, "can we ever achieve tranquility and security." To another audience he said, "There will be no permanent position of serenity and confidence for the Western World as long as we are confronted with the Communist menace."[77] The key to security and serenity, Eisenhower insisted, was European unity. Without it, he told a press conference, NATO might "produce temporarily a military equilibrium." But "the peace and security of the world" required more than this; it required "a healthy and stable economy" and "long term security" in Western Europe. That was "a matter of the indefinite future." And the only way to achieve it was European unity.[78]

On this topic he occasionally allowed himself to indulge in utopian language, which was otherwise now rare in his public rhetoric. "Aroused and united, there is nothing which the nations of the Atlantic Community cannot achieve," he said in his first broadcast from Paris. In the address to the English Speaking Union he predicted that a united Europe "will produce miracles for the common good. . . . Europe could build adequate security and, at the same time, continue the march of human betterment that has characterized western civilization." But he rarely spoke about change or improvement in civilization. He was far more likely to dwell on the imperative need to defend the civilization already achieved. In that same speech, for example, he went on to describe NATO as a "team for defense . . . defending for all mankind those things that allow personal dignity to the least of us—those things that permit each to believe himself important in the eyes of God."[79]

As chief of staff, Eisenhower had spoken of peace primarily as a future state to be attained; peace represented change for the better. Now, though, peace meant primarily maintaining the status quo, avoiding change for the worse. In early 1952, speaking over the BBC, he told the British public of "the cause that lies nearest our hearts today—*the preservation of peace*. . . . our true objective is to *prevent war*." NATO's ultimate goal, he concluded, was to provide "*security and peace*." [80] Peace could be so readily and so often identified with security because war was now openly identified with the communist threat. This made peace, above all, the prevention of the ultimate disaster of communist-initiated war.

Peace and European unity became inseparable terms. Only a united Europe could build a wall strong enough to ward off communism and war, Eisenhower argued. Indeed he often spoke as if the nations of Western Europe, united politically and militarily, would themselves become the "wall of peace." He promoted unity, as he promoted all his NATO plans, on the basis of "enlightened self-interest": "If we can make everybody believe that what he is doing in this thing is good for him, then we achieve unity." These words to a Senate subcommittee might have been meant to placate those Republicans who wanted to put "America first." Eisenhower took great pains to insist that Europe would eventually have to defend itself. The only aim of the United States was "to give the people the umbrella under which they can start building this thing, to give them the confidence that the U.S. is here with them."[81]

His principal theme was partnership among the United States and its European allies. Commemorating D day, he said: "We know—out of tragic experience—that peace can never be the portion of the divided, the fearful. . . . We shall be strong only as we are one. . . . Where, among partners, strength is demanded in its fullness, unity is the first requisite." "We must press forward with the mobilization of our spiritual and intellectual strength; we must develop promptly the material force that will assure the safety of our friends upon the continent and the security of the free world."[82]

As SACEUR, Eisenhower often emphasized the importance of spiritual and economic as well as military strength. He did not want to appear to be just one more general asking for money for the military. To Congress, for example, he stressed that morale was a central issue because the cold war was "definitely a struggle to capture men, their loyalties, their beliefs, their convictions. . . . It involves understanding, it involves heart, it involves courage, fortitude, basic purpose."Europe had to be united in its purpose to resist communism and the United States had to inspire Europe by its example and leadership: "This faith in America is one that lies at the bottom of this whole thing. Faith that the leadership she can provide will inspire the same kind of feeling, the same kind of effort in our friends abroad. . . . We must by example inspire and get everybody to do his maximum. . . . We must make sure that the heart and soul of Europe is right."[83]

"Right" in this case meant as strenuously and permanently anticommunist as the exemplary United States. Unlike the Soviets, the United States could not enforce "a unity achieved by ignorance, by force, by the NKVD. What we have got to do, the only thing we have to do, is to meet that unity with a higher type of unity." Eisenhower's view of military leadership told him that unity of belief required leadership. Only the United States, he argued, now had the wherewithal to be that leader.[84]

Eisenhower's public discussions of strength typically began with the spiritual and proceeded through the economic to the military. This appeared to relegate military strength to the last place. At the same time, though, it made the other forms of strength rhetorical preliminaries; it allowed him to dwell in greater detail on the military, his true province of expertise. When he told the English Speaking Union, "The hand of the aggressor is stayed by strength—and strength alone,"[85] the context made it clear that he referred primarily to military strength. If peace meant, above all, a secure defensive wall, then it was perfectly logical to identify peace with a powerful military establishment. The military establishment was the central building block of the wall.

On occasion he could make the point with simplicity rather than rhetorical flourish: "If you make Western Europe strong enough, the Russians will just turn somewhere else where the picking is easier." In such an extreme (and atypical) formulation, peace was reduced merely to keeping Soviet armies out of Western Europe. More typically, the SACEUR used the word *peace* to mean keeping Soviet armies out of any territory, anywhere in the world, that they did not already control. Peace and military security thus became inseparable, and virtually interchangeable: "In a secure peace attained through strength is now the safety and security of the free nations."[86]

## PUBLIC AND PRIVATE

Eisenhower's public language as SACEUR marked a return to the global vision and concern for peace of the chief of staff years, but with some significant changes. As chief of staff, Eisenhower had spoken publicly of rapprochement with the Soviets, while privately doubting its possibility. As SACEUR, his private language of vigorous cold war was equally public. The tension between public and private discourse was, on this point, eliminated. This allowed him to resolve another tension. As chief of staff, he held out an eschatological vision of peace as a global harmony, which would render military forces unnecessary. So he had to promote military strength only as a temporary protection for those traveling the road to peace. As SACEUR, he offered no hope of global harmony, at least in the foreseeable future. On most occasions, instead of an eschatological vision, he offered only a permanently invulnerable wall built out of Western strength. So he could, and indeed had to, speak of peace and military strength as virtually synonymous. This equation, which had always been implicit and sometimes explicit in the private discourse, now became public too.

These changes marked an important step in synthesizing his discourse. He blended the focus on global affairs and concern for peace of the chief of staff years with the overt anticommunism and defense of free enterprise of the Columbia years. Foreign and domestic affairs were melded together, most fully in the private discourse, but quite noticeably in the public as well. Nothing in the previous discourse was rejected. The new elements were perfectly consistent with the ideological commitments of the earlier discourse. The result was not to change, but to expand, the discourse and the ideology embedded in it. Freedom was now equated with economic free enterprise, political liberal democracy, and a unified "free world" system of economic, political, and military interdependence. But Eisenhower's discourse valued all these expressions of freedom primarily as ways to preserve the status quo in the "free world" and particularly in the United States. That preservation, behind a wall of military security, was now the essence of peace. This was truly a Pax Americana, for both the means and the purpose of that peace were realizations of the "American system" throughout the "free world." Peace and freedom meant, above all, a permanent defense of the "American system" against the seemingly permanent communist threat to it.

This discursive edifice was based on the premise of continuing threat. Alarmism was a key feature, and a logical precondition, of the whole structure. The threat of apocalyptic catastrophe still had to be introduced in the public discourse, but the leader's obligation to boost morale required it to be somewhat muted beneath official expressions of optimism. As before, alarmism was more prominent, and its expressions more apocalyptic, in the private discourse. Likewise, the discursive construction of positive goals for U.S. policy entailed continuing construction of threats to the attainment of those goals. Indeed, as Eisenhower synthesized his previous discursive patterns, he synthesized all the ironies of these patterns, and made them even more inescapable. Once peace and freedom were reduced to security behind a defensive wall, there was no way to talk about these ideals except by heightening the sense of danger.

With all the ideals of the "American system" linguistically unified, and all the threats to those ideals equally unified, the "wall" and its geopolitical equivalent, the Iron Curtain, took on the greatest importance. It was the image of the place where the two great discursive blocs, representing the cosmic forces of good and evil, met. Precisely by separating those blocs, a necessary relationship was created between them. One had no meaning without the other. In a sense, Eisenhower's discourse had come full circle. It had emerged in the early months of World War II as an expression of an ideology of spiritual struggle. The struggle itself, being waged within every human being, was the key fact. Since both contending sides were innate in human nature, there was clearly no way to separate them, much less eliminate either one; speaking of one necessarily entailed speaking of the other. Now the SACEUR's discursive synthesis projected the same totalizing and simplifying vision onto a global scale. The individual spiritual struggle and the global superpower struggle became, in public as well as in private, mirror images of each other. Eisenhower's discourse had been moving inexorably in this direction. By the time he returned home to run for president, in June 1952, the process was virtually complete.

## CHAPTER 13

# Presidential Candidate: 1952

Throughout the winter of 1951–52, Eisenhower continued to resist the mounting pressure to declare himself a candidate for president. He may very well have been genuinely ambivalent. Even if he had privately determined to run, he still waited to be drafted by a seemingly unsought groundswell of public demand. This air of reticence could be a valuable political asset. "His most powerful weapon was his image," writes Herbert Parmet. His image of not seeking the office was, in Robert Divine's words, "precisely how most Americans want their prospective presidents to act." Eisenhower understood all this. He wrote to Harry Bullis, a key Republican booster in Minnesota, that any public efforts he made on his own behalf "would do much to destroy such reputation [as] I have had for a disinterested and loyal public servant." "The seeker is never so popular as the sought," he told his friends. "People want what they think that they can't get."[1]

By late March, though, it was evident that Eisenhower would have to campaign in person if he wanted to be assured of victory. The Republican professionals directing his campaign (most notably Henry Cabot Lodge, Jr.) feared with good reason that if he waited too long it would be too late. On 2 April he formally asked President Truman to relieve him of his duty as SACEUR, as of 1 June.[2]

### "A High Plateau of Tension"

On 4 June the general began his campaign with a speech at the rodeo arena in his hometown of Abilene. That first speech was widely seen as an inauspicious beginning. All historians who have written on it have noted that it was delivered in the rain, to a disappointingly small crowd, which was soon bored by its uninspired, pedantic tone. Perhaps the most important point about this speech, though, was its rhetorical structure. "Only her citizens—who comprise America—can do her mortal hurt," the candidate declared at the outset. Then he went on to enumerate all of the ways in which Americans might destroy their own nation. "Alert recognition of external as well as internal dangers" was essential, he warned, for "the salvation of every free land," and most especially to save the United States. As Parmet says, "millions were hearing confirmation of their fears spoken by one of undisputed integrity."[3]

This approach made sense for a Republican, who would have to run against the record of the incumbent administration. He could hardly reap advantage by urging his audience to feel satisfied about the present. He had to address sources of discontent. Of course he could have framed the issues in terms of public anger or indignation or confusion. Likewise, he could have stressed not the evils of the present, but his plans for a better future. But he chose none of these as his main theme. In fact, he offered no kind of concrete hope for the future. He spoke only about fears and dangers, and how he would forestall those dangers. He made it the nation's highest goal "to preserve important areas from communism," while admitting that the billions this was costing might "bankrupt" the nation. Danger lurked on every side, it seemed. "Alarmist Ike" had come home.

What about the goal of bringing peace to the world? His advisors agreed that peace was his strongest issue, and they urged him to make this the theme of his kick-off speech. William Robinson, the acknowledged expert on public relations, wrote to him that no one had ever "made a great speech on peace. . . . No one was equipped to do it . . . no one but you. . . . The people need your leadership—not on the 'issues' (to hell with the issues)—on their greatest unfulfilled ambition—peace." Cliff Roberts, another highly respected friend, agreed. After the Abilene speech he advised the candidate: "The chief reason that people want to vote for you is because they think you have more ability to keep us out of another war." And the influential publisher Henry Luce called on Eisenhower personally to advise him to give a speech on peace, to get back "on the high level of broad purposes and principles and stay there." As Blanche Wiesen Cook notes, "Whenever Eisenhower became tempted to debate questions of politics, the domestic economy, or the fiscal future, his friends reminded him to return to the primary principle," which was peace.[4]

Eisenhower started to take their advice the day after the initial Abilene fiasco, when he recouped with a masterful performance at a press conference. "The thing that is causing us our great problem today is the issue of real peace and security in the world," he told the assembled reporters. But he developed the theme in a most revealing way. The essence of the problem, he said, was to find a way to wage cold war without "living under such an umbrella of fear and doubt and hysteria. First, it's un-American and second it is completely stultifying." Yet as he went on, he seemed to justify the fear: "We're in sort of a new thing. We're not in an emergency [i.e., total war mobilization] but we're certainly not at peace. I prefer to call it sort of a high plateau of tension. . . . It means we've got to accustom ourselves to living in sort of a tense basis until we can get these things straightened out and we can again experience the tranquility, the serenity that we should have." Later in the year he would say, "Today this world dwells in a twilight zone between peace and war—a zone we call 'cold war.'"[5]

Of course, Eisenhower had long ago acknowledged his view that it would take decades to "get these things straightened out," which meant decades of tension. And he had brought back from Europe an alarmist language that could only heighten the tension. While he deplored "fear and doubt and hysteria," he wanted every American to look at things "squarely in the face" and see that, if Western Europe were to "fall" to the communists, "the cost [to the U.S.] will be so great as to be back-breaking and we'll be in mortal danger." Therefore, the United States would have to live, for decades at least, at a high plateau of tension.[6]

Even as he tried to initiate a hopeful message of peace, "Alarmist Ike's" words confirmed the very fears he decried. He wanted to distinguish "realistic" alarm from hysterical fear. But *fear* and *hysteria* were still only code words for views and policies different from his own. Throughout the campaign Eisenhower held to this pattern. He promoted himself as the man who could bring peace, which meant tranquility and serenity rather than fear and doubt. When he spoke about peace, however, he consistently articulated the nation's fears much more specifically and vividly than he articluated its hopes.

Just two days after the Abilene press conference, for example, he repeated the performance in New York,[7] explaining why he intended to speak often about peace: "I cannot conceive in this day and time of anything that is more important to any American citizen than the question of the secure peace in the world. We justifiably worry about such things as recurring deficits, vast expenditures by our Federal government. . . . We worry about inflation." But the cause of all these domestic fears, he argued, was "the threat hanging over the world, the fact that the basic issue of our time is 'can we make a free system, such as we know, work?'" The problem, as always for "Alarmist Ike," was of apocalyptic magnitude. And for those who expected him to become president and supply the solution, he had a humble response: "If I knew any real panacea for this great tribulation through which the poor old world is going, and which threatens the great values on which we place so much value, I would most certainly make a speech on which I would work for weeks." In Eisenhower's discourse, a "panacea" was the only alternative to an endless plateau of high tension.

One reporter asked about a small step that might ease tension a bit, namely, a meeting between the U.S. president and Stalin. Eisenhower's answer (which merited the headline in the next day's *New York Times*) saw little value in such a meeting: "Had I the slightest reason to believe that such a meeting would be welcome [by Stalin, presumably], I would go to any place in this world" to promote peace. But there was really nothing to negotiate as long as the communists refused the possibility of coexistence with capitalism. He continued, "We can produce a situation in the world where they may modify that statement, that intention, and therefore get to a position at least where we can work out a method of living with them." That modus vivendi was, apparently, the path to peace of mind.

## THE PRIMARY CAMPAIGN: CONTAINMENT, LIBERATION, AND FEAR

The modus vivendi was also a matter of great political controversy. Would an Eisenhower administration accept the present borders of the communism bloc, rather than rolling it back? That was the gist of the very next question: "Would you conquer subversion by helping resistance behind the Iron Curtain?" "My dear sir," the candidate responded cryptically, "when I am in a thing like this, I believe in helping everybody who is on my side."

Evasion was the politic thing. Like all candidates, Eisenhower wanted to identify evils and announce his plans for mitigating them; unlike many other candidates, he intended to proclaim a crusade to wholly eliminate the worst evils. The whole framework of his ideological discourse made the idea of a modus vivendi logically dubious, at best. Moreover, he could hardly afford to rule out "liberation" completely if he wanted mainstream Republican support in the fall campaign. He planned to use his predilection for apocalypticism to serve pragmatic rhetorical purposes. Yet pragmatism also moved him to embrace a distinctly nonapocalyptic modus vivendi. He intended to campaign as a man of peace, and he knew better than anyone the anxieties stirred up among the NATO allies by U.S. talk of "liberation." He needed to reassure European allies that there would be no war of "liberation." Caught between these conflicting imperatives, he would walk (or skirt) the line between the two positions without endorsing either one.

Eisenhower's ambiguity also addressed a more immediate political problem. Taft, an advocate of "liberation," was busy trying to persuade the world that he and the general essentially agreed on foreign policy matters. In order to woo delegates, the Eisenhower forces had to put distance between their man and Taft. Given the pitfalls of the "liberation" debate, they hoped to avoid that issue (though it was still widely seen as the major foreign policy difference between the two factions). Instead, they focused on the charge that Taft was an isolationist.

On 20 June Eisenhower promoted this view in a letter to Dulles, who was charged with drafting the foreign policy plank for the party's platform.[8] (The letter was made public four days later.) Though the general promised to "accept almost any revision of my own views" on details, he clearly laid out his "minimum requirement" for the platform. He said nothing about "liberation" or of working out "a way of living with them." Instead he insisted that the platform be premised on the essential need for international trade and access to raw materials: "Any thought of 'retiring within our own borders' will certainly lead to disaster for the U.S.A. . . . . America cannot live alone." America's "form of life is threatened by Communistic dictatorship," which hoped to cut off U.S. access to trading partners. To avoid that fate, the United States needed more than "a mere power of retaliation" (a favorite Taft theme). It needed the kind of collective security for which he had worked as SACEUR. "Only chaos in the world and eventual distress and worse for us would result from abandonment of the principle of collective security."[9]

In this letter, the candidate was relating his warnings of chaos and disaster to a difference only in cold war means, not goals. He had acknowledged as much at his 7 June press conference, when he said that his difference with Taft was "really a disagreement as to methods. We all have the same basic objective."[10] Taft had already signaled to Eisenhower that he was "anxious" to see the latter's NATO project "carried through to completion. . . . I can see no difference between us on that subject." Taft had also told John Foster Dulles (who would write the platform's foreign policy plank) that there was "a large area of possible agreement" between himself and the Eisenhower wing of the party. Taft may have exaggerated. He and the general differed strongly on the need for formal collective security agreements with, and U.S. troops in, the Western European nations. These differences, though, were matters of means, as Eisenhower said. Taft certainly agreed with his opponent on the basic ends—the need for trade and the need to contain the threat of communism. Indeed, Taft was arguably more anticommunist than Eisenhower.[11]

In the letter to Dulles, Eisenhower made the difference in means sound like a difference in basic goals, a difference on which U.S. survival depended. In effect, he insisted that the fundamentals of his own ideology, in its most recent version, must also be the fundamentals of the Republican platform. He did not insist on specific words such as *disaster* and *chaos* in the platform. These were merely his accustomed ways of expressing himself; he knew no other language in which to couch his views. When he added that he trusted Dulles to find the right words to reflect "these essentials," he was surely confident that Dulles would be right at home with such language.

Of course Eisenhower did not see himself as an alarmist, or in any way excessively fearful. On the same day he wrote to Dulles, he also responded to a letter from an investment banker, Abraham Sakier. Sakier urged Eisenhower, in impassioned terms, to "turn his back upon the fearful thinking of the past thirty-five years" and say, "Enough of this shameful and unmanly . . . cowardly fear of enemies." Eisenhower replied: "I find myself in full agreement with your main thesis—that America and the free world have nothing to fear from Communism," as long as they used their resources effectively in the ideological struggle. He could say this only because he translated Sakier's thesis into his own ideological terms, clearly missing Sakier's point.

It simply was not possible, in Eisenhower's discursive frame, to imagine that he himself might be excessively frightened. So he continued blithely: "Manifestly it would be idle to attempt to minimize the character of the threat." The only solution, he said, was the "self-confidence" that came from collective security among nations with sound economies. Once the "free world" was in "a completely sound and solid position," it could "begin to work effectively toward a permanent and secure peace."[12] In other words, to move toward peace the noncommunist world would have to gird itself for cold war, which meant first adopting Eisenhower's own sense of threat—precisely the obstacle to peace and progress, in Sakier's opinion. It is possible, of course, that Eisenhower understood Sakier well enough but chose to sidestep the issue. Even so, this letter shows how easily he could deny his own alarmism by reinterpreting words, to adapt them to his own discursive patterns.

Having moved his headquarters to Denver for the latter part of June, the candidate continued to show that Sakier's criticism was on target. In a speech devoted to peace, "the problem closest to our hearts," he warned that "aggressive communism is cunning, it is godless; it aims to destroy all freedom—and most of all, yours and mine, because America is its final and chief target." Without an internationalist policy and strong alliances, he continued, the United States would end up as "a gaunt America, surrounded by a savage wolf pack." His antidote to all this fear was to make the United States so strong that the Soviet Union would "feel obliged to accept a plan for peace and disarmament." But strength meant more than just soldiers and weaponry, he maintained. This speech introduced a theme he would sound many times before the fall election: "To be strong we must have an unshakeable spiritual depth. Let us constantly proclaim to all peoples our belief in God and our devotion to the ideals and causes that spring from such belief."

This was the way to "courage and confidence instead of defeatism; hope instead of despair"—not to stop fearing, but to respond to increasing fear with increasing military-cum-spiritual strength.[13]

Alarmist language could be applied just as readily to domestic political concerns. "If the Republican party should not win," Eisenhower exhorted Texas Republicans, "we should see the end or risk the end of the two-party system in the United States." A few days later, in Denver, he began to tell the nation why this would be such a disaster. "Eisenhower Says Democrats Failed at Home and Abroad," the New York Times headlined; "Strongest Attack Yet On Democrats." Yet relatively little of the speech dealt directly with Democratic shortcomings. It was an address about the fears of the young. The older generation had bequeathed to them the legacy of "two world wars, continuing years of instability, an astronomical debt, crushing taxes . . . a feeling of insecurity, tension, even fear. . . . For the first time in history young Americans find their country, as it faces the world, fearful and indecisive." The candidate put this question in the mouths of the young people: "What's happening to America, and what, as a result, is going to happen to us?" Youth wanted to better themselves, he noted, but "most of all they want to be freed from the dreadful uncertainties of the present without fear that all of their planning will come to nothing because of war."[14]

Eisenhower blamed all of this fear on "the party too long in power" (his consistent euphemism for the Democrats). It had been "too ready for too long to trust a godless dictatorship." The claim that Truman, Acheson, et al. had been "trusting" the Soviet Union might have stretched the credulity of an objective observer, but it made fine campaign rhetoric. His strategy was to evoke the fear of war as a symbol of and focal point for all of the public's fears, so that he could offer himself as the champion of both peace and confidence. Privately, Eisenhower continued to doubt that there was much reason to fear a U.S-Soviet war in the foreseeable future. Just four days after the Denver speech he wrote to his old confidante, Bernard Baruch: "I do not believe that the Soviets would in their own best interests, deliberately provoke global war. I believe that war is possible." In public, though, he had to arouse fears of war so that he could establish peace as the opposite of and antidote to fear. The Democrats were to blame for the fear of war, and therefore for every fear, he wanted to argue; only Republicans could bring peace and therefore (by the logic of his argument) banish fear. Having dwelt for many minutes on insecurity and anxiety, he concluded that there was yet "no reason for defeatism." A Republican administration would not "trust" the communists, but it would make the United States so strong—militarily, economically, and spiritually—that "the Communists will fairly understand our language and agree, at the least, to live and let live. . . . Once we are on that course, our fears will begin to subside." Truman and the Democrats were to fears of war as Eisenhower and the Republicans were to peace of mind.[15]

How would an Eisenhower administration produce this peace? His brief acceptance speech to the nominating convention set forth the understanding of peace implicit in all his campaign rhetoric to come. The Republicans would sweep away the "heavy burdens and anxieties" of years of Democratic rule and "strengthen freedom. . . . We will so undergird our freedom that today's aggressors and those who tomorrow may rise up to threaten us, will not merely be deterred but stopped in their tracks. Then we will at last be on the road to real peace." The candidate did not promise to preserve or even attain peace, but only to set the nation on the road to it; the essence of that road to peace lay in the barriers placed across the communists' path of expansion. The acceptance speech also made clear the capstone of Eisenhower's rhetorical argument: "You have summoned me . . . to lead a great crusade." More than ever before, he would rely on the language of spiritual battle. The United States, he said, "under God," was now "the mightiest temporal power and the mightiest spiritual force on earth. The destiny of mankind" would be decided by the contest between U.S. Republicans and Democrats. He would frame the election as a moment of apocalyptic decision. And he would argue consistently that spiritual strength was the source of all other strengths and thus the key to world peace and peace of mind.[16]

## THE FALL CAMPAIGN: WAR, PEACE, AND FEAR

Eisenhower's full argument was laid out in the first major address of the fall campaign, delivered in late August to the American Legion convention. The Soviets aimed at "the economic strangulation of America," Eisenhower explained. "There may have to be another international war." Only a great military effort could prevent it, but that effort might "break our great competitive system. . . . Our peril circumscribes our industrial goal . . . our very attitudes are covered by this great threat. . . . Dire peril stalks every free nation today." Even fear itself could create disaster: "Fear is a climate that nourishes bankruptcy. . . . In a climate of fear long endured, we can find the death rattle of a nation." After all this, the audience might have been surprised when the speaker suddenly shifted gears: "I assure you, ladies and gentlemen, that there is no cause for fear." The *New York Times* epitomized the seeming paradox in two adjoining sub-headlines: "[Eisenhower] Sees U.S. in Greatest Peril; No Time for Fear." But the implicit logic was clear: there was no cause for fear because Ike was here. An Eisenhower presidency would "banish from the free world every last probability of Communist aggression. The course to peace is the establishment of conditions that will abolish fear and build confidence." The great war hero would find a way "of living peacefully and permanently with communism in the world."[17]

This promise of peaceful accommodation was counterbalanced (and, in some minds, contradicted) by the speech's most controversial words: "We can never rest . . . until the enslaved nations of the world have in the fullness of freedom the right to choose their own path." This promise of a "liberation" policy seemed to make good political sense, for it appealed to right-wing Republicans and voters of Eastern European descent. As Parmet notes, however, such words created "fear among American allies of Yankee adventures unleashing an aggressive military force." "Europeans were horrified," as Divine says, and "the Democrats, sensing that Eisenhower had gone too far, hit back hard."[18]

In his next major speech, a week later in Philadelphia, Eisenhower had to try to resolve the apparent contradiction. He assured the world that he would pursue liberation "only by peaceful means." Years later he claimed that he had counseled Dulles to include the same explicit proviso in the latter's speeches.[19] After that the "liberation" theme, and Dulles's influence in speechwriting, quickly dwindled to a few vague generalities.[20] Eisenhower was never enthusiastic about the "liberation" theme and he never wanted to make it a major issue. It had too many liabilities whichever way he played it; it was still safer to downplay it, and even to admit (though only occasionally) that the United States would have to accept the communist bloc as a fact of life.[21]

What he wanted to stress, to the American Legion, in Philadelphia, and throughout the fall campaign, was not the geopolitical or even the economic dimensions of war and peace, but the feelings and attitudes they evoked. The Philadelphia speech echoed the previous speech's catalogue of fears. It began with a flat assertion that the only issue of the campaign was "the mess in Washington"; it was time to get rid of "the bunglers, the incompetents." Then it shifted to the dangers of war: "Today freedom falters and communism crusades. . . . This Administration has bungled us perilously close to World War III. . . . The awful fact of war reaches into every American family. . . . Time after time in a single generation, our people, loving peace, have been involved in war." In this speech Eisenhower raised the stakes, sounding a new note he would often repeat: "In this atomic age, in this day of terrible new weapons, victory is impossible in a global war. The beginning of such a war would be a loss from which the world could not recover in a millennium. Only the losing of a modern war could be more disastrous than winning it. The one—the only—way to win World War III is to prevent it."

Having blamed the Democrats for this unprecedented danger and fear, Eisenhower went on to spell out a ten-step program for preventing war, all in suitably vague and general terms. "Our minimum goal," he said, was "to make sure that there can be no move against us to threaten our nation's security, its economy, its peace." Stopping all inimical movement would "restore tranquility and confidence." As he neared his conclusion he got a bit carried away and promised to bring "secure and permanent peace. . . . We will always strive for permanent peace." (A moment later he would scale back the promise, offering only "a world from which war and the threats of war have at last begun to disappear.") After explaining the roles played by military strength, economic prosperity, and collective security, he reached his climax, which was the need for spiritual strength: "We can save freedom by making the cause of freedom again a crusade."[22]

The American Legion speech a week earlier had built to a similar conclusion. It had framed the cold war as an assault not only on the United States but also on universal values, for the United States was "the spiritual and material realization of the dreams that men have dreamt since the dawn of history . . . the symbol of man's hopes and goals everywhere." It promised peace, above all, to ease the fear that those values might disappear. But the positive values and attitudes that it set as a goal were also the means to achieving that goal. The key to stopping communist "paganism" was a "common front" of people united by "the certainty that we and the free world are defending common values. . . . Spiritual values are the ultimate source of . . . every material advantage we enjoy."[23]

Eisenhower continued to stress these themes throughout the campaign. He could promote his candidacy as the antidote to fear only by first evoking fear. It was "a weary, worn and almost defeated world," he told Michigan voters. The Russian vision of an empire encompassing all of Europe was "closer to fact than fantasy," he said in a major address in New York; the growth of the Soviet empire had been "so fast and so fabulous as to make all prior fears seem conservative." "At this rate, there will soon be nothing left but the Western Hemisphere," he warned, decrying the specter of isolationism. Compounding the dangers were "ominous weaknesses in the free world's economic structure," he warned the *New York Herald Tribune* Forum; if not relieved they would be "transformed into political catastrophe."[24]

Summarizing his message to a South Carolina audience, he said: "The danger of war fills our future. . . . The uncertainties that hang over every American family are bred of war and the threats of war." If threats of war were the fundamental source of fear, and peace meant the end of fear, then logically peace had to be defined as the absence of threats of war: "Our deepest desire—the desire of every

American—is for a just and lasting peace; for the end of war and the threats of war." To campaign workers in Washington he defined the meaning of peace: an international "state of understanding where at least we can abjure war and keep away from it." Here he added again that "the only way to win it is to prevent it."[25]

Eisenhower was using this definition of peace as a symbolic vehicle to promise more. In his Philadelphia speech he had set as a minimum goal, "no moves against us." The premise that all "moves against us" would come from communists hardly needed to be spoken. Both candidates made that point with equal emotion; at times the campaign seemed to be a contest about who could be more ardently anticommunist. Regardless of who won, U.S. public discourse was reconfirming and deepening the symbolic role of "the communists" as the primary vehicle for expressing every feeling of threat and anxiety.

In the larger context of Eisenhower's discursive pattern, though, this phenomenon had a more specific meaning. As SACEUR he had committed himself to building a "wall of peace" that would keep the United States secure. He had made peace virtually identical with the image of a wall of nations, bound together in collective security, protecting the West from communist aggression. Now he brought that image home. He told a Portland audience that only the United States could "lead the free nations of the world into a voluntary association which will bind them together firmly in opposition to the spread of Communism." In Bridgeport, Connecticut, he defined peace as the United States leading the "free world" in "a combination of protection that will stop communism right where it is and gradually allow it to atrophy and recede of its own evil elements within itself." He told Chicagoans that "this cloud of fear, of worry, of doubt" would be lifted if the "free world" could "keep the communists where they belong—in their own territory." If his rhetoric reconfirmed the premise of "the communists" as the source of all evil, it simultaneously created an equally powerful premise: an impregnable wall between the United States and "the communists," making war between the two sides impossible, would be the essence of peace and the source of all good.[26]

Eisenhower could associate the Republicans with the public's desire for a wall to protect them not merely against communism, but against every disruption of their comfortable daily routine. The word *peace* became a symbol, not merely of the avoidance of war, the end of all war, or of national security, but a symbol of every desire for permanently guaranteed safety, ease, and enjoyment of life. (The Eisenhower campaign distributed buttons with slogans such as "Mighty Tower Eisenhower" and "Eisenhower Will Guard My Future.") In his peace rhetoric, as in so much else, Eisenhower offered—and indeed became—as Marquis Childs wrote, "a clean slate on which each citizen could write his own hopes and aspirations."

Tutored by Eisenhower's rhetoric, however, citizens learned that they could write their hopes only if they first inscribed their fears.[27]

Eisenhower summed up all of the complex meanings he had woven around the word *peace* when he spoke in a small town in northern California:

> A united strong United States can lead the free nations of the world into that kind of collective security program that will lift a great burden from our hearts: the burden of fear abroad. As I said before it won't immediately produce that kind of tranquil world which we all hope to establish in our time, but it will be in that process which will bring the Soviets to understand there is nothing for them to gain by force and threat of force, and gradually these great burdens will be lifted from our hearts and our young men can stay home on the farms and in the stores and in the schools instead of going into uniform abroad.[28]

When Eisenhower spoke of collective security, or when he said that "peace for America is inseparable from peace for the world," he was again offering a "clean slate." He never intended to define any precise doctrine or specific strategy for his administration. His words were created only for the purpose of winning the election. They were meant to be vague generalities, written and spoken in the rush of political battle. So there was plenty of room for ambiguity, and plenty of political profit from it. Internationalists could understand him to be calling for U.S. integration into and leadership of a true world community. But in the full context of his campaign discourse, the statement could easily mean something quite different. "The peace of the world" was a euphemism for the secure wall that would permanently end disturbances from abroad. In most of his discourse, in other words, world peace was only a means to American peace of mind. If the well-being of people in the Soviet Union was now largely irrelevant, even the well-being of people in allied nations was a secondary issue, a means to an end. In that sense, Eisenhower's consistent condemnations of isolationism had a bit of a hollow ring. Although he later claimed that he had run for president solely to forestall the drift toward isolationism, and during the campaign he often pronounced isolationism "dead," he was obviously shaping his rhetoric to placate the isolationist sentiment that remained so strong in his own party. Politics had made him, however indirectly, an "America-firster."

Sometimes the candidate could speak as if peace already existed and needed only to be defended. He told the American Federation of Labor, for example, that the nation's task was "to make secure the peace . . . making the Free World so strong of heart and sinew that aggression becomes unthinkable." This was logical enough; if peace meant preventing unwanted movement, it meant preserving the status quo. The problem was that Eisenhower was running against the incumbent administration, which meant opposing the status quo. So for the most part he talked about peace as a thwarted hope, a desire yet to be fulfilled. He promised to "win the peace that has escaped us." Occasionally he lapsed into the public language of his years as chief of staff, promising eventual peace for the entire world.[29]

The bulk of his rhetoric, however, was more modest, speaking only of a future peace for the "free world." Peace became a state of collective security within the "free world"; in an election eve statement he set as his goal "peace in the world for ourselves and for all free people." When he proposed "a practical plan for world peace," he meant a plan for keeping the two geopolitical halves of the world wholly asunder. Peace meant securing the "free world" by preventing any adverse happenings from impinging upon it. That was now the essence of good. What happened to those on the other side of the wall was a distinctly secondary concern. The image of a "wall of peace" implied that peace meant not a new kind of relationship, but rather a new absence of relationship, with the adversary.

This image went far toward solving the dilemma Eisenhower faced over the contradiction between pursuing "liberation" and working out "a way of living with them." His professed goal was now to stop the Soviet Union "in its tracks" and then leave it alone. As long as the Soviets refrained from aggression (the implicit argument went), they could be safely left alone, because they would be forever contained. This was the sum total of the modus vivendi Eisenhower sought, the goal of "living peacefully and permanently with communism in the world."[30] It was easy enough to tack on a quick reference to the enemy's internal atrophy, proclaim this goal as the new image of total victory, and thereby sidestep the whole "liberation" issue. Working out "a way of living with them" became the new image of apocalyptic triumph.

Even living with the communists, he often said, would be a long, difficult road; he admitted that he had no easy solutions to the problems of war and peace. When advertising consultant Rosser Reeves wanted to bill him as "the man who will bring us peace," he demurred, for he would make no such guarantees. He was content to accept Reeves's alternative proposal: "Eisenhower, man of peace." This limitation, too, could be blamed on the communists: "We do not have to hold anyone up to the responsibility of producing a perfect peace. Of course we can't have that as long as Soviet Communism is the militant aggressive dictatorship it is." The "man of peace" could promise only that if elected he would, some day, see to it that the United States was securely sheltered behind a "wall of peace."[31]

As chief of staff, Eisenhower had equated peace with the global triumph of "the American way." Now, though, peace meant the spread of the "American way" only up to the borders of the communist bloc. He gave lip service to the value of diversity within the "free world," but he always returned to his conviction that the United States must be the ideal model if the "free world" were to live in peace. In San Francisco, for example, he called for the United States to "prevail in this 'cold war' struggle for the minds and wills of men." He assured the world that "we are not trying to remake the world in the image of America." But then he immediately undermined his own assurance: "We have an appointment to keep with history. If we can show to all the peoples of this earth . . . that their hope is our hope, that their goal is our goal, then we shall keep that appointment with history. And that appointment is the most important that history has ever made, for it can bring peace on earth." Addressing the Alfred E. Smith Dinner, he tried to resolve the seeming contradiction. Unity in the "free world" did not mean "dull uniformity"; it meant "a true harmony of distinct and varied colors. Only on the total, final effect must we agree—and that is: the stout defense of freedom."[32]

In the context of Eisenhower's discourse, the intertwining of peace, "free world" unity, the "defense of freedom," and "the American way" was tautological. Just as every individual's selfish impulses had to be restrained either by voluntary self-control or externally imposed control, so every nation had to live either in freedom (i.e., voluntary self-control) or totalitarianism (i.e., external control). There was no third possibility. If peace meant the "free world" united as a wall to block out totalitarian communism, then peace meant a permanent and absolute separation between the two realms. Peace meant, by definition, keeping the "free world" forever free. And freedom, of course, meant political democracy and economic free enterprise as practiced in the United States, "the spiritual and material realization . . . of man's hopes and goals everywhere." So peace had to require the extension of "the American way" throughout the "free world." Variations might be accepted on details, but not on the fundamentals.[33]

## "I SHALL GO TO KOREA"

Early in the campaign, the peace theme did not seem to be the decisive winner that Republican strategists expected. The candidate admitted as much to campaign workers on 11 September: "That subject does not seem to be uppermost in those terms, at least, in the minds of the people I encountered. It is this desire for a change [that is uppermost]." Just a few days later, Republican pollsters began to find a way to link the themes of peace and change. In their quest to determine which particular fears their candidate should focus upon, they discovered that the greatest fear in the minds of the voters was not a future global war, but the present war in Korea.

Responding immediately, Eisenhower and his speechwriters began pounding home the theme of "a peace that would eliminate the chances of a new Korea, a peace that would bring the present Korea to a satisfactory close, a peace that would allow us to keep our youngsters at home." The strategy was to focus on public concerns, turn them into fears, and blame them on the Democrats. Since Korea was such an overwhelming concern, it became the rhetorical symbol for all of the nation's fears. And of course it could be labeled "the Democrats' war," implying that a Republican president would wage cold war so fiercely that the enemy would never even start a "hot" war.

The candidate told a St. Louis audience of his "one personal dedication, which transcends all others. That dedication is to help bring lasting peace to the world; to help make sure that your sons and their sons will never have to be sent to fight in another war." He wanted to lead the nation, he said a few days later in West Virginia, "toward the end of this Korea and the prevention of other Koreas so that we do not have to live with the shadow of fear across all our doorsteps that our young sons and grandsons may be taken away." On many occasions he added that he wanted to bring peace so that fewer of the nation's financial resources would have to be put into preparation for war. "Thousands of our workers toil to fire the furnaces, to speed the assembly lines to tool the machines—from which will come the weapons of war. . . . This is the shadow that haunts the hopes of all of us," he told Ohio voters. The great costs in both blood and money "creep into our hearts, they create fear and on top of that they cause us to spend our substance."[34]

The "Eisenhower, man of peace" theme culminated on 24 October, in Detroit. The candidate blamed the Korean War on the Democrats' failure "to check and to turn back Communist ambition . . . to read and outwit the totalitarian mind." The implication was clear: his greater military experience and fiercer anticommunism would never allow him to make such a mistake. Then he offered his famous pledge: "I shall go to Korea." Martin Medhurst's close reading of the text shows how it drew on familiar contexts of public discourse about the cold war, foreign policy, and Korea, as well as Eisenhower's own persona. Weaving these together, the speech seemed to be powerful evidence of his intent to end the war, even though there was "no plan, or promise, or program beyond an inspection tour." As Piers Brendon says, "the pledge smacked of action but committed Ike to nothing more than making the journey. It implied to hawks that he would win the war and to doves that he would end it." He certainly did not say what he would do after he got to Korea. Indeed he explained that he needed to make the trip "to learn" how best to bring peace. It was apparently an admission that he did not know how to proceed toward ending the war. Yet the pledge itself seemed sufficient to swing the necessary votes into his column.[35]

In fact, though, the candidate did have some specific ideas on how to proceed toward peace, both in Korea and in the world. He offered them immediately after his famous promise to go to Korea, and his words offered a fair preview and epitome of his future cold war strategy as president. "Progress along at least two lines can instantly begin," he continued. "We can—first—step up the program of training and arming the South Korean forces." He had offered this idea to Republican convention delegates back in June as "far from a satisfactory solution, but it is the only one that looks to me to have any sense at this moment." In early October he began to make it a theme of his campaign rhetoric. The fighting in Korea was "a job for the Koreans," he told an Illinois audience. "If there must be a war there, let it be Asians against Asians." From the speechwriting headquarters in New York, C.D. Jackson cabled his concern to the campaign train: "The way it sounded here was that the General thought it was a fine [idea] to have Asians killing Asians." The general did think this was a fine idea, assuming that the war had to go on, one way or another. He repeated the idea often during the campaign, despite Jackson's misgivings.[36]

More important, perhaps, he was beginning to speak of this, in private, as a principle that could be generalized. When he wrote to his running mate, Richard Nixon, on 1 October that "the early and important thing to do is organize, train and equip South Koreans," he added at the last moment "and other Asiatic non-communist nations." The sentence continued, "and thus minimize, if not eliminate, the drain on Western manpower." Just a few days after his election, he wrote to Secretary of Defense Robert Lovett that training and equipping more South Koreans "might be able to minimize American and other western casualties." Then he generalized the point: "I sincerely believe that the only way our national interests are going to be protected around the world is to encourage—indeed to insist upon—every local area contributing the maximum to its own defense." Eisenhower was not suggesting that the United States abandon Asian anticommunist warriors. As he said in the Detroit speech, though, he wanted U.S. troops only "in reserve positions and supporting roles [as] assurance that disaster would not again strike." His announcement at the outset of the speech that he was treating Korea as "the supreme symbol" of the entire U.S. foreign policy proved significant. This speech set out two central facets of his emerging foreign policy and understanding of peace: keeping "American boys" out of war while still preventing "disaster."[37]

The Detroit speech went on to mention another approach that could begin "instantly": "We can—secondly—shape our psychological warfare program into a weapon capable of cracking the Communist front." Eisenhower had already devoted a major address to this subject at San Francisco, on 8 October. That speech had explained the notion of psychological warfare in the context of the candidate's larger notion of peace. He had come to San Francisco, he said, to talk about "the calamities that have come to our nation. . . . The psychological strategists of communism have crept into our citadel." The cold war had put the world in "a twilight zone between war and peace." The West Coast was in just as much danger as the rest of the country: "The vast Pacific is no longer the sure guardian of your homes." In this speech, more than any other, he articulated "the peaceful tools that must be used in the waging of this fight." Eisenhower had been interested in psychological warfare since the early days of World War II. Now he was also using the idea to keep alive the "liberation" theme without committing the United States to any overt military risks: "Our first objective is to render unreliable in the minds of the Kremlin rulers the hundreds of millions enslaved in the occupied and satellite nations. Peace will then have her triumph no less than war." Psychological warfare was the way "to gain a victory without casualties, to win a contest that can quite literally save peace."[38]

This was more than effective rhetoric. It foreshadowed an important facet of the Eisenhower administration's cold war strategy, a strategy that entailed a new, more complex relationship between war and peace. By renouncing military means of "liberation" and tacitly allowing the Soviet Union to pursue its own internal course, Eisenhower was redefining not only peace but also war. The crusade of the cold war ("a twilight zone between peace and war," according to the San Francisco speech) would be quite different from Eisenhower's "crusade in Europe." Victory would not mean occupation or even conquest of the enemy. Victory would mean only a permanent absence of direct engagement between the opposing sides. It would be, in effect, an endless truce, a permanent "way of living with them." Eisenhower's decision to downplay the liberation theme left open the possibility that the communist satellites might even be allowed to remain on the communist side of the Iron Curtain (though his literal words excluded that possibility). When, and only when, this new kind of victory was obtained, there would be "world peace." So the effective definition of victory and the effective definition of peace were now identical. In that sense, victory would "quite literally save peace"—and peace would be both the means to and the sign of victory in war.

This convergence of war and peace was crucial to Eisenhower's success, for it enabled him to be a "clean slate" on the most crucial of issues in 1952—the battle against communism. As Lloyd Gardner has noted, he convinced many liberal internationalists that he sincerely wanted peace and could get along with the Russians; at the same time, he convinced many earnest cold warriors that he could stand up to the Russians and "lick the hell out of them."[39] He accomplished this feat by defining both peace and victory as permanent successful resistance to communism, stopping it "in its tracks" with a "wall of peace." Once those definitions were accepted, it followed logically that the only man who could bring peace was the man who could stand up most firmly to the Russians. So the real feat was not projecting two contradictory images at once, but getting such a wide spectrum of voters to accept his rhetorical definitions. Once that acceptance was secured, the rest followed quite naturally.

## THE CRUSADE

Peace was certainly not Eisenhower's only theme. He warned at length about Democratic corruption, Democratic mismanagement of the economy, oppressive Democratic bureaucracy, and Democratic toleration of domestic subversives. He sounded the alarm on as many fronts as his speechwriters could realistically manage to invent. He won votes on the far right and helped to unify the Republican Party when he warned of spies and subversives, "experts in treason," whose damage could not even be calculated. He wooed more liberal voters by promising to preserve federal social programs "that keep all of us from falling into the pit of disaster." Alarmist language could be used for every political purpose. But time and again he heeded the original advice of his advisors and returned to the theme of peace. Each time he would articulate a variety of fears, link all to the fear of war, and proclaim spiritual strength the key to peace.[40]

The greatest danger of all, he said at one press conference, was not paying attention to the relationship between external and internal threats. Beneath any specific relationships he might discuss, there was always the deeper implicit link. The internal threats—particularly government corruption, the favorite theme— were always described as moral and spiritual weaknesses. The "scandal-a-day" administration was a clear sign of spiritual pollution and disease; it had tolerated the "malignant growth" of domestic subversion. It had failed to stop "this hideous disease that attacks the world today." The "malignant growth" had to be completely excised. Only a total change could "clean up and clean out" the "mess in Washington." Purification was the moral task to which the candidate called the nation. Sometimes he made an explicit link between domestic health and purity and world peace. The United States could lead an alliance to stop communism only if it could offer a model of a better way. How could it do so if its own government were not pure? With the honest Republicans in the White House, he promised, "all the world" would once again recognize the United States as the embodiment of universal values and enlist in the battle against communism.[41]

Although he usually left the link between external and internal pollution implicit, it was clear enough. He framed both the presidential campaign and the cold war as spiritual battles, in which moral virtue and purity were the winning weapons. Many of his speeches culminated in an apocalyptic summons to practice spiritual values. In his speech on psychological warfare, he described the cold war as "the struggle for the minds and wills of men. . . . The decisive fact will be the spirit, the resolve, the determination with which we bend to our task." Although he might occasionally deny his apocalyptic bent ("I bring you no prophecy of doom; neither do I promise Utopia"), he generally found it more politically effective as well as more natural to resort to the language of global crisis.[42]

He pronounced himself "actively and urgently enlisted in the cause of preserving for the young and the future young of America those unique characteristics of our civilization that have privileged us above all other peoples of the globe." "The worldwide Communist conspiracy seeks to destroy the spiritual convictions on which our civilization is based," he warned in Los Angeles. The freedom that communism threatened was "that glorious gift of the Judeo-Christian traditions." "In this election our country's future is at stake," he warned in South Carolina; "We will need single-mindedness born of moral conviction and wisdom, and courage born of the spirit—a spirit rooted in our own deep and uncompromising religious belief." The future of this country would determine the future of the world, either peace or chaos: "A strong, united America is the very cornerstone of peace. We must have that or we will have only turmoil in the world." This apocalyptic phrasing reached its peak in Milwaukee, where Eisenhower had to woo McCarthyite voters. Communism and freedom represented "two distinct worlds," he told them, "opposed as danger is to safety, as sickness is to health, as weakness is to strength, as darkness to light." The future would belong to "men who—today—are ready to bear spiritual and intellectual arms against an alien army of Communist ideas."[43]

In his speech accepting the Republican nomination, Eisenhower had reinforced this apocalypticism by proclaiming his campaign a "crusade." He made much of that word throughout the campaign. All the major events in his life had held "that extra spiritual factor to make them a crusade," he told Massachusetts voters. Now he was crusading "to liberate the American people from the shackles of expensive corruption" and inflation and taxes, as well as from "the terrifying shadow of war." Concluding the "I shall go to Korea" speech, he called his effort for peace a crusade because it was "devoted to a just cause of the purest meaning" and "victory can come only with the gift of God's help."[44]

The West's greatest asset, he said in New York, was its "matchless spiritual strength . . . a civilization believing in man as made in the image of God." The West could meet the Soviet challenge only by uniting in its faith in "the infinitely precious, utterly unique individual of living flesh, whose spirit has such strength that he can endure and survive oppression, and poverty disease, and imprisonment—to keep alive his soul's love of freedom." Of course freedom, for Eisenhower, meant the freedom to restrain one's own desires and willingly endure deprivation. This was still the essence of spiritual virtue. So he called for "triumph over the temptations of economic nationalism" and "the patience to check our tempers" in dealing with allies. He applied the same values in domestic politics, telling Texas Republicans, "first and foremost, above everything else, we must have moral and spiritual strength. . . . This requires us to put our party above ourselves and our country above our party."[45]

Because the cold war was a struggle between two ways of life, he told Boston voters, it would have to be won on a spiritual level: "The enemy we face is, above all . . . a moral enemy. . . . Our salvation demands much more than clever compromise or neat negotiations. You can pay ransom for the body—but never for the soul."[46]

It is hardly surprising to find a political candidate uttering such pieties on the campaign trail. Many who do are simply reading words supplied by their speechwriters. But this was hardly the case with Eisenhower. Several of his aides later testified that he edited nearly all of his speeches, some of them quite carefully. All the major themes of his rhetoric were rooted in his long-standing discursive patterns, private as well as public. Certainly this was true of his emphasis on spiritual values.

As a candidate for president, Eisenhower had little time for private correspondence on any substantive issues. But in the few letters he did write, stray remarks reflected the importance he attached to religious language. Shortly after the Republican convention he wrote to a personal friend and important Republican figure, Paul Hoffman, of "our struggle to keep the crusade moving along." When an even closer friend, Cliff Roberts, suggested that it would be politically advantageous for Eisenhower to join a specific church, the candidate replied that he and his brothers were "all very earnestly and seriously religious." Of course Eisenhower had his own notion of religiosity. He alluded to it in a letter to his son on the same day that he wrote to Roberts about religion. Citing Robert E. Lee's words, "We cannot do more than our duty, we do not wish to do less," he admonished John to "do your duty in whatever function or office to which you may be assigned." Duty meant "complete self-control," and this was the basis of "enduring value." Ultimately, all of the values for which Eisenhower was "crusading" could be traced back to this notion of self-control.[47]

He drew on this ideological nexus of ideas when he had to explain to the French Defense Minister, Rene Pleven, a controversial remark he had made at the Republican convention. News reports had him saying that half the French people were atheists or agnostics. This was not quite accurate reporting, he complained to Pleven. But he did allow that if it were substantially true, it "would explain some of France's political troubles. Manifestly, if there is such a general lack of faith in basic religious tenets, then the support of any government based upon the equality and dignity of men will be weakened." He added his "fervent hope that spiritually and intellectually [France] would rally one hundred percent behind the banner of freedom and against Communism."[48]

This was not a particularly politic response. Eisenhower was strongly invested, personally and politically, in Pleven's own plan for a European defense force. He might have been expected to bend over backward to placate Pleven in this seemingly trivial incident. To Eisenhower, though, it was apparently not trivial. He would offer Pleven only this half-hearted apology, which actually confirmed the spirit, if not the letter, of his published remark. He could not speak about political freedom, cold war victory, or peace without invoking, or at least assuming, his own understanding of religion. *Freedom, victory, peace,* and *faith* were now virtually synonymous terms in Eisenhower's discourse. Any one could be substituted for any other, because each was a synecdochical representation of the whole web of his ideological values.

As a candidate for president the former general, freed of the constraints of the military, was doing what he had always wanted to do: preaching spiritual revival to the entire nation, exhorting it to enlist on the side of right and virtue in an apocalyptic crusade. The essence of his campaign message was the essential spiritual virtue of self-restraint. He called Americans to return to that virtue precisely because communism threatened to prevent them from practicing it. He proclaimed himself the man who could promote self-restraint throughout the 'free world," creating an impregnable wall that would shield Americans from every threat. Thus he would lead the nation back to geopolitical peace, mental clarity, and moral purity. Augustinian virtues would create an Augustinian peace, with the forces of order permanently walling out the forces of chaos. And this victory in a new kind of crusade would become the new meaning for both peace and apocalyptic salvation.

Like every good preacher, the candidate used his words to create an entire self-defining world in which his congregation could safely dwell. He used his rhetorical definition of virtue to identify the threats to virtue. Then he used those rhetorical threats, and the prospect of victory over them, to stimulate a return to virtue. Finally, he promised that those who embraced his entire package of ideological discourse would be repaid with permanent peace of mind. In all of this, he offered words—particularly his own inspirational words—as the crusaders' winning weapon. There was a profound note of truth in what Eisenhower wrote to Edward Meade Earle the day before the Philadelphia speech: "The farther I proceed in political life, the more I believe that I, as an individual, should have striven to be worthy of the pulpit as an avenue of public service instead of the political podium."[49] This was the task he had imagined himself fulfilling as president of a university. On 4 November 1952, he received an overwhelming mandate to fulfill it as president of the United States.

# Conclusion

On 7 December 1941, Dwight Eisenhower held the permanent rank of lieutenant colonel in the United States Army. He was well known to and respected by the army's officer corps, but virtually unknown beyond it. Less than three years later, he had become one of the most famous war heroes in the nation's history, known to and admired by the vast majority of his compatriots and millions of others around the world. By 7 December 1952, he was returning home after fulfilling his campaign promise to go to Korea. On board a cruiser in the Pacific, he was meeting with new cabinet members and top advisers, preparing to take control of the most powerful government in the history of the world.

Reviewing this rapid rise, one would expect to see significant changes in the man's ideology and discourse. One would expect to see evidence of revision, innovation, and creative development. In fact, though, there were no major changes in the basic patterns and structures. These were almost fully articulated by the time he watched his troops invade Italy in the summer of 1943. From then on, the logic of his ideological framework was firmly in place.

There would be numerous developments, of course. As he moved on from wartime commander to occupation commander, chief of staff, university president, NATO military chief, and finally presidential candidate, he skillfully adapted his discourse, both private and public, to each new situation. New elements were incorporated; old elements were dropped and sometimes brought back in, as the situation demanded. But these were all logical extensions of the basic pattern. It was very much like a house always under construction. Rooms, and occasionally even whole wings or stories, might be added, removed, or remodeled. But the foundation and the overall architectural design remained the same.

## THE "GOD TERMS"

One useful way to trace this process of creative adaptation is to look at the key words Eisenhower used to represent the highest rung on his scale of values.

Various words played this role at various times, including *duty, self-sacrifice, teamwork, freedom, democracy, peace, order,* and *civilization.* All the key terms could be subsumed in the overarching category of religious or spiritual values. This makes it quite appropriate to give all these words a label sometimes used by scholars of rhetoric: "god terms."

During the war, the primary words were *duty, self-sacrifice,* and *teamwork.* Once the general proclaimed the war a crusade against fascism, words such as *freedom* and *democracy* began to appear, but they remained rather secondary. As head of the occupation in Germany, he added *peace, order,* and *civilization* to the list. Not until he returned home as chief of staff did *freedom* and *democracy* begin to play a central role. None of the other terms was abandoned, though, at least in the public rhetoric. The achievement of his rhetoric as C/S was to weave together a rich and unified texture, by identifying all these key terms as virtual synonyms for each other. In the private discourse, *peace* was far less prominent; *security, strength,* and *stability* were more likely to take its place.

Once free of the constraints of active military service, Eisenhower made *peace* much less prominent in the public rhetoric, while the other key words remained central in his vocabulary. The major change during the Columbia years was bringing *capitalism* and *free enterprise* to the fore. He made it clear that when he used *freedom* as a "god term," in both public and private, it necessarily entailed the freedom to own and amass private wealth. It would be misleading to say that this was his primary meaning of freedom, but equally misleading to say that any other kind of freedom was primary for him. His central point was, rather, that all the types of freedom he praised were interlaced and indivisible—just as he had previously proclaimed peace in all parts of the world indivisible.

This indivisibility was a logical outgrowth of his discursive structure. The various forms of freedom, like the various key terms, were interwoven because they had to have equal weight and value, and they had to form a single system that stood or fell together. This was a logical implication of his ideological system. The many forms of freedom were all threatened by the same evil, the innate selfishness of human nature, whether manifest in social chaos or state control. Just as all the "god terms" pointed to a single sacred principle, so all the "devil terms" pointed to a single principle of evil. Whenever that evil triumphed, Eisenhower affirmed in many ways, it destroyed every form of freedom simultaneously. Whatever form it took, *freedom* meant, above all, preventing that ultimate disaster. Since every kind of freedom was part of a single ideological "team" fighting the same foe, all freedoms had to be viewed as indivisible, for the sake not only of logic but also to avoid defeat in the great spiritual battle.

Eisenhower's primary ideological problem was that he urged the world on to final victory in that battle while simultaneously denying that it could ever be achieved. Privately, he had already moved toward resolving this contradiction while chief of staff, when he confessed that perhaps the best to hope for was permanent containment of the enemy. With this linguistic move he was at least tempted to equate permanent containment with ultimate victory. In the public discourse through 1950, though, he continued to offer utopian promises of international peace and a domestic "middle way." His return to military service in Europe in 1951 forced him to bring his public language more in line with the private. Now the wartime "god terms" were highly serviceable once again. Containment took on an aura of eschatological promise. It became the effective working definition of peace; the return to military leadership required him to return *peace* to an integral place in the list of key words.

*Containment* was never itself a "god term" for Eisenhower. Rather, he continued to frame his discourse around the prerequisites for containment: *duty, self-sacrifice, teamwork.* By 1951, all the key words that Eisenhower had ever used were joined together in a unified discursive structure that would carry him to the White House. And all of it could be traced back to the single, simple spiritual battle he had depicted in the early months of World War II. He endowed the cold war with meaning, as he had endowed World War II with meaning, by making the global superpower struggle a reflex and mirror image of the individual spiritual struggle.

Just below this highest echelon of "god terms" in Eisenhower's discourse, there was a complex network of secondary key words sustaining and enriching the whole ideological edifice. Prominent among these, and virtually a "god term" itself, was *leadership.* The key to leadership was the officer's exemplary behavior, which would inspire the troops to emulate him. Always heavily influenced by his life's work as a soldier, Eisenhower charged the whole U.S. citizenry to be to the world what a good officer was to his troops. Yet his view of human nature prevented him from trusting the entire citizenry to heed his call. Most people, he assumed, were like the millions of enlisted men he had led during World War II; they needed strong leaders to weld them into a unified team that performed in exemplary ways.

Eisenhower heard endless praise for the teamwork his leadership had created during the war. It was perhaps natural that he would nominate himself as the leader needed for postwar victory. Since few Americans would observe his own behavior directly (though he was always sensitive to any hint of impropriety in his behavior), he focused primarily on his words as the source of motivation and inspiration. For Eisenhower leadership was, above all, a matter of effective public discourse.

During World War II, he pronounced himself firmly convinced that virtuous ideas among his troops were the key to victory; in a very real sense, he sought victory over the Axis only as a means to the victory of virtue among the Allies. As head of the occupation in Germany, he focused far more on public relations than on policy determination; his chief goal was to pronounce the right words. As chief of staff, he argued both in private and in public that victory in the cold war depended on making U.S. domestic life an example that would inspire emulation around the world. Domestic reform was the key to successful foreign policy. But since he always found the source of societal problems in individual behavior and values, not in political or economic institutional structures, the reform he called for was not political or economic, but spiritual. Successful exhortation to spiritual virtue was thus the most practical of policy goals.

As president of Columbia, Eisenhower had little discernible impact on university policy, apart from initiating a few pet projects; his overriding practical goal was raising money. He had taken the presidency because it offered such a tempting platform to preach to the nation, and that preaching was arguably his highest concern. As head of SHAPE, he made it clear once again that cold war victory depended on the inculcation of proper attitudes both at home and among allied populations. This was his own task; the details of policy were left to subordinates. Similarly, as a candidate for president, he showed far more interest in the spiritual reform he hoped to spur with his words than in specific policy positions. He constructed the cold war as essentially a war of the spirit. Words were its most crucial weapons.

Eisenhower said repeatedly that he wanted to lead the nation and accomplish all his goals by speaking persuasive words. His efforts were directed more toward that goal than to influencing policy at the highest levels. In fact, throughout the period studied here, he had relatively little direct influence on important policy developments. The policies with which he was involved would probably have turned out much the same had someone else been in charge. This is one more reason to credit his own claim that he was most concerned with effective words.

## THE IRONY OF CLARITY

Clarity, like leadership, was a key term for Eisenhower, and the two were closely related. He often urged upon others, in private and in public, the importance of clear planning, clear analysis, clear speech, and clear thinking. Clarity was particular important for leaders, he claimed, because their clear minds and clear words were needed to create mental clarity for others. Only a leader who could forge a well-defined, shared understanding within a group, be it a platoon or a whole nation, could unify, inspire, and motivate that group. From the day World War II ended, the general took his main task to be the articulation of the specific values and worldview of "the American way." He wanted to provide the nation with a vision sufficiently clear and unified to spark a spiritual reform. He held that reform to be the winning weapon in the war against all enemies, foreign and domestic. The essence of that reform, as he described it, was widespread public affirmation of the ideological words that he himself pronounced.

To be sure, he denied that he was offering ideology. He took it for granted that ideologies were found only among the "isms," which were spawned by selfishness. In order to set himself off from that most grievous fault, he had to declare himself free of ideology. Within his absolute dualistic framework, he could do that only by fervently proclaiming his devotion to the absolute opposite of ideology: moderate, sober logical reasoning. Still, the rigidity and totalizing urge of his discourse resembled the discourse he disdained.

It was the longing for clarity, in others as well as himself, that led Eisenhower to be an ideologue. His passion for a clarity that would banish all ambiguities was a line of defense, perhaps the primary line of defense, against his innate alarmism and his fear of a rapidly changing world.[1] He assumed that his audiences would instantly recognize and share his sense of living in an unfamiliar, bewildering, frightening country. His ideological language conjured up appealing (if largely illusory) images of a bygone era of clearly defined, universally shared American values. He employed a long series of catchwords, each of which denoted the whole system of values. In addition, he was always ready to offer his own personal hopes and fears as synecdochical signs representing the hopes and fears of the nation.

This may be the key to the mystery of Eisenhower's astonishing popularity. It was accepted as almost an axiom of U.S. politics that he was popular enough to be elected president on either party's ticket. *Time* magazine praised "his poise, tact, and amazing popularity," which made him "a perfect presidential candidate." The general may have been happier when a *New York Times* editorial credited his success to the content of his public words as well as his manner of delivery: "One reason for General Eisenhower's steadily mounting prestige is his commonsense approach to difficult and intricate problems. A second reason is his ability to express the problem clearly. A third is his always evident sincerity." Here was praise for the kind of clarity he hoped to provide.[2]

His words, however, were not reported in the media nearly as often as he might have liked (at least until he became a candidate for president). The spotlight was more on his personality and presence, as well as the ever-present issue of his political future. *Newsweek* columnist Raymond Moley offered a valuable insight when he ascribed his popularity to "the prevalent sense of foreboding about foreign relations and the people's desire to have a wise experienced hand at the helm." Sociologists Kenneth Morris and Barry Schwartz find this sense of fore-boding the key factor. They argue that Eisenhower became so popular precisely because there was such a widespread sense of crisis about the viability of cultural traditions in the 1940s and 1950s. Eisenhower was particularly well suited to symbolize and enact the traditions called into doubt, thereby providing reassurance to the public. In a troubled time, he continued to tell and represent an official story that was persuasive because it was simple, reassuring, and seemingly sincere. Martin Medhurst adds, "Eisenhower not only delivered discourses; he was, himself, a discourse," embodying traditional virtues such as sincerity, humility, duty, and a "down-home sense of self." In other words, his personality as well as his words served the basic function of ideology: inspiring hope through what Geertz calls "retraditionalization."[3]

Of course only a few intimates were informed that his expressions of hope were usually artificially induced, consciously willed responses to his fears. While using his images of the past to assuage his fears as well as those of his audience, he acknowledged that there could be no full return to naive traditionalism. He understood that something like retraditionalization was the best he could hope for. He did hope for it ardently, too, clinging to his ideological roadmap of "the American way of life" as the only way to escape the unfamiliar reality of his country.

Through retraditionalization Eisenhower sought clarity, in order to unify the nation and make possible the teamwork so essential to winning a war, hot or cold. An equal argument can be made that he sought teamwork because it would foster ideological unity, which in turn would create a conviction of clarity; with all alternative opinions marginalized, the regnant ideology would appear to be self-evidently true. It would be fruitless to debate whether sociopolitical unity or ideological unity was Eisenhower's chief goal. Putting the question that way misses the key point that he sought both simultaneously, for he could not separate one from the other. Sociopolitical and ideological categories were both essential to his vision of a national unity that would ultimately lead to global unity. Clarity was supposed to be the path to unity, and unity in turn was supposed to lead to reassurance and hope.

The irony of Eisenhower's discourse was that his quest for perfect clarity actually led to a decrease in clarity. The general never intended to be a philosopher, of course. Ultimately he wanted to exhort and edify. Yet he wanted his exhortations to bring clarity, he said, not only to enhance security but also to give people peace of mind and hope for a better future. Judged against his own stated criteria, he failed more than he succeeded. His words constantly and sometimes promiscuously blended logically inconsistent ideas, values, and cultural traditions. The resulting confusion and instability underscored the confusion and instability of the world he was reflecting and creating. This could only make those who heard or read his words more fearful about the present and future. It need not have been this way, since he had a single premise from which all important elements in his discourse flowed. Yet he did not (or perhaps could not) make that internal consistency clear to others. Occasionally this could be attributed to limitations placed upon him by offices he held. Much more often, though, he simply missed obvious opportunities to show the consistency in his discourse. His rhetoric laid spokes of his ideological wheel side by side, responding to the needs of the moment. Rarely, though, did he trace those wheels back to their unifying hub.

This irony was compounded by another: the discourse that was supposed to provide security and hope was built upon and suffused with the language of fear. The two ironies were closely linked. When clarity is pursued via a rigid, totalizing ideological wheel, it is bound to breed fear. Ideology must insist on becoming all-encompassing. It must go around and around in the same circle, with no alternative views allowed. Every new issue that comes into view is interpreted within the circumference of the wheel, so every new issue becomes another spoke. With every new spoke that is added, the wheel enlarges itself and thus confirms and reinforces itself. Since the wheel is self-legitimating, nothing can challenge the system. Because all the spokes of the ideological wheel are interconnected, stemming from the same hub, any uncertainty about one spoke threatens the validity of all and, especially, the validity of the hub. When new or alternative approaches to specific issues come into view, they deepen the sense of living in unfamiliar territory, precisely the feeling the ideology is intended to banish. So they must be perceived as a frightening harbinger of total chaos, the collapse of the wheel.

The ideologue's natural response to any alternative is to banish it from consciousness, to reaffirm the wheel and its every spoke as the only possible interpretation of reality. Every new issue that arises must become a new spoke in order to legitimize the entirety of the wheel. This explains the typically rigid stance, the penchant for speaking in absolutes, and the tendency to exaggerate every danger. In Eisenhower's discourse these features were all openly articulated, and often openly legitimized. Ideology and absolutism are mutually reinforcing parts of a single process, or perhaps simply two different ways of describing the same process. Once inside such a self-perpetuating wheel, a person can find it quite difficult to break out. Of course, with all alternative interpretations banished, it is difficult to see any reason even to try to break out of the wheel. This problem is compounded when (as is usually the case) the individual surrounds himself or herself with others who simply confirm, reinforce, and enlarge the wheel.

Such a characterization seems to fit Eisenhower's situation. He was determined to interpret every facet of the contemporary scene, and indeed of human life, as a manifestation of the universal spiritual civil war. All the spokes of his discourse could be logically interlinked because all stemmed from a single hub, the "age-old battle" between selfishness and self-restraint. Despite his occasional gestures of intellectual humility, his discourse exuded an air of certainty. Everything had to be woven into the system (as loosely articulated as it was) and circumscribed within its absolute demarcations between truth and falsehood, right and wrong. Therefore, all realities had to be dichotomized; everything had to be treated only in relation to its absolute opposite. Dichotomizing and polarizing were the only methods he could discern that would lead to clarity. In political terms, freedom, capitalism, and "the American way" could be meaningful only if pitted against their absolute opposites. This created the need to construct discursively an imminent foreign and domestic "Red menace," so that the nation could be called upon to make a decisive choice between the opposites.

### PEACE, COLD WAR, AND FEAR

This part of the Eisenhower record is easily misunderstood. Most historians have assumed that, in the first postwar years, the general upheld the Wilsonian vision of global harmony. Historians generally agree that he sincerely wanted to make the cooperative values of liberal internationalism the foundation of U.S. discourse and policy, but that he was soon dissuaded by the shifting political winds. This view is hardly tenable. In all his various official capacities, he neither made nor suggested any effort to compromise the differences between the United States and the Soviet Union. He never suggested any specific diplomatic overtures toward the Soviets. He neither initiated nor offered any concrete steps that would foster a closer relationship or any sense of mutuality between the two great powers.

Nor is this at all surprising. Eisenhower's ideology provided no role or motive for genuine mutuality, understanding, and cooperation between nations—and certainly not between the two superpowers. Within his discursive framework, cooperation was essentially a negative process of individuals or groups restraining their selfish desires for the sake of a common goal. His praise of cooperation always assumed that the common goal already existed; cooperation meant simply joining the team to achieve the goal. Rarely did he show any interest in how the common goal was initially determined. Rarely did he urge the public to foster the skills of sharing ideas, making compromises, and setting goals together. Nor did he say much about these skills in private. When Eisenhower spoke of cooperation and mutual understanding, he applied those virtues to the pursuit, not the determination, of goals.

Perhaps this was natural for a military man. He assumed the goal as a given. He admitted that he was uncomfortable when there was no pre-existing, clearly articulated, shared goal to pursue. The absence of a pre-existing goal was confusing and therefore disturbing for a man who valued mental clarity and order so highly. Perhaps this helps to explain why he showed relatively little interest in the political give-and-take of policy formulation. Even in World War II, where he was responsible for developing and implementing so many policies, they were all means to an end. The goal of unconditional surrender had been handed down to him by his civilian superiors, and he simply assumed it. That was apparently the process he preferred.

Eisenhower's understanding of spirituality fit hand-in-glove with his military training. Cooperation as self-restraint meant doing one's duty without questioning the validity of the goal. When it came to the fundamental goals and purposes of life, there could be no question; these were determined by spiritual truths, which were by definition universal. His private discourse made it clear that he would accept no compromise on basic goals, but only on means to achieve them. So his spiritual views and his military temperament combined to make cooperation more a matter of conformity than shared decision-making. A team would be successful if its members restrained themselves, did not obtrude on each other, and thus worked side by side toward the common goal. On the ideal team there would be no political life, in the broadest sense of that term, no interplay of claims and counterclaims, no searching for a negotiated middle ground. When Eisenhower said he hated politics because it was an expression of selfishness, he was also saying (necessarily, by the logic of his discourse) that he hated the uncertainty, the imprecision, and the compromise on basic goals that political life always demands.

When Eisenhower spoke of peace as a matter of mutual understanding and cooperation, he could mean only a shared understanding of goals already given from on high, and cooperative effort to achieve those goals. In terms of U.S.-Soviet relations, this could only mean shared understanding of and striving toward liberal democratic capitalist ideals—"the American system." On that point there could be no compromise, so there was no need to listen to a fundamentally different point of view. For tactical reasons, Eisenhower the chief of staff could explain quite eloquently the value of understanding the Soviets' fundamentally different view. His own ideology, though, allowed no possibility of, nor reason for, accommodating U.S. policy to that view. Therefore, there was no motivation to listen to it seriously, and there was certainly no motivation to search for a genuine middle ground between the superpowers.

Once released from the constraints of military office, he quickly brought his public rhetoric into line with these implications of his private discourse. Certainly his self-proclaimed philosophy of the "middle way" could never mean a compromise between the superpowers or their respective ideological systems. The "middle way" was rather the "American way," the polar opposite of everything that the Soviets symbolized in Eisenhower's discourse. It represented the ideal of a life of perfect rational balance, based on a perfectly clear and ordered set of ideas. This ideal was translated into geopolitical terms in the language of containment. Perfect containment promised a world permanently divided into two immutable spheres of influence and hence perfectly balanced—a world of immutable stability.

Eisenhower's discourse of peace would allow no genuine interchange between the two great nations; it denied the possibility of harmonious interaction so basic to the Wilsonian internationalist ideal. It used Wilsonian language only as a tactic to ensure that there would always be a firm Augustinian wall between the realm of order and the realm of chaos. This meant that there could be no dynamic give-and-take between the superpowers. Such a scenario was unacceptable because it would be unpredictable, leading to uncontrollable changes in the world situation. The outcome of any interchange had to be guaranteed in advance to conform to the universal goals that Eisenhower held inviolable. The outcome had to reinforce existing realities, not create new ones. It had to ensure that all fundamental change was held in check, because any such change threatened an apocalyptic overthrow of the existing reality.

In a geopolitical sense, the outcome also had to reinforce the existing situation. The goal of all interaction would be to provide a vehicle for acting out and securing a bipolar world, not to furnish an arena for genuine mutuality and compromise. The superpowers would be like members of an ideal team, working side by side but not impinging upon each other. Both would serve the interests of rational balance and the "middle way," which was "the American way." Unless there was prior commitment to that universal goal, any interaction would be a threat to the United States and would have to be avoided. The goal was always to ensure that the "Red menace" would be contained within its existing borders. But Eisenhower's discursive framework would be meaningful only as long as the sense of menace persisted. The "Red menace" could never be allowed to conquer, but neither could it be allowed to disappear. The "twilight zone between peace and war" would have to continue indefinitely. So the discourse that was meant to offer reassurance and hope for stable order had to perpetuate and heighten a fear of growing disorder.

As a speaker and writer, Eisenhower entered into an implicit contract with his audiences, and the common currency of that contract was fear. He was responding to the fears of others with words that he claimed were clear and hopeful. His awareness of growing fear impelled him to speak confidently about a better future.

But the process also worked simultaneously in reverse: his language of hope promoted an ever greater sense that the American system was under deadly attack and needed Herculean efforts merely to secure its survival. The more he spoke of the need to protect the American system, the more firmly he constructed that system out of an unending series of purported threats to its very existence. The language of stability and control had to construct the very fears of instability it was designed to control. The crusade to abolish all enemies ensured that the nation would view itself as an island surrounded by a sea of enemies. So hopeful and frightening words generated each other in a vicious circle. In this way, as Robert Ivie has argued, Eisenhower's cold war rhetoric contributed powerfully to what H.W. Brands, Jr., has called the "national insecurity state." "In short," Ivie concludes, "Ike's rhetorical legacy as a cold warrior was to institutionalize an age of peril. . . . Eisenhower sanctioned—and thereby helped to perpetuate—a cultural pathology of peril."[4]

The general's "realism," his "idealism," and his apocalypticism all contributed to this discursive circle. In practical terms, he was a true "realist," accepting the de facto spheres of influence that had emerged from the war as a fact of life. For a "realist," geopolitical polarization was inevitable, and so was the fear that went with it. For an "idealist," this fact had to be only temporary, but the unnatural "twilight zone" it connoted, and the prospect of enduring in that state for many years, had to raise fears. For an apocalypticist, it simply meant that absolute evil was still unvanquished, which certainly meant a continuing state of fear.

Eisenhower constructed his distinctive vision of peace by blending these three elements. He typically used an "idealist" image of perfect world peace in his public rhetoric, in order to boost support for the Augustinian "realist" project of containment. Thus he constructed the communist peril in global, apocalyptic proportions. But he offered no apocalyptic solution. So he and his public were left with only an endlessly bifurcated world posing endless apocalyptic danger. The world he depicted, condemned to a permanent war, was a mirror image of the self he depicted, condemned to be forever at war with itself. The threatening other was a product and a mirror image of the forces threatening within every self. In this discursive context, every expressed hope for progress became a reminder of the immutable limits to progress posed by human nature, the ultimate source of the unending peril. Every expressed hope for containment of the enemy did the same. Although he might promote and defend policies with the language of "realist" or "idealist" hope, the underlying motive force was always fear of disaster. Whenever he spoke of his hope for peace, then, Eisenhower tightened the circle of hope and fear, ensuring that each would entail the other. This circle, built of words, was fitted to all the changing circumstances of cold war events. The result was always the same: to raise ever higher the discursive construction of permanent apocalyptic fear.

To some extent, of course, this was the point; "Alarmist Ike" had every intention of sounding the alarm. He never intended to raise excessive fear, though. He hoped to control his public discourse to create "the middle way," the perfect balance between fear and hope. In this respect, though, as in so many others, he could never define "the middle way" with any precision. Without that precision, "the middle way" served no purpose, since its whole discursive function was to provide a balance and clarity that would yield a reassuring sense of certainty. In this it was bound to fail, for the task was impossible. Eisenhower was using absolute dualism in public to mask the rather different absolute dualisms of his private discourse. The two had to be related to each other, since the public language was meant to achieve goals defined by the private. For this reason the masking could never be complete. In both, he remained caught between genuine global harmony and containment, between stable order and chaos, between hope and fear. He could not speak of one without speaking of the other.

His language, therefore, reinforced the growing sense of defensiveness that could so easily turn to belligerence. Even though Eisenhower chose his language in hopes of keeping the war cold, he was part of a cultural wave that swept the nation toward the deep freeze of cold war enmity and the immense risks of the nuclear arms race. Perhaps he acknowledged indirectly that he was playing with atomic fire, when he criticized the "hysterical" voices warning of imminent war. In contrast to these, he could present himself as the reasonable, moderate alternative. But he never acknowledged how much he had in common with the "hysterical" voices. He never showed any conscious awareness that his language would inevitably exacerbate cold war tensions, undermine the public's sense of stability, and perhaps lead the world to the ultimate instability of war. It didn't go that far, of course, and Eisenhower's genuine desire to avoid global war deserves some of the credit. But the whole body of his discourse, including its eschatological promises of peace, the "middle way," and endless containment, did move the nation in that dangerous direction.

This is the final irony of Eisenhower's discourse. It was part of a profound change in the public discourse of the whole nation. Yet the fear that it bred created a profound aversion to change. As Anthony James Joes has put it, Eisenhower "sought consensus behind limited aims, often expressed in terms of preventing bad things from happening."[5] In his discourse, all of the "god terms" pointed to the same ideal: protection against bad things happening. The idea of peace as an organic harmony among constantly changing and interacting partners could have no positive meaning for him. Nor could he even promote the expansion of the

American system (or the extension of U.S. economic dominance) as his primary goal. Those were only means to ensure a more perfect protection of the status quo. As he spoke of duty, the prevention of chaos, the preservation of civilization, the "middle way," global stability, and the "wall of peace," he made it clear that stasis, not dynamism, was his ideal. And this ideal flowed directly from the hub of his discourse: the demand for self-restraint in the eternal, internal spiritual battle. If peace, freedom, and all the other "god terms" were virtues, and if political life were to be virtuous, they had to bear the hallmark of every virtue. The "god terms" had to be ways of preventing the bad things inside every human being from bursting out, ways of permanently managing the ever-impending internal apocalypse.

Within this discursive framework, political life and the political process took on a very restricted meaning. The liberal internationalist vision had been rooted in, and lent credence to, classical liberal political thought. It assumed that political life brought people together to debate rationally, decide upon, and implement plans for improving the world. Although Eisenhower used the Lockean and Wilsonian language of liberalism to speak about peace, his actual ideological vision reflected a very different sense. It was dedicated to restraining the threatening other, as a logically necessary part of the larger project of restraining the threatening self. The two forms of restraint were two elements in the same process of maintaining social order. To maintain order, leaders were obliged to frame policies, particularly foreign and national security policies, which would provide enough stability to prevent disaster. Since the masses of people often blocked those efforts, out of ignorance and selfishness, domestic politics was largely a matter of preventing the masses from hindering the leaders' efforts at prevention. Eisenhower's own explanation of his decision to run for president turned on this double movement. He wanted to prevent either Taft or any Democrat from becoming president, because none of them would ward off the triple threat of communism, financial collapse, and war. He also wanted the opportunity to rally the domestic masses, through his rhetoric, to support his own plans for preventing all three forms of disaster.

All the "god terms" in Eisenhower's discourse represented a political mode of salvation. But salvation was a fundamentally static quality. Salvation meant endless containment, stable order, predictable outcomes, clear fixed boundaries, universal restraint, and conformity to immutable universal goals. This made any kind of substantial change appear to be a fundamental threat to the United States and its people. Change evoked fear; hope meant the hope for a dependable continuing stasis. The language of hope for a better future was still employed. Whenever it was uttered, though, it now evoked fear of change. So hopeful words of improvement and progress ended up reaffirming the more basic hope of preventing change.

The world is never static, however. The advent of nuclear weapons, the end of the colonial empires, and other global developments made substantial change inevitable, which meant that threat was inevitable. There could be no perfect stasis. The more that hope was identified with stability, the more it evoked fear—especially when the vain quest for stability was pursued through cold war and a nuclear arms race. That lent powerful credibility to Eisenhower's warning that the permanent threat was of apocalyptic dimensions. As cold war language seemed to move the world toward the brink of hot war, the fear of change became a fear of catastrophe. The only way to prevent catastrophe, it seemed, was to prevent significant change of any kind. Since it was impossible to stop change, it was impossible to alleviate fear. Caught in this vicious circle, Eisenhower's words again exacerbated the very fears he hoped to assuage.

## EISENHOWER AND US

Dwight Eisenhower did not create the ideology and discourse of the cold war. He is a valuable subject for study, not because he was unusual or innovative, but because he was in many ways so typical of his times. Historians studying Eisenhower's presidency have often depicted him as a prototypical figure of his era. They have used their studies to illuminate what they see as larger truths of the cold war era. The revisionist historians of the 1980s cast him as a symbol of the "best" kind of cold warrior: resisting communism firmly yet with restraint, and always seeking peace. During the 1990s, postrevisionists began to recognize the dangerous excesses of his anticommunism. Their Eisenhower was a tragic hero, a good man with one fatal flaw. With the cold war over, he could serve as a metaphor for the entire nation: always committed to peace and justice, but somehow sadly derailed for four decades by the fatal flaw of overzealous anticommunism. Now, this interpretation suggested, we could get back on track and pursue our true aim more fruitfully.

Since there is as yet no sign of the reorientation expected by the postrevisionists, it would appear that we need another stage in Eisenhower scholarship, one that can illuminate the most relevant truth of the cold war today: its enduring grip on U.S. culture and society. The specific policies of the cold war era may be rather irrelevant, since they presuppose a geopolitical situation that has almost vanished. But the discourse formed within that situation still forms the core of our public discourse today. The blend of liberal internationalist language, global power politics, and apocalyptic dualism that led to our cold war stance is still very much with us, and it shows few signs of disappearing any time soon. Our leaders and pundits tell us that the world is not less but more dangerous than before. Our public discourse is still framed almost solely in terms of apocalyptic threats and how to contain them. Any policy or leader that can manage apocalyptic threats is considered successful.

Our society's highest political aspiration might best be termed "apocalypse management." Nothing more is asked for. No greater goal is pursued, or even imagined. The public is eager to hear about apocalyptic dangers and plans for containing them, but hardly able to imagine options for meaningful change in positive directions. With positive change so difficult to talk about or even imagine, there is little chance for large-scale meaningful efforts to pursue change. There is every chance that the public will organize only to try to protect itself against an ever-shifting array of perceived threats. The fear of change that prevented Eisenhower from responding to new realities with genuinely new policies has a similar effect on U.S. public discourse today.

His ideology and discourse exert their most lasting influence upon us because he brought them into the White House, where he was able to shape the discursive pattern of a whole era. In a world of hydrogen bombs and nuclear parity, the ironies and anxieties inherent in the pattern were magnified. Growing fears elicited more urgent presidential appeals for optimism and hope. As always, though, these were couched in language that reinforced fear. The circle became a spiral. As it rose, the fear of change—the sense that any substantial change meant intolerable risk—rose with it. This spiral holds the key to understanding the continuing power of the cold war framework.[6]

Eisenhower is an important figure for us today because his pattern of ideology and discourse typified so much of the pattern of the early cold war years. The key to understanding that pattern, and the spiral of fear it generated, lies in the years before he became president, the years studied in this book. Public language is the matrix, the source, and the determinant of public action. If we do not understand the confusions in our public language, we will perpetuate those confusions. Our political culture will be less stable, and insecurity will grow, bringing with it more fear of change. To clarify the prevailing mode of public action—or inaction—today we must understand more clearly the ideology and discourse of apocalypse management. We can come one step closer to that understanding by studying the ideology and discourse of Dwight D. Eisenhower.

# Notes

## INTRODUCTION

1. Michael H. Hunt, *Ideology and U.S. Foreign Policy* (New Haven: Yale University Press, 1987), 12–16; Michael J. Hogan, *A Cross of Iron: Harry S. Truman and the Origins of the National Security State, 1945–1954* (New York: Cambridge University Press, 1998), x; Frank Ninkovich, *The Wilsonian Century: U.S. Foreign Policy Since 1900* (Chicago: University of Chicago Press, 1999), 2–9. See also Michael H. Hunt, "Ideology," in *Explaining the History of American Foreign Relations,* ed. Michael J. Hogan and Thomas G. Paterson (New York: Cambridge University Press, 1991).

2. Fred I. Greenstein, *The Hidden-Hand Presidency: Eisenhower as Leader* (New York: Basic Books, 1982), 20.

3. Richard H. Immerman, "Confessions of an Eisenhower Revisionist: An Agonizing Reappraisal," *Diplomatic History* 14 (summer 1990): 325; Robert Griffith, "Dwight D. Eisenhower and the Corporate Commonwealth," *American Historical Review* 87 (1982): 88, 96.

4. Clifford Geertz, "Ideology as a Cultural System," in *Interpretation of Cultures,* by Clifford Geertz (New York: Basic Books, 1973), 193–233; Hunt, *Ideology and U.S. Foreign Policy,* xi.

5. Geertz, *Interpretation of Cultures,* 90, 112.

6. Ibid., 218, 219. I cite Geertz here not to say that his idea of ideology is the best or truest, but only to say that it is strikingly congruent with Eisenhower's own claims about the nature and function of his discourse. For recent discussions of different approaches to the definition and study of ideology, see David Hawkes, *Ideology* (London: Routledge, 1996); David McLellan, *Ideology,* 2d ed. (Minneapolis: University of Minnesota Press, 1995); Terry Eagleton, *Ideology: An Introduction* (London and New York: Verso, 1991).

7. Since I want to avoid drawing any conclusions about inner mental events, I have tried to refrain from any psychological observations. At a few places in my text, however, the temptation has been too great to resist completely. There is a large literature on the cognitive psychology of political decision-making, and Eisenhower has received some attention in this literature, particularly in relation to his foreign policy as president. I have not, however, employed this approach in the present study. For a good overview of this approach as applied to foreign policy, see Richard Immerman, "Psychology," in *Explaining the History of American Foreign Relations.*

8. John Fiske, *Television Culture* (London: Routledge, 1989), 14.

9. Francis A. Beer and Robert Hariman, "Realism and Rhetoric in International Relations," in *Post-Realism: The Rhetorical Turn in International Relations,* ed. Francis A. Beer and Robert

Hariman (East Lansing: Michigan State University Press, 1996), 20; Daniel T. Rodgers, *Contested Truths: Keywords in American Politics Since Independence* (New York: Basic Books, Inc., 1987), 5.

10. Martin J. Medhurst, "Eisenhower's Rhetorical Leadership: An Interpretation," 288, 289, in *Eisenhower's War of Words: Rhetoric and Leadership*, ed. Martin J. Medhurst (East Lansing: Michigan State University Press, 1994); Martin J. Medhurst, "Eisenhower, Little Rock, and the Rhetoric of Crisis," in *The Modern Presidency and Crisis Rhetoric*, ed. Amos Kiewe (Westport, Conn.: Praeger Publishers, 1994), 23; Robert L. Ivie, "Eisenhower as Cold Warrior," in *Eisenhower's War of Words*, 22; J. Michael Hogan, "Eisenhower and 'Open Skies,'" in *Eisenhower's War of Words*, 138. Medhurst's phrase became the title of his book, *Dwight D. Eisenhower: Strategic Communicator* (Westport, Conn.: Greenwood Press, 1993). Here Medhurst follows the lead of Fred Greenstein, who finds Eisenhower following "an unspoken axiom that public language was to be adapted to the circumstances at hand and toward the best possible consequences" (*Hidden-Hand Presidency*, 69n.).

11. Geertz, *Interpretation of Cultures*, 202–3. For thoughtful discussions of this issue in the context of the history of U.S. foreign relations, see Frank Ninkovich, "Interests and Discourse," *Diplomatic History* 13 (spring 1989) and Melvyn Leffler, "New Approaches, Old Configurations, and Prospective Reconfigurations," in *America in the World; The Historiography of American Foreign Relations Since 1941*, ed. Michael J. Hogan (Cambridge: Cambridge University Press, 1995).

12. Greenstein, *Hidden-Hand Presidency*, 53, 54.

13. Peter Lyon, *Eisenhower: Portrait of the Hero* (Boston: Little, Brown, Co., 1974), 402.

14. Halford Ross Ryan, "A Rhetorical Analysis of General Eisenhower's Public Speaking From 1945 to 1951," Ph.D. diss (University of Illinois at Urbana-Champaign, 1972), 81, 82, 86, 87, 103–11, 123.

15. Martin J. Medhurst, "Rhetoric and Cold War: A Strategic Approach," in *Cold War Rhetoric: Strategy, Metaphor, and Ideology*, ed. Medhurst et al., rev. ed. (East Lansing: Michigan State University Press, 1997), 19.

16. Lynn Boyd Hinds and Theodore Otto Windt, Jr., *The Cold War as Rhetoric: The Beginnings, 1945–1950* (New York: Praeger Publishers, 1991), 251, 250.

17. Paul A. Chilton, "The Meaning of Security," in *Post-Realism*, 202; Hans Morgenthau, *Politics Among Nations*, 4th ed. (New York: Alfred A. Knopf, 1967), 87.

18. William Graebner, *The Age of Doubt: American Thought and Culture in the 1940s* (Boston: Twayne Publishers, 1991), 42, 49, 65, 119, 146, 148.

19. Hinds and Windt, *Cold War as Rhetoric*, 67, citing Norman Graebner, ed. *Ideas and Diplomacy* (New York: Oxford University Press, 1964), 690. See also Martin Medhurst, "Truman's Rhetorical Reticence, 1945–1947: An Interpretive Essay," *Quarterly Journal of Speech* (February 1988): 52–70. The views of Graebner and Hinds and Windt are compatible with Medhurst's conclusion that, through early 1947, Truman was motivated primarily by his desire to adhere to Wilsonian beliefs.

20. Athan Theoharis, "The Rhetoric of Politics," in *Politics and Policies of the Truman Administration*, ed. Barton Bernstein (Chicago: Quadrangle Books, 1970), 213, 217.

21. Robert Underhill, *The Truman Persuasions* (Ames: Iowa State University Press, 1981), 315–16; Thomas G. Paterson, *On Every Front: The Making of the Cold War* (New York: W.W. Norton & Co., 1979), 124, 123, 116; Theoharis, "Rhetoric of Politics," 217, 201.

22. Robert Ivie, "Declaring a National Emergency," in *Modern Presidency and Crisis Rhetoric*, 1, 2, 3; Theoharis, "Rhetoric of Politics," 216; Robert Ivie, "Literalizing the Metaphor of Soviet Savagery: President Truman's Plain Style," *Southern Speech Communication Journal* 51 (1986): 91–105. For further illustrations of the "fragility" theme in Truman's rhetoric, see

Ivie, "The Ideology of Freedom's 'Fragility' in American Foreign Policy Argument," *Journal of the American Forensic Association* 24 (1987): 27–36.

23. Robert L. Ivie, "Realism Masking Fear: George F. Kennan's Political Rhetoric," in *Post-Realism,* 55, 56, 66. See also Anders L. Stephanson, *Kennan and the Art of Foreign Policy* (Cambridge, Mass.: Harvard University Press, 1989).

24. Hogan, *Cross of Iron.* Hogan summarizes these points on pp. 10–18.

25. For a good survey of these "other voices," see Hogan, *Cross of Iron,* chap. 10.

26. John Morton Blum, ed., *The Price of Vision: The Diary of Henry A. Wallace, 1942–1946* (Boston: Houghton Mifflin, 1973), 589–601. For rhetorical analyses of Wallace's efforts, see Hinds and Windt, *Cold War as Rhetoric,* 208–16, and Robert L. Ivie, "Metaphor and the Rhetorical Invention of Cold War 'Idealists,'" in *Cold War Rhetoric,* 107–12.

27. Hogan, *Cross of Iron,* 466–68. When he became president, Eisenhower often warned his advisors about the dangers of making the United States a "garrison state." Curiously, he rarely used the term in his pre-presidential years; see chap. 10, note 20, below.

28. Eisenhower's parents were both devout adherents of sectarian evangelical Christianity. His father was raised in the River Brethren Church. His mother and father met while attending a college of the United Brethren in Christ. His parents, particularly his mother, later became involved with the Jehovah's Witnesses. Jerry Bergman has suggested a strong influence of the latter tradition on Eisenhower, but his argument adduces no substantial evidence ("Steeped in Religion: President Eisenhower and the Influence of the Jehovah's Witnesses," *Kansas History* 21:148–67). The evidence for direct influence of these traditions on Eisenhower is so slim and inconclusive that it has not seemed to me worthwhile to speculate on it. The Christian influences upon him do not bear the marks of any particular denomination. After leaving home, he joined no church and prided himself on being a religious freethinker. He did join a church (Presbyterian, his wife's denomination) just before he became president, in order, he said, to set a good example for the nation. The best bibliography for a study of Eisenhower's religion can be found in the notes to the relevant chapter in Richard V. Pierard and Robert D. Linder, *Civil Religion and the Presidency* (Grand Rapids, Mich.: Academie Books, 1988).

29. Ryan, "A Rhetorical Analysis," 75; Graebner, *Age of Doubt,* 101. Ryan's dissertation offers a brief summary of the major themes in Eisenhower's speeches from 1945 to 1951, along with some interesting comments on style and delivery. It makes no effort to link the public rhetoric with private discourse.

30. Theoharis, "Rhetoric of Politics," 204, 212.

31. This was the title of the second volume of his presidential memoirs: Dwight D. Eisenhower, *The White House Years, Waging Peace, 1956–1961* (Garden City, N.Y.: Doubleday and Co., 1965).

32. C. Wright Mills, *The Causes of World War Three* (London: Secker and Warburg, 1959), 117–18.

33. The large collection of prewar documents in Daniel D. Holt and James W. Leyerzapf, eds., *Eisenhower: The Prewar Diaries and Selected Papers, 1905–1941* (Baltimore: Johns Hopkins University Press, 1998) has only scant, fragmentary material relevant to the ideological patterns that emerged during and after the war.

## CHAPTER 1

1. Stephen E. Ambrose, *Eisenhower, Soldier, General of the Army, President Elect,* vol. 1 (New York: Simon and Schuster, 1983), 119.

2. H. W. Brands, Jr., *Cold Warriors: Eisenhower's Generation and American Foreign Policy* (New York: Columbia University Press, 1988), 195, 200.
3. Dwight D. Eisenhower, *Crusade in Europe* (Garden City, N.Y.: Doubleday and Co., 1948), 157. During the war, Eisenhower used the term *crusade* on several occasions to describe the war. His D-day message to the Allied troops, "You are about to embark upon a Great Crusade" (PDDE 3:1913; see Bibliographic note, p. 351), was perhaps the most famous. For other references to Allied troops as crusaders, see Eisenhower to All Commanders, 23 July 1943, PDDE 3:1276, and Eisenhower to American Forces, NATOUSA, 8 November 1943, PDDE 3:1552. Eisenhower often referred to a cause about which he felt strongly as a "crusade." Addressing ROTC students in 1939, he had urged them to be "crusaders" for the spirit of cooperation (Holt and Leyerzapf, *Eisenhower,* 428).
4. Ambrose, *Eisenhower,* 1:207; Merle Miller, *Ike the Soldier: As They Knew Him* (New York: G.P. Putnam's Sons, 1987), 421.
5. Piers Brendon, *Ike: His Life and Times* (New York: Harper and Row, 1966), 96; Robert F. Burk, *Dwight D. Eisenhower: Hero and Politician* (Boston: Twayne Publishers, 1986), 66; Lyon, *Eisenhower,* 194.
6. Eisenhower to Edgar Eisenhower, 30 March 1942, PDDE 1:218. The only other antifascist expression in the first sixteen months is in Eisenhower to Edgar Eisenhower, 16 November 1942, PDDE 2:724: "I have developed such a violent hatred of the Axis and all that it stands for, I sincerely hope the drubbing we give them will be one that will keep that crowd from wanting another war for the next two hundred years." Edgar was the most outspokenly conservative of the brothers; perhaps Dwight wrote these letters only because he knew this was something Edgar in particular wanted to hear. There is also a cursory nod to "the Four Freedoms" in a public relations statement quoted in "The Foot-Slogging Soldier," *Life,* 22 January 1943, 32. Before the United States entered the war, Eisenhower had privately condemned Hitler as an individual (Holt and Leyerzapf, *Eisenhower,* 446, 540). But he never condemned fascism, and he even praised Mussolini in his diary (see note 38, below).
7. Even when he thanked a second grade class for naming their Citizenship Club after him, he said nothing about the moral or ideological issues of the war (Eisenhower to Janice Polley, 2 December 1942, PDDE 2:786). See also messages cited in the *New York Times,* 12 January 1943, 3; 27 November 1942, 7; 1 March 1943, 21.
8. Eisenhower to Charles Herron, 4 April 1943, PDDE 2:1069. Eisenhower took political thought seriously and would later take the time to read and think (albeit rather superficially) about Marxist-Leninist theory. Yet he never once alluded to any study of or interest in the concepts or theories of fascism, which is another indication of his lack of interest in the issue.
9. Eisenhower to Edward Hazlett, Jr., 7 April 1943, PDDE 2:1082.
10. Eisenhower to Harold Alexander, 8 April 1943, PDDE 2:1083.
11. Eisenhower to John Eisenhower, 8 April 1943, PDDE 2:1084. The same day he privately told an Abilene friend that the war demanded a concerted effort of "all Democratic nations" (Eisenhower to Charles Harger, 8 April 1943, PDDE 2:1085).
12. Eisenhower to George Marshall, 6 April 1943, PDDE 2:1077–78.
13. Eisenhower's views are well documented in Holt and Leyerzapf, *Eisenhower,* 138–88.
14. Diary, 12 January 1942, PDDE 1:52.
15. Eisenhower to Alfred Gruenther, 24 February 1942, PDDE 1:131; Burton Barr, quoted in Miller, *Ike the Soldier,* 310; Holt and Leyerzapf, *Eisenhower,* 507 (see also 508). He later credited his prescience to his early mentor, Fox Conner, who taught him to expect another war with Germany. But Conner's view of inevitable German aggression was shaped before Hitler was ever heard of; the issue he stressed was nationalistic power, not political ideology

(Miller, *Ike the Soldier,* 210, 301). In 1929, touring Europe, he wrote in a travel diary that the German people were quite friendly and that he liked Germany, though in September, 1918, he had told troops under his command that the German "war machine" was created by "lust, selfishness, and sinful conceit" (Holt and Leyerzapf, *Eisenhower,* 90, 18).

16. Holt and Leyerzapf, *Eisenhower,* 465. When World War II began, in September 1939, Eisenhower predicted in his diary that the United States would not enter the war. Apparently he changed his mind in the following months. By September 1940, he admitted in the diary that Americans had "at least begun to awaken to their own peril" (Holt and Leyerzapf, *Eisenhower,* 446, 494).

17. Diary, 22 January 1942, PDDE 1:66; diary, 19 March 1942, Robert H. Ferrell, ed., *The Eisenhower Diaries,* (New York: W.W. Norton & Co., 1981), 51; diary, 5 May 1942, PDDE 1:282; Harry C. Butcher, *My Three Years With Eisenhower* (New York: Simon and Schuster, 1946), 29. See also diary, 27 January 1942, PDDE 1:75; diary, 22 February 1942, PDDE 1:126; diary, 28 March 1942, PDDE 1:213; Eisenhower to George Marshall and Ernest King, 19 July 1942, PDDE 1:393; memorandum, 26 July 1942, PDDE 1:417.

18. Ambrose, *Eisenhower,* 230; Eisenhower to Harry Butcher, 15 September 1942, PDDE 1:559–60; Eisenhower to Harry Butcher, 2 September 1942, PDDE 1:526; Eisenhower to Russell Hartle, 15 January 1943, PDDE 2:904; Eisenhower to Leonard Gerow, 24 February 1943, PDDE 2:986.

19. Diary, 29 June 1942, Ferrell, *Diaries,* 67; Eisenhower to George Van Horn Mosely, 27 August 1942, PDDE 1:504; diary, 22 January 1942, PDDE 1:66; diary, 20 April 1942, PDDE 1:260. See also diary, 23 February 1942, PDDE 1:129; diary, 22 January 1942, PDDE 1:66. Eisenhower expressed these views (which were common enough for an officer) before the war too. See, e.g., Eisenhower to Manuel Quezon, 8 August 1940, and Eisenhower to Everett Hughes, 26 November 1940 (Holt and Leyerzapf, *Eisenhower,* 474–76, 509). Throughout this book, all emphasis in quotations is in the original source.

20. Dwight D. Eisenhower, *Letters to Mamie,* ed. John S.D. Eisenhower (Garden City, N.Y.: Doubleday and Company, 1978), 74 (16 December 1942), 172 (11 March 1944); see also 156 (19 November 1943). For other references to this often repeated theme, see diary, 22 January 1943 and 29 June 1942, Ferrell, *Diaries,* 43, 44, 67; Eisenhower to George Van Horn Mosely, 27 August 1942, PDDE 1:504; diary, 20 April 1942, PDDE 1:260; Eisenhower to George Marshall, 5 April 1943, PDDE 2:1070–71.

21. Fred Greenstein, "Eisenhower's Leadership Style," in *Eisenhower: A Centenary Assessment,* ed. Stephen E. Ambrose and Gunter Bischof (Baton Rouge: Louisiana State University Press, 1995), 63.

22. Eisenhower to John Eisenhower, 27 June 1942, PDDE 1:366; Eisenhower to John Eisenhower, 22 May 1943, PDDE 2:1151; Eisenhower to Gen. Harold Alexander, 29 March 1943, PDDE 2:1064. This theme is repeated in documents too numerous to cite here.

23. Eisenhower to William Lee, 29 March 1943, PDDE 2:1063–64; Eisenhower to John Lee, 19 February 1944, PDDE 3:1741. See also Eisenhower to John Eisenhower, 20 March 1943, PDDE 2:1050; Eisenhower to Russell Hartle, 19 July 1942, PDDE 1:398–99.

24. General Vernon Prichard, 29 March 1943, PDDE 2:1063; Eisenhower to John Eisenhower, 20 March 1943, PDDE 2:1050. When Eisenhower suggested to Marshall that a smarter looking uniform would improve discipline, he argued: "Given a uniform which tends to look a bit tough, and the natural proclivities of the American soldier quickly create a general impression of a disorderly mob" (Eisenhower to George Marshall, 5 May 1943, PDDE 2:1115).

25. Eisenhower to Charles Harger, 23 April 1943, PDDE 2:1099; Eisenhower to Edgar Eisenhower, 21 August 1943, PDDE 2:1351; Eisenhower, *Letters to Mamie* 104 (2 March

312 CHAPTER 1 NOTES

1943); see the numerous references in PDDE, vol. 5, Eisenhower Index, s.v., "Home Front: popular expectations of easy victory."

26. Eisenhower to Edgar Eisenhower, 30 March 1942, PDDE 1:218; Eisenhower to Arthur Eisenhower, 24 July 1943, PDDE 2:1278; Eisenhower to John Doud, 18 August 1943, PDDE 2:1345; Eisenhower to Charles Harger, 8 April 1943, PDDE 2:1085; Eisenhower to Vernon Prichard, 1 March 1943, PDDE 2:1000; Eisenhower to Arthur Eisenhower, 18 May 1943, PDDE 2:1148. In the early 1930s Eisenhower was already writing that modern warfare demanded a total mobilization and centralized coordination of all civilian as well as military resources; see, e.g., Holt and Leyerzapf, *Eisenhower,* 139, 141, 153.

27. Morris Janowitz, *The Professional Soldier* (Glencoe, Ill.: Free Press, 1960), 242–55, esp. 248 (see also 228).

28. Russell F. Weigley, *The American Way of War* (New York: Macmillan, 1973). The following discussion of this approach to war draws upon the theoretical observations in James A. Aho, *Religious Mythology and the Art of War* (Westport, Conn.: Greenwood Press, 1981). For more detail see Ira Chernus, *Dr. Strangegod: On the Symbolic Meaning of Nuclear Weapons* (Columbia: University of South Carolina Press, 1986), chap. 7. Eisenhower's penchant for a single decisive attack led him to support an early all-out assault on northwest Europe; hence his bitter disappointment when Operation Sledgehammer was cancelled (see note 13, above).

29. Eisenhower might thus have said of World War II what Chris, the hero of Oliver Stone's *Platoon,* said of the United States' Vietnam War: we were actually fighting against ourselves; two forces were contending within us for our very soul.

30. Eisenhower, *Letters to Mamie,* 140 (12 August 1943).

31. Lyon, *Eisenhower,* 143, 141.

32. Eisenhower to Gen. Joseph McNarney, 19 January 1943, PDDE 2:914; Eisenhower to George Marshall, 20 October 1942, PDDE 1:628; Eisenhower to Walter Smith, 12 November 1942, PDDE 2:702. "To a certain extent," he concluded to Marshall, "a man must merely believe in his luck and figure that a certain amount of good fortune will bless us when the critical day arrives." One is reminded here of the Roman Stoics' worship of the goddess Fortuna. Though the specific reference to good fortune is uncharacteristic for Eisenhower, the broader stoic attitude is not. In addition to his efforts at stoic calm, he often voiced the typically stoic view that once decisions were made, fate would inevitably decide the outcome. Yet a psychological interpreter might ask why he made the disclaimer about not crying wolf unless he suspected he might in fact be crying wolf?

33. Eisenhower to John Eisenhower, 8 September 1943, PDDE 2:1396; Miller, *Ike the Soldier,* 391.

34. Eisenhower to George Marshall, 12 October 1942, PDDE 1:606; Miller, *Ike the Soldier,* 443, 411.

35. Eisenhower to Charles Gailey, Jr., 1 January 1943, PDDE 2:885; Eisenhower to Gen. Andrew Cunningham, 23 February 1944, PDDE 3:1747; Eisenhower, *Letters to Mamie,* 175 (16 April 1944); Eisenhower to Edgar Eisenhower, 24 July 1942, PDDE 1:415; diary, 11 March 1942, PDDE 1:183.

36. Diary, 12 March 1942, PDDE 1:184 (where he recorded that he did cease work for thirty minutes to remember his father). A voluntary restraint of normal human emotions also allowed a good soldier to avoid confronting his own emotions and desires. It is hard to avoid speculating that Eisenhower's alarmism and his insistence on duty and self-restraint were related, to some extent, to his personal doubts and insecurities. By viewing his alarmism as compelling evidence of self-restraint and obedience to duty, he was able (how-

ever unconsciously) to legitimate his fear of failure and give it positive meaning, which must have made it easier to bear. Perhaps even deeper than his fear of failure lay his fear of his own emotions. It would seem at least plausible that Eisenhower, always the good soldier, found something frightening in his own feelings and used his good soldiering as a way to avoid those fears by avoiding the feelings themselves. If so, then understandably he could admit no compromise with absolute adherence to duty, for that would compromise the rigidity of his own defenses. It would seem equally plausible that such a strongly defended soldier would view obedience to duty as a sacred calling and war as an uncompromising crusade.

Eisenhower's biographers to date have done remarkably little psychological interpretation of any real value. The material is rich, and it should prove quite rewarding in the hands of trained psycho-historians. Reading his remarks upon the death of his father, for example, the psycho-historian might note that in the hundreds of pages of prewar documents published by Holt and Leyerzapf, there are several warm letters to his father-in-law, but barely a word to his father (or to his mother).

37. Total commitment to the war effort was also the essential theme of his early letter to his brother Edgar (see note 6 above). The warning about enslavement to fascism was a secondary point.

38. The exception to this rule occurred in numerous references to Italian fascism. But in that case *fascism* was simply a shorthand reference to Mussolini's government. Eisenhower was willing to accept a highly reactionary government in Italy after Mussolini fell. He was opposed to Mussolini's government because it was fighting the Allies, not because of its political ideology or domestic policies. Before the United States entered the war, Eisenhower expressed in his diary "some degree of admiration for Mussolini" as an able administrator (Holt and Leyerzapf, *Eisenhower,* 446).

39. Eisenhower to American Forces, NATOUSA, 8 November 1943, PDDE 3:1522–3; 5 July 1943, PDDE 1241. For antifascist sentiments in other official statements, see Eisenhower to All Commanders, 23 July 1943, PDDE 2:1276–77; Eisenhower to Troops of the A.E.F., 6 June 1944, PDDE 3:1913; *New York Times,* 4 September 1944, 15; Eisenhower to All Members of the Royal Air Force, 18 September 1944, PDDE 4:2163.

40. Eisenhower, *Letters to Mamie,* 130 (20 June 1943); Eisenhower to Gertrude Gough, 5 August 1943, PDDE 2:1322. These appear to be the only two explicit antifascist statements among Eisenhower's fairly numerous private letters in the last two years of the war.

41. Eisenhower to Milton Eisenhower, 31 May 1944, PDDE 3:1897; Eisenhower, *Letters to Mamie,* 184 (31 May 1944).

42. Holt and Leyerzapf, *Eisenhower,* 446 (see also Kevin McCann, *Man From Abilene* [Garden City, N.Y.: Doubleday and Co., 1952], 53); Eisenhower, *Letters to Mamie,* 42–43 (15 September 1942). These were Eisenhower's only substantive comments about the postwar world to anyone during the duration of the war.

43. Holt and Leyerzapf, *Eisenhower,* 248, 249, 254 (see also similar diary entries, 251, 256); Kenneth S. Davis, *Soldier of Democracy* (Garden City, N.Y.: Doubleday, Doran and Company, 1945), 230, 234. In an article ghostwritten for the assistant secretary of war in 1930, Eisenhower wrote that in a national "emergency," the necessary economic control "can come from the central Government alone" (Holt and Leyerzapf, *Eisenhower,* 141). Though he was speaking of war, he later applied the same idea to the Depression. Davis (242) reports one occasion on which Eisenhower supported the anti-Roosevelt views of his brother Edgar against the pro-FDR sentiments of his brothers Milton and Arthur, but the context and the questions at issue are not at all clear. On the common use of war metaphors for the New Deal, see William E. Leuchtenberg, "The New Deal and the Analogue of War,"

in *Change and Continuity in Twentieth-Century America,* ed. John Braeman et al. (Columbus: Ohio State University Press, 1964).

44. Holt and Leyerzapf, *Eisenhower,* 235, 236, 246. Years later he partially retracted this view of the Bonus March (*At Ease: Stories I Tell My Friends* [Garden City, N.Y.: Doubleday and Co., 1967], 216). Geoffrey Perret shows that this later account is inaccurate in several respects, and he suggests that Eisenhower probably generally supported the harsh action (*Eisenhower* [New York: Random House, 1999], 114–15). The report may reflect the official story as MacArthur, his superior, wanted it told. On the other hand, on 10 August 1932, he wrote in his private diary that the report was "as accurate as I could make it" (Holt and Leyerzapf, *Eisenhower,* 233). The report does comport well with Eisenhower's continuing fears of social disorder and with a fear of "mobocracy" and anarchy that was evident in the military at the time; see also Janowitz, *The Professional Soldier,* 250.

45. Eisenhower to Swede Hazlett, 20 October 1943, PDDE 3:1520; Eisenhower to Helen Eisenhower, 18 October 1943, PDDE 3:1515.

46. Eisenhower to Arthur Eisenhower, 18 May 1943, PDDE 2:1148.

47. Eisenhower to Harry Butcher, 2 September 1942, PDDE 1:527.

48. Stephen E. Ambrose, *The Supreme Commander: The War Years of General Dwight D. Eisenhower* (Garden City, N.Y.: Doubleday and Co., 1970), 135; Brendon, *Ike,* 93; Lyon, *Eisenhower,* 181.

49. Eisenhower to Harry Butcher, 2 September 1942, PDDE 1:527; Darlan's authority over the French army uncertain (Eisenhower to Walter Smith, 12 November 1942, PDDE 2:701); Eisenhower to Combined Chiefs of Staff, 12 November 1942, PDDE 2:697; little chance of military performance from French (Eisenhower to George Patton, Jr., 15 November 1942, PDDE 2:716); Eisenhower to Walter Smith, 16 January 1942, PDDE 2:718; Eisenhower to George Marshall, 17 November 1942, PDDE 2:729 [a reference to the "so-called North African Army and Navy"]; Eisenhower to George Marshall, 19 November 1942, PDDE 2:739n. 4; bringing French fleet to Allied side: Eisenhower to George Marshall, 11 November 1942, PDDE 2:691; Eisenhower to John Eisenhower, 12 November 1942, PDDE 2:696; Eisenhower to Combined Chiefs of Staff, 13 November 1942, PDDE 2:706; position already favorable: Eisenhower to Walter Smith, 14 November 1942, PDDE 2:712.

50. Eisenhower to Mark Clark, 12 November 1942, PDDE 2:699; Eisenhower to Walter Smith, 18 November 1942, PDDE 2:735; Ambrose, *Eisenhower,* 1:205; Ambrose, *Supreme Commander,* 135.

51. Burk, *Dwight D. Eisenhower,* 66; Eisenhower to George Marshall, 3 December 1942, PDDE 2:789 (see also Eisenhower to George Marshall, 5 January 1943, PDDE 895); Eisenhower to Cordell Hull and George Marshall, 30 August 1943, PDDE 2:1372; Eisenhower to George Marshall, 7 April 1945, PDDE 4:2589.

52. Lyon, *Eisenhower,* 164; Eisenhower to John Eisenhower, 19 February 1943, PDDE 2:965–66.

53. Brendon, *Ike,* 96; Blanche Wiesen Cook, *The Declassified Eisenhower* (Garden City, N.Y.: Doubleday and Co., 1981), 17 (citing McCloy to Eisenhower, 1 March 1943).

54. Eisenhower, *Letters to Mamie,* 66 (27 November 1942). Eisenhower to John Eisenhower, 20 November 1942, PDDE 2:746; Miller, *Ike the Soldier,* 437; Ambrose, *Eisenhower,* 207. If the Arabs seemed so content, as he told Smith, why fear a revolt from them? This suggests even more strongly that Eisenhower's fears were principally the result of irrational prejudice.

55. Eisenhower to Walter Smith, 9 November 1942, PDDE 2:677 ("Oh well—by the time this thing is over I'll probably be as crooked as any of them," he added, rather uncharacteristically); Eisenhower to Walter Smith, 11 November 1942, PDDE 2:693; Eisenhower to Walter Smith, 18 November 1942, PDDE 2:735.

56. Eisenhower to Arthur Hurd, 29 January 1943, PDDE 2:931. Peyrouton was appointed to replace Darlan when the latter was assassinated.
57. Eisenhower to John Eisenhower, 20 December 1942, PDDE 2:855; Harold MacMillan, *The Blast of War, 1939–1945* (New York: Harper and Row, 1968), 174 (2 January 1943). Eisenhower, caught in apocalyptic dualism, had not yet found the possibility of a "middle way," which would later become his own favorite image for his political stance.
58. Eisenhower to Walter Smith, 18 November 1942, PDDE 2:735; Eisenhower to Edgar Eisenhower, 18 February 1943, PDDE 2:962; Eisenhower, *Letters to Mamie,* 94–95 (15 February 1943). Merle Miller calls this the most personally revealing letter Eisenhower ever wrote (*Ike the Soldier,* 477). But many historians suggest that, while Eisenhower expected some criticism, he was certainly unprepared for the intensity of it. And his disclaimer, "I'm not—and never have—attempted to defend anything," sounds unconvincing here, especially since he had just asserted that the Darlan deal had been necessary for the capture of Tunisia. See the equally unconvincing disclaimer to John in Eisenhower to John Eisenhower, 20 December 1942, PDDE 2:855.
59. Eisenhower to John Eisenhower, 20 January 1943, PDDE 2:916; Eisenhower to George Marshall, 5 January 1943, PDDE 2:895; Eisenhower to George Marshall, 30 November 1942, PDDE 2:781. Ten years earlier, Eisenhower had written off critics of MacArthur's attack on the Bonus Marchers with the same charge: "A lot of furor has been stirred up but mostly to make political capital" (Brendon, *Ike,* 63).

## CHAPTER 2

1. Edward N. Peterson, *The American Occupation of Germany: Retreat to Victory* (Detroit: Wayne State University Press, 1977), 55, 97; Stimson Diary, 7/27/45, cited in Barton Bernstein, "Ike and Hiroshima: Did He Oppose It?" *Journal of Strategic Studies* 10 (September 1987): 380; Lyon, *Eisenhower,* 368. Eisenhower was involved in establishing the partition of Germany, and thus he helped to fix the framework for later cold war tensions (see PDDE 6:166). But this was essentially President Truman's decision, and it seems likely that Germany would have been partitioned, with the Soviet Union retaining control of the eastern zone, in any event.
2. Cook, *Declassified Eisenhower,* 40. The only detailed studies of Eisenhower's months as head of the German occupation are found in the biographies. Cook's (36–50) is the most perceptive and interesting. The other notable discussions of this period are in Ambrose, *Eisenhower,* 1:409–30; Brendon, *Ike,* 188–94; Lyon, *Eisenhower,* 365–85. Eisenhower himself wrote briefly about this period in *At Ease,* 298–308.
3. For some brief comments on Eisenhower's words in this period, see Medhurst, *Eisenhower,* chap. 1.
4. William Robinson to Helen Rogers Reid, 21 June 1948, William Robinson Papers, Box 6, "Diary—WER and DDE"; Eisenhower to Marshall, 25 September 1945, PDDE 6:373.
5. Eisenhower to Marshall, 1 June 1945, PDDE 6:115; Eisenhower to Marshall, 2 June 1945, PDDE 6:126; Eisenhower to Combined Chiefs of Staff, 2 June 1945, PDDE 6:125. Eisenhower also told a congressional committee that "public opinion wins wars" (testimony to the House Committee on Military Affairs, 15 November 1945, Pre-Presidential Papers, Principal Series, Box 144, "Hearings Volume 1 November 1945–January 1945 [1]"). See also a memo to his subordinate commanders, in which he said that he didn't want "the whole public effect [of the war] ruined in America" (14 May 1945, PDDE 6:40), and a letter to Patton, 23 August 1945, PDDE 6:307.

6. Eisenhower to Butcher, 12 October 1945, PDDE 6:432, and Eisenhower to Clay, 15 October 1945, PDDE 6:444; see also Eisenhower to Marshall, 13 October 1945, PDDE 6:433. Eisenhower even hesitated to allow the American Friends Service Committee into Germany because it "may react on American opinion" (Eisenhower to Marshall, 1 August 1945, PDDE 6:237).

7. Rudolph L. Treuenfels, *Eisenhower Speaks: Dwight D. Eisenhower in His Messages and Speeches* (New York: Farrar, Strauss, & Co., 1948), 15.

8. For a useful discussion of postwar rhetoric, focusing on presidential rhetoric, see Kenneth Zagacki, "Rhetoric, Redemption, and Reconciliation: A Study of Twentieth Century Postwar Rhetoric" (Ph.D. diss., University of Texas, 1986), esp. chap.1.

9. Victor Turner, *The Ritual Process: Structure and Anti-structure* (New York: Aldine de Gruyter, 1995).

10. Aho, *Religious Mythology*, 28.

11. Ibid., 29. For the classic psychoanalytic interpretation of this phenomenon, see Sigmund Freud, *Totem and Taboo*, trans. James Strachey (New York: W.W. Norton, 1950), 39–41. Many writers on the Vietnam War have noted the lack of rites of reintegration for U.S. soldiers in that war and the subsequent damaging effects. Thomas M. Holm has suggested that Native American veterans had lower rates of post-traumatic stress because their tribes provided ritual reintegration for them: "American Indians and the Vietnam War," in *The Vietnam Reader*, ed. Walter Capps (New York: Routledge, 1990), 191–204.

12. Ambrose, *Eisenhower*, 1:420.

13. William Robinson to Helen Rogers Reid, 21 June 1948, William Robinson Papers, Box 6, "Diary—WER and DDE"; Eisenhower to Marshall, 29 September 1945, PDDE 6:392. In fact these themes were not as prevalent in Eisenhower's speeches as he claimed. In Treuenfels's representative collection UMT is not explicitly discussed in any major speech from this period; for service unification, see Treuenfels, 23, 34–35.

14. Treuenfels, *Eisenhower Speaks*, 23 (see also ibid., 9, 36); Daniel Yergin, *Shattered Peace: The Origins of the Cold War and the National Security State* (Boston: Houghton Mifflin, Sentry Editions, 1978), 211.

15. Treuenfels, *Eisenhower Speaks*, 41, 43; see also ibid., 44.

16. Treuenfels, *Eisenhower Speaks*, 39

17. Eisenhower to Marshall, 13 October 1945, PDDE 6:436.

18. Peterson suggests that Eisenhower expected a civilian government to take over within a few weeks of the surrender (*American Occupation of Germany*, 55). On the army's planning during the war for its occupation role, see John L. Gaddis, *The United States and the Origins of the Cold War, 1941–1947* (New York: Columbia University Press, 1972), 102–4, 116–25.

19. Treuenfels, *Eisenhower Speaks*, 33, 47, 16.

20. Speech at Belfast University, 24 August 1945, Pre-Presidential Papers, Principal Series, Box 192, "Speeches 1939–November 1945 (1)"; Treuenfels, *Eisenhower Speaks*, 18, 12; Radio Forum, 29 September 1945, Pre-Presidential Papers, Principal Series, Box 192, "Speeches 1939–November 1945 (1)."

21. Treuenfels, *Eisenhower Speaks*, 39; Gaddis, *Origins of Cold War*, 122–25; Paterson, *The Making of the Cold War*, 13. JCS 1067 laid all blame for the chaos upon Germany itself, thus justifying a harsh occupation; see PDDE 6:41.

22. Testimony to the House Committee on Military Affairs, 15 November 1945, Pre-Presidential Papers, Principal Series, Box 144, "Hearings Volume 1 November 1945–January 1945 (1)"; message for the National War Fund, 11 September 1945, Pre-Presidential Papers, Principal Series, Box 192, "Speeches 1939–November 1945 (1)"; see also e.g., Treuenfels, *Eisenhower Speaks*, 44. See chap. 1, note 42.

23. Melvyn Leffler, *A Preponderance of Power* (Stanford: Stanford University Press, 1992), 35–36; Treuenfels, *Eisenhower Speaks,* 44; speech at Belfast University, 24 August 1945, Pre-Presidential Papers, Principal Series, Box 192, "Speeches 1939–November 1945 (1)"; testimony to the House Committee on Military Affairs, 15 November 1945, Pre-Presidential Papers, Principal Series, Box 144, "Hearings Volume 1 November 1945–January 1945 (1)."
24. Radio Forum, 29 September 1945, Pre-Presidential Papers, Principal Series, Box 192, "Speeches 1939–November 1945 (1)."
25. Eisenhower to Col. Arthur Goodfriend, 15 February 1945, 5: 2480; Treuenfels, *Eisenhower Speaks,* 10 (emphasis in original), 39, 14. As early as February 1945, he had written for a popular magazine: "The job is far from done. Even when the shooting finally ceases, to struggle to perfect a lasting peace will still remain a fight."
26. Speech at Belfast University, 24 August 1945, Pre-Presidential Papers, Principal Series, Box 192, "Speeches 1939–November 1945 (1)"; Treuenfels, *Eisenhower Speaks,* 39; see also ibid., 36 and transcript of recording, 28 July 1945, Pre-Presidential Papers, Principal Series, Box 192, "Speeches 1939–November 1945 (1)."
27. Treuenfels, *Eisenhower Speaks,* 14; speech at Belfast University, 24 August 1945, Pre-Presidential Papers, Principal Series, Box 192, "Speeches 1939–November 1945 (1)."
28. Treuenfels, *Eisenhower Speaks,* 29, 45; speech at Louvain University, 19 October 1945, Pre-Presidential Papers, Principal Series, Box 192, "Speeches 1939–November 1945 (1)."
29. Treuenfels, *Eisenhower Speaks,* 32.
30. Interview with the Patch-Simpson Board, 23 September 1945, PDDE 6:340.
31. Message written for a history of World War II, 21 August 1945, PDDE 6:190n. 2.
32. Treuenfels, *Eisenhower Speaks,* 47–50.

## CHAPTER 3

1. Cook, *Declassified Eisenhower,* 59.
2. Press conference, 14 August 1945, in Treuenfels, *Eisenhower Speaks,* 15; Eisenhower to Wallace, 28 August 1945, PDDE 6:315. For a good summary of Eisenhower's public remarks on peaceful relations with the Soviets, see Ambrose, *Eisenhower,* 1:427. See also Treuenfels, *Eisenhower Speaks,* 23.
3. Lyon, *Eisenhower,* 387; Treuenfels, *Eisenhower Speaks,* 76, 165, 81, 130.
4. Hearings of House Committee on Appropriations, 5 June 1947, Pre-Presidential Papers, Principal Series, Box 144, "Hearings, volume 2: January 1946–June 1946 (2)"; Treuenfels, *Eisenhower Speaks,* 233.
5. Ambrose, *Eisenhower,* 1:427, 435; Brendon, *Ike,* 194. Other major Eisenhower biographers who share Brendon's view include Cook, *Declassified Eisenhower,* 41, and Lyon, *Eisenhower,* 378.
6. Eisenhower, *At Ease,* 329; diary, 11 June 1949, PDDE 10:627. At a Forrestal memorial dinner in 1954, President Eisenhower said: "At my first meeting with him, during World War II, he expressed his grave fear that Communist Russia would emerge from the war as a threat to individual liberty and freedom" (25 October 1954, *Public Papers of the Presidents, Dwight D. Eisenhower, 1954,* 951). This was apparently an ad lib, since it does not appear in the draft text of the speech in William Robinson Papers, Box 2, "Eisenhower—July–December, 1954," Eisenhower Library. See also Eisenhower to Walter Kerr, 9 April 1951, PDDE 12:203.
7. Eisenhower, *At Ease,* 329; Dwight D. Eisenhower, *Crusade in Europe* (Garden City, N.Y.: Doubleday, 1948), 194, 284; speech to Associated Press, 24 April 1950, *Vital Speeches of*

*the Day* 16 (1 June 1950): 485; Eisenhower to Louis Johnson, 31 July 1950, PDDE 13:1240.

8. Eisenhower, *At Ease*, 319; Cook, *Declassified Eisenhower*, 86.

9. Cook, *Declassified Eisenhower*, 37. She makes no effort to square this with her claim (41) that he continued to believe in the U.S–Soviet alliance.

10. Diary, 26 May 1946, Robert H. Ferrell, ed., *The Eisenhower Diaries* (New York: W.W. Norton, 1981), 136–37.

11. Diary, 16 September 1947, Ferrell, *Diaries*, 143.

12. Eisenhower allowed here for the possibility of dictatorships that were not expansionist. He never addressed this issue in theoretical terms, as many other cold warriors did to legitimate their fierce anti-Soviet stance. But he took it for granted that the Soviet Union was, in the late 1940s, both dictatorial and expansionist.

13. Eisenhower to Kenyon Joyce, 7 March 1947, PDDE 8:1567; Eisenhower to Henry Wilson, 30 October 1947, PDDE 9:2022. Historians who see Eisenhower as genuinely friendly toward the Soviets make much of his warm feelings for Marshall Zhukov. But the general himself never saw Zhukov's amiability as evidence of Soviet policy. He told Lucius Clay that they were lucky to have dealt with Zhukov: "We might not have had such good luck if we had met other individuals" (Eisenhower to Lucius Clay, 9 March 1946, PDDE 7:915; see also Eisenhower, *Crusade in Europe*, 438). He wrote to Henry Wilson that he was sure that not only Zhukov, but Stalin himself, had wanted "to be friends with the Western democracies" at the war's end. He was baffled by their rapid change of view and suspected that they were swayed by a majority of the Soviet leadership, who had held a more belligerent view (Eisenhower to Wilson, 30 October 1947, PDDE 9:2022).

14. Eisenhower to Smith, 20 May 1944, PDDE 3:1872; Eisenhower to Marshall, 27 September 1944, PDDE 3:1875; Eisenhower to Marshall, 22 October 1944, PDDE 4:2242.

15. Eisenhower to Marshall, 17 May 1945, PDDE 6:57, and 23 May 1945, PDDE 6:91; see also James F. Schnabel, *History of the Joint Chiefs of Staff*, vol. 1, *The Joint Chiefs of Staff and National Policy, 1945–1947* (Washington, D.C.: Office of the Chairman of the Joint Chiefs of Staff, 1996), 23.

16. Eisenhower to George Marshall, 17 October 1945, PDDE 6:449. Benes is quoted in PDDE 6:453; see also the detailed discussion of the whole episode in PDDE 6:450–54. For Murphy's view see *FRUS, 1945,* 4: 499–502. Geoffrey Perret notes that after the war's end Eisenhower urged Truman to be flexible in terminating lend-lease arrangements with Britain and France, "but he said not a word about the Soviet Union, whose people were in worse straits than the British or French" (*Eisenhower,* 354).

17. PDDE 7:1106n. 3.

18. Eisenhower to JCS, 5 March 1947, PDDE 8:1550–51; see also 1552n. 6. Eisenhower offered his view on troop reductions tentatively, and apparently he made no effort to argue it strongly once he saw that the other chiefs disagreed with him. On the UNO, see PDDE 7:878–79n. 1.

19. Eisenhower to JCS, 9 January 1946, PDDE 7:744; Eisenhower to JCS, 21 February 1946, PDDE 7:877–79 (see also JCS 1592/2 in *FRUS, 1946,* 1:1165); Eisenhower to JCS, 10 May 1947, PDDE 8:1701.

20. Eisenhower to JCS, 9 January 1946, PDDE 7:742, 743; Eisenhower to John M. Palmer, 30 January 1946, PDDE 7:811; Compton Commission Report on UMT, PDDE 8:1694n. 4; Eisenhower to JCS, 11 February 1946, PDDE 7:849; Eisenhower to JCS, 22 December 1947, PDDE 9:2155. Eisenhower later insisted that planners should assume that Britain would ally with the United States in the next war. Several historians have commented on the tendency, in postwar military planning, to assume that the next war would resemble

World War II. See, for example, Steven T. Ross, *American War Plans, 1945–1950* (New York: Garland Publishing, 1988), 154, 155.

21. Eisenhower to all War Department officials, 30 April 1946, PDDE 7:1049; Eisenhower to McNarney, 17 April 1946, PDDE 7:1010; Eisenhower to Forrestal and Patterson, 13 March 1947, PDDE 8:1593–94. See the discussion of JCS fears of Soviet motives in Schnabel, *Joint Chiefs of Staff,* 46–47.

22. Eisenhower to Lauris Norstad, 19 June 1947, PDDE 8:1763; Eisenhower to Forrestal, 17 November 1947, PDDE 9:2062; Eisenhower to JCS, 5 June 1946, PDDE 7:1105.

23. Eisenhower to JCS, 10 May 1947, PDDE 8:1700–01.

24. Eisenhower to JCS, 17 December 1947, PDDE 9:2142–43.

25. Eisenhower to MacArthur, 13 February 1947, PDDE 8:1519; Committee of Three meeting, 1 February 1947, PDDE 8:1660n. 5.

26. Eisenhower to Forrestal, 7 February 1948, PDDE 9:2254.

27. Eisenhower to JCS, 9 January 1946, PDDE 7:744; Eisenhower to Forrestal, 17 November 1947, PDDE 9:2063n. 4.

28. Eisenhower to Forrestal and Patterson, 13 March 1947, PDDE 8:1593–4; Eisenhower to Kenneth Royall, 22 October 1947, PDDE 9:1997–99; Eisenhower to JCS, 29 October 1947, PDDE 9:2012; Eisenhower to William Morgan, 4 December 1947, PDDE 9:2103; Schnabel, *Joint Chiefs of Staff,* 59; see also 222n. 67. Eisenhower did not indiscriminately recommend placing U.S. troops in every country. For example, he advised the JCS not to promise too much military support to Italy, where he saw no immediate threat of communist takeover. He also urged a gradual withdrawal of U.S. troops from the Philippines, to avoid public unrest and maintain public support for the United States in "weaker countries," which were more susceptible to communist subversion (Eisenhower to JCS, 22 November 1946, PDDE 8:1389). These cases indicate that he was focusing primarily on perceived Soviet threats in making his troop recommendations.

29. Medhurst, *Dwight D. Eisenhower,* 13–18.

30. Treuenfels, *Eisenhower Speaks,* 29.

31. Hearings of House Committee on Military Affairs, 15 November 1945, Pre-Presidential Papers, Principal Series, Box 144, "Hearings, volume 1: November 1945–January 1946 (1)."

32. Montgomery to Eisenhower, 1 February 1947, PDDE 8:1531n. 1; Eisenhower to Montgomery, 20 February 1947, PDDE 8:1530.

33. Ambrose, *Eisenhower,* 1:435.

34. Eisenhower to Charles Portal, 4 February 1947, PDDE 8:1477.

35. Ann Whitman File, Ann C. Whitman Diary Series, Box 2, "ACW Diary, June 1954 (1)."

36. Patterson to Lewis Brown, 17 October 1947, and Eisenhower to Patterson, 20 October 1947, PDDE 9:1993.

37. Eisenhower to Chynoweth, 7 March 1946, PDDE 7:903; press conference, 25 September 1946, Pre-Presidential Papers, Principal Series, Box 156, "Press Statements and Release, 1944–1946 (1)." Many years earlier, Eisenhower had advised his brother Milton to leave government service so that Milton could "publish what *you believe,* not what administration policy supports. . . . I would regard this as a tremendous advantage" (Eisenhower to Milton Eisenhower, 3 January 1939, in Holt and Leyerzapf, *Eisenhower,* 417).

38. Treuenfels, *Eisenhower Speaks,* 256, 64; speech to American Legion, 20 November 1945, Pre-Presidential Papers, Principal Series, Box 192, "Speeches November 1945–April 1946 (2)."

39. Eisenhower to Cornelius Vanderbilt, Jr., 29 October 1947, PDDE 9:2017; Eisenhower to John Doud, 23 August 1946, PDDE 8:1250.

40. Treuenfels, *Eisenhower Speaks,* 244, 259, 125; speech to American Meat Institute, 4 September 1947, Pre-Presidential Papers, Principal Series, Box 192, "Speeches January 1947–October 1947 (1)."
41. Ambrose, *Eisenhower,* 1:427, citing the diary of Eisenhower's aide, Capt. Harry Butcher.

## CHAPTER 4

1. Robert Griffith, "Dwight D. Eisenhower and the Corporate Commonwealth," *American Historical Review* 87 (1982): 87–122.
2. Halford Ross Ryan, "A Rhetorical Analysis of General Eisenhower's Public Speaking From 1945 to 1951" (Ph.D. diss., University of Illinois at Urbana-Champaign, 1972), 53. The text is in Treuenfels, *Eisenhower Speaks,* 190–91. Although all of Eisenhower's speeches sounded similar themes, each was tailored to the particular audience he addressed. Apparently, he assumed the DAR would have a special interest in the nation's first principles and ideological foundations.
3. Treuenfels, *Eisenhower Speaks,* 233, 77, 164. Eisenhower was fond of quoting these words of Wilson; see also, e.g., Treuenfels, *Eisenhower Speaks,* 101, 119. See also Treuenfels, *Eisenhower Speaks,* 101, 112, and speech to Advisory Council to Women's Interests Unit, Public Relations Division, 14 November 1946, Pre-Presidential Papers, Principal Series, Box 192, "Speeches May 1946–December 1946 (2)." He had already used Wilson's words in public speaking before World War II; see Holt and Leyerzapf, *Eisenhower,* 428. The theme of cooperation for the good of the nation had become prominent in his discourse in the early 1930s; see chap. 1, note 19, above.
4. Treuenfels, *Eisenhower Speaks,* 118–19; speech at University of West Virginia, 23 September 1947, Pre-Presidential Papers, Principal Series, Box 192, "Speeches January 1947–October 1947 (1)."
5. Speech to Inter-American Defense Board, 15 April 1946, Pre-Presidential Papers, Principal Series, Box 192, "Speeches November 1945–April 1946 (1)."
6. Treuenfels, *Eisenhower Speaks,* 256, 248.
7. Ibid., 99, 257, 258.
8. Ibid., 144, 168, 103, 120.
9. Ibid., 119, 262; Richard A. Melanson, "The Foundations of Eisenhower's Foreign Policy," in *Reevaluating Eisenhower: American Foreign Policy in the 1950s,* ed. Richard A. Melanson and David Mayers (Urbana and Chicago: University of Illinois Press, 1987). See also Michael Sherry, *In the Shadow of War* (New Haven: Yale University Press, 1995), chap. 1.
10. Treuenfels, *Eisenhower Speaks,* 219, 96, 79.
11. Address at Cambridge University, 11 October 1946, Pre-Presidential Papers, Principal Series, Box 192, "Speeches May 1946–December 1946 (2)."
12. Diary, 26 May 1946, Ferrell, *Diaries,* 136; Eisenhower to Henry Wilson, 30 October 1947, PDDE 9:2022; Eisenhower to John Doud, 23 August 1946, PDDE 8:1250; Eisenhower to Al Browning, 27 January 1948, PDDE 9:2213; Eisenhower to James Forrestal, 7 February 1948, PDDE 9:2251; Eisenhower to Geoffrey Keynes, 5 March 1947, PDDE 8:1564.
13. Diary, 12 November 1946, Ferrell, *Diaries* 138; Eisenhower to Eddie Rickenbacker, 17 December 1947, PDDE 9:2145; Eisenhower to Milton Eisenhower, 16 October 1947, PDDE 9:1986–87; Eisenhower, Doolittle Board Remarks, April 1946, PDDE 7:906. Once Eisenhower described to his brother Milton a conversation with some businessmen. They had agreed that if Americans ate more frugally and showed it possible to save food "through the voluntary action of the entire American population, it would be a

most heartening declaration of the working ability of democracy" (16 September 1947, PDDE 9:1922). Here he was able to commend the disciplining of appetite quite literally, while affirming democracy's dependence on voluntary cooperation, the only rational course.

14. William Robinson to Helen Rogers Reid, 21 June 1948, William Robinson Papers, Box 6, "Diary–WER and DDE." Robinson's summary of Eisenhower's views was not verbatim, and it was probably written to promote the general as a presidential candidate. But it does fit well with the verbatim opinions Eisenhower expressed elsewhere.

15. Eisenhower to Swede Hazlett, 19 July 1947, PDDE 8:1837; diary, 26 May 1946, Ferrell, *Diaries*, 137.

16. Eisenhower to John Eisenhower, 14 November 1946, PDDE 8:1381; Eisenhower to Milton Eisenhower 15 March 1946, PDDE 7:942; Eisenhower to Gen. Geoffrey Keyes, 5 March 1947, PDDE 8:1564.

17. See Patrick Henry, "'And I Don't Care What It Is': The Tradition-History of a Civil Religion Proof-Text," *Journal of the American Academy of Religion* 49 (March 1981): 35–50; Robert Morse Crumden, *Ministers of Reform: The Progressives' Achievement in American Civilization, 1889–1920* (New York: Basic Books, 1982). It was especially appropriate that he should so often quote perhaps the greatest "minister of reform" to inhabit the White House, Woodrow Wilson.

18. Eisenhower to Roy Roberts, 30 January 1948, PDDE 9:2217; Eisenhower to Leonard Finder, 27 January 1948, PDDE 9:2202; Eisenhower to Walter Bedell Smith, 18 September 1947, PDDE 9:1934; Eisenhower to Swede Hazlett, 25 August 1947, PDDE 9:1897.

19. Diary, 8 March 1947, Ferrell, *Diaries*, 140.

20. Eisenhower to Gen. Jonathan Wainwright, 28 June 1946, PDDE 7:1155.

21. Treuenfels, *Eisenhower Speaks*, 186; speech to Inter-American Defense Board, 15 April 1946, Pre-Presidential Papers, Principal Series, Box 192, "Speeches November 1945–April 1946 (1)"; press conference, 25 September 1946, Pre-Presidential Papers, Principal Series, Box 156, "Press Statements and Releases, 1944–1946 (1)."

22. Treuenfels, *Eisenhower Speaks*, 244, 117, 113, 86, 68; speech to U.S. Conference of Mayors, 20 January 1947, Pre-Presidential Papers, Principal Series, Box 192, "Speeches January 1947–October 1947 (3)."

23. Eisenhower, *Crusade in Europe*, 30; Treuenfels, *Eisenhower Speaks*, 74, 112, 68, 65.

24. Treuenfels, *Eisenhower Speaks*, 74, 153, 112.

25. Speech to Roosevelt Memorial Association, 27 October 1946, Pre-Presidential Papers, Principal Series, Box 129, "Speeches May 1946 - December 1946 (2)"; speech to Women's Peace Conference, 28 March 1947, Pre-Presidential Papers, Principal Series, Box 192, "Speeches January 1947–October 1947 (3)"; speech to U.S. Conference of Mayors, 20 January 1947, Pre-Presidential Papers, Principal Series, Box 192, "Speeches January 1947–October 1947 (3)."

26. Speech to Women's Peace Conference, 28 March 1947, Pre-Presidential Papers, Principal Series, Box 192, "Speeches January 1947–October 1947 (3)"; Treuenfels, *Eisenhower Speaks*, 119, 254; speech to Cleveland Aviation Club, 11 April 1946, Pre-Presidential Papers, Principal Series, Box 192, "Speeches November 1945–April 1946 (1)."

27. Treuenfels, *Eisenhower Speaks*, 144, 217, 219.

28. Ibid., 153, 103, 71; speech to Cleveland Aviation Club, 11 April 1946, Pre-Presidential Papers, Principal Series, Box 192, "Speeches November 1945–April 1946 (1)"; press conference, 28 September 1946, Pre-Presidential Papers, Principal Series, Box 156, "Press Statements and Releases, 1944–46 (1)"; D-day address, Kansas City, 6 June 1947, Pre-Presidential Papers, Principal Series, Box 192, "Speeches January 1947–October 1947 (2)";

notes for speech to Poor Richard Club, Philadelphia, 17 January 1948, Pre-Presidential Papers, Principal Series, Box 195 "Poor Richard Club."

29. See Eisenhower to Cornelius Vanderbilt, Jr., 29 October 1947, PDDE 2017; Eisenhower to Swede Hazlett, 19 July 1947, PDDE 1837; diary 16 September 1947, Ferrell, *Diaries*, 143; all discussed below, p. 119. On 27 January 1948, Eisenhower told newspaper publisher Leonard Finder of his "fanatical devotion to the purpose of perpetuating peace" (PDDE 2202). Finder was a major booster of the "Eisenhower for president" movement, and there was intense public interest in Eisenhower's response to Finder. So this letter must be seen as something of a public relations matter, if not technically a public statement.

## CHAPTER 5

1. Treuenfels, *Eisenhower Speaks*, 77, 102.
2. Speech at Boston, 12 November 1945, Pre-Presidential Papers, Principal Series, Box 192, "Speeches November 1945–April 1946 (2)" (italics in original); message to Congress, 15 January 1946, Pre-Presidential Papers, Principal Series, Box 144, "Hearings Volume 1 November 1945–January 1945 (2)" (in the entire typed text, Eisenhower underlined only these words); Treuenfels, *Eisenhower Speaks*, 96.
3. See Joyce and Gabriel Kolko, *The Limits of Power: The World and United States Foreign Policy, 1945–1951* (New York: Harper and Row, 1972), 337.
4. Speech to women writers, 5 June 1946, Pre-Presidential Papers, Principal Series, Box 192, "Speeches May 1946–December 1946 (3)"; Treuenfels, *Eisenhower Speaks*, 58, 177, 200, 248, 249. By mid-1947, "the shadow of enslavement" was clearly a public warning about the dangers of communism, but it exemplified the rhetorical power of Eisenhower's theoretical paradigm.
5. Treuenfels, *Eisenhower Speaks*, 122, 256. See also address to Women's Peace Conference, 28 March 1947, Pre-Presidential Papers, Principal Series, Box 192, "Speeches January 1947–October 1947 (3)": "Millions of people grope along concerned entirely with the difficult job of finding the day's bread. In this supine state they are likely victims of militant minorities."
6. Treuenfels, *Eisenhower Speaks*, 154, 64; speech to American Legion, 20 November 1945, Pre-Presidential Papers, Principal Series, Box 192, "Speeches November 1945–April 1946 (2)." Eisenhower warned a congressional committee that lack of military preparation would "encourage future Hitlers" (testimony to the House Committee on Military Affairs, 15 November 1945, Pre-Presidential Papers, Principal Series, Box 144, "Hearings Volume 1 November 1945–January 1945 [1]").
7. At the congressional hearing on 15 November 1945 (see preceding note), when prodded to name Russia as "a potential aggressor," he refused to take the bait, answering only (for the record) that Russia had no reason to start a war and wanted "friendship with the United States" (Lyon, *Eisenhower*, 387).
8. Letter to National Conference of Christians and Jews, 19 November 1947, PDDE 7:1069; Treuenfels, *Eisenhower Speaks*, 71; hearings of House Subcommittee of Committee on Appropriations, 19 February 1947, Pre-Presidential Papers, Principal Series, Box 144, "Hearings, volume 3: June 1946–May 1947"; Treuenfels, *Eisenhower Speaks*, 219, 145, 179, 186. See also Treuenfels, *Eisenhower Speaks*, 113: peace "can be achieved if every nation realizes that its very survival may depend on its earnest co-operation in the peaceful settlement of disputes"; Treuenfels, *Eisenhower Speaks*, 65: "Unless the world breaks away from traditional habits in the international field, humanity can look forward to nothing but suffering, impoverishment, and possible self-destruction."

9. Treuenfels, *Eisenhower Speaks,* 244, 259; *New York Times,* 1 October 1946, 17; Treuenfels, *Eisenhower Speaks,* 141; speech to American Meat Institute, 9/4/47, Pre-Presidential Papers, Principal Series, Box 192, "Speeches January 1947–October 1947 (1)." See also Treuenfels, *Eisenhower Speaks,* 125, 238. The *New York Times* was more than willing to publicize Eisenhower's jeremiads. On one occasion he mentioned "the possibility of insane attack on those who work for peace." It was quite an atypical remark, made in passing in a speech full of much more typical Eisenhower rhetoric, but the *Times* used it as a headline (5 July 1947, 12).

10. Treuenfels, *Eisenhower Speaks,* 262.

11. Ibid., 256, 162, 255; see also PDDE 9:2051 and Treuenfels, *Eisenhower Speaks,* 254.

12. Treuenfels, *Eisenhower Speaks,* 55, 249; *New York Times,* 4 October 1946, 5.

13. D-day address, 6 June 1947, Pre-Presidential Papers, Principal Series, Box 192, "Speeches January 1947–October 1947 (2)."

14. Army Day speech, 6 April 1946, Pre-Presidential Papers, Principal Series, Box 192, "Speeches November 1945–April 1946 (2)"; Treuenfels, *Eisenhower Speaks,* 90, 127 (see also 57, 145); speech to Bond Club, N.Y., 23 January 1947, Pre-Presidential Papers, Principal Series, Box 192, "Speeches January 1947–October 1947 (3)." See also D-day address, 6 June 1947, Pre-Presidential Papers, Principal Series, Box 192, "Speeches January 1947–October 1947 (2)"; speech to U.S. Conference of Mayors, 20 January 1947, Pre-Presidential Papers, Principal Series, Box 192, "Speeches January 1947–October 1947 (3)"; testimony to the House Military Affairs Committee, 21 March 1946, and testimony to Senate Committee on Military Affairs, 8 April 1946, both in Pre-Presidential Papers, Principal Series, Box 144, "Hearings Volume 2 January 1946–June 1946 (1)."

15. Treuenfels, *Eisenhower Speaks,* 64, 65, 77, 120, 115. On Eisenhower 's use of military metaphors, see Ryan, "A Rhetorical Analysis," 117–18.

16. Message to Congress, 15 January 1946, Pre-Presidential Papers, Principal Series, Box 144, "Hearings Volume 1 November 1945–January 1946 (2)"; Treuenfels, *Eisenhower Speaks,* 77, 116; Christmas message, 11 December 1946, PDDE 8:1431.

17. Treuenfels, *Eisenhower Speaks,* 112.

18. Address to American Legion, 20 November 1945, Pre-Presidential Papers, Principal Series, Box 192, "Speeches November 1945–April 1946 (2)"; address to Women's Peace Conference, 28 March 1947, Pre-Presidential Papers, Principal Series, Box 192, "Speeches January 1947–October 1947 (3)"; Treuenfels, *Eisenhower Speaks,* 112, 114.

19. See Ernest L. Tuveson, *Redeemer Nation: The Idea of America's Millennial Role* (Chicago: University of Chicago Press, 1968), chap. 1, on the historical roots of the idea of the apocalypse as a process.

20. *New York Times,* 10 August 1946, 6.

21. Ambrose, *Eisenhower,* 1:435.

22. Christmas message, 11 December 1946, PDDE 8:1431; draft press statement, 5 January 1948, Pre-Presidential Papers, Principal Series, Box 156, "Press Statements and Releases, 1947–1952 (4)" (the statement was issued on 15 January 1948).

23. Speech to Women's Action Committee for Lasting Peace, 28 March 1947, PDDE 8:1640n. 3; Treuenfels, *Eisenhower Speaks,* 90.

24. Address to American Legion, 20 November 1945, Pre-Presidential Papers, Principal Series, Box 192, "Speeches November 1945–April 1946 (2)." On the Augustinian roots of the idea of peace through strength, see James Turner Johnson, *The Quest for Peace* (Princeton: Princeton University Press, 1987), 56–66. Johnson points out that Augustine's understanding of peace was uniquely suited to the political context of a powerful central government, such as the Roman empire.

25. Treuenfels, *Eisenhower Speaks*, 68, 175 (see also 244, 250); speech to Bond Club, New York, 23 January 1947, Pre-Presidential Papers, Principal Series, Box 192, "Speeches January 1947–October 1947 (3)"; speech to U.S. Conference of Mayors, 20 January 1947, Pre-Presidential Papers, Principal Series, Box 192, "Speeches January 1947–October 1947 (3)"; Treuenfels, *Eisenhower Speaks*, 266 (see also 72, 113).

26. Ryan, "A Rhetorical Analysis," 76; Treuenfels, *Eisenhower Speaks*, 77 (see also 88, 107, 175, 253); speech to Advisory Council to Women's Interests Unit, Public Relations Division, 14 November 1946, Pre-Presidential Papers, Principal Series, Box 192, "Speeches May 1946–December 1946 (2)."

27. Treuenfels, *Eisenhower Speaks*, 251. Eisenhower was likely to label any emotion or opinion of which he disapproved "hysteria." He dismissed the public clamor for faster postwar demobilization as "hysteria," according to Steve Neal, *The Eisenhowers: Reluctant Dynasty* (Garden City, N.Y.: Doubleday, 1978), 228. He even applied the term to himself, telling Swede Hazlett that when he tried to express his strong determination not to run for president, "I merely get so vehement that I grow speechless, if not hysterical" (3 March 1946, PDDE 7:922).

28. Treuenfels, *Eisenhower Speaks*, 220; speech to Women's Peace Conference, 28 March 1947, Pre-Presidential Papers, Principal Series, Box 192, "Speeches January 1947–October 1947 (3)."

29. *Time*, 25 June 1945, 16; *Newsweek*, 25 June 1945, 30; *Time*, 2 July 1945, 19. As C/S, Eisenhower was usually lobbying for higher military budgets. Occasionally he did sound a note that would be a central theme of his presidency, the need to avoid spending too much, "to see that you do not go bankrupt to support duplication or obsolete formations" (Treuenfels, *Eisenhower Speaks*, 129).

30. Treuenfels, *Eisenhower Speaks*, 161, 118, 166.

31. Ibid., 219; testimony to Subcommittee of Senate Committee on Armed Service, Pre-Presidential Papers, Principal Series, Box 145, "Hearing Volume 4 May 1947–April 1948 (2)"; Treuenfels, *Eisenhower Speaks*, 129, 77, 174.

32. Treuenfels, *Eisenhower Speaks*, 114, 117, 118.

33. Ibid., 168, 176, 85; address to American Legion, 20 November 1945, Pre-Presidential Papers, Principal Series, Box 192, "Speeches November 1945–April 1946 (2)." See also Treuenfels, *Eisenhower Speaks*, 76: Those who work for peace would "stand for co-operation as against domination and know that co-operation implies readiness to give as well as to receive."

34. Treuenfels, *Eisenhower Speaks*, 110, 128, 126, 243; *New York Times*, 7 June 1947, 1.

35. Treuenfels, *Eisenhower Speaks*, 240; hearings of Senate Subcommittee of Committee on Foreign Relations, 3 March 1947, Pre-Presidential Papers, Principal Series, Box 144, "Hearings, volume 3: June 1946–May 1947."

36. John Winthrop, "A Model of Christian Charity," in *The Puritans*, vol. 1, ed. Perry Miller and Thomas H. Johnson (New York: Harper Torchbooks, 1963), 199; Treuenfels, *Eisenhower Speaks*, 121, 163. On the two cultural traditions, see John F. Wilson, *Public Religion in American Culture* (Philadelphia: Temple University Press, 1979), 28–31.

37. Speech to Advisory Council to Women's Interests Unit, Public Relations Division, 14 November 1946, Pre-Presidential Papers, Principal Series, Box 192, "Speeches May 1946–December 1946 (2)"; Treuenfels, *Eisenhower Speaks*, 112, 205. See the classic study by R. W. B. Lewis, *The American Adam: Innocence, Tragedy, and Tradition in the Nineteenth Century* (Chicago: University of Chicago Press, 1955).

38. Sacvan Bercovitch has argued that, in the original jeremiads of the seventeenth-century Puritan clergy, the condemnation of public immorality served to legitimate the Puritans'

claim to be the "New Israel," with a divinely appointed eschatological mission. See *The American Jeremiad* (Madison: University of Wisconsin Press, 1978).

39. Diary, 1 November 1946, Ferrell, *Diaries,* 137; diary, 15 May 1947, Ferrell, *Diaries,* 141; Eisenhower to Gen. Ike Eichelberger, 1 March 1947, PDDE 8:1546; Eisenhower to John Doud, 23 August 1946, PDDE 8:1249; Eisenhower to Walter Bedell Smith, 30 August 1946, PDDE 1267; Eisenhower to John Eisenhower, 28 August 1947, PDDE 9:1902.

40. Eisenhower to Louis Marx, 9 March 1946, PDDE 7:911.

41. Diary, 12 November 1946, Ferrell, *Diaries,* 138; Eisenhower to John Eisenhower, 3 March 1946, PDDE 7:882; Eisenhower to Walter Bedell Smith, 29 October 1947, PDDE 9:2014.

42. Notes for speech in Boston, 12 November 1945, Pre-Presidential Papers, Principal Series, Box 192, "Speeches, November 1945–April 1946 (2)"; Treuenfels, *Eisenhower Speaks,* 77.

43. Eisenhower to John Eisenhower, 14 November 1946, PDDE 8:1381; Eisenhower to Walter Bedell Smith, 30 August 1946, PDDE 8:1267. In another letter he complained to John that on economic, military, and foreign policy issues, "no one seems to have a complete program on which he is ready to stand or fall. Personally, I consider this merely typical of the state of confusion that the world was bound to experience following upon the global war" (3 March 1946, PDDE 7:882).

44. Eisenhower to Bernard Baruch, 5 January 1946, PDDE 7:736; diary, 2 December 1946, Ferrell, *Diaries,* 139; diary, 26 May 1946, Ferrell, *Diaries,* 137.

45. Diary, 16 September 1947, Ferrell, *Diaries,* 143; diary, 26 May 1946, Ferrell, *Diaries,* 136; diary, 15 May 1947, Ferrell, *Diaries,* 142; Eisenhower to Walter Bedell Smith, 18 September 1947, PDDE 9:1934.

46. Eisenhower to Thomas Hargrave, 18 November 1947, PDDE 9:2067; Eisenhower to Sen. Walter Judd 9 May 1947, PDDE 8:1699 (see also *New York Times,* 20 April 1947); Eisenhower to Walter Andrews, 30 January 1948, PDDE 9:2215. These letters to legislators, like all his rhetoric of continuing war, were explicitly intended to promote Universal Military Training bills in Congress. But they were embedded in and reflected the larger patterns of Eisenhower's discourse. Yet he did not want to state this view openly. Asked at a congressional hearing whether the United States could be "devastated by foreign attack," he would only answer off the record (testimony to Subcommittee of House Committee on Appropriations, 19 February 1947, Pre-Presidential Papers, Principal Series, Box 144, "Hearings Volume 3 June 1946–May 1947 [2]").

47. Eisenhower to Walter Bedell Smith, 28 November 1947, PDDE 9:2085.

48. Diary, 16 September 1947, Ferrell, *Diaries,* 143.

49. Diary, 26 May 1946, Ferrell, *Diaries,* 137.

50. Eisenhower to Cornelius Vanderbilt, Jr., 29 October 1947, PDDE 9:2017.

51. Eisenhower to Swede Hazlett, 25 August 1947, PDDE 9:1897 and 19 July 1947, PDDE 8:1837.

52. Diary, 8 March 1947; Ferrell, *Diaries,* 140.

53. Eisenhower to Frederick Morgan, 26 December 1947, PDDE 9:2165.

54. Eisenhower to JCS, 10 May 1947, PDDE 8:1701.

# CHAPTER 6

1. Memorandum for the Chief of Staff, 12 April 1946, RG 165, P&O Decimal File 1946–1948 (TS), Box 1, 000.5 to 000.9, "(Section II) (Cases 2–10)," National Archives. See also Hull to Eisenhower, 12 March 1946, PDDE 7:1078. Several documents in this folder demonstrate Groves's great influence upon Baruch.

2. Memorandum of meeting, 15 April 1946, RG 165, Box 170, ABC File 471.6 Atom (17 August 1945), "Section 6-A," National Archives.
3. The memo to Baruch (14 June 1946) cited here and in the following paragraphs is in PDDE 7:1125–27. In a brief cryptic personal letter two weeks earlier, he told Baruch that disarmament would be difficult if all nations were as disinterested in it as the United States. He wrote, "Because of the obvious complications and obstacles, I am doubly ready" to help (RG 165, Records of the War Department General and Special Staffs, Office of the Chief of Staff, Classified General Correspondence 1942–1947, Box 258, WDCSA No. 000.9, National Archives).
4. Eisenhower testimony, 5 June 1946, PDDE 7:1094; Eisenhower to JCS, 26 November 1946, 8:1394n. 3; Rusk to Petersen, 15 January 1947, FRUS, 1947, 1:362 (see also PDDE 8:1485n. 4).
5. Eisenhower to Baruch, 14 June 1946, PDDE 7:1126.
6. McGeorge Bundy, Danger and Survival: Choices About the Bomb in the First Fifty Years (New York: Random House, 1988), 236. Eisenhower did once tell an audience (in July 1946) that international cooperation was especially important because of "terrifying new weapons" (Treuenfels, Eisenhower Speaks, 119).
7. Norstad to Eisenhower, 24 June 1946, RG 319, Plans and Operations Division Decimal File 000.9, Box 6, "(Section IV) (Cases 41–50)," National Archives.
8. Eisenhower to Lauris Norstad, 5 February 1947, PDDE 8:1483–84
9. Memorandum for the Chief of Staff, 17 July 1946, and Eisenhower to JCS, 18 July 1947, both in RG 165, BX 170, ABC File 471.6 Atom (17 August 1945), "Section 6-B," National Archives; testimony to Subcommittee of Senate Committee on Appropriations, 28 June 1947, Pre-Presidential Papers, Primary Series, Box 145, "Hearings Volume 4 May 1947–April 1948 (2)."
10. Ridgway to Eisenhower, 3 February 1947; Marshall to Patterson, 18 February 1947 (with Eisenhower's notation stressing the public relations campaign); Norstad to Ridgway, 21 February 1947; all in RG 165, P&O Decimal File 1946–1948 (TS), Box 1, 000.5 to 000.9, "(Section II) (Cases 2–10)," National Archives. The same folder contains a letter from Ridgway to Eisenhower, 1 August 1947, suggesting that such a publicity effort would contribute to "the defeat of Russian aims."
11. In a letter approved by Eisenhower, Gen. A. D. Surles told Henry Pringle that the Army Chief of Staff was "definitely circumscribed in what he has to say" about control of atomic weapons, because he was required to endorse official administration positions (RG 165, Records of the War Department General and Special Staffs, Office of the Chief of Staff, Classified General Correspondence 1942–1947, Box 322, WDCSA No. 471.6, National Archives). All the evidence, both during and after his tenure as C/S, indicates that had he not been circumscribed he would have been more, not less, of a hawk on disarmament.
12. Bernard Brodie, ed., The Absolute Weapon: Atomic Power and World Order (New York: Harcourt, Brace, 1946). On 25 March 1946, Eisenhower's aide, Lt. Col. James Stack, wrote a memo indicating that Eisenhower had received The Absolute Weapon and wanted it made available to all senior officials of the War Department (RG 165, Records of the War Department General and Special Staffs, Office of the Chief of Staff, Classified General Correspondence 1942–1947, Box 322, WDCSA No. 471.6, National Archives). An anonymous memo, circulated in the P&O division, provided selected quotes from Brodie's book. The crucial and famous quotation cited above was not included in the memo. Rather, the memo found the "basic proposition of atomic bomb warfare" in Brodie's contention that the military could only "fight back" after atomic attack if its facilities were not located in big cities. In general, the memo stressed the need to build atomic arsenals and prepare for a

war that would be fought in a very compressed time span. It is unclear whether Eisenhower ever saw this memo, but it did accord well with his views on the atomic bomb. A copy is in RG 319, Plans and Operations Division Decimal File 000.9, Box 6, "(Section III) (Cases 32–40)," National Archives.

13. Eisenhower to Dorothy Thompson, 25 June 1946, PDDE 7:1149–50.

14. Treunfels, *Eisenhower Speaks,* 115. Eisenhower and the other joint chiefs were particularly concerned about shaping public reaction to the Bikini tests. Secretary of War Robert Patterson wrote to W. G. Chandler, president of the American Newspaper Publishers Association, that the JCS were "studying the problem from all angles" (Patterson to Chandler, 11 March 1946, RG 165, Records of the War Department General and Special Staffs, Office of the Chief of Staff, Classified General Correspondence 1942–1947, Box 322, WDCSA No. 471.6, National Archives; this file contains numerous relevant documents). A public relations unit assembled for this purpose, called "Joint Task Force One," sent Eisenhower "Suggested Remarks" as early as 13 May: "Suggested Remarks for General Eisenhower," RG 319, Plans and Operations Division Decimal File 000.9, Box 6, "(Section IV) (Cases 41–50)," National Archives.

15. Treuenfels, *Eisenhower Speaks,* 173

16. RG 165, Box 170, ABC File 471.6 Atom (17 August 1945), "Section 6-B," National Archives. This was a rare foreshadowing during Eisenhower's term as C/S of the concern that would guide his planning as president.

17. See PDDE 6:205 for sources. Barton Bernstein raises serious doubts about Eisenhower's supposed qualms in "Ike and Hiroshima," 377–89.

18. Perret, *Eisenhower,* 371, citing Eisenhower to JCS, 3 December 1945, PDDE 7:575. See also Eisenhower to Bernard Baruch, 14 June 1946, PDDE 7:1126; Eisenhower to JCS, 12 March 1947, PDDE 8:1582; Eisenhower to Robert Patterson, 17 March 1947, PDDE 8:1606; Eisenhower to JCS, 22 December 1947, PDDE 9:2157. The latter document suggests that the United States should plan not only for the likelihood of using atomic weapons in war, but also for the very real possibility of using, and even initiating, biological and chemical warfare.

19. Eisenhower to JCS, 16 January 1946, PDDE 7:760–62; Gregg Herken, *The Winning Weapon: The Atomic Bomb in the Cold War, 1945–1950* (New York: Vintage Books, 1982), 213; RG 319, Plans and Operations Division Decimal File 000.9, Box 5, "(Section I) (Cases 1–20)," National Archives. See Eisenhower's praise of Groves in Eisenhower to Bourke Hickenlooper, 6 June 1946, PDDE 7:1104.

20. Steven T. Ross, *American War Plans, 1945–1950* (New York: Garland, 1988), 154, 155. Similarly, Samuel R. Williamson, Jr. and Steven L. Rearden speak of "the operating assumption that nuclear weapons, though clearly more powerful, were essentially no different from other weapons" (*The Origins of U.S. Nuclear Strategy, 1945–1953* [New York: St. Martin's Press, 1993], 194).

21. Ross, *War Plans,* 154. Ross notes that by 1949–50 this had become the consensus opinion. The important point here is that Eisenhower was already advocating this view two years earlier.

22. Eisenhower to JCS, 3 December 1945, PDDE 7:575; Eisenhower to JCS, 17 December 1945, PDDE 7:639–42; Eisenhower to JCS, 16 January 1946, PDDE 7:760–62.

23. Eisenhower to JCS, 12 March 1947, PDDE 8:1582; Eisenhower to Robert Patterson, 17 March 1947, PDDE 8:1606.

24. Williamson and Rearden, *Origins of U.S. Nuclear Strategy,* x, 194.

25. Treuenfels, *Eisenhower Speaks,* 43. On the links between economic concerns and early nuclear strategy, see Michael Sherry, *The Rise of American Air Power: The Creation of Armageddon* (New Haven: Yale University Press, 1987), passim, and Lawrence Freedman, *The Evolution of Nuclear Strategy,* 2d ed. (New York: St. Martin's Press, 1989), 47–48.

26. Sherry, *Rise of American Air Power,* 323, 327.
27. See Spencer Weart, *Nuclear Fear: A History of Images* (Cambridge, Mass.: Harvard University Press, 1988) and Chernus, *Dr. Strangegod.*
28. For a good overview of this theological difference as a preface to understanding U.S. political culture, see Tuveson, *Redeemer Nation,* chap. 1.
29. Lyon, *Eisenhower,* 398.
30. Words could be aimed indirectly at the enemy. Having supported pioneering efforts in psychological warfare during World War II, Eisenhower continued to be a strong proponent of plans for psychological warfare in the next war. He told his director of plans and operations to "keep alive the arts of psychological warfare . . . [and] a nucleus of personnel capable of handling these arts in case an emergency arises" (Eisenhower to Lauris Norstad, 19 June 1947, PDDE 8:1763). See also Eisenhower to James Forrestal, 17 November 1947, PDDE 9:2062.
31. Treuenfels, *Eisenhower Speaks,* 87.
32. Ibid., 165.
33. Ibid., 130. See also Eisenhower, *Crusade in Europe,* 452, where Eisenhower claimed that if the Soviet Union "could have been as closely knit into the team as were the others . . . the peace would have rested on a more secure foundation."
34. Treuenfels, *Eisenhower Speaks,* 233.
35. Eisenhower did admit in one congressional hearing that the United States had been imperialistic in the past, but "that was a long time ago. We have reformed. We don't do those things any more. . . . We do honestly believe in the purity of our motives today" (Treuenfels, 205).
36. Ibid., 204.
37. *New York Times,* 29 July 1947, 12.
38. Treuenfels, *Eisenhower Speaks,* 249, 250. The hard line cold warrior tone of this speech earned a front-page banner headline and a laudatory editorial in the *New York Times,* 30 August 1947.
39. For a somewhat different view, see Lyon, *Eisenhower,* 398.
40. Speech to Women's Peace Conference, 28 March 1947, Pre-Presidential Papers, Principal Series, Box 192, "Speeches January 1947–October 1947 (3)"; Treuenfels, *Eisenhower Speaks,* 147, 188, 115, 70; speech at University of Pennsylvania, 18 June 1947, quoted in Ambrose, *Eisenhower,* 1:436. Months earlier, under the heading "Eisenhower Sees Too Much Despair," the *New York Times* had quoted him: "At the risk of being called pollyanish I think there's too much pessimism" (1 October 1946, 17).
41. Press conference, 11 October 1946, Pre-Presidential Papers, Principal Series, Box 156, "Press Statements and Release, 1944–1946 (1)"; *New York Times,* 6 May 1947, 13; Treuenfels, *Eisenhower Speaks,* 65.
42. 10 December 1945, PDDE 7:610.
43. Eisenhower to Charles Portal, 4 February 1947, PDDE 8:1477.
44. Eisenhower to P.A. Hodgson, 23 October 1947, PDDE 9:2007; Eisenhower to Walter Bedell Smith, 29 October 1947, PDDE 9:2014; Eisenhower to Henry Wilson, 30 October 1947, PDDE 9:2021.
45. Eisenhower to Swede Hazlett, 29 October 1947, PDDE 9:2016; Eisenhower to James B. Conant, 20 October 1947, PDDE 9:1992. Anyone who has spent time in Abilene, even in the 1990s, might be tempted to agree with its most famous son about the relative absence of change, though not necessarily with his evaluation of the results.
46. Eisenhower to Walter Bedell Smith, 18 April 1947, PDDE 8:1649 and 28 November 1947, PDDE 9:2084; Eisenhower to Yousef Karsh, 20 September 1947, PDDE 9:1938;

Eisenhower to Freddie Morgan, 26 December 1947, PDDE 9:2165; Eisenhower to H. Lionel Ismay, 13 July 1946, PDDE 7:1192.

47. Speech to Advisory Council to Women's Interests Unit, Public Relations Division, 14 November 1946, Pre-Presidential Papers, Principal Series, Box 192, "Speeches May 1946–December 1946 (2)." See also comments to the House Subcommittee of Committee on Appropriations, 28 June 1947, Pre-Presidential Papers, Principal Series, Box 144, "Hearings, volume 3: June 1946–May 1947" and speech to U.S. Conference of Mayors, 20 January 1947, Pre-Presidential Papers, Principal Series, Box 192, "Speeches January 1947–October 1947 (3)."

48. Hearings of House Committee on Military Affairs, 15 November 1945, Pre-Presidential Papers, Principal Series, Box 144, "Hearings, volume 1: November 1945–January 1946 (1)."

49. Address to chaplains, 24 April 1946, Pre-Presidential Papers, Principal Series, Box 192, "Speeches November 1945–April 1946 (1)" (see also *New York Times,* 25 April 1946, sec. 5, p. 2); Treuenfels, *Eisenhower Speaks,* 165, 112. See also Eisenhower to Hazlett, 26 January 1948, PDDE 9:2197: "We need crusaders."

# CHAPTER 7

1. Eisenhower rarely if ever used the phrase "new world order," perhaps because its use by the Nazis was still fresh in public memory. But the phrase effectively sums up the goal he was articulating.

2. For classic theories of religion stressing the importance of words in creating a sense of social stability, see, e.g., the works of Mircea Eliade, as well as Peter Berger, *The Sacred Canopy* (Garden City, N.Y.: Doubleday, 1967).

3. Among historians of religions, Jonathan Z. Smith has raised this question in particularly pointed form; see his "Map Is Not Territory," in Jonathan Z. Smith, *Map Is Not Territory: Studies in the History of Religions* (Leiden: E.J. Brill, 1978), as well as various essays in his collection, *Imagining Religion* (Chicago: University of Chicago Press, 1982). The question has also been raised, in a different and very influential form, by the work of Michel Foucault. It seems plausible to speculate that the insistence on stability is especially characteristic of urban hierarchical societies.

4. A received story (believed to be quite unchanging) about the Revolution of 1776 has been a major source of stability in U.S. discourse. Yet that discourse has typically frowned upon any other revolutions; see Hunt, *Ideology and U.S. Foreign Policy*, chap. 4. This is just one symptom of the widespread reluctance to accept any kind of radical change, and the desire to use language to achieve lasting stability. For a broader discussion of this desire, see David Campbell, *Writing Security,* 2d ed. (Minneapolis: University of Minnesota Press, 1998).

5. David Campbell argues in *Writing Security* that this paradoxical pattern is typical of the history of U.S. public discourse about foreign affairs.

6. Thomas Paterson, *Meeting the Communist Threat: Truman to Reagan* (New York: Oxford University Press, 1988), 3.

7. On Augustine and apocalypticism, see Tuveson, *Redeemer Nation,* chap. 1.

# CHAPTER 8

1. Eisenhower to Swede Hazlett, 19 July 1947, PDDE 1837; Eisenhower to Vernon Sturdee, 3 February 1948, PDDE 2225, (see also Eisenhower to Charles Herron, PDDE 1811, 9 July

1947); press conference, 21 May 1948, Pre-Presidential Papers, Principal Series, Box 156, "Press Statements and Releases, 1947–1952 (4)."

2. Testimony to Senate Committee on Armed Services, 2 April 1948, Pre-presidential Papers, Principal Series, Box 145, "Hearings Volume 4 May 1947–April 1948 (3)."

3. Diary, 27 January 1949, PDDE 10:449; Eisenhower to James Forrestal, 27 September 1948, PDDE 10:231; Eisenhower to Walter Winchell, 15 March 1948, PDDE 10:28; Eisenhower to James Forrestal 4 October 1948, PDDE 10:239; Eisenhower to Lewis Brown, 7 February 1949, PDDE 10:477.

4. Michael Wala, "An 'Education in Foreign Affairs for the Future President': The Council on Foreign Relations and Dwight D. Eisenhower," in *Reexamining the Eisenhower Presidency,* ed. Shirley Anne Warshaw (Westport, Conn.: Greenwood Press, 1993), 7 (this meeting was on 10 January 1949); diary 29 April 1950, PDDE 11:1092 (P.I. = Philippine Islands; N.E.I. = Netherlands East Indies).

5. Herken, *Winning Weapon,* 246; Russel D. Buhite and Wm. Christopher Hamel, "War for Peace: The Question of an American Preventive War against the Soviet Union, 1945–1955," *Diplomatic History* 14 (summer 1990): 375; press conference, 3 May 1948, Pre-Presidential Papers, Principal Series, Box 156, "Press Statements and Releases, 1947–1952 (4)." On the debate over preventive war, see the article by Buhite and Hamel, as well as Marc Trachtenberg, *History and Strategy* (Princeton: Princeton University Press, 1991), 103–6. In January 1949, Eisenhower went so far as to say that a "strong element" in the Politburo wanted cooperation with the West, although Stalin was not part of this element (speech to New York State Bar Association, 29 January 1949, *New York Times,* 30 January 1949, 46).

6. Diary, 27 January 1949, PDDE 10:449.

7. Herken, *Winning Weapon,* 246.

8. David Alan Rosenberg points to the specific convergence of strategic and economic concerns: "President Eisenhower was not happy with the crisis-oriented defense program and record peacetime defense budgets he had inherited from the Truman administration. He was convinced that budgeting to meet a projected 'year of maximum danger' would result in runaway expenditures and undermine the American economy" ("Origins of Overkill: Nuclear Weapons and American Strategy," in *The National Security: Its Theory and Practice, 1945–1960,* ed. Norman A. Graebner [New York: Oxford University Press, 1986], 142).

9. Address to New York Chamber of Commerce, 7 May 1948, *Vital Speeches of the Day* 14 (15 May 1948): 461; draft report for House Armed Services Committee, 3 January 1950, PDDE 11:900; Eisenhower to Swede Hazlett, 27 April 1949, PDDE 10:564 (see also Eisenhower's testimony to Senate Committee on Armed Services, 2 April 1948, Pre-presidential Papers, Principal Series, Box 145, "Hearings Volume 4 May 1947–April 1948 [3]"); testimony to the House Subcommittee on Defense Appropriations, 24 February 1950, summarized in PDDE 11:971n. 5; Eisenhower to Swede Hazlett, 12 September 1950, PDDE 11:1311); *New York Times,* 3 March 1950, 2; speech at Franklin and Marshall College, 2 March 1950, Pre-presidential Papers, Principal Series, Box 193, "Speeches, January 1950–December 1950 (2)."

10. Eisenhower to Swede Hazlett, 27 April 1949, PDDE 10:564; diary, 8 January 1949, PDDE 10:401, 402; testimony to the Senate Subcommittee on Military Appropriations, *New York Times,* 30 March 1950, 1; *New York Times,* 21 October 1949, 1; see also PDDE 10:793n. 2.

11. Herken, *Winning Weapon,* 244. See the expressions of uncertainty about the bomb's effects in PDDE 10:380, 448–49.

12. Eisenhower to Forrestal, 21 December 1948, PDDE 10:381; diary, 13 December 1948, PDDE 10:366.

13. Eisenhower to JCS 1844/37, cited in PDDE 10:517; Eisenhower to Louis Johnson, 3 May 1949, PDDE 10:568. The JCS used the public code phrase "air offensive" for an attack with atomic weapons; see the memo by Navy Chief of Staff Chester Nimitz, initialed by Eisenhower, in RG 165, Box 170, ABC File 471.6 Atom (17 August 1945), "Section 7," National Archives.

14. Eisenhower to Louis Johnson, 14 July 1949, PDDE 10:700–1, and 29 August 1949, PDDE 10:740 (see also Eisenhower to Stuart Symington, 29 August 1949, PDDE 738).

15. Eisenhower to Louis Johnson, 14 July 1949, PDDE 10:700–1; Eisenhower to Bernard Baruch, 10 October 1949, PDDE 10:773; Eisenhower to Swede Hazlett, 12 September 1950. PDDE 11:1311.

16. Diary 27 January 1949, PDDE 449; Eisenhower to James Forrestal, 21 December 1948, PDDE 381. Here Eisenhower was touting the advantage of a new naval carrier task force, which could also be used in an "emergency."

17. *New York Times,* 24 September 1949, 2; PDDE 10:800nn. 2, 3. On the public's nuclear fears, see Paul Boyer, *By the Bomb's Early Light: American Thought and Culture at the Dawn of the Atomic Age* (New York: Pantheon Books, 1985), esp. chaps. 23, 25.

18. Speech to Moles Dinner, 9 February 1950, *New York Times,* 10 February 1950, 9; speech to Scholastic Press Association, 11 March 1950. The *New York Times* reported this speech on 12 March 1950, under the title "Eisenhower Urges Brighter Outlook" (40).

19. Speech to Scholastic Press Association, 11 March 1950, *New York Times,* 12 March 1950, 40; Eisenhower to Regis Colasanti, 21 March 1950, PDDE 11:1019. These remarks reflect a powerful emotional response. Along with his insistent demands for "a brighter outlook," they would probably strike most psychologists as evidence that the fears being repressed were quite intense. And some might see his claim that "everyone seems to enjoy the terror," and his assurance that no one is going to drop a bomb and make the United States disappear, as curious examples of the return of the repressed. Although Eisenhower and his biographers have stressed the centrality of the Bible in his childhood home, there are virtually no references to biblical phraseology in the several thousand pages of PDDE. "The twinkling of any eye" is one of the very rare exceptions.

20. Eisenhower to Douglas Fairbanks, 3 May 1950, PDDE 11:1100; Eisenhower to Mary E.T. Bull, 27 February 1948, PDDE 10:17; Eisenhower to Thomas Hopper, 19 October 1948, PDDE 10:255 (see also Eisenhower to James Moore, 19 May 1948, PDDE 10:78; Eisenhower to Clifford Lee, 29 January 1949, PDDE 10:458; Eisenhower to Frank Page, 28 March 1950, PDDE 11:1037; Eisenhower to George Sokolsky, 23 May 1950, PDDE 11:1123). In 1940, in a rare early reference to the spiritual/material dichotomy, Eisenhower wrote to his son John that "when you begin to consider the question of man's origin, his mission and his destiny," man consisted of something more than just "chemicals and elements" (Holt and Leyerzapf, *Eisenhower,* 465).

21. Eisenhower to Richard Davies, 22 March 1948, PDDE 10:31; diary, 4 June 1949, PDDE 10:607.

22. Eisenhower to Louis Smith, 25 May 1948, PDDE 10:85. In this letter he was defending the propriety of teaching college students about communism, arguing implicitly that he was as concerned as the critics of Columbia about the dangers of communism; see also Eisenhower to Tooey Spaatz, 4 April 1950, PDDE 11:1062: the U.S. public needed a "true awakening to the facts of the world situation and to our own opportunities and responsibilities." Many years earlier, Eisenhower had advised his brother Milton to leave government service so that Milton could "publish what *you believe,* not what administration policy supports. . . . I would regard this as a tremendous advantage" (Eisenhower to Milton Eisenhower, 3 January 1939, in Holt and Leyerzapf, *Eisenhower,* 417).

23. Diary, 25 November 1949, PDDE 10:840; diary, 7 July 1949, PDDE 10:678; see also a similar conversation with Clare Booth Luce recorded in a diary entry of 27 September 1949, PDDE 10:755. For similar comments from other Republican notables, see Robert Griffith, "Dwight D. Eisenhower and the Corporate Commonwealth," *American Historical Review* 87 (February 1982): 99n. 26.

24. Eisenhower to Phillip Murray, 17 January 1949, PDDE 10:439; Eisenhower to Albert Volk, 21 June 1949, PDDE 10:650; Eisenhower to Lewis Brown, 18 January 1949, PDDE 10:440; Eisenhower to George Sokolsky, 20 January 1949, PDDE 10:445. Months earlier he had written that "the practice of democracy rests upon the retention of the greatest possible amount of authority in the community and . . . [the] state" rather than the federal government (Eisenhower to Frank Caffey, 25 September 1948, PDDE 10:230; see also Eisenhower to Paul Hawley, 2 June 1949, PDDE 10:605).

25. Diary, 14 January 1949, PDDE 10:431. Several months earlier he had already written of his concerns about federal aid to education: "One of my abiding convictions is that the more we permit the Federal Government to get into such matters, except on a basis of research, the more we are drifting toward an undesirable centralization of authority and power. That I am against" (to Roger Williams, 15 September 1948, PDDE 10:194). He did approve of Social Security, however, as posing a negligible risk of governmental control (Eisenhower to Ward Bannister, 22 September 1949, PDDE 10:751); see also Eisenhower to Rhoda Graves, 10 January 1949, PDDE 10:406.

26. Eisenhower to Albert Volk, 8 June 1949, PDDE 10:613.

27. Eisenhower to Eddie Rickenbacker, 23 December 1949, PDDE 11:872; Eisenhower to Amon Carter, 27 June 1949, PDDE 10:666 (see also Eisenhower to Leonard McCollum, 31 May 1950, PDDE 11:1145); Eisenhower to Felix Frankfurter, 18 October 1948, PDDE 10:250; Eisenhower to Thomas Watson, 22 August 1949, PDDE 10:733.

28. Eisenhower to Percy Bishop, 4 January 1950, PDDE 11:914; Eisenhower to Dr. Herbert Black, 20 December 1949, PDDE 11:857.

29. Eisenhower to J. Meyrick Colley, 22 December 1949, PDDE 11:864.

30. Eisenhower to John Wells, 18 January 1950, PDDE 11:934; Eisenhower to Albert Volk, 21 June 1949, PDDE 10:650; see also Eisenhower to Averrell Harriman, 12 December 1950, PDDE 11:1471: "It is only human nature to try to throw responsibility on others."

31. On the history of populist fears of government, see, among many other works, Bernard Bailyn, *The Ideological Origins of the American Revolution* (Cambridge, Mass.: Harvard University Press, 1967) and Michael Kazin, *The Populist Persuasion* (New York: Basic Books, 1995).

32. Eisenhower to Palmer Hoyt, 20 December 1949, PDDE 11:855.

33. Eisenhower to Thomas Jefferson Davis, 14 October 1949, PDDE 10:783; Eisenhower to Jock Whiteley, 17 October 1949, PDDE 10:790.

34. Eisenhower to Jock Whiteley, 17 October 1949, PDDE 10:790.

35. Brendon, *Ike,* 202; see, e.g., Craig Allen, *Eisenhower and the Mass Media* (Chapel Hill: University of North Carolina Press, 1993), 15: "His lesson on what he called a moderate 'middle way' was a pretext and springboard for his entry into the next presidential campaign."

36. Diary, 1 January 1950, PDDE 11:886.

37. See also diary, 27 September 1949, PDDE 10:758: "No one has condemned paternalism, yielding to pressure groups, raiding the federal treasury in favor of any class, etc., etc., more than I have."

38. Diary, 14 October 1949, PDDE 10:778; see also William Robinson to Helen Rogers Reid, 21 June 1948, William Robinson Papers, Box 6, "Diary–WER and DDE," Eisenhower Library, discussed in chapter 4, note 16, above. In a diary entry of 5 April 1950 (PDDE

11:1067), Eisenhower wrote that Republicans in Kansas "know of course that I believe we must have a Republican victory in '52." See also Greenstein, *The Hidden-Hand Presidency,* 50. Perhaps Eisenhower eschewed explicit attacks on the Democrats to avoid the appearance of being a presidential candidate. This was increasingly difficult to do as his speeches became obvious attacks on Truman's policies (see also PDDE 11:1090n. 3).

39. Diary, 27 September 1949, PDDE 10:756.

40. Griffith, "Dwight D. Eisenhower and the Corporate Commonwealth," 98.

41. Ibid., 97, 98.

42. Peter Berger and Thomas Luckmann, *The Social Construction of Reality* (Garden City, N.Y.: Anchor Books, 1967).

43. Pre-Presidential Papers, Principal Series, Box 195, "Endicott, NY, 14 July 1948."

44. Griffith, "Dwight D. Eisenhower and the Corporate Commonwealth," 94n.16; Eisenhower to Millicent McIntosh, 9 February 1949, PDDE 10:484; Eisenhower to Edwin Newsom, 9 March 1950, PDDE 11:1006; diary, 2 May 1950, PDDE 11:10969–70. Years later, when he reviewed his accomplishments at Columbia with his brother, Eisenhower prided himself on the financial improvements during his regime (Ann Whitman File, Ann Whitman Diary Series, Box 4, "ACW Diary, March 1955 [4]"); see also Eisenhower, *At Ease,* 343.

45. Eisenhower to Swede Hazlett, 24 February 1950, PDDE 11:990. Piers Brendon suggests that Eisenhower expected to get a rest at Columbia and be "little more than a figurehead" (*Ike,* 198–99).

46. Eisenhower to Frank Chambers, 12 July 1949, PDDE 10:696. He immediately went on to contradict himself and protest, rather too much, that he would never allow Columbia's financial woes "to dictate, in the slightest degree, my choice of friends and of social contacts." But he was admitting that those contacts, once made for whatever reason, tended to get involved with fundraising.

47. Eisenhower to Amon Carter, 27 June 1949, PDDE 10:667, 668.

48. Eisenhower to Richard Simon, 10 October 1949, PDDE 10:776.

49. Eisenhower to Alumni and Friends, 24 February 1949, PDDE 10:507; see also Eisenhower to Alumni and Friends, 20 January 1949, PDDE 10:444.

50. Eisenhower to Alumni and Friends, 3 February 1949, PDDE 10:463, 464; *New York Times,* 29 November 1949, 22.

51. Neal, *The Eisenhowers,* 249–50.

52. Eisenhower to Swede Hazlett, 19 July 1947, PDDE 11:1837; Lyon, *Eisenhower,* 396. Lyon seems to credit Eisenhower's own explanation, which is curious, since he scoffs at Eisenhower's endless insistence that he would become president only if he saw it as his clear duty.

53. Eisenhower to James Forrestal, 7 May 1948 and 11 May 1948, PDDE 10:61, 62; Eisenhower to Drew Middleton, 21 June 1948, PDDE 10:120; see also diary 14 October 1949, PDDE 10:778. Harry Truman said that it was "of importance to the government" that Eisenhower continue making his speeches (PDDE 10:63n. 8).

54. Eisenhower to Richard Jones, 2 June 1949, PDDE 10:601; Eisenhower to Marion Huff, 4 February 1948, PDDE 9:2227.

55. Eisenhower to George Van Horn Moseley, 10 May 1950, PDDE 11:1105; Eisenhower to John Danaher, 4 March 1949, PDDE 10:529. See also diary, 1 January 1950, PDDE 11:883; Eisenhower to Kaufman Keller, 11 January 1949, PDDE 10:407; Eisenhower to Sen. Arthur Capper, 27 November 1948, PDDE 10:328; Eisenhower to Drew Middleton, 21 June 1948, PDDE 10:121; Eisenhower to William Standley, 21 October 1948, PDDE 10:259.

56. Diary 27 November 1949, PDDE 10:755–56; Eisenhower to Walter Bedell Smith, 18 September 1947, PDDE 9:1933; diary, 3 November 1949, PDDE 10:809. See the comments of Peter Lyon, *Eisenhower,* 402.

57. See, e.g., Col. Ralph Jones to Eisenhower, 18 September 1949, PDDE 10:757n. 4: "You are now the sole remaining hope of the world."

58. Diary, 1 January 1950, PDDE 11:883; Eisenhower to Nicholas Murray Butler, 26 June 1947, PDDE 9:1784.

59. Eisenhower to Bernard Baruch, 8 June 1949, PDDE 10:617. For similar self-characterizations of his speaking efforts, see e.g., PDDE 10:733, 758, 779, 11:1104.

60. Eisenhower to Arthur Page, 10 June 1949, PDDE 10:621.

61. Eisenhower to Bruce Barton, 2 September 1950, PDDE 11:1293.

62. Eisenhower to Walter Bedell Smith, 11 April 1949, PDDE 10:556–57; diary 27 April 1950, PDDE 11:1089; Eisenhower to Frank Page, 4 January 1950, PDDE 11:908; Eisenhower to Milton Eisenhower, 19 December 1949, PDDE 11:851; see also chap. 9nn. 19, 20, below. Eisenhower avoided preparing speeches by doing most of them extemporaneously. He repeated the same themes so often that he soon had no need to prepare at all.

63. Eisenhower to Swede Hazlett, 19 July 1947, PDDE 9:1837. For more detail on Eisenhower's tenure as president of Columbia, see Travis Beal Jacobs, *Eisenhower at Columbia* (New Brunswick, N.J.: Transaction Publishers, 2001). Unfortunately, this book was published after the present chapter was completed.

# CHAPTER 9

1. Eisenhower, *Crusade in Europe*, 1–4; Medhurst, *Dwight D. Eisenhower*, 13. Eisenhower's unpublished draft for an introduction to the book began by distinguishing between "the private and the general": the former endured only intermittent tension, while the latter's "pressure and strain" was constant (unpublished draft, Pre-Presidential Papers, Miscellaneous Series, Box 11, "DDE Memoir Introduction").

2. Medhurst (*Dwight D. Eisenhower*, 14) stresses the book's tendency to understate Eisenhower's own achievement ("the story, after all, was about the team, not the individual"), while still depicting him as a decisive leader: "The image created was one of firm resolve tempered by deep respect for the opposing view." This suggested that there was no contradiction between being a team player and being a responsible individual, fully in charge; a virtuous leader would be both.

3. Barton Bernstein points out that Eisenhower's claim to have dissented from the decision to use the atomic bomb first appeared in *Crusade in Europe* (443). Bernstein suggests that Eisenhower invented this story to enhance "his image as a moral military man" and to salve his conscience at a time when he was actively involved in planning to use nuclear weapons in a future war ("Ike and Hiroshima," 386).

4. *New York Times*, 24 November 1948, 21. Most of the unpublished introduction was devoted to explaining the "dual advantages" of cheerfulness and optimism for a military commander: repressing his own anxiety and helping others to do the same. Eisenhower said in this introduction that he wrote the book because he hoped it would have the same effect upon the reading public. He was drawing a clear parallel between his wartime troops and his postwar readers.

5. Drew Middleton wrote in his review that the book's analyses of the war were "interesting but not particularly penetrating. What is important is Eisenhower's reasoned judgments on communism and democracy" (*New York Times*, 21 November 1948, sec. 7, p.1).

6. Eisenhower, *Crusade*, 474.

7. Ibid., 451–52, 475.

8. Eisenhower took time off from writing the book to testify to a Senate committee that the Soviet Union wanted to destroy democracy and would make no effort to get along with the United States (Pre-Presidential Papers, Principal Series, Box 145, "Hearings, vol. 4, May 1947–April 1948 [3]").

9. Eisenhower, *Crusade,* 476. The "world [was] a keg of dynamite—HST [Truman] shouldn't start it," Marshall said, fearing that a bellicose speech by the president would "pull the trigger" (Daniel Yergin, *Shattered Peace: The Origins of the Cold War and the National Security State* [Boston: Houghton Mifflin, Sentry Editions, 1978], 351, 353).

10. Eisenhower, *Crusade,* 478.

11. "An Open Letter to Parents," *Reader's Digest,* February 1949, 11.

12. "An Open Letter to America's Students," *Reader's Digest,* October 1948, 4.

13. Interview with Milton Eisenhower for B. Kornitzer's biography of the Eisenhower brothers, 3/17/55, Ann Whitman File, Ann C. Whitman Diary, Box 4, "ACW Diary March 1955 (4)." The text adds a parenthetical note, presumably recording President Eisenhower's own comment: "Given at a time when the President thought he had forever removed himself from political consideration." Perhaps this was intended to emphasize that its contents were wholly sincere, having no political motivation. The whole list of "finest speeches" also includes the Guildhall speech of June 1945, the public letter to Leonard Finder (January 1948) refusing presidential candidacy, and three from his presidency: the Inaugural, the Chance for Peace, and Atoms for Peace. A comment following the list (again, presumably the president's) says that the dominant theme in all these speeches was the importance of world peace. It adds: ("Passages to illustrate can be found.") In fact, though, the lengthy speech to the ABA contained no reference at all to world peace.

14. Address to American Bar Association, 5 September 1949, *Vital Speeches of the Day* 15 (15 September 1949): 708–11.

15. A May 1948 headline, over a report on Eisenhower's talk given to boost the Columbia Business School, was telling: "Eisenhower Ready to Aid U.S. System; His First Talk as Civilian" (*New York Times,* 5 May 1948, 37).

16. Peter Lyon calls this brief reference "the ceremonial frown at the Right" (*Eisenhower,* 431).

17. See the same theme in, e.g., a speech for the New York Central Railroad, 15 September 1948, *New York Times,* 16 September 1948, 32. See the brief discussion in Griffith, "Dwight D. Eisenhower and the Corporate Commonwealth," 91. Quotations in this and the following two paragraphs are from the address to the American Bar Association.

18. Richard E. Crable, "Dwight David Eisenhower," in *American Orators of the Twentieth Century,* ed. Bernard K. Duffy and Halford R. Ryan (Westport, Conn.: Greenwood Press, 1987), 117.

19. Travis Beal Jacobs, "Eisenhower, the American Assembly, and the 1952 Elections," in *Reexamining the Eisenhower Presidency,* ed. Shirley Anne Warshaw (Westport, Conn.: Greenwood Press, 1993), 19. Jacobs adds, "and he did so much more than any president of the United States since Woodrow Wilson, also a university president." Perhaps Herbert Hoover, though never a university president, should be included in this company; on Hoover as a model for Eisenhower, see Griffith, "Dwight D. Eisenhower and the Corporate Commonwealth," 96.

20. *New York Times,* 23 October 1949, 62; Inaugural Address, Columbia University, 12 October 1948, *Vital Speeches of the Day* 15 (1 November 1948): 35. Martin Medhurst (*Eisenhower,* 24) finds the Columbia inaugural speech especially important for revealing "the initial indicators of a developing rhetorical stance."

21. Inaugural Address, Columbia University, 35–38. See also the same point in an earlier speech (Pre-Presidential Papers, Principal Series, Box 195, "Endicott, NY 7/14/48"). His

message supporting the National Committee for Free Europe, on the tenth anniversary of the Nazi invasion of Poland, merged foreign and domestic threats: "Only when we know that the assurance of individual freedoms has been permanently established here and in the other countries which desire it will we have achieved the aims for which we fought and won a great war" (Eisenhower to Joseph Grew, 18 August 1949, PDDE 10:729).

22. Eisenhower to Rep. Ralph Gwinn, 7 June 1949, 10:609.

23. Inaugural Address, Columbia University, 12 October 1948, 35–38.

24. Ryan, "A Rhetorical Analysis," 55. Ryan points out (84) that Eisenhower never gave logical arguments to support his claim that "statism" was a serious impending danger; he merely asserted the danger.

25. Here Eisenhower was quoting the conservative British historian Macauley, who was speaking specifically about the United States.

26. Eisenhower argued to another university audience that whenever government disbursed money it was morally obliged to impose "some form of supervision." Precisely for that reason, it was dangerous to take any government funds (address at University of the State of New York, Albany, 15 October 1948, New York Times, 16 October 1948, 17).

27. Pre-Presidential Papers, Principal Series, Box 195, "IBM, 6/26/48." A few weeks earlier, Eisenhower told a press conference, "I am one of the most deeply religious men I know. That doesn't mean that I necessarily adhere to any particular sect or organization. I do not believe that Democracy can exist without religion and I do believe in Democracy" (Press Conference, 3 May 1948, Pre-Presidential Papers, Principal Series, Box 156, "Press Statements and Releases, 1947–1952 [4]"). Later he told a Jewish Theological Seminary audience that the army fought to defend doctrines rooted in the biblical belief that "the soul is not of this world" (New York Times, 28 September 1948, 49). This particular audience may have been rather surprised to hear the Hebrew Bible interpreted in such an unorthodox manner.

28. Address at Columbia University, 23 March 1950, in Dwight D. Eisenhower, Peace With Justice: Selected Addresses of Dwight D. Eisenhower (New York: Columbia University Press, 1961), 15.

29. Eisenhower, Peace With Justice, 15.

30. Speech to Columbia College Forum on Democracy, 12 February 1949, Vital Speeches of the Day 15 (15 March 1949): 335.

31. New York Times, 1 December 1949, 23. The next day the Columbia student newspaper commented: "We are willing to bet beer and hot dogs weren't on the menu at the Waldorf-Astoria [where Eisenhower spoke] last night" (Lester David and Irene David, Ike and Mamie [New York: Putnam, 1981], 172–73).

32. Speech to Houston Chamber of Commerce, 7 December 1949, Pre-Presidential Papers, Principal Series, Box 193, "Speeches, July 1949–December 1949 (1)"; speech to Galveston Chamber of Commerce, 8 December 1949, Pre-Presidential Papers, Principal Series, Box 193, "Speeches July 1949–December 1949 (1)"; speech at Columbia, 28 September 1949, cited in Ryan, "A Rhetorical Analysis," 58. See also Cook, Declassified Eisenhower, 79. The following year Eisenhower told a Pittsburgh audience that "regimented men . . . never knowing the turmoil of freedom or its hazards can never feel the stimulus of its rewards" (speech at Pittsburgh, 19 October 1950, Pre-Presidential Papers, Principal Series, Box 193, "Speeches January 1950–December 1950 [1]").

33. Cook, Declassified Eisenhower, 79.

34. Eisenhower to Milton Eisenhower, 19 December 1949, PDDE 11:851.

35. Cook, Declassified Eisenhower, 80; Pre-Presidential Papers, Principal Series, Box 195, "Columbia Summer Session, 7/6/48"; Eisenhower to DeWitt Wallace, 8 June 1949, PDDE 10:614. The Reader's Digest series never materialized.

36. Commencement Exercises of Columbia University, 1 June 1949, *Vital Speeches of the Day* 15 (15 June 1949): 518, 519

37. Speech to *New York Herald Tribune* Forum, 25 October 1949, *Vital Speeches of the Day* 16 (15 November 1949): 66, 67.

38. Speech to *New York Herald Tribune* Forum, 67, 66; see also Eisenhower to Amon Carter, 27 June 1949, PDDE 10:666. For an interpretation of "the middle way" quite different from that presented here, see Griffith, "Dwight D. Eisenhower and the Corporate Commonwealth," 91–92.

39. Address at Riverdale Country School, 16 October 1948, Pre-Presidential Papers, Principal Series, Box 193, "Speeches, August 1948 - June 1949 (2)"; "An Open Letter to America's Students," *Reader's Digest,* October 1948, 3.

40. "An Open Letter to America's Students," *Reader's Digest,* October 1948, 2–4.

41. Eisenhower to Leonard McCollum et al., 12 September 1950, PDDE 11:1306, 1309; see also Eisenhower to George Shellenberger, 6 July 1950, PDDE 11:1202–4. In the memoir *At Ease* (350), Eisenhower wrote of the American Assembly: "Working toward this idea became an absorbing pursuit for me through most of 1949. . . . Much of the time I think its beginnings were my principal success as University President." In the 1955 interview, when his brother Milton asked about his achievements at Columbia, he mentioned the American Assembly first (Ann Whitman File, Ann C. Whitman Diary Series, Box 4, "ACW Diary, March 1955 [4]"). The idea of the assembly may have originated in a suggestion from Bernard Baruch for a commission to study where to draw "the dividing line between government and personal responsibility" (Baruch to Eisenhower, 22 June 1949, PDDE 10:773n. 2).

42. Travis Beal Jacobs suggests that by the fall of 1949, Eisenhower realized that the faculty was largely uninterested in using the conventional university apparatus to support his goals and directions. So he undertook pet projects such as the American Assembly and the Institute of War and Peace to redirect the university's resources regardless of faculty desires. See Jacobs, "Eisenhower," 19.

## CHAPTER 10

1. Eisenhower to Aksel Nielsen, 26 May 1949, PDDE 10:595; Eisenhower to Adm. William Furlong, 9 March 1950, PDDE 11:1009.

2. Wala, "An 'Education in Foreign Affairs,'" 8.

3. Eisenhower to Joseph Davies, 7 June 1949, PDDE 10:611; Eisenhower to Amon Carter, 27 June 1949, PDDE 10:668.

4. Eisenhower to Edwin Clark, 5 April 1950, PDDE 11:1065.

5. Eisenhower to Edwin Clark, 18 January 1950, PDDE 11:932 (see also PDDE 11:933n. 1; Eisenhower's disclaimer to Clark, "I could not remember whether your concept of teaching or researching military history in Columbia was necessarily tied up with the project of bringing here the Military Institute," seems disingenuous); Eisenhower to Ed Bermingham, 10 February 1950, PDDE 11:962, and 10 March 1950, PDDE 11:1010. See also PDDE 11:1011nn. 1, 2; 10:692n. 5; 11:950n. 2.

6. Eisenhower to Edward Bermingham, 22 May 1950, PDDE 11:1117–18.

7. Eisenhower to George Kennan, 3 November 1950, PDDE 11:1403.

8. Eisenhower to Godfrey Cabot, 3 November 1950, PDDE 11:1401. See also, e.g., Eisenhower to Wallace Speers, 3 June 1950, PDDE 11:1153.

9. In February 1950, Eisenhower told the Moles Dinner that Columbia wanted to do nuclear research (*New York Times,* 10 February 1950, 9).

10. Eisenhower to Freddie de Guingand, 23 March 1950, PDDE 11:1031; Eisenhower, *At Ease,* 357. See also diary, 22 March 1950, PDDE 11:1023.

11. Address at Columbia University, 23 March 1950, in Eisenhower, *Peace With Justice,* 25.

12. Ibid., 22, 3; see also the extended praise of Britain at the beginning of the speech, 3–5.

13. Address at Columbia University, *Peace With Justice,* 6, 19; Eisenhower to Gretchen Waldo, 4 April 1950, PDDE 11:1064 (see also the same theme in a speech to the American Arbitration Association, 16 May 1950, *New York Times,* 17 May 1950, 33).

14. Address at Columbia University, *Peace With Justice,* 7, 13, 17, 23. Although Eisenhower said "there is no need to remake the world in the likeness of the United States" (17), the rest of his text seems to imply the opposite. The Silver address was written at the same time that drafts of NSC-68 were circulating among top government officials. (Dean Acheson and Paul Nitze presented it to Secretary of Defense Louis Johnson on the very day the address was delivered [Acheson, *Present at the Creation,* 373].) The two documents embody generally similar, though hardly identical, premises and conclusions. I have found no evidence that Eisenhower took any direct interest at the time in NSC-68. Andrew Goodpaster, one of Eisenhower's closest presidential aides, later said: "I doubt that he would have identified it by number, but he was aware of this study" (Goodpaster Oral History, OH 477).

15. Address at Columbia University, *Peace With Justice,* 8, 18; *New York Times,* 24 March 1950, 1: "Eisenhower Sees Nation Disarming Past Safety Limit."

16. *New York Times,* 30 March 1950, 1, 2; see also the discussion of this testimony in chapter 8, p. 165, above. See an aide's memorandum warning him that he might be the victim of a "squeeze plan" designed to pin responsibility for the budget upon him, and advising a rather hawkish anti-Soviet stance, in Pre-Presidential Papers, Principal Series, Box 156, "Press Statements and Releases, 1947–1952 (4)." In his testimony Eisenhower avoided taking responsibility and moderated the anti-Soviet language.

17. Press conference, 27 June 1947, Treuenfels, *Eisenhower Speaks,* 238–42. Eisenhower echoed these sentiments at another press conference, around the time he took over at Columbia: "The average soldier thought he was fighting to save his type of nation . . . It is this that I am trying to continue to do, but in a different field. . . . The strength of the United States is the greatest source for peace in the world" (Pre-Presidential Papers, Principal Series, Box 156, "Press Statements and Releases, 1947–1952 [4]").

18. Address at Riverdale Country School, 16 October 1948, Pre-Presidential Papers, Principal Series, Box 193, "Speeches, August 1948–June 1949 (2)." In this speech at an elite prep school he began by telling the audience that he had been "assigned the title, the subject, Education for Peace." Perhaps he accepted the assignment because he hoped to persuade wealthy parents in the audience to send their children to, and generously support, Columbia. In his inaugural address at Columbia, just four days earlier, he had not mentioned peace at all. Other speeches in the spring and summer of 1948 had purely perfunctory and tangential references to peace as a goal; see also, e.g., Pre-Presidential Papers, Principal Series, Box 195, "Endicott, NY, July 14, 1948" and Speech to Chamber of Commerce, State of New York, 7 May 1948, *Vital Speeches of the Day* 14 (15 May 1948): 463.

19. Message for North American Newspaper Alliance, 11 June 1948, Pre-Presidential Papers, Principal Series, Box 149, "Messages, December 1947–November 1948"; Ryan, "A Rhetorical Analysis," 95.

20. Speech at Franklin and Marshall College, 2 March 1950, Pre-Presidential Papers, Principal Series, Box 193, "Speeches, January 1950–December 1950 (2)." Michael J. Hogan has

shown that many U.S. leaders in the late 1940s worried that excessive military expenditures would turn the U.S. into a "garrison state." For this reason they resisted the Truman administration's rapid promotion of internationalism and the "national security state" (*A Cross of Iron: Harry S. Truman and the Origins of the National Security State, 1945–1954* [New York: Cambridge University Press, 1998]). As president, Eisenhower would often warn his advisors about the "garrison state." Surprisingly, he used the term rarely during his years at Columbia. Perhaps, as a committed internationalist, he hesitated to use a term that had become a code word for limited international involvements. His election signaled that this battle was over, so as president he felt free to use the term, indicating that he had always shared some of the concerns of his political opponents.

21. Pre-Presidential Papers, Principal Series, Box 195 "Endicott, NY- 7/14/48." Earlier in the same speech he asserted that his main ambition was to perpetuate the system of "freedoms of the American Heritage," while his greatest fear was "forces in the world endangering the American Way of Life."

22. Speech to Associated Press, 24 April 1950, *Vital Speeches of the Day* 16 (1 June 1950): 485.

23. Eisenhower to Averell Harriman, 26 June 1950, PDDE 11:1173.

24. Diary, 30 June 1950, PDDE 11:1190. In August Eisenhower would tell the author of a paper urging the use of atomic bombs in Korea that "G-2 of the Department of the Army would be interested in your views" (PDDE 11:1279); this may have been sincere, or simply a polite way of avoiding a specific response.

25. Diary, 30 June 1950, PDDE 11:1190 (see also PDDE 12:150); Eisenhower to Kenneth Strong, 29 June 1950, PDDE 11:1184–85 (see also Eisenhower to H.E. Schlichter, 14 August 1950, PDDE 11:1274); Eisenhower to Alfred Gruenther, 16 September 1950, PDDE 11:1320. By October he would tell a former aide that he was no longer so confident the Russians would not start a war (Eisenhower to Craig Campbell, 10 October 1950, PDDE 11:1371).

26. Eisenhower to Clare Booth Luce, 29 June 1950, PDDE 11:1186; diary, 6 July 1950, PDDE 11:1212; Eisenhower to Bernard Baruch, 31 July 1950, PDDE 11:1243; Eisenhower to Alfred Gruenther, 30 November 1950, PDDE 11:1450; diary, 5 December 1950, PDDE 11:1459.

27. Eisenhower to Swede Hazlett, 12 September 1950, PDDE 11:1311–12; Eisenhower to Milton Reckord, 15 December 1950, PDDE 11:1484.

28. Eisenhower to James Black, 14 August 1950, PDDE 11:1276 (see also Eisenhower to William Burnham, 16 September 1950, PDDE 11:1322); Eisenhower to Donald Kennedy, 1 August 1950, PDDE 11:1253; Eisenhower to Leonard McCollum et al., 12 September 1950, PDDE 11:1306; Eisenhower to Mirdza Silis-Ozolins, 27 September 1950, PDDE 11:1345.

29. Eisenhower to Louis Johnson, 31 July 1950, PDDE 11:1240; diary, 6 November 1950, PDDE 11:1409; Eisenhower to H.E. Schlichter, 14 August 1950, PDDE 11:1275, where Eisenhower also added an uncharacteristic comment that the Soviet Union, like the empire of Genghis Khan, might fall apart internally.

30. Eisenhower to Lucile Sleinkofer, 5 September 1950, PDDE 11:1294.

31. Eisenhower to Swede Hazlett, 12 September 1950, PDDE 11:1312; Eisenhower to Harry Bullis, 17 September 1950, PDDE 11:1328; Eisenhower to Arthur Compton, 9 October 1950, PDDE 11:1365; Eisenhower to Leonard McCollum et al., 12 September 1950, PDDE 11:1309.

32. Eisenhower to William Jeffers, 25 September 1950, PDDE 11:1336; diary 6 July 1950, PDDE 11:1212; Eisenhower to Forrest Sherman et al., 30 December 1950, PDDE 11:1510.

33. Eisenhower to Ferdinand Eberstadt, 31 December 1950, PDDE 11:1514 and 21 August 1950, PDDE 11:1282; diary 6 November 1950, PDDE 11:1409.

34. Speech to Columbia Summer Session, 10 July 1950, *New York Times,* 11 July 1950, 19; speech to Boy Scouts, 4 July 1950, Pre-Presidential Papers, Principal Series, Box 193, "Speeches January 1950–December 1950 (1)."

35. Speech at Pittsburgh, 19 October 1950, Pre-Presidential Papers, Principal Series, Box 193, "Speeches January 1950–December 1950 (1)."

36. Martin J. Medhurst, "Eisenhower and the Crusade for Freedom: The Rhetorical Origins of a Cold War Campaign," *Presidential Studies Quarterly* 27 (fall 1997): 654, 659.

37. "Crusade for Freedom" speech, Denver, 4 September 1950, *Vital Speeches of the Day* 26 (1 October 1950): 747.

## CHAPTER 11

1. Eisenhower to Swede Hazlett, 19 July 1947, PDDE 9:1837.

2. Perhaps this reflected a personal scale of values. Perhaps it was harder to find evidence of direct threats to U.S. democracy (though the purported "evidence" of an immediate threat to the capitalist system rather strains credulity, so someone thinking along such lines might easily have "discovered" evidence of an immediate threat to democracy). Most likely, this simply reflected Eisenhower's own experience. Having served in Panama and the Philippines, he had seen capitalism functioning full tilt in the absence of democracy, so he could hardly argue that capitalism required democracy. He had never seen democracy outside of a capitalist system, so he assumed that democracy required capitalism.

3. His leadership style also reflected the military paradigm. Biographers always note that university faculty and administrators had to get past a pair of military aides-de-camp in order to see the general, and were not often successful.

4. *New York Times,* 4 September 1949, 13.

5. James T. Kloppenberg, "The Virtues of Liberalism," *Journal of American History* 74 (June 1987): esp. 23; Tuveson, *Redeemer Nation.*

6. Speech to *New York Herald Tribune* Forum, 25 October 1949, *Vital Speeches of the Day* 26 (15 November 1949): 67, 66. See also Eisenhower to Amon Carter, 27 June 1949, PDDE 10:666.

7. Geertz, *Interpretation of Cultures,* 218.

8. Message to New York Convention of the Army and Navy Union, 22 July 1948, *New York Times,* 23 July 1948, 8

9. Richard Hofstadter, *The Paranoid Style in American Politics and Other Essays* (New York: Vintage Books, 1967).

10. Ibid., xi, xii, 29–32, 36, 39.

## CHAPTER 12

1. For an insightful analysis of the background and context of this decision, see Trachtenberg, *History and Strategy,* 107–24.

2. Cook, *Declassified Eisenhower,* 88, 116; see also PDDE 12:101.

3. The official letter of appointment from President Truman, dated 19 December 1950, is in *FRUS, 1950,* 3:604.

4. Acheson, *Present at the Creation,* 493, 494. See Thomas M. Sisk, "Forging the Weapon: Eisenhower as NATO's Supreme Allied Commander, Europe, 1950–52," in *Eisenhower: A Centenary Assessment,* ed. Stephen E. Ambrose and Gunter Bischof (Baton Rouge: Louisiana State University Press, 1995), 65–71, and the literature cited there. Sisk's article is the best comprehensive overview of Eisenhower's sixteen months as SACEUR.

5. Brendon, *Ike,* 203–6. Peter Lyon (*Eisenhower,* 444) also suggests that Eisenhower's move helped him by preventing his own political bandwagon from peaking too soon. Joyce and Gabriel Kolko (*The Limits of Power* [New York: Harper & Row, 1972], 675) have suggested that Truman, trusting Eisenhower to continue his "Europe-first" foreign policy, sent him to Europe precisely to boost Eisenhower's presidential chances and head off the Taft-MacArthur "Asia-first" forces.

6. Years later, Eisenhower wrote that in January 1951 he considered a formal repudiation of all presidential ambition. He rejected this option when Sen. Robert Taft, the other Republican contender, refused to endorse the Truman administration's NATO plans (*At Ease,* 370–72).

7. In fact he was probably distressed by the new job and took it reluctantly; see the incident recounted in Lyon, *Eisenhower,* 440, in which Eisenhower admitted to Henry Wriston, "No, I'm not happy."

8. Eisenhower to Cliff Roberts, 4 January 1951, PDDE 12:11 (see also diary, 5 March 1951, PDDE 12:91); Eisenhower to Edward Bermingham, 8 February 1951, PDDE 12:38. Many historians have pointed out that most conservative Republicans in 1951 were unilateralist, but not isolationist. Yet Eisenhower, like most others who styled themselves international-ist, used the term *isolationist* to denote those who opposed large U.S. troop contingents abroad. The term is used here in that sense.

9. Eisenhower to Edward Bermingham, 28 February 1951, PDDE 12:75–77.

10. Wala, "'Education in Foreign Affairs,'" 6–7. See also chap. 8, note 4, above.

11. Notes on a Meeting at the White House, 31 January 1951, *FRUS,* 1951, 3:450–457.

12. Leslie S. Stevens, "A National Strategy for the Soviet Union," 25 January 1951, Pre-Presidential Papers, Principal Series, Box 55, "Harriman, W. Averell (4)"; Eisenhower to Leslie Stevens, 22 February 1951, PDDE 12:61.

13. Stevens, "A National Strategy for the Soviet Union"; Eisenhower to Earl Schaefer, 22 January 1952, PDDE 13:905. See also Eisenhower to Thomas Campbell, 1 September 1951, PDDE 12:510: "Sometimes it would almost appear that they deliberately seek open conflict."

14. Eisenhower to Gruenther, 23 March 1951, PDDE 12:150; Wala, "'Education in Foreign Affairs,'" 10; Stevens, "A National Strategy for the Soviet Union"; Eisenhower to Paul Hoffman, 28 August 1951, PDDE 12:500. On the NATO doctrine, see Strategic Concept for the Defense of the North Atlantic Area, *FRUS, 1949,* 4:355. The final draft of the letter to Truman removed the explicit reference to Russia, but it clearly implied that without the U.S. atomic threat, Russia would already have initiated a war (Cook, *Declassified Eisenhower,* 89), though Eisenhower's notes to the Stevens paper cast strong doubt on this claim.

15. Eisenhower to Joseph Collins, 28 February 1951, PDDE 12:80, 81; diary, 14 June 1951, PDDE 12:354; diary, 15 October 1951, PDDE 12:647.

16. Eisenhower to Sterling Morton, 28 July 1951, PDDE 12:445; Eisenhower to Lucius Clay, 10 April 1952, PDDE 13:1173 (see also Eisenhower to Martin Clement, 9 January 1952, PDDE 13:865); Eisenhower to Edgar Eisenhower, 6 December 1951, PDDE 12:756, 757 (see also Eisenhower to Julius Schaefer, 27 December 1951, PDDE 12:820). In his diary, Eisenhower worried about the Asian dominos falling, from Indochina to Indonesia to India, though he already acknowledged that no military victory was possible in Indochina (diary, 17 March 1951, PDDE 12:138).

17. Eisenhower to DeWitt Wallace, 21 July 1951, PDDE 12:430; Eisenhower to George Sloan, 20 March 1952, PDDE 13:1101, 1102; Eisenhower to George Whitney, 4 September 1951, PDDE 12:518; Eisenhower to Thomas Campbell, 1 September 1951, PDDE 12:510. A few weeks later, when Whitney replied that controls might be acceptable in a national emergency, Eisenhower responded gratefully that he now had "a basis for developing a sort of doctrine" (22 September 1951, PDDE 12:561). See his comments in the diary entry for 22 January 1952, PDDE 13:897.

18. Diary, 22 January 1952, PDDE 13:896–99. Eisenhower made a similar point a year earlier in his comments on Leslie Stevens's paper. When Stevens wrote that "for many, many years we shall be confronted with much the same sort of dangerous, uneasy world in which we now live," Eisenhower wrote: "The very foundation of logical policy today" (Stevens, "A National Strategy for the Soviet Union").

19. Eisenhower to Milton Eisenhower, 30 May 1951, PDDE 12:304; Cook, *Declassified Eisenhower*, 115, quoting Eisenhower to Reed, 20 December 1951.

20. Eisenhower to Robert Kleberg, 18 December 1951, PDDE 12:794; Eisenhower to Robert Lovett, 25 September 1951, PDDE 12:567, 568; Pre-Presidential Papers, Principal Series, Box 196 "Staff Talk - 6/14/51"; Eisenhower to Edgar Eisenhower, 30 January 1952, PDDE 13:935.

21. Cook, *Declassified Eisenhower*, 87–89; Wala, "'Education in Foreign Affairs,'" 9–10; Eisenhower to George Sloan, 20 March 1952, PDDE 13:1099; see also Eisenhower to Lucius Clay, 2 March 1952, PDDE 12:86.

22. Eisenhower to George Whitney, 26 March 1952, PDDE 13:1125; Eisenhower to Earl Eisenhower, 5 October 1951, PDDE 12:619; Eisenhower to Robert McConnell, 29 June 1951, PDDE 12:391; Eisenhower to Fred Gurley, 22 September 1951, PDDE 12:558; Eisenhower to Charles E. Wilson, 20 October 1951, PDDE 12:659.

23. Diary, 8 October 1951, PDDE 12:651; Eisenhower to Truman, 24 February 1951, PDDE 12:68; diary, 18 October 1951, PDDE 12:650.

24. Eisenhower to Martin Clement, 21 July 1951, PDDE 12:431 (see also Eisenhower to Martin Clement, 4 December 1951, PDDE 13:1754); Eisenhower to Henry Cabot Lodge, 20 May 1952, PDDE 13:1233. Eisenhower did agree, on the advice of Robinson and Bermingham, to stop praising "capitalism" and speak instead about "free enterprise" or "the customer economy" (Eisenhower to William Robinson, 15 March 1951, PDDE 12:131; Cook, *Declassified Eisenhower*, 117–18; Lyon, *Eisenhower*, 420).

25. Eisenhower to George Whitney, 4 September 1951, PDDE 12:518; Eisenhower to Earl Schaefer, 3 December 1951, PDDE 12:751; diary, 9 May 1951, PDDE 12:329; Eisenhower to Roy Cullen, 26 June 1951, PDDE 12:387; Eisenhower to George Whitney, 14 June 1951, PDDE 12:352; Eisenhower to Kenyon Joyce, 15 March 1952, PDDE 13:1072.

26. Eisenhower to Douglas Southall Freeman, 20 September 1951, PDDE 12:554; Eisenhower to Lucius Clay 30 May 1951, PDDE 12:307; Eisenhower to Milton Eisenhower, 23 February 1952, PDDE 13:1011; Eisenhower to Earl Schaefer, 22 January 1952, PDDE 13:905; Eisenhower to Joseph Collins, 28 February 1951, PDDE 12:81; Eisenhower to George Whitney, 26 March 1952, PDDE 13:1125–26.

27. Eisenhower to Elizabeth Rankin, 11 December 1951, PDDE 12:773; Eisenhower to Gabriel Stilian, 23 August 1951, PDDE 12:488–89. See also Eisenhower to Lee duBridge, 28 December 1951, PDDE 12:824, where Eisenhower pronounced himself glad that scientists were helping to "preserve the peace."

28. Eisenhower to Paul Hoffman, 4 October 1951, PDDE 12:611; Eisenhower to John Cowles, 3 October 1951, PDDE 12:603; see also 604n. 6.

29. Eisenhower to George Sloan, 20 March 1952, PDDE 13:1103; Eisenhower to George Whitney, 26 March 1952, PDDE 13:1125–26.

30. Eisenhower to Milton Eisenhower, 20 September 1951, PDDE 12:555; Eisenhower to Swede Hazlett, 21 June 1951, PDDE 12:369; diary, 9 April 1951, PDDE 12:200; Eisenhower to Harry Butcher, 7 May 1951, PDDE 12:271.

31. Eisenhower to Martin Clement, 9 January 1952, PDDE 13:867; Eisenhower to Drew Pearson, 27 March 1952, PDDE 13:1134. This letter is a particularly good example of quasi-public discourse (private letters meant to send a public message). It was written to a syndicated columnist, thus obviously intended for political effect. And the editors of PDDE note (13:1135n. 1) that it was drafted by an Eisenhower aide, Gen. Charles Lanham, so it contained only typical stock themes of Eisenhower's discourse. By this time the fundamentals of Eisenhower's quasi-public letters were so well fixed that his aide could state the argument for him. But the idea that the Soviet satellites were part of the "free world" was a standard theme only in the public, not in the private, discourse. The "of course" in this quotation may have been a nod to the obligatory nature of such an affirmation for any political candidate.

32. Diary, 11 June 1951, PDDE 12:340; diary, 2 July 1951, PDDE 12:399 (see also Eisenhower to George Marshall, 3 August 1951, PDDE 12:458–59); Eisenhower to Harriman, 30 June 1951, PDDE 12:398 (see also Eisenhower to Cliff Roberts, 14 September 1951, PDDE 12:538); Eisenhower to Harry Truman, 4 January 1952, PDDE 12:840; Eisenhower to George Sloan, 3 January 1952, 12:837; Eisenhower to Samuel Paley, 29 March 1952, PDDE 13:1147. In the diary entry of 2 July 1951, Eisenhower characteristically complained that back in 1945 he and Clay had warned that U.S. policies would make Germany "ineffective on *our* side," but they were "told to mind our own business."

33. Eisenhower to Lucius Clay, 16 April 1951, PDDE 12:211 (see also Eisenhower to Joseph Collins, 2 April 1951, PDDE 12:185); Eisenhower to Brian Horrocks, 2 October 1951, PDDE 12:591; Eisenhower to Averell Harriman, 2 April 1951, PDDE 12:180; Eisenhower to Joseph Collins, 2 April 1951, PDDE 12:185; Eisenhower to Swede Hazlett, 21 June 1951, PDDE 12:369.

34. Eisenhower to Paul Hoffman, 9 February 1952, PDDE 13:955; Cook, *Declassified Eisenhower,* 135; Eisenhower to George Sloan, 20 March 1952, PDDE 13:1100; Eisenhower to Kenyon Joyce, 15 March 1952, PDDE 13:1072.

35. Eisenhower to Brian Horrocks, 2 October 1951, PDDE 12:591; Eisenhower to Thomas Campbell, 1 September 1951, PDDE 12:511; Eisenhower to Kenyon Joyce, 15 March 1952, PDDE 13:1072; Eisenhower to Averell Harriman, 1 June 1951, PDDE 12:315.

36. Eisenhower to Robert Lovett, 13 December 1951, PDDE 12:780 (see the whole interesting discussion about "cynicism" in this letter); Eisenhower to Lucius Clay, 30 March 1951, PDDE 12:171; Thomas M. Sisk, "Forging the Weapon: Eisenhower as NATO's Supreme Allied Commander, Europe, 1950–52," in *Eisenhower: A Centenary Assessment,* ed. Stephen E. Ambrose and Gunter Bischof (Baton Rouge: Louisiana State University Press, 1995), 74.

37. Eisenhower to Robert Lovett, 25 September 1951, PDDE 12:566, 568; diary, 10 October 1951, PDDE 12:629; Eisenhower to Frank Caffey, 28 July 1951, PDDE 12:447.

38. Eisenhower to Robert Lovett, 25 September 1951, PDDE 12:566; Eisenhower to Lucius Clay, 30 March 1951, PDDE 12:171.

39. Eisenhower to Joseph Collins, 19 June 1951, PDDE 12:365; Eisenhower to Robert McConnell, 29 June 1951, PDDE 12:391; Eisenhower to Arthur Sulzberger, 14 January 1952, PDDE 13:881; Cook, *Declassified Eisenhower,* 116.

40. Diary, 10 October 1951, PDDE 12:629; Eisenhower to Martin Clement, 9 January 1952, PDDE 13:866; Eisenhower to Arthur Summerfield, 11 March 1952, PDDE 13:1057; Eisenhower to George Sloan, 20 March 1952, PDDE 13:1103; see also Eisenhower to Tracy Voorhees, 27 February 1952, PDDE 13:1016.

41. Diary, 9 April 1951, PDDE 12:200; Eisenhower to Samuel Goldwyn, 4 October 1951, PDDE 12:612.
42. Eisenhower to Ruth Hagy, 18 March 1952, PDDE 13:1082; Eisenhower to Edgar Eisenhower, 6 December 1951, PDDE 12:755.
43. Eisenhower to George Whitney, 22 September 1951, PDDE 12:561, and 26 March 1952, PDDE 13:1125; Eisenhower to Swede Hazlett, 4 September 1951, PDDE 12:514; Eisenhower to Ruth Hagy, 18 March 1952, PDDE 13:1083.
44. Eisenhower to Sid Richardson, 20 June 1951, PDDE 12:367 (see also diary, 2 March 1951, PDDE 12:83); diary, 27 April 1951, PDDE 12:245; diary, 11 June 1951, PDDE 12:341; Eisenhower to Arthur Eisenhower, 11 September 1951, PDDE 12:535; Eisenhower to Edgar Eisenhower, 6 December 1951, PDDE 12:756; diary, 2 March 1951, PDDE 12:83; diary, 27 April 1951, PDDE 12:245; diary, 11 June 1951, PDDE 12:341.
45. Eisenhower to George Sloan, 29 January 1952, PDDE 13:929; Eisenhower to Milton Eisenhower, 21 March 1952, PDDE 13:1106.
46. Eisenhower to William Robinson, 12 February 1952, PDDE 13:985–91.
47. Eisenhower to Robert Lovett, 25 September 1951, PDDE 13:567, 568. By the time he became president, Eisenhower developed a more specific economic understanding of the sacrifices needed in Europe. He told financier Clarence Dillon (8 January 1953, PDDE 13:1491) that "the real problem for every country is to produce and export those things the world needs." Every country should shift to an export-oriented economy, to earn the foreign currency needed for imports. "We of course know that in the early stages of such an effort, certain hardships will be endured by some groups and possible a general reduction in already low living standards will be experienced. Incidentally, there is raised the question of whether the political leaders would and could withstand the pressures. . . . Resentment, brought about by lack of general understanding," might force governments to enact a New Deal approach "that of course leads finally either to bankruptcy and poverty or to dictatorship and regimentation." These "clear facts" had to be understood in Europe, he continued. Intending no irony, he added that since the United States exported far more than other nations, "it is other countries who would have to go through a general wringing-out process rather than the United States."
48. Eisenhower to Henry Luce, 8 January 1952, PDDE 13:859. "The longer I live the more I thank the good Lord that he allowed me to be born an American," Eisenhower told Luce, in a rather uncharacteristic but highly quotable patriotic flourish.
49. Eisenhower to William Robinson, 12 February 1952, PDDE 13:985–91.
50. Eisenhower to George Sloan, 8 February 1952, PDDE 13:949; Eisenhower to Clifford Roberts, 28 January 1952, PDDE 13:922.
51. Eisenhower to Swede Hazlett, 14 November 1951, PDDE 12:714. There is nothing in the corpus of Eisenhower's writing to indicate why he chose precisely 3,000 years. Perhaps he held a common view that the religion of ancient Israel, reflected in the Hebrew Bible, began roughly 1,000 years B.C.E.
52. Eisenhower to Averell Harriman, 17 September 1951, PDDE 12:545; Eisenhower to George Sloan, 20 March 1952, PDDE 13:1100.
53. Eisenhower to Victor Emanuel, 29 March 1952, PDDE 13:1146.
54. Eisenhower to Elizabeth Rankin, 11 December 1951, PDDE 12:773; Eisenhower to George Sloan, 20 March 1952, PDDE 13:1103.
55. Eisenhower to George Sloan, 29 January 1952, PDDE 13:930.
56. Eisenhower to George Sloan, 20 March 1952, PDDE 13:1100; Eisenhower to Lucius Clay, 9 February 1952, PDDE 13:963.

57. Eisenhower to Arthur Eisenhower, 11 November 1951, PDDE 12:535; Eisenhower to George Sloan, 1 March 1952, PDDE 13:1039; Eisenhower to Victor Emanuel, 29 March 1952, PDDE 13:1146.

58. Eisenhower to Drew Pearson, 27 March 1952, PDDE 13:1134; see also note 6 above.

59. Medhurst, *Dwight D. Eisenhower,* 28.

60. Address to British Parliament, 15 January 1952, Pre-Presidential Papers, Principal Series, Box 193, "Speeches January 1951–May 1952 (2)."

61. Broadcast speech from Washington, 2 February 1951, Pre-Presidential Papers, Principal Series, Box 197, "Report to the Nation 2/2/51"; see also the same theme in his published testimony to a Senate subcommittee: "Eisenhower Reveals Europe's Plight," *U.S. News & World Report,* 7 September 1951, 82.

62. Speech to Congress, 1 February 1951, *Vital Speeches of the Day* 17 (15 February 1951): 258–60; "Eisenhower Reveals Europe's Plight," 83.

63. Speech to Congress, 258; address to English Speaking Union, London, 3 July 1951, *Vital Speeches of the Day* 17 (1 August 1951): 614; extracts from address to news media, 20 November 1951, Pre-Presidential Papers, Principal Series, Box 197, "News Media Address 11/20/51"; address to North Atlantic Council, 27 November 1951, Pre-Presidential Papers, Principal Series, Box 193, "Speeches January 1951–May 1952 (2)"; remarks to press, 21 January 1952, Pre-Presidential Papers, Principal Series, Box 197, "News Media Address 11/20/51"; speech to Congress, 261.

64. Halford Ross Ryan finds that Eisenhower used rhetorical appeals to fear (as well as patriotism) noticeably more often at SHAPE than previously ("A Rhetorical Analysis," 93, 97, 101). This judgment seems to overlook the consistent appeals to fear before 1951.

65. Remarks to press, 21 January 1952, Pre-Presidential Papers, Principal Series, Box 197, "News Media Address 11/20/51"; speech to Congress, 261; annual report to SHAPE, 2 April 1952, Pre-Presidential Papers, Principal Series, Box 197, "2nd Anniversary of SHAPE 4/2/52 (1)"; address to English Speaking Union, London, 613. Occasionally Eisenhower described peace and his goals for NATO in terms of improving Western civilization by creating something that did not yet exist. For example, "With unity achieved, Europe could build adequate security and, at the same time, continue the march of human betterment that has characterized western civilization" (remarks at opening of SHAPE headquarters at Marly, 23 July 1951, Pre-Presidential Papers, Principal Series, Box 197, "Opening of SHAPE HQ 7/23/51"). But such formulations were quite rare.

66. Pre-Presidential Papers, Principal Series, Box 197, "Academy of Moral and Political Sciences, 1/21/52"; address to English Speaking Union, London, 614; speech to Congress, 258–60.

67. Broadcast speech from Washington, 2 February 1951, Pre-Presidential Papers, Principal Series, Box 197, "Report to the Nation 2/2/51"; extracts from address to news media, 20 November 1951, Pre-Presidential Papers, Principal Series, Box 197, "News Media Address 11/20/51"; "Eisenhower Reveals Europe's Plight," 86, 85.

68. Broadcast speech from Washington, 2 February 1951, Pre-Presidential Papers, Principal Series, Box 197, "Report to the Nation 2/2/51."

69. Statement broadcast from Paris, 7 January 1951, Pre-Presidential Papers, Principal Series, Box 193, "Speeches January 1951–May 1952 (2)"; broadcast speech from Washington, 2 February 1951, Pre-Presidential Papers, Principal Series, Box 197, "Report to the Nation 2/2/51"; speech to Congress, 259, 260; report on SHAPE, Pre-Presidential Papers, Principal Series, Box 197 "Second Anniversary of SHAPE–4/2/52 (1)."

70. Draft for General Eisenhower–Television, 1 November 1951, Box 197, "Edward Morrow [sic] Program, 11/1/51"; address to English Speaking Union, London, 614.

71. Annual report to SHAPE, 2 April 1952, Pre-Presidential Papers, Principal Series, Box 197, "2nd Anniversary of SHAPE 4/2/52 (1)"; "Eisenhower Reveals Europe's Plight," 88.

72. Broadcast speech from Washington, 2 February 1951, Pre-Presidential Papers, Principal Series, Box 197, "Report to the Nation 2/2/51"; speech to Congress, 259, 260; address to North Atlantic Council, 27 November 1951, Pre-Presidential Papers, Principal Series, Box 193, "Speeches January 1951–May 1952 (2)."

73. Remarks to press, 21 January 1952, Pre-Presidential Papers, Principal Series, Box 197, "News Media Address 11/20/51."

74. See, e.g., "General Eisenhower's Latest Size-Up of the World Situation," *U.S. News & World Report,* 1 February 1952, 23; address to English Speaking Union, London, 613.

75. "General Eisenhower's Latest Size-Up," 24; "Eisenhower Reveals Europe's Plight," 85; statement broadcast from Paris, 7 January 1951, Pre-Presidential Papers, Principal Series, Box 193, "Speeches January 1951–May 1952 (2)."

76. Remarks to press, 21 January 1952, Pre-Presidential Papers, Principal Series, Box 197, "News Media Address 11/20/51"; address at D-day commemoration, Bayeux, France, 6 June 1951, Pre-Presidential Papers, Principal Series, Box 193, "Speeches January 1951–May 1952 (2)."

77. Address to North Atlantic Council, 27 November 1951, Pre-Presidential Papers, Principal Series, Box 193, "Speeches January 1951–May 1952 (2)"; Annual Report to SHAPE, 2 April 1952; extracts from address to news media, 20 November 1951, Pre-Presidential Papers, Principal Series, Box 197, "News Media Address 11/20/51"; see also address to English Speaking Union, London, 613; statement broadcast from Paris, 7 January 1951, Pre-Presidential Papers, Principal Series, Box 193, "Speeches January 1951–May 1952 (2)."

78. "General Eisenhower's Latest Size-Up," 23.

79. Statement broadcast from Paris, 7 January 1951, Pre-Presidential Papers, Principal Series, Box 193, "Speeches January 1951–May 1952 (2)"; address to English Speaking Union, London, 614.

80. Pre-Presidential Papers, Principal Series, Box 197, "BBC Talk 1/31/52"; see also press release, 2 April 1952, Pre-Presidential Papers, Principal Series, Box 197, "Second Anniversary of SHAPE–4/2/52 (1)."

81. "Eisenhower Reveals Europe's Plight," 83. Here Eisenhower foreshadowed the later common image of the "nuclear umbrella."

82. Address at D-day commemoration, Bayeux, France, 6 June 1951, Pre-Presidential Papers, Principal Series, Box 193, "Speeches January 1951–May 1952 (2)"; address to English Speaking Union, London, 613.

83. "Eisenhower Reveals Europe's Plight," 82; speech to Congress, 261.

84. Speech to Congress, 260.

85. Address to English Speaking Union, London, 613.

86. "Eisenhower Reveals Europe's Plight," 91; remarks at opening of SHAPE headquarters at Marly, 23 July 1951, Pre-Presidential Papers, Principal Series, Box 197, "Opening of SHAPE HQ 7/23/51."

## CHAPTER 13

1. Herbert Parmet, *Eisenhower and the American Crusades* (New York: Macmillan, 1972), 47; Robert A. Divine, *Foreign Policy and U.S. Presidential Election, 1952–1960* (New York: New Viewpoints, 1974), 13; Eisenhower to Harry Bullis, 3 December 1951, PDDE 12:753;

Stephen E. Ambrose, *Eisenhower,* vol.1 (New York: Simon & Schuster, 1983), 521. The most thorough study of Eisenhower's decision to run for president is William B. Pickett, *Eisenhower Decides to Run: Presidential Politics and Cold War Strategy* (Chicago: Ivan Dee, Inc., 2000). Unfortunately, this book was published after the present chapter was completed.

2. Eisenhower to Truman, 2 April 1952, PDDE 13:1155. Lucius Clay later claimed that he had already persuaded Eisenhower to commit to this decision in early February; see Lyon, *Eisenhower,* 458, 460.

3. Speech at Abilene, 4 June 1954, *Vital Speeches of the Day* 17 (15 June 1952): 514–17; Parmet, *Eisenhower,* 5.

4. Cook, *Declassified Eisenhower,* 146–47, quoting William Robinson to Eisenhower, 18 February 1952 and Cliff Roberts to Eisenhower, 16 June 1952; Eisenhower to Cliff Roberts, 19 June 1952, PDDE 13:1251; see also Robinson to Eisenhower, 19 June 1952, quoted in Ambrose, *Eisenhower,* 1:534.

5. *New York Times,* 6 June 1952, 10; speech at San Francisco, 8 December 1952, *New York Times,* 9 October 1952, 24. See also Eisenhower to Bernard Baruch, 30 June 1952, PDDE 13:1263: "We find ourselves in circumstances that are neither war nor peace."

6. *New York Times,* 6 June 1952, 10.

7. *New York Times,* 8 June 1952, 52.

8. Divine has argued that Dulles stressed "liberation" because it offered "a unifying slogan that effectively disguised the differences between isolationists and internationalists" (*Foreign Policy,* 25). In this respect he was serving Taft's interests (perhaps unwittingly, or perhaps quite wittingly positioning himself to become secretary of state, no matter who won the Republican nomination). For a less likely interpretation, see Townsend Hoopes, *The Devil and John Foster Dulles* (Boston: Little, Brown, and Co., 1973), 129.

9. Divine, *Foreign Policy,* 31; Eisenhower to John Foster Dulles, 20 June 1952, PDDE 13:1254.

10. *New York Times,* 8 June 1952, 52

11. James T. Patterson, *Mr. Republican: A Biography of Robert A. Taft* (Boston: Houghton Mifflin Company, 1972), 519; Louis L. Gerson, *John Foster Dulles* (New York: Cooper Square Publishers, 1967), 82. For good overviews of Taft's foreign policy views, see Patterson, *Mr. Republican,* 474–96 and Russell Kirk and James McClellan, *The Political Principles of Robert A. Taft* (New York: Fleet Press Corporation, 1967), 158–89. The similarities between Taft and Eisenhower are rather more striking than the differences.

12. 20 June 1952, PDDE 13:1258–59; see also Eisenhower to Abraham Sakier, 8 July 1949, PDDE 10:680.

13. Speech at Denver, 23 June 1952, Pre-Presidential Papers, Principal Series, Box 197 "Denver, CO June 1952."

14. Speech in Dallas, 21 June 1952, *New York Times,* 22 June 1952, 35; speech in Denver, 26 June 1952, *New York Times,* 27 June 1952, 10.

15. Eisenhower to Bernard Baruch, 30 June 1952, PDDE 13:1263 (emphasis in original); speech in Denver, 26 June 1952, *New York Times,* 27 June 1952, 10.

16. Address to Republican National Convention, 11 July 1952, *Vital Speeches of the Day* 18 (1 August 1952): 610, 611.

17. Speech to the American Legion, 25 August 1952, *New York Times,* 26 August 1952, 12, 1.

18. Parmet, *Eisenhower,* 124; Divine, *Foreign Policy,* 51, 52

19. Speech at Philadelphia, 4 September 1952, *Vital Speeches of the Day* 18 (15 September 1952): 708–10; Parmet, *Eisenhower,* 125; Ambrose, *Eisenhower,* 1:548. There is no independent confirmation, apart from Eisenhower's own memory, for the often-repeated story of Eisenhower's admonition to Dulles.

20. Divine, *Foreign Policy,* 54; John Robert Greene, *The Crusade: The Presidential Election of 1952* (Lanham, Md.: University Press of America, 1985), 188.

21. The ultimate wording of the platform plank, with its aggressive calls for "liberation" of communist-dominated lands, was widely seen as representing the Taft wing of the party. Emmet Hughes, a principal campaign speechwriter on foreign policy, later claimed that Eisenhower never even bothered to read the platform (Hoopes, *The Devil and John Foster Dulles,* 130).

22. Speech at Philadelphia, 4 September 1952, 709–10. Eisenhower added a desire for "general disarmament," if there were "dependable assurances of good faith"; this would not be a prominent theme in his campaign oratory.

23. Speech to the American Legion, 25 August 1952, *New York Times,* 26 August 1952, 12.

24. Address to Alfred E Smith Dinner, 16 October 1952, *Vital Speeches of the Day* 19 (15 October 1952): 37; Emmet John Hughes, *Ordeal of Power* (New York: Athenaeum, 1963), 31–32; speech at Worcester, Mass., 20 October 1952, *New York Times,* 21 October 1952, 24; speech at *New York Herald Tribune* Forum, 21 October 1952, *New York Times,* 22 October 1952, 1.

25. Speech at Columbia, S.C., 30 September 1952, *Vital Speeches of the Day* 19 (15 October 1952): 3; speech at Republican National Headquarters, 10 September 1952, *New York Times,* 11 September 1952, 26.

26. Speech at Portland, Oregon, 7 October 1952, cited in Campaign Statements of Dwight D. Eisenhower: A Reference Index (typescript in Eisenhower Library), 321; speech at Bridgeport, Conn., 20 October 1952, *New York Times,* 21 October 1952, 24; speech at Chicago, 5 September 1952, Campaign Statements, 315.

27. Kenneth E. Morris and Barry Schwartz, "Why They Liked Ike: Tradition, Crisis, And Heroic Leadership," *Sociological Quarterly* 34 (spring 1993): 138 (see chap. 11, note 14, above); Marquis Childs, *Eisenhower, Captive Hero* (New York: Harcourt, Brace, 1958), 145. The slogan "Mighty Tower Eisenhower" surely reminded many Protestant voters of the well-known hymn, "A Mighty Fortress Is Our God." The "blank slate" phenomenon continued throughout Eisenhower's presidency. In a 1955 Gallup poll, two-thirds of self-identified liberals saw Eisenhower as a liberal, while two-thirds of self-identified conservatives saw him as conservative (Walter LaFeber, *America, Russia, and the Cold War,* 5th ed. [New York: Alfred A. Knopf Co., 1985], 141).

28. Speech at Fairfield, Calif., 10/8/52, Campaign Statements, 321.

29. Speech to AFL, 17 September 1952, *Vital Speeches of the Day* 18 (1 October 1952): 738 (see also address to Alfred E. Smith Dinner, 16 October 1952, *Vital Speeches of the Day* 19 [1 November 1952]: 39); speech at Boston, 3 November 1952, *New York Times,* 4 November 1952, 23. On opposition to the status quo, see *New York Times* Magazine, 2 November 1952, 9.

30. *New York Times,* 2 November 1952, 78; speech at Detroit, 24 October 1952, in Medhurst, *Dwight D. Eisenhower,* 156; *New York Times,* 26 August 1952, 12, 1.

31. David Halberstam, *The Fifties* (New York: Villard Books, 1993), 229; speech at Taunton, Mass., 20 October 1952, Campaign Statements, 322.

32. Speech in San Francisco, 8 October 1952, *New York Times,* 9 October 1952, 24; address to Alfred E. Smith Dinner, *Vital Speeches of the Day* 19 (1 November 1952): 40.

33. Eisenhower continued to speak of the "free world's" values as those of Western civilization (see below). Since he expected those values to prevail throughout the noncommunist world, he could quite logically tell some Republican convention delegates that Japan was "the real outpost of our civilization" (cited in Ambrose, *Eisenhower,* 2:33).

34. Speech at Joliet, Illinois, 15 September 1952, Campaign Statements, 316; speech at St. Louis, 20 September 1952, Campaign Statements, 318; speech at Parkersburg, West

Virginia, 24 September 1952, Campaign Statements, 319; speech at Cincinnati, 22 September 1952, Campaign Statements, 318; speech at Dayton, 23 September 1952, Campaign Statements, 326.

35. Speech at Detroit, 24 October 1952, Medhurst, *Strategic Communicator,* 155; Martin J. Medhurst, "Text and Context in the 1952 Presidential Campaign: Eisenhower's 'I Shall Go To Korea' Speech," *Presidential Studies Quarterly* 30 (September 2000): 480; Brendon, *Ike,* 226.

36. Speech at Detroit, 24 October 1952, Medhurst, *Strategic Communicator,* 155; *New York Times,* 19 June 1952, 14; Eisenhower to Cliff Roberts, 20 June 1952, PDDE 13:1251; Jackson to Gabriel Hauge, 3 October 1952, cited in Divine, *Foreign Policy,* 71. In his speech at San Francisco (8 October 1952), Eisenhower quoted the South Korean ambassador as saying: "Give us guns; spare your sons."

37. Eisenhower to Richard Nixon, 1 October 1952, PDDE 13:1368 (perhaps this letter planted a seed in Nixon's mind that would later germinate as "Vietnamization"); Eisenhower to Robert Lovett, 8 November 1952, PDDE 13:1416; speech at Detroit, 24 October 1952, Medhurst, *Strategic Communicator,* 155.

38. Speech at Detroit, 24 October 1952, Medhurst, *Strategic Communicator,* 155; speech at San Francisco, 8 October 1952, *New York Times,* 9 October 1952, 24.

39. Lloyd Gardner, *Architects of Illusion* (Chicago: Quadrangle Books, 1972), viii. Morris and Schwartz argue that Eisenhower's popularity rested in part on a similar "blank slate" dynamic in domestic policy, because "he integrated libertarianism and equalitarianism into a corporate ideal specifically suited to the domestic opportunities and international challenges of his age" ("Why They Liked Ike," 144).

40. Speech at Milwaukee, 3 October 1952, Medhurst, *Strategic Communicator,* 146; speech at Boise, 20 August 1952, *Vital Speeches of the Day* 18 (1 September 1952): 677; see also speech to American Federation of Labor, 17 September 1952, *Vital Speeches of the Day* 18 (1 October 1952): 741.

41. Press conference, 7 June 1952, *New York Times,* 8 June 1952, 52; speech at Milwaukee, 3 October 1952, Medhurst, *Strategic Communicator,* 146, 147; *U.S. News & World Report,* 21 August 1952; speech to American Legion, 25 August 1952, *New York Times,* 26 August 1952, 12; see also speech at Frederick, Md., 25 September 1952, Campaign Statements, 319.

42. Speech at San Francisco, 8 October 1952, *New York Times,* 9 October 1952, 24; speech to American Federation of Labor, 17 September 1952, *Vital Speeches of the Day* 18 (1 October 1952): 741.

43. Speech in Denver, 26 June 1952, *New York Times,* 27 June 1952, 10; speech at Los Angeles, 9 October 1952, Campaign Statements, 213; address at Alfred E. Smith Dinner, 16 October 1952, *Vital Speeches of the Day* 19 (1 November 1952): 40; speech at Columbia, S.C., 30 September 1952, *Vital Speeches of the Day* 19 (15 October 1952): 5; speech at Duluth, 4 October 1952, *New York Times,* 5 October 1952, 80; speech at Milwaukee, 3 October 1952, Medhurst, *Strategic Communicator,* 145, 150.

44. Speech at Worcester, 20 October 1952, *New York Times,* 21 October 1952, 24; speech at Detroit, 24 October 1952, Medhurst, *Strategic Communicator,* 156.

45. Address at Alfred E. Smith Dinner, 16 October 1952, *Vital Speeches of the Day* 19 (1 November 1952): 39, 41; speech at Dallas, 21 June 1952, *New York Times,* 22 June 1952, 35.

46. Speech at Boston, 3 November 1952, *New York Times,* 4 November 1952, 23. The secret of America's "genius and power" was found only in its churches. He added: "America is great because America is good."

47. Eisenhower to Paul Hoffman, 17 July 1952, PDDE 13:1276; Eisenhower to Cliff Roberts, 29 July 1952, PDDE 13:1284–85; Eisenhower to John Eisenhower, 29 July 1952, PDDE 13:1283. He had avoided commitment to any specific church, he told Roberts, because he was "a little bit 'non-conformist.' . . . I have always sort of treasured my independence because I like to note the difference in the several Protestant denominations." In the several thousand pages of published letters and documents, there is not a single reference to any differences among Protestant denominations. During the campaign, Clare Booth Luce persuaded him to join a church and start attending, because a non-churchgoing president would give millions of American children an excuse to refuse to go to church. The argument persuaded the candidate; with no denominational preference of his own, he joined Mamie's Presbyterian church. See Clare Booth Luce Oral History, Columbia Oral History Project, as cited in Perret, *Eisenhower,* 428.
48. Eisenhower to Rene Pleven, 13 August 1952, PDDE 13:1217.
49. Eisenhower to Edward Meade Earle, 2 September 1952, PDDE 13:1346.

## CONCLUSION

1. Perhaps Eisenhower was uncomfortable with the intellectuals on the Columbia faculty, as he admitted, because they would not settle for simple truths that denied or evaded ambiguity.
2. *Time,* 2 December 1946, 25; *New York Times,* 27 April 1946, 16.
3. *Newsweek,* 22 September 1947, 100; Morris and Schwartz, "Why They Liked Ike," 133–51; Medhurst, "Text and Context in the 1952 Presidential Campaign," 469.
4. Robert L. Ivie, "Eisenhower as Cold Warrior," in *Eisenhower's War of Words,* 8, 21; H. W. Brands Jr., "The Age of Vulnerability: Eisenhower and the National Insecurity State," *The American Historical Review* 94 (October 1989).
5. Anthony James Joes, "Eisenhower Revisionism and American Politics," in *Dwight D. Eisenhower: Soldier, President, Statesman,* ed. Joan P. Krieg (Westport, Conn.: Greenwood Press, 1987), 294.
6. On Eisenhower's ideology, rhetoric, and discourse as president, see my monograph *Eisenhower's Atoms for Peace* (College Station: Texas A & M University Press, 2002) and my study in preparation of Eisenhower's discourse of national security during his eight years as president.

# Bibliography

## UNPUBLISHED SOURCES

All unpublished documents cited in the following notes are held in the Eisenhower Library, Abilene, Kansas, unless otherwise noted.

The following abbreviations are used throughout the notes for published collections of original source documents:

PDDE = *The Papers of Dwight David Eisenhower* (Baltimore: Johns Hopkins University Press), Volumes 1–5, *The War Years and Occupation 1945,* edited by Alfred Chandler and Louis Galambos (1978); Volume 6, *Occupation: 1945,* edited by Alfred Chandler and Louis Galambos (1978); volumes 7–9, *The Chief of Staff,* edited by Louis Galambos ([1978)]; volumes 10–11, *Columbia University,* edited by Louis Galambos, (1984); volumes 12–13, *NATO and the Campaign of 1952,* edited by Louis Galambos (1989); volumes 14–17, *The Presidency: The Middle Way,* edited by Louis Galambos and Daun Van Ee ([1996). PDDE is cited by volume and page number (not document number).

Treuenfels, *Eisenhower Speaks* = Rudolph L. Treuenfels, *Eisenhower Speaks: Dwight D. Eisenhower in His Messages and Speeches* (New York: Farrar, Strauss, & Company, 1948). This collection of speeches and other public statements, from May 1945 to January 1948, is cited by page number.

FRUS = *Foreign Relations of the United States. FRUS* is cited by year, volume, and page number. PDDE = *The Papers of Dwight David Eisenhower* (Baltimore: Johns Hopkins University Press), volumes 1–5, *The War Years and Occupation 1945,* edited by Alfred Chandler and Louis Galambos (1978); volume 6, *Occupation: 1945,* edited by Alfred Chandler and Louis Galambos (1978); volumes 7–9, *The Chief of Staff,* edited by Louis Galambos (1978); volumes 10–11, *Columbia*

*University,* edited by Louis Galambos (1984); volumes 12–13, *NATO and the Campaign of 1952,* edited by Louis Galambos (1989); volumes 14–17, *The Presidency: The Middle Way,* edited by Louis Galambos and Daun Van Ee (1996). PDDE is cited by volume and page number (not document number).

Treuenfels, *Eisenhower Speaks* = Rudolph L. Treuenfels, *Eisenhower Speaks: Dwight D. Eisenhower in His Messages and Speeches* (New York: Farrar, Strauss, & Company, 1948). This collection of speeches and other public statements, from May 1945 to January 1948, is cited by page number.

*FRUS* = *Foreign Relations of the United States. FRUS* is cited by year, volume, and page number.


Published Sources


Aho, James A. *Religious Mythology and the Art of War.* Westport, Conn.: Greenwood Press, 1981.

Allen, Craig. *Eisenhower and the Mass Media.* Chapel Hill: University of North Carolina Press, 1993).

Ambrose, Stephen E. *Eisenhower.* Vol. 1, *Soldier, General of the Army, President Elect.* New York: Simon and Schuster, 1983.

————. *The Supreme Commander: The War Years of General Dwight D. Eisenhower.* Garden City, N.Y.: Doubleday, 1970.

Bailyn, Bernard. *The Ideological Origins of the American Revolution.* Cambridge, Mass.: Harvard University Press, 1967.

Beer, Francis A., and Robert Hariman. "Realism and Rhetoric in International Relations." In *Post-Realism: The Rhetorical Turn in International Relations,* edited by Francis A. Beer and Robert Hariman, 1–30. East Lansing: Michigan State University Press, 1996.

Bercovitch, Sacvan. *The American Jeremiad.* Madison: University of Wisconsin Press, 1978.

Berger, Peter. *The Sacred Canopy.* Garden City, N.Y.: Doubleday, 1967.

Berger, Peter, and Thomas Luckmann. *The Social Construction of Reality.* Garden City, N.Y.: Anchor Books, 1967.

Bergman, Jerry. "Steeped in Religion: President Eisenhower and the Influence of the Jehovah's Witnesses." *Kansas History* 21(1998): 148–67.

Bernstein, Barton. "Ike and Hiroshima: Did He Oppose It?" *Journal of Strategic Studies* 10 (September 1987): 377–89.

Blum, John Morton, ed. *The Price of Vision: The Diary of Henry A. Wallace, 1942–1946.* Boston: Houghton Mifflin, 1973.

Brands Jr., H. W. "The Age of Vulnerability: Eisenhower and the National Insecurity State." *The American Historical Review* 94 (October 1989): 963–89.

——. *Cold Warriors: Eisenhower's Generation and American Foreign Policy.* New York: Columbia University Press, 1988.

Brendon, Piers. *Ike: His Life and Times.* New York: Harper and Row, 1966.

Brodie, Bernard, ed. *The Absolute Weapon: Atomic Power and World Order.* New York: Harcourt, Brace, 1946.

Buhite, Russel D., and Wm. Christopher Hamel. "War for Peace: The Question of an American Preventive War against the Soviet Union, 1945–1955." *Diplomatic History* 14 (summer 1990): 367–85.

Bundy, McGeorge. *Danger and Survival: Choices About the Bomb in the First Fifty Years.* New York: Random House, 1988.

Burk, Robert F. *Dwight D. Eisenhower: Hero and Politician.* Boston: Twayne Publishers, 1986.

Butcher, Harry C. *My Three Years With Eisenhower.* New York: Simon and Schuster, 1946.

Campbell, David. *Writing Security.* 2d ed. Minneapolis: University of Minnesota Press, 1998.

Childs, Marquis. *Eisenhower, Captive Hero.* New York: Harcourt, Brace, 1958.

Chilton, Paul A. "The Meaning of Security." In *Post-Realism: The Rhetorical Turn in International Relations,* edited by Francis A. Beer and Robert Hariman, 193–216. East Lansing: Michigan State University Press, 1996.

Chernus, Ira. *Eisenhower's Atoms for Peace.* College Station: Texas A & M University Press, 2002.

——. *Dr. Strangegod: On the Symbolic Meaning of Nuclear Weapons.* Columbia: University of South Carolina Press, 1986.

Cook, Blanche Wiesen. *The Declassified Eisenhower.* Garden City, N.Y.: Doubleday, 1981.

Crable, Richard E. "Dwight David Eisenhower." In *American Orators of the Twentieth Century,* edited by Bernard K. Duffy and Halford R. Ryan, 115–22. Westport, Conn.: Greenwood Press, 1987.

Crumden, Robert Morse. *Ministers of Reform: The Progressives' Achievement in American Civilization, 1889–1920.* New York: Basic Books, 1982.

David, Lester, and Irene David. *Ike and Mamie.* New York: Putnam, 1981.

Davis, Kenneth S. *Soldier of Democracy.* Garden City, N.Y.: Doubleday, Doran and Co., 1945.

Divine, Robert A. *Foreign Policy and U.S. Presidential Election, 1952–1960.* New York: New Viewpoints, 1974.

Eagleton, Terry. *Ideology: An Introduction*. London and New York: Verso, 1991.

Eisenhower, Dwight D. *Letters to Mamie*. Edited by John S. D. Eisenhower. Garden City, N.Y.: Doubleday, 1978.

———. *At Ease: Stories I Tell My Friends*. Garden City, N.Y.: Doubleday, 1967.

———. *The White House Years, Waging Peace, 1956–1961*. Garden City, N.Y.: Doubleday, 1965.

———. *Peace With Justice: Selected Addresses of Dwight D. Eisenhower*. New York: Columbia University Press, 1961.

———. *Crusade in Europe*. Garden City, N.Y.: Doubleday, 1948.

Ferrell, Robert H., ed. *The Eisenhower Diaries*. New York: W.W. Norton, 1981.

Fiske, John. *Television Culture*. London: Routledge, 1989.

Freedman, Lawrence. *The Evolution of Nuclear Strategy*. 2d ed. New York: St. Martin's Press, 1989.

Freud, Sigmund. *Totem and Taboo*. Translated by James Strachey. New York: W.W. Norton, 1950.

Gaddis, John L. *The United States and the Origins of the Cold War, 1941–1947*. New York: Columbia University Press, 1972.

Gardner, Lloyd. *Architects of Illusion*. Chicago: Quadrangle Books, 1972.

Geertz, Clifford. "Ideology as a Cultural System." In *Interpretation of Cultures*, by Clifford Geertz, 193–233. New York: Basic Books, 1973.

Gerson, Louis L. *John Foster Dulles*. New York: Cooper Square Publishers, 1967.

Graebner, Norman, ed. *Ideas and Diplomacy*. New York: Oxford University Press, 1964.

Graebner, William. *The Age of Doubt: American Thought and Culture in the 1940s*. Boston: Twayne Publishers, 1991.

Greene, John Robert. *The Crusade: The Presidential Election of 1952*. Lanham, Md.: University Press of America, 1985.

Greenstein, Fred I. "Eisenhower's Leadership Style." In *Eisenhower: A Centenary Assessment*, edited by Stephen E. Ambrose and Gunter Bischof, 55–63. Baton Rouge: Louisiana State University Press, 1995.

———. *The Hidden-Hand Presidency: Eisenhower as Leader*. New York: Basic Books, 1982.

Griffith, Robert, "Dwight D. Eisenhower and the Corporate Commonwealth," *American Historical Review* 87 (1982): 87–122.

Halberstam, David. *The Fifties*. New York: Villard Books, 1993.

Hawkes, David. *Ideology*. London: Routledge, 1996.

Henry, Patrick. "'And I Don't Care What It Is': The Tradition-History of a Civil Religion Proof-Text." *Journal of the American Academy of Religion* 49 (March 1981): 35–50.

Herken, Gregg. *The Winning Weapon: The Atomic Bomb in the Cold War, 1945–1950.* New York: Vintage Books, 1982.

Hinds, Lynn Boyd, and Theodore Otto Windt, Jr. *The Cold War as Rhetoric: The Beginnings, 1945–1950.* New York: Praeger Publishers, 1991.

Hofstadter, Richard. *The Paranoid Style in American Politics and Other Essays.* New York: Vintage Books, 1967.

Hogan, J. Michael. "Eisenhower and 'Open Skies.'" In *Eisenhower's War of Words: Rhetoric and Leadership,* edited by Martin J. Medhurst, 137–55. East Lansing: Michigan State University Press, 1994.

Hogan, Michael J. *A Cross of Iron: Harry S. Truman and the Origins of the National Security State, 1945–1954.* New York: Cambridge University Press, 1998.

Holm, Thomas M. "American Indians and the Vietnam War." In *The Vietnam Reader,* edited by Walter Capps, 191–204. New York: Routledge, 1990.

Holt, Daniel D., and James W. Leyerzapf, eds. *Eisenhower: The Prewar Diaries and Selected Papers, 1905–1941.* Baltimore: Johns Hopkins University Press, 1998.

Hoopes, Townsend. *The Devil and John Foster Dulles.* Boston: Little, Brown, and Co., 1973.

Hughes, Emmet John. *Ordeal of Power.* New York: Athenaeum, 1963.

Hunt, Michael H. *Ideology and U.S. Foreign Policy.* New Haven: Yale University Press, 1987.

———. "Ideology." In *Explaining the History of American Foreign Relations,* edited by Michael J. Hogan and Thomas G. Paterson. New York: Cambridge University Press, 1991.

Immerman, Richard H. "Confessions of an Eisenhower Revisionist: An Agonizing Reappraisal," *Diplomatic History* 14 (summer 1990): 319–43.

———. "Psychology." In *Explaining the History of American Foreign Relations,* edited by Michael J. Hogan and Thomas G. Paterson, 151–64. New York: Cambridge University Press, 1991.

Ivie, Robert L. "Metaphor and the Rhetorical Invention of Cold War 'Idealists.'" In *Cold War Rhetoric: Strategy, Metaphor, and Ideology,* rev. ed., edited by Martin J. Medhurst, Robert L. Ivie, Philip Wander, and Robert L. Scott, 103–27. East Lansing: Michigan State University Press, 1997.

———. "Eisenhower as Cold Warrior." In *Eisenhower's War of Words: Rhetoric and Leadership,* edited by Martin J. Medhurst, 7–25. East Lansing: Michigan State University Press, 1994.

———. "Declaring a National Emergency." In *The Modern Presidency and Crisis Rhetoric,* edited by Amos Kiewe, 1–18. Westport, Conn.: Praeger Publishers, 1994.

———. "Literalizing the Metaphor of Soviet Savagery: President Truman's Plain Style." *Southern Speech Communication Journal* 51 (1986): 91–105.

———. "The Ideology of Freedom's 'Fragility' in American Foreign Policy Argument." *Journal of the American Forensic Association* 24 (1987): 27–36.

———. "Realism Masking Fear: George F. Kennan's Political Rhetoric." In *Post-Realism: The Rhetorical Turn in International Relations,* edited by Francis A. Beer and Robert Hariman, 55–74. East Lansing: Michigan State University Press, 1996.

Jacobs, Travis Beal. *Eisenhower at Columbia.* New Brunswick, N.J.: Transaction Publishers, 2001.

———. "Eisenhower, the American Assembly, and the 1952 Elections." In *Reexamining the Eisenhower Presidency,* edited by Shirley Anne Warshaw, 17–32. Westport, Conn.: Greenwood Press, 1993.

Janowitz, Morris. *The Professional Soldier.* Glencoe, Ill.: Free Press, 1960.

Joes, Anthony James. "Eisenhower Revisionism and American Politics." In *Dwight D. Eisenhower: Soldier, President, Statesman,* edited by Joan P. Krieg, 283–96. Westport, Conn.: Greenwood Press, 1987.

Johnson, James Turner. *The Quest for Peace.* Princeton: Princeton University Press, 1987.

Kazin, Michael. *The Populist Persuasion.* New York: Basic Books, 1995.

Kloppenberg, James T. "The Virtues of Liberalism." *Journal of American History* 74 (June 1987): 9–33.

Kirk, Russell, and James McClellan. *The Political Principles of Robert A. Taft.* New York: Fleet Press Corporation, 1967.

Kolko, Joyce, and Gabriel Kolko. *The Limits of Power: The World and United States Foreign Policy, 1945–1951.* New York: Harper and Row, 1972.

LaFeber, Walter. *America, Russia, and the Cold War.* 5th ed. New York: Alfred A. Knopf, 1985.

Leffler, Melvyn. "New Approaches, Old Configurations, and Prospective Reconfigurations." In *America in the World; The Historiography of American Foreign Relations Since 1941,* edited by Michael J. Hogan, 63–92. Cambridge: Cambridge University Press, 1995.

———. *A Preponderance of Power.* Stanford: Stanford University Press, 1992.

Leuchtenberg, William E. "The New Deal and the Analogue of War." In *Change and Continuity in Twentieth-Century America,* edited by John Braeman et al., 81–143. Columbus: Ohio State University Press, 1964.

Lewis, R. W. B. *The American Adam: Innocence, Tragedy, and Tradition in the Nineteenth Century.* Chicago: University of Chicago Press, 1955.

Lyon, Peter. *Eisenhower: Portrait of the Hero.* Boston: Little, Brown, Co., 1974.

McCann, Kevin. *Man From Abilene.* Garden City, N.Y.: Doubleday, 1952.

McLellan, David. *Ideology.* 2d ed. Minneapolis: University of Minnesota Press, 1995.

MacMillan, Harold. *The Blast of War, 1939–1945.* New York: Harper and Row, 1968.

Medhurst, Martin J. "Text and Context in the 1952 Presidential Campaign: Eisenhower's 'I Shall Go To Korea' Speech." *Presidential Studies Quarterly* 30 (September 2000): 155–96.

———. "Rhetoric and Cold War: A Strategic Approach." In *Cold War Rhetoric: Strategy, Metaphor, and Ideology,* rev. ed., edited by Martin J. Medhurst, Robert L. Ivie, Philip Wander, and Robert L. Scott, 19–27. East Lansing: Michigan State University Press, 1997.

———. "Eisenhower's Rhetorical Leadership: An Interpretation." In *Eisenhower's War of Words: Rhetoric and Leadership,* edited by Martin J. Medhurst, 285–97. East Lansing: Michigan State University Press, 1994.

———. "Eisenhower, Little Rock, and the Rhetoric of Crisis." In *The Modern Presidency and Crisis Rhetoric,* edited by Amos Kiewe, 19–46. Westport, Conn.: Praeger Publishers, 1994.

———. *Dwight D. Eisenhower: Strategic Communicator.* Westport, Conn.: Greenwood Press, 1993.

———. "Truman's Rhetorical Reticence, 1945–1947: An Interpretive Essay." *Quarterly Journal of Speech* (February 1988): 52–70.

Melanson, Richard A. "The Foundations of Eisenhower's Foreign Policy." In *Reevaluating Eisenhower: American Foreign Policy in the 1950s,* edited by Richard A. Melanson and David Mayers, 31–64. Urbana and Chicago: University of Illinois Press, 1987.

Miller, Merle. *Ike the Soldier: As They Knew Him.* New York: G.P. Putnam's Sons, 1987.

Mills, C. Wright. *The Causes of World War Three.* London: Secker and Warburg, 1959.

Morgenthau, Hans. *Politics Among Nations.* 4th ed. New York: Alfred A. Knopf, 1967.

Morris, Kenneth E., and Barry Schwartz. "Why They Liked Ike: Tradition, Crisis, and Heroic Leadership." *Sociological Quarterly* 34 (spring 1993): 133–51.

Ninkovich, Frank. *The Wilsonian Century: U.S. Foreign Policy Since 1900.* Chicago: University of Chicago Press, 1999.

———. "Interests and Discourse." *Diplomatic History* 13 (spring 1989): 135–62.

Neal, Steve. *The Eisenhowers: Reluctant Dynasty.* Garden City, N.Y.: Doubleday, 1978.

Parmet, Herbert. *Eisenhower and the American Crusades.* New York: Macmillan, 1972.

Paterson, Thomas G. *Meeting the Communist Threat: Truman to Reagan.* New York: Oxford University Press, 1988.

———. *On Every Front: The Making of the Cold War.* New York: W.W. Norton, 1979.

Patterson, James T. *Mr. Republican: A Biography of Robert A. Taft.* Boston: Houghton Mifflin Company, 1972.

Perret, Geoffrey. *Eisenhower.* New York: Random House, 1999.

Peterson, Edward N. *The American Occupation of Germany: Retreat to Victory.* Detroit: Wayne State University Press, 1977.

Pickett, William B. *Eisenhower Decides to Run: Presidential Politics and Cold War Strategy.* Chicago: Ivan Dee, Inc., 2000.

Pierard, Richard V., and Robert D. Linder. *Civil Religion and the Presidency.* Grand Rapids, Mich.: Academie Books, 1988.

Rodgers, Daniel T. *Contested Truths: Keywords in American Politics Since Independence.* New York: Basic Books, Inc., 1987.

Rosenberg, David Alan. "Origins of Overkill: Nuclear Weapons and American Strategy." In *The National Security: Its Theory and Practice, 1945–1960,* edited by Norman A. Graebner, 123–95. New York: Oxford University Press, 1986.

Ross, Steven T. *American War Plans, 1945–1950.* New York: Garland Publishing, 1988.

Ryan, Halford Ross. "A Rhetorical Analysis of General Eisenhower's Public Speaking From 1945 to 1951." Ph.D. diss. University of Illinois at Urbana-Champaign, 1972.

Schnabel, James F. *History of the Joint Chiefs of Staff.* Vol. 1, *The Joint Chiefs of Staff and National Policy, 1945–1947.* Washington, D.C.: Office of the Chairman of the Joint Chiefs of Staff, 1996.

Sherry, Michael. *In the Shadow of War.* New Haven: Yale University Press, 1995.

———. *The Rise of American Air Power: The Creation of Armageddon.* New Haven: Yale University Press, 1987.

Sisk, Thomas M. "Forging the Weapon: Eisenhower as NATO's Supreme Allied Commander, Europe, 1950–52." In *Eisenhower: A Centenary Assessment,* edited by Stephen E. Ambrose and Gunter Bischof, 64–83. Baton Rouge: Louisiana State University Press, 1995.

Smith, Jonathan Z. *Map Is Not Territory: Studies in the History of Religions.* Leiden: E.J. Brill, 1978.

———. *Imagining Religion.* Chicago: University of Chicago Press, 1982.

Stephanson, Anders L. *Kennan and the Art of Foreign Policy.* Cambridge, Mass.: Harvard University Press, 1989.

Theoharis, Athan. "The Rhetoric of Politics." In *Politics and Policies of the Truman Administration,* edited by Barton Bernstein, 196–241. Chicago: Quadrangle Books, 1970.

Trachtenberg, Marc. *History and Strategy.* Princeton: Princeton University Press, 1991.

Treuenfels, Rudolph L. *Eisenhower Speaks: Dwight D. Eisenhower in His Messages and Speeches.* New York: Farrar, Strauss, & Co., 1948.

Turner, Victor. *The Ritual Process: Structure and Anti-Structure.* New York: Aldine de Gruyter, 1995.

Tuveson, Ernest L. *Redeemer Nation: The Idea of America's Millennial Role.* Chicago: University of Chicago Press, 1968.

Underhill, Robert. *The Truman Persuasions.* Ames: Iowa State University Press, 1981.

*Vital Speeches of the Day.* New York: The City New Publishing Co., 1934–.

Wala, Michael. "An 'Education in Foreign Affairs for the Future President': The Council on Foreign Relations and Dwight D. Eisenhower." In *Reexamining the Eisenhower Presidency,* edited by Shirley Anne Warshaw, 1–16. Westport, Conn.: Greenwood Press, 1993.

Weart, Spencer. *Nuclear Fear: A History of Images.* Cambridge, Mass.: Harvard University Press, 1988.

Weigley, Russell F. *The American Way of War.* New York: Macmillan, 1973.

Williamson, Jr., Samuel R., and Steven L. Rearden. *The Origins of U.S. Nuclear Strategy, 1945–1953.* New York: St. Martin's Press, 1993.

Winthrop, John. "A Model of Christian Charity." In *The Puritans,* Vol. 1, edited by Perry Miller and Thomas H. Johnson, 195–99. New York: Harper Torchbooks, 1963.

Wilson, John F. *Public Religion in American Culture.* Philadelphia: Temple University Press, 1979.

Yergin, Daniel. *Shattered Peace: The Origins of the Cold War and the National Security State.* Boston: Houghton Mifflin, Sentry Editions, 1978.

Zagacki, Kenneth. "Rhetoric, Redemption, and Reconciliation: A Study of Twentieth Century Postwar Rhetoric." Ph.D. Diss. University of Texas, 1986.

# Index

as Supreme Allied Commander,
Europe, 251–52, 255

as presidential candidate in
1952, 280

and ideology, relations between, 8,
293, 295–98, 301

as Army Chief of Staff, 83

as president of Columbia
University, 173, 224–25,
229–30, 233–34

as presidential candidate in
1952, 289

logic in, 3, 11, 97, 194, 267

objectivity in, 6, 200

as main concern, 8, 293–95

in occupation of Germany, 52

as Army Chief of Staff, 84

as president of Columbia
University, 166, 182, 218, 220,
225, 226

as Supreme Allied Commander,
Europe, 251

as presidential candidate in
1952, 290

motives for, 8–10, 296

as Army Chief of Staff, 84–85,
92, 97, 152, 320n. 2

as president of Columbia
University, 168, 175–78,
180–86, 195, 207–8, 218, 224

as Supreme Allied Commander,
Europe, 248, 251

as presidential candidate in
1952, 272, 280, 289–90

paranoid style, 232–234

in public and in private, 9, 302

as Army Chief of Staff, 83,
92–93, 98, 117, 134, 150

as president of Columbia
University, 192, 213, 226–27

as Supreme Allied Commander,
Europe, 239, 266–67, 343n. 31

as presidential candidate in
1952, 288

Military career, 25, 33, 49, 77, 161,
182, 198, 227, 237–38

Mobilization for war, views on, 28–29,
117, 128, 164, 224, 243–44, 246,
283, 312n. 26. *See also* Soviet
Union, preparations for war against

Nuclear weapons, views on, 124–34,
144–45, 157, 165–67, 215, 224,
277, 326n. 12, 334n. 3

Occupation of Germany, as head of

Emphasis on public relations, 49–50,
54, 76

Fear about army's role, 53, 54

Public speaking role, 50–52

Relations with Soviets, 76

Political career, 295–96, 303

as Army Chief of Staff, 83–84, 91,
92

as president of Columbia
University, 175–77, 183–84,
199, 332n. 38

as Supreme Allied Commander,
Europe, 238–39, 246–47,
341 nn. 5, 6

as presidential candidate in
1952,269–90 passim

as President of Columbia University,
161, 179–80, 202, 207–8, 227,
333n. 44

Psychological warfare, support for,
73, 74, 251–52, 285, 328n. 30

as Supreme Allied Commander,
Europe, 237–38, 240, 244,
250–51, 269

Self-image, 296

in WW II, 36–37, 312–13n. 36

in occupation of Germany, 49, 53

as Army Chief of Staff, 92, 117,
143–46

as president of Columbia
University, 162, 180, 183–85, 218